ML

REA

**ACPL ITEM
DISCARDED**

The Heart of Charles Dickens

Charles Dickens in 1839

From a painting by Daniel Maclise

THE HEART OF
Charles Dickens

AS REVEALED IN HIS LETTERS
TO ANGELA BURDETT-COUTTS,
SELECTED AND EDITED FROM
THE COLLECTION IN THE PIER-
PONT MORGAN LIBRARY, WITH
A CRITICAL AND BIOGRAPHICAL
INTRODUCTION BY

EDGAR JOHNSON

GREENWOOD PRESS, PUBLISHERS
WESTPORT, CONNECTICUT

Library of Congress Cataloging in Publication Data

Dickens, Charles, 1812-1870.
  The heart of Charles Dickens.

    Reprint of the ed. published by Duell, Sloan, and
Pearce, New York.
    Includes index.
    1. Dickens, Charles, 1812-1870--Correspondence.
2. Burdett-Coutts, Angela Georgina Burdett-Coutts,
Baroness, 1814-1906. I. Burdett-Coutts, Baroness,
1814-1906. II. Johnson, Edgar. III. Title.
[PR4581.A4B77 1976]   823'.8 [B]   75-25254
ISBN 0-8371-8397-9

Originally published in 1952 by Duell, Sloan and Pearce,
New York and Little, Brown and Company, Boston

Reprinted with the permission of Hawthorn Books, Inc.

Reprinted in 1976 by Greenwood Press,
a division of Williamhouse-Regency Inc.

Library of Congress Catalog Card Number 75-25254

ISBN 0-8371-8397-9

Printed in the United States of America

To the
IMMORTAL MEMORY

Preface and Acknowledgments

*I*N THE FALL *of 1950 the Pierpont Morgan Library added to its magnificent accumulation of Charles Dickens manuscripts, letters, and mementos the famous Burdett-Coutts Collection of his letters. For many years, unknown to Dickens students, they had lain in the possession of Miss Coutts and her heirs. Even when they were sold to an American collector in 1922, they still remained almost entirely unavailable to scholars. The tremendous light they shed on Dickens's character and career can hardly be exaggerated. Totaling almost seven hundred, there are more than five hundred from Dickens to Angela Burdett-Coutts alone, and a considerable number to her friend and companion Hannah Meredith (later Mrs. William Brown) and to Dr. William Brown, as well as letters to Miss Coutts and to Dickens from other persons. Not long after their acquisition, Mr. Frederick B. Adams, Jr., the Director of the Library, asked me to edit a selection of them for publication.*

Hardly more than a quarter of Dickens's letters to Miss Coutts have ever appeared in print, and to the best of my knowledge only one of those to Mrs. Brown. Many of the inclusions in C. C. Osborne's edition of 1932 consisted of no more than a few paragraphs from letters considerably longer, and the few additional parts of letters to Miss Coutts in Walter Dexter's three-volume Nonesuch edition of Dickens's letters in 1938 were often limited to a few sentences or fragments of sentences quoted from sales catalogues. A dozen not included by either Osborne or Dexter were privately printed in The Charity of Charles Dickens, *edited by Edward F. Payne, and Henry H. Harper for the Bibliophile Society in 1929 in an edition limited to four hundred and twenty-five copies for members, and therefore not generally available. A few more, taken from transcripts made by Osborne, appeared in an article by K. J. Fielding in the London* Times Literary Supplement, *March 2 and 9, 1951. That is the sum total that has so far appeared in any form.*

Except for two that are incomplete in manuscript, all the letters in the present selection are given complete. They have been chosen to reveal a characteristic and illuminating picture of Dickens's activities, especially of the comparatively little known charitable enterprises and welfare work that he and Miss Coutts for so many years carried on together. I have not tried to avoid all duplication whatever of previous publication: when a letter was outstandingly important or when it was needed to make clear a narrative sequence or to explain letters following it, I have not hesitated to use material printed elsewhere.

There are two hundred and eighty letters in this volume. Of these, one hundred and fifty-one have never been printed before, eighty-two have appeared only in fragmentary forms, and twelve have been privately printed in the Bibliophile Society limited edition already mentioned; two hundred and forty-five, therefore, are either new or virtually new. Of the remaining thirty-five, considerable portions of twenty-seven have been published before, but only eight have appeared in their entirety.

The overwhelming bulk of these letters has been drawn from the Pierpont Morgan Library, but there are a few from other sources. Mr. Roger W. Barrett of Kenilworth, Illinois, has kindly permitted me to use the texts of five letters in his possession; the authorities of the New York Public Library and Dr. John W. Gordan, Curator of the Berg Collection, have allowed me to use two letters in that collection; the late Comte Alain de Suzannet of Lausanne, Switzerland, sent me a transcript of one in his possession, with his permission to use it; and Mr. K. J. Fielding has generously allowed me to reprint one letter and a part of another, both of which he published in the London Times *Literary Supplement. Although these debts are individually acknowledged in their proper places, I desire to express my warm gratitude for them here. And for an inclusive permission to use them all I am deeply grateful to Mr. Henry Charles Dickens, O.B.E., of London.*

Scores of scholars and librarians, responding to countless queries, both written and oral, have enabled me to clarify many allusions in the letters, but these cannot be isolated from those who aided in my biography, Charles Dickens: His Tragedy and Triumph. *Let me simply repeat to them all that I thank them no less heartily for their help with this book.*

There are three people, however, who must receive special thanks. First, Mr. Frederick B. Adams, Jr., the Director of the Morgan Library, who suggested the book, and who has aided me in every way. Second, Dr. George Kenneth Boyce, Curator of Autograph Manuscripts of the Library, who superintended making the transcripts from the original letters and checked them all for accuracy. And third, and most of all, my wife Eleanor Johnson, whose critical comment has been even more valuable than all of her laborious and devoted help in the physical preparation of my text.

At the Annual Conference and Banquet of the Dickens Fellowship held in May each year, the climax of the evening is the toast "To the Immortal Memory of Charles Dickens." From those words I have borrowed my dedication.

EDGAR JOHNSON

The City College
New York
April 18, 1952

Note

*T*O *AVOID a good deal of space-consuming repetition, the saluta-
tions and complimentary closings of all the letters are omitted. For
the most part, these were entirely formal. Dickens never used any salu-
tation except "My Dear Miss Coutts" or "Dear Miss Coutts," more often
the former. His usual conclusion was "Faithfully Yours" or some per-
mutation of "Ever faithfully yours" or "Always faithfully yours," although there were many slight variations: "Ever Dear Miss Coutts,
Faithfully yours," "Faithfully your friend," "Your most obliged and
faithful friend," "Yours faithfully and obliged," "Ever believe me, With
the truest regard, Faithfully yours," and similar phrases.*

*In the headings, for the reader's convenience, the dates are printed
first and the address follows. Dickens, however, always gave the address
first, usually in some detail, as "1 Devonshire Terrace, York Gate,
Regent's Park." Many of the letters from Tavistock House, and, later,
almost all those from the office of* Household Words, *the office of*
All the Year Round, *and Gad's Hill, are on printed letterheads, with
only the date written in by hand. His dates are almost always written
out in full, "Twenty Fourth May 1855," sometimes with the day of the
week as well — "Tuesday Twenty Ninth May 1855," and even "Tuesday
Night Twentieth May 1856." He very seldom fails to date a letter or
dates it merely with the day of the week.*

*Aside from these details, the letters are printed in their entirety with-
out change. I have not taken it upon myself to correct Dickens's capi-
talization, spelling, or punctuation, or to rationalize inconsistencies or
variations in his usage. The flavor of any writer of strong individuality
often lies partly in his deviations from conventional norms, and even a
patent slip is not without interest. The texts of these letters are therefore (except for possible errors in transcription) exactly as Dickens
wrote them, including his highly personal use of initial capitals to
emphasize a word.*

In numbering the footnotes I have borrowed from Professor Frederick A. Pottle a revival of the eighteenth-century system used in Boswell's Life of Johnson. Instead of beginning again with each letter, or carrying through each part, the numbers run in recurring series of nine, a system which avoids the unsightly use of double reference figures. Inasmuch as the same number never recurs on the same page, I am sure the reader will find its use entirely clear.

— E. J.

Contents

Miss Angela Burdett-Coutts

From a portrait by J. R. Swinton, first exhibited in 1865

The Heart of Charles Dickens

Introduction

ONE EVENING, probably in the year 1835, a banker named Edward Marjoribanks had two young people to dinner at his table. The host was in the great banking house of Coutts and Company, and in 1838 was to become a partner. Over six feet in height and colossal in build, he presented a sharp contrast to the slim, almost fragile vitality of his two younger guests. One of these was a newspaper reporter of twenty-three, who had written a number of clever sketches that had been appearing for the past year in the Monthly Magazine, Bell's Life in London, *and the columns of the* Evening Chronicle. *Little more than five foot eight, with delicate features, he had blue eyes, thick brown hair that descended in waving locks almost to his shoulders, and a face as smooth as a girl's. The second guest was a girl of twenty-one, slender in figure, with shining dark hair, an aquiline nose, and piercing eyes.*

The writer was Charles Dickens, still hardly known outside of newspaper circles. The girl was Miss Angela Burdett, youngest daughter of Sir Francis Burdett, the radical politician, and a granddaughter of Thomas Coutts, the largest shareholder in the bank that bore his name. (On falling heiress to her grandfather's fortune she took his surname and became Angela Burdett Coutts.) How Dickens had made the acquaintance of Edward Marjoribanks has not been discovered. Journalists, however, are brought into contact with many people, and from the moment that he had entered the reporters' Gallery of the House of Commons at the age of nineteen or twenty, Dickens had moved rapidly to a distinction outranking even the seasoned veterans of his profession. A keen-minded banker might easily identify him as a young man with a future. The quality of Angela Burdett was still to be revealed. Even in 1835, however, it must have been clear to Edward Marjoribanks that she was as far from ordinary as his other young guest. Nineteenth-century bankers did not make a habit of presenting reporters, however brilliant, who were earning only seven guineas a week, to the daughters of baronets with a fortune of twenty thousand pounds a year.

Not that there was any dangerous likelihood of a romance between them. Dickens was either already engaged or soon to be engaged to Catherine Hogarth, daughter of George Hogarth, music critic and editor of the Evening Chronicle. The close and enduring bonds that were to knit the young author and the young heiress together, although warm with personal admiration and devotion, were those of a shared zeal for the public welfare. Angela Burdett did not despise the social privileges of her rank. She mingled in the most glittering circles, and was to entertain on a grand scale. But she was an earnest young woman determined to be no mere butterfly dancing at balls and shimmering with jewels at the opera. She intended to use her position and her fortune to aid her fellow beings. And Dickens, despite his magnificent gifts as a writer, his command of comic laughter, dramatic character portrayal, and pathos, seethed with a volcanic resolution to battle suffering and oppression that far transcended any possibility of concentrating his energies exclusively in the paths of the literary artist. He was a liberal, a progressive, a reformer — a radical, he proclaimed defiantly — a fighter from tip to toe of his taut body.

The rapport between these two was irresistible and creative. So Dickens certainly felt in later years. Their meeting was among those events in his life that he felt to be fated. He had developed the mild superstition that everything of crucial importance to him had taken place on a Friday. "I was born on a Friday, and it is a most astonishing coincidence that I have never in my life, whatever projects I may have determined on otherwise — never begun a book or begun anything of interest to me, or done anything of importance to me, but it was on a Friday." More than twenty years after this initial meeting with Angela Burdett, when their association had ripened into a devoted friendship, "It must have been on a Friday," he wrote fervently, "that I first dined with you at Mr Marjoribanks."

I I

The paths that brought them together were very different. Dickens was born on February 7, 1812, in a little rented house at Landport, on the island of Portsea, Portsmouth. His father, John Dickens, was a son of the steward and the housekeeper at Crewe Hall, and through *the influence of their employer, John Crewe, M.P., the young fellow received a government appointment in the Navy Pay Office when he was twenty. Able and energetic, John Dickens was also convivial, cheerfully and ornately voluble, and improvident. Although his salary rose gradually to £350 a year, he never managed to live within his income. Before Charles was six months old the family had to move to a cheaper house; in Chatham, to which John Dickens was transferred when Charles was five, the same story of expenditure and increasingly desperate straits was presently repeated.*

Little Charles, however, was not aware of these troubles, and his childhood years in Chatham were a happy time. He romped in the hayfields, watched the bright regiments drilling at Fort Pitt and the ships sailing down the Medway out to sea, learned to read and became a precocious singer of comic songs, went to birthday parties and Twelfth Night celebrations. Even in the whitewashed tenement to which the Dickenses presently descended, Charles's life was unclouded. He was too busy roaming the lower town and the clanging dockyard, exulting in his rapid progress at school, and gulping down great draughts of Tom Jones, Peregrine Pickle, Roderick Random, Don Quixote, The Vicar of Wakefield, The Arabian Nights, *and* Robinson Crusoe, *which he had found in a little back room in the house. As he grew older, kind friends sometimes took him to the little theater in Rochester, where he delighted in the great clown Joe Grimaldi and thrilled to* Macbeth. *With his father, too, he wandered on long, talkative walks exploring the precincts of Rochester's gray Norman cathedral, clambering the ruins of its crumbling old castle, crossing Rochester Bridge and climbing the long hill of the Dover Road to ramble through Cobham Wood and come out by Gad's Hill, where Falstaff robbed the travelers. Here the boy would always gaze with admiration on the rose-brick front of Gad's Hill Place, and heave a deep sigh of incredulity and longing while his father elegantly informed him that if he were to work very hard he might some day come to dwell there.*

Like an enchanted dream these days suddenly vanished. In the winter of 1822 John Dickens was ordered back to London. The family finances were now very bad. The parents, with their six children, were crowded into a four-room house in Camden Town, a neighborhood of small artisans, washerwomen, and Bow Street runners, where the surrounding fields were dotted with garbage dumps. Instead of con-

tinuing school Charles found himself running errands, drudging about the house, and blacking the family boots. The small, well-fingered collection of books was sold; Charles was sent to the pawnbroker with teaspoons, silver teapots, and other small articles that yielded a few shillings; little by little even the family furniture disappeared, until they were camping in the downstairs rooms with a kitchen table, a few chairs, and the beds. At the hall door, unpaid tradesmen bawled angry demands to have their bills settled, while John Dickens trembled in a room above. Between husband and wife there were worried discussions of a "deed," a financial agreement with the creditors, which their small son's frightened imagination confused with some horrible Satanic compact or with the unnamed deed of the witches in Macbeth.

All at once there fell a worse blow. A relation by marriage offered Charles six shillings a week to tie up and label bottles in a blacking warehouse from eight in the morning to eight at night. In their distress his parents accepted the offer, and on his twelfth birthday, despairingly, the child found himself condemned to monotonous toil among rough men and common boys. The blacking warehouse was a crazy, tumbledown building on the river at the foot of Hungerford Stairs, odorous with dirt and decay, rotten floors and dank cellars overrun with old gray rats. A fortnight later John Dickens was arrested for debt and imprisoned in the Marshalsea.

Weeping in the jail lodge, his father told Charles that the sun had set upon him forever. The boy thought that his heart was broken. Escape from the blacking warehouse seemed hopeless. Even twenty-five years later, "No words can express the secret agony of my soul," he wrote, "as I sunk into this companionship; compared these every day associates with those of my happier childhood; and felt my early hopes of growing up to be a learned and distinguished man, crushed in my breast. . . . My whole nature was so penetrated with the grief and humiliation of such considerations, that even now, famous and caressed and happy, I often forget in my dreams that I have a dear wife and children; even that I am a man; and wander desolately back to that time of my life."

His mother and the younger children went to live with John Dickens in the Marshalsea, but Charles had a small room outside the jail, from which he trudged to and from the blacking warehouse. His breakfast of bread and milk and his supper of bread and cheese he provided for himself out of his small earnings. "They made a hole in the six or seven shillings, I know well; and I was out at the blacking-warehouse all day, and had to support myself upon that money all the week. . . . I certainly had no other assistance . . . No advice, no counsel, no encouragement, no consolation, no support, from anyone that I can call to mind, so help me God. . . . I know that I do not exaggerate, unconsciously and unintentionally . . . I know that I have lounged about the streets, insufficiently and unsatisfactorily fed. I know that, but for the mercy of God, I might easily have been, for any care that was taken of me, a little robber or a little vagabond."

Even when a small legacy luckily enabled his father to pay his debts and obtain his release from prison, his parents did not think of sending Charles back to school. The weary months dragged on. Once his father came to the warehouse and saw him engaged in his menial toil, and Charles wondered how he could bear it. But at last, one day, his father quarreled with the relation for whom Charles worked, quarreled about him, violently, and said he should go back to the warehouse no more, but be sent again to school. His mother, appalled at even this small loss to the family income, tried to patch up the quarrel and brought next day an invitation for Charles to return to the warehouse. But John Dickens stood firm. "I do not write resentfully or angrily," Dickens said, "for I know how all these things have worked together to make me what I am; but I never afterwards forgot, I never shall forget, I never can forget, that my mother was warm for my being sent back."

The time the boy spent in the blacking warehouse was no more than four or five months. For him, though, it was an eternity of despair from which he had felt no prospect of ever being released, and the agony ate its way indelibly into his soul. The experience was both formative and corrosive. Deep within him, his spirit made the decision that never should such things happen to him again. He would fall prey to none of the slipshod imprudence that had ruined his father. He would subject himself to a discipline of steel. No obstacle should stand between him and ambition; no grief or frustration arrest his strivings. But the blacking warehouse that made him a man of insuperable resolve and deadly determination, also made him for life a sympathizer with all suffering and with all victims of injustice.

Meanwhile, he was sent as a day pupil to Wellington House Academy in the Hampstead Road (an institution whose proprietor he later pilloried as Mr. Creakle in David Copperfield*). This second school* *time did not last long. The Navy Pay Office would not retain a man who had been in debtors' prison, and John Dickens was forced to resign, although in consideration for his years of service and his family of six children he was granted a pension of £145. This was not enough to live on; industriously John Dickens fitted himself to become a newspaper reporter and obtained employment in the London press. As always, he was able and hard-working, but, as always, he was unable to live within his income. In March 1827 the Dickenses were evicted from their house at 29 Johnson Street for failure to pay their rent, and around the same time Charles left school.*

He became an office boy for the law firm of Ellis and Blackmore, where his salary rose from ten shillings to thirteen and six and then to fifteen shillings. But he found the work dull and advancement slow, and the law seemed to him an involved hocus-pocus in which lawyers entangled its victims. He wanted a speedier and more exciting path to prosperity. Through his father he knew that the crack reporters who took down the debates of Parliament earned as much as fifteen guineas a week. Better still, many distinguished men had begun as parliamentary reporters. With enormous vigor Dickens taught himself shorthand. Two months before he was seventeen, at the end of November 1828, he threw up his job with Ellis and Blackmore and became a freelance reporter in the law courts of Doctors' Commons, hiring himself out to take down stenographic records. By the time he was twenty he was a reporter for the Mirror of Parliament *and a new paper named the* True Sun; *within two years he was on the* Morning Chronicle, *the most important Whig newspaper in London.*

His determined drive had entailed a struggle all the more desperate because for almost four of those years he had been unhappily in love. In 1829 he had met Maria Beadnell, a diminutive siren with dark ringlets, the brightest of eyes, and a "prettily pettish manner" that soon reduced him to abject slavery. Her father was a bank manager who at first paid little attention to Dickens among the other young men who danced attendance on his three attractive daughters. Charles and Maria exchanged letters and little gifts and he believed that she loved him. He lived in a mist of shining dreams and wretched happiness; all delight was in being with her, all misery in separation from her.

Mr. and Mrs. Beadnell, however, did not take long to make up their minds that this sparkling but ineligible young man was dangerous. A shorthand reporter was not a banker's dream for his daughter, and Mr.

Beadnell had also learned of John Dickens's incarceration in the Marshalsea. Suddenly Maria was sent to Paris "to finish her education." When she returned in 1832 she was strangely altered. Now there were coldnesses, quarrels, caprices, reproaches. Dickens was bewildered and sick and miserable. Maria coquetted and tormented him, and he stumbled on from month to month through a fog of complex misery and fruitless devotion. At last he perceived that his suit was hopeless. While Maria still alternately frowned and relented, he found the strength and courage to say good-by and go his way.

The wounds left in Dickens's heart by this unhappy love merge with the shadow cast by the spiked wall of the Marshalsea and the imprisoning shades of the blacking warehouse. They deepened his intense capacity for suffering, and for feeling with suffering. They hardened his determination to slash through all material obstacles. He well knew how much his shabby background and his mediocre prospects had to do with his ineligibility as a suitor. The hope of winning Maria had steeled his ambitious efforts, and he had lost that hope just as he was achieving recognition. The experience not only focused into burning clarity his impassioned resolve never again to be the victim of indigence, it made him adamantine when his will was pitted against the will of others. And linked with this domineering and overbearing tendency, rooted in the same causes, was his excessive vulnerability to psychological pain. He was both sensitive and truculently assertive, at once eager for affection and sympathy and habitually armored in a reserve no less real for all the bright exuberance with which he faced the world.

Such was the background of experience that had made Charles Dickens the man he was when he and Angela Burdett first met.

I I I

She was born April 25, 1814. Although her heritage united the pride of an ancient family name and enormous wealth, her father, Sir Francis Burdett, gave a blazing support to all the most radical and uncompromising reform movements of the day. At the age of twenty-three, in 1793, he had married Sophia, the third daughter of Thomas Coutts, and it is probable that the conservative financier, who was a friend of Georgiana, Duchess of Devonshire, and banker to the Prince Regent, was often somewhat embarrassed by his firebrand son-in-law. Young Sir Francis was a stormy figure in British politics. He had been in

Paris during the early days of the French Revolution and attended meetings of the political clubs. As a member of Parliament in 1796 he joined the Constitutional Association for promoting parliamentary reform. In 1797 he delivered a vehement indictment of the Government's encroachment on popular rights and stigmatized the war against France as an attempt to stifle the flame of liberty. He made repeated protests against the restraints on freedom of speech, protested the suspension of habeas corpus, demanded an inquiry into the mismanagement of Coldbath Fields Prison, where persons suspected of being subversive were detained and treated like convicted felons.

Angry opponents bawled that his aim was merely to win the applause of the mob. Between 1802 and 1806 determined efforts were made to void his election to Parliament, vast sums were spent on both sides, and his election alternately declared legal and illegal. In 1806 he was finally ejected. He was promptly elected as Member for Westminster. A public dinner was held in celebration of his victory, and he was borne through the streets in a triumphal car. In Parliament he was more uncompromising than ever. He spoke against corporal punishment in the army, supported a motion to inquire into the alleged parliamentary corruption of the ministers, made a speech against the exclusion of listeners from the proceedings of the House of Commons.

When he published this speech as a pamphlet the Speaker of the House ruled it a breach of privilege and issued a warrant for his arrest. Burdett announced that he would refuse to surrender except to force. Lord Eldon, the Lord Chancellor, was not certain that the authorities could legally break down his door; Lord Redesdale suggested an act of attainder. Mobs gathered in Westminster and Burdett's house was garrisoned by volunteers. On the fourth day of this siege the Government made forcible entry, Burdett was taken to the Tower, and London was guarded by thousands of soldiers. He was in prison for only a few weeks when Parliament was prorogued and he was released. He promptly brought legal action against the Speaker and the sergeant-at-arms, but lost. Meanwhile he had won re-election from Westminster with flying colors. He held the same seat for the next thirty years.

He did not cease to be both progressive and violently outspoken. In 1820 he was convicted at the Leicester assizes for a flaming attack on the conduct of the authorities after the "Peterloo Massacre," when an unarmed and orderly crowd of 60,000 men, women, and children in St. Peter's Fields, Manchester, had been charged by a regiment of cavalry who slashed at them with sabers and trampled them under the horses' hoofs. He was fined £2000 and sentenced to three months' imprisonment. In 1828 he carried a motion to consider the laws affecting Roman Catholics; that very year the Test and Corporation Acts were repealed and the following year saw Catholic emancipation achieved. He was a vigorous supporter of Lord Grey in bringing about the Reform Bill of 1832. When the death of William IV and the accession of Victoria to the throne entailed the dissolution of Parliament in 1837, he resigned his seat for Westminster, but in the general election was brought in for North Wiltshire, where he had large estates. This seat he occupied until his death in 1844.

Although Burdett's youngest daughter had none of her father's hotheaded impetuosity, there can be no doubt that all her social sympathies were deeply permeated with his influence. She was always to regard her position in society as a responsibility and its use for the welfare of others as a duty. But in her a deep sense of balance and sobriety, perhaps inherited from her shrewd and cautious banker grandfather, tempered the passions with judgment. Her will was obstinate but imperturbable, moving unalterably upon its course, never losing sight of its purposes and pressing them with relentless determination. Deliberate in making up her mind, she could neither be hurried nor deflected. Beneath her still calm of manner, however, this deep-eyed girl burned with an intense earnestness of feeling.

Her childhood was largely passed at her father's country estates at Ramsbury in Wiltshire and Foremark in Derbyshire, with occasional visits to Bath. When she was nine, Miss Hannah Meredith was chosen as her governess, and later became and remained her companion and lifelong friend. At her father's town house in St. James's Place, in girlhood, Angela Burdett met Wordsworth, Thomas Moore, the old banker-poet Samuel Rogers, the painter Sir Thomas Lawrence, the aging Duke of Wellington, and the young Disraeli, resplendent in gold-flowered waistcoats. With Miss Meredith she traveled abroad for three years, learning to speak French, German, and Italian. But while she was still a girl her prospects had dazzlingly changed. As the youngest of Sir Francis Burdett's six children she could have hoped for no more than a settlement of a few thousand pounds a year upon marriage. In 1824 she became the heiress to her grandfather's enormous fortune of over £50,000 a year.

The circumstances were complicated. Of plebeian origin, Thomas

Coutts had spent half a century building up the power of the bank that bore his name. He had sent his three daughters to a fashionable school in Queen Square, Bloomsbury, and the eldest and youngest — the second was delicate in health — to finishing school in Paris. The eldest, Susan, had married the Earl of Guilford; the second, Frances, had married the Marquis of Bute; and the third, Sophia, had married Sir Francis Burdett. To each of his daughters their father had given £45,000, and the Burdetts presently came to live at 1 Stratton Street, in a house belonging to Thomas Coutts and adjoining the house at 78 Piccadilly which he occupied himself.

In 1814 his wife died. Within a fortnight the old man — he was at this time eighty years of age — married an actress named Harriot Mellon, who was more than forty years his junior. Although his daughters had no belief in the scandalous rumors of her being his mistress that had long circulated in the newspapers, and had at times written her affectionate letters, they were furious at the match. Thomas Coutts took a house in Southampton Street, Covent Garden, alternately living there and in his suburban villa of Holly Lodge, Highgate. Sir Francis, outspoken as always, voiced his hostility, and was angrily ordered to vacate Stratton Street. When the old man died in 1822 it seemed that the family's worst fears had been realized. Four years earlier he had made a will mentioning the provision he had already made for his daughters and leaving his entire fortune to his widow.

But Harriot Coutts was not a fortune huntress. In that first year she gave her three stepdaughters £9000 each; two years later she gave them about £30,000 out of an income of £53,000. And she had already made it clear that when she died the bulk of her inheritance would return to the family. The sincerity, simplicity, and tenderness of her nature are revealed in a letter written to her friend Sir Walter Scott when, in 1827, she was about to marry Aubrey de Vere, the ninth Duke of St. Albans:

> *What a strange eventful life has mine been, from a poor little player child, with just food and clothes to cover me, dependent on a precarious profession, without talent or a friend in the world! "to have seen what I have seen, seeing what I see." Is it not wonderful? is it true? Can I believe it — first the wife of the best, the most perfect being that ever breathed, his love and unbounded confidence in me, his immense fortune so honourably acquired by his own industry, all at my command . . . and now*

the wife of a Duke. You must write my life; the History of Tom Thumb, Jack the Giant-Killer, and Goody Two-Shoes will sink compared with my true history written by the author of Waverley.

Lady Bute had hoped that her son, Lord Dudley Coutts Stuart, would enter the bank and wield the Coutts control there, and Harriot Coutts had indeed at first intended to make him her heir. But in 1824 he married the daughter of Lucien Bonaparte and was at once disinherited. His cousin Angela was installed in his place, with the provision that if she married a foreigner her interest in the bank must go to one of her sisters. When Lady St. Albans died in 1837, it was learned that she had left her widower an annuity of £10,000 and the use of Holly Lodge and her town house for his lifetime, and that on his death even these were to revert to Angela Burdett. All the rest, including 78 Piccadilly, Thomas Coutts's half of all the shares in the bank, and his casting vote in case of a tie between the shareholders, came to her at once. Still only twenty-three, she dazzled rumor as "the richest heiress in all England."

With her inheritance she added to her name the surname of Coutts. Barham's *Ingoldsby Legends* describes her at the coronation of Queen Victoria in 1838 as

that swate charmer,
The female heiress, Miss Anja-lay Coutts.

Society was breathless about whom she might marry. Within the next two years every eligible young man in England was supposed to have asked her hand. Gossip included even the old Duke of Wellington among her suitors, and said that she had refused Prince Louis Napoleon, the nephew of Bonaparte. But when she attended the marriage of Queen Victoria and Prince Albert in 1840, glittering with famous jewels that included the tiara of Marie Antoinette, she was still unmarried. Even then no one would have imagined that she would remain a spinster for another forty years.

She moved in the most distinguished circles, political, social, and intellectual. Wilberforce and Sir Robert Peel were among her intimates. She was on cordial terms with the Duke and Duchess of Cambridge and with the Duc d'Aumale. After Louis Napoleon became Emperor of the French she visited him and Eugénie at Compiègne. Men of science, too, were her friends: Faraday, Tyndall, Hooker, and the geologist Pengelly. Among American men of letters

and statesmen she knew Motley, Bancroft, Lowell, Webster, and Ever-
ett. Through Dickens she became friendly with William Charles Mac-
ready, the famous actor; in later years she knew Sir Henry Irving. In
1855 she bought many of the famous pictures in the collection of Sam-
uel Rogers. But the heart of her life was in her numerous philanthropic
activities, both public and private, and it was these that deepened her
intimacy with Dickens.

I V

The more than five hundred of his letters to her that have survived
extend from a time about three years after Dickens's rise into fame
to within almost three years of his death. Although the greater part
of them are primarily concerned with the welfare work and the in-
dividual charities he and Miss Coutts carried on together, there is no
part of his life, either personal or literary, that they do not strikingly
illumine. Not even his surviving letters to his close friend John Forster
are nearly so numerous and complete — many of these exist only in the
excerpts that Forster quoted in his biography of Dickens — nor do they
throw upon Dickens's character and career a more searching light.

In these letters to Miss Coutts we see Dickens almost as he lived
from day to day, his amusements and vacations, his magazine editing,
his play-acting and directing, his literary career from The Old Curiosity Shop *to* Our Mutual Friend, *together with his struggles, his*
peaks of elation, his angers, his high spirits, and his bitter gulfs of de-
pression. There are sharp diatribes against the state of the world and
wildly hilarious pieces of foolery, earnest outpourings of plans, clear
accounts of practical work accomplished, vivid portraits of friends and
acquaintances, colorful and sometimes dramatic anecdotes of the
day's adventures, generous tributes to the deeds and characters of
other people, unpretentious but noble affirmations of his own social
creed. The whole man is in these letters.

No one more constantly worked for others in the midst of a laborious
career. While he was pouring out The Old Curiosity Shop, Barnaby
Rudge, *and* Martin Chuzzlewit, *Dickens was devoting nights to*
visiting the "ragged schools," where slum children were provided free
instruction, helping them find new and cleaner quarters, giving and
obtaining financial support. He spent days advancing the welfare of
the orphaned Elton children, whose father had drowned in the Irish
Sea; even while he was rushing The Chimes *through the press he was*

looking after the orphans of the poor carpenter John Overs. In the midst of Dombey and Son *he planned, established, and superintended Miss Coutts's Home for Fallen Women at Shepherd's Bush. As he drove through the long monthly installments of* David Copperfield *he was vigorously supporting Mrs. Caroline Chisholm's Family Colonization Loan Society to help poor people emigrate to Australia, and publishing articles about her work in his newly established weekly magazine* Household Words. *At the same time, "I dream of Mrs Chisholm's housekeeping," he wrote Miss Coutts. "The dirty faces of her children are my continual companions"; and her neglect of her own family partly inspired the character of Mrs. Jellyby in his next novel,* Bleak House. *All these busy activities of his life are in these letters, as well as a constant stream of speaking engagements at lyceums and mechanics' institutes and of theatrical benefits for charitable causes.*

The amusements and relaxations of Dickens's life are here too. From his pen we learn of "the children's Fairy-plays" at Tavistock House on Twelfth Night, of Fortunio and His Seven Gifted Servants *and of Fielding's* Tom Thumb, *with the small hero "represented by one of our tiniest babies" and all the other childish actors looking "like little pieces of china." In 1853, worn out by almost two years of toil on* Bleak House, *Dickens took a vacation trip through Italy with his friends Wilkie Collins and the artist Augustus Egg. The coastal steamer from Genoa to Naples was so crowded that there were no staterooms available, but Dickens was able to cajole the captain into finding special accommodations for them — in consequence of which Collins and Egg slept in a storeroom whence they emerged "profoundly innocent" of the fact that they smelt of pickles and Gloucester cheese, and Dickens bunked on a narrow pallet down in the bowels of the ship with "the engine under the pillow" and an "extremely nervous" wall "in a profuse perspiration of warm oil." The lively letters in which Dickens revealed these and the other events of their three months of companionship are almost a journal of the tour.*

Such concrete details paint in new and brilliant coloring even those parts of Dickens's life that are known from other sources. But more important still, these letters throw a flood of light into significant areas of which little has been known until now, sometimes into the almost totally unknown. An unending stream of them reveals his painstaking care in bringing up and educating his children and his thoughtful efforts to provide a good start in life for each of his seven sons, from his eldest born, Charley, down to the baby, "Plorn," of whose beauty, size, and vigor Dickens constantly makes grandiose parental boast.

The letters dealing with Charley fill many pages. Miss Coutts, as his godmother, had begged to be allowed to defray the expenses of his schooling, and her generosity paid for his education at King's College School in London, at Eton, and abroad in Germany. Although he was, Dickens said, "the best of boys," and gave ground for hope that he would "not be among anything but the best of men," his lack of energy and industry filled his father with concern. Dickens thought him "quick and sensitive," but observed about him even in childhood what he called "a strange kind of fading" developing with youth into "an indescribable lassitude of character" — inherited, Dickens feared, from his mother — and indicating a lack of fixed purpose that his resolute father found disquieting. "I believe him to have fewer active faults than ninety-nine boys out of a hundred at his age; but his virtues and merits all want activity too." He vacillated between going into the army, studying for the bar, and entering upon a mercantile career, and only after long uncertainty settled down, through Dickens's aid and Miss Coutts's financial connections, to a business calling with a position in the great firm of Baring Brothers.

Walter, the second son, Dickens feared was "a little slow," but praised as "a hard-working, patient capable child," steady and reliable. He decided on a military career, and, although he was not good enough at mathematics to enter the engineers, obtained through Miss Coutts's influence a cadetship in India. Frank was even more indecisive than Charley. He wanted to be a doctor, then a gentleman farmer, then a doctor again; he went into business and didn't like it, was tried out unsuccessfully in the office of Household Words, entered for the bar but disliked law; ultimately expressed a desire to join the Bengal Mounted Police, which Dickens enabled him to do. Alfred was trained for the artillery, changed his mind and decided to go into business. After a short trial he gave it up, feeling that he would like to try Australia, and emigrated with Dickens's aid. Throughout the years we see Dickens wrestling with such problems in an anxious and loving endeavor to ensure the welfare of his brood.

No less revealing are the letters in which Dickens speaks of his wife. None of his other correspondence — not even with Forster and Collins, *the two men in whom he confided most intimately — tells so much about his unhappy marriage as the letters he addressed to Miss Coutts on the verge of his separation from Catherine and in the years that followed. (To Forster and Collins it is not improbable, of course, that he spoke directly and had no need to resort to writing.) If his words to Miss Coutts are distorted by anguish and do not contain the perfect truth about what Catherine Dickens was like or about all the accumulating causes of their domestic misery, they illumine with distressing clarity how it seemed to Dickens and what wounds were left upon his heart. Whenever he recurs to this agonizing theme his words throb with an intensity that agitates his very life-blood.*

"No two people were ever created," he cries, "with such an impossibility of interest, sympathy, confidence, sentiment, tender union of any kind between them, as there is between my wife and me. It is an immense misfortune to her — it is an immense misfortune to me . . . I merely mention a fact which may induce you to pity us both, when I tell you that she is the only person I have ever known with whom I could not get on somehow or other . . ." Nor, he insists, does she love the children, or they her. "Mary and Katey (whose dispositions are of the gentlest and most affectionate conceivable) harden into stone figures of girls when they can be got to go near her . . ." "From Walter away in India to little Plornish at Gad's Hill there is a grim knowledge among them as familiar to them as the knowledge of Day Light, that what I now write is the plain bare fact."

Miss Coutts tried gently but vainly to bring Dickens and Catherine together again. Even with the passage of time, after the separation, his scars did not entirely heal. When Miss Coutts made another effort in 1860 he remained adamantine. "In the last two years, I have been stabbed too often and too deep, not to have a settled knowledge of the wounded place. . . . That figure is out of my life for evermore (except to darken it) and my desire is, Never to see it again." Four years later still, the bitterness had dwindled, but Dickens's only desire was to forget. "Do not think me unimpressed by certain words in your letter concerning forgiveness and tenderness when I say that I do not claim to have anything to forgive — that if I had, I hope and believe I would forgive freely — but that a page in my life which once had writing on it, has become absolutely blank, and that it is not in my power to pretend that it has a solitary word upon it."

V

The largest and most important single theme of these letters, however, is the work that Dickens and Miss Coutts were carrying on together. In a way hardly more than hinted elsewhere, they reveal him as a practical and active figure in the field of social welfare. He was not only the creative imagination behind many of Miss Coutts's efforts, but their directing force and executive arm. He drew her attention to the ragged schools and enlisted her aid in their support; he conducted surveys in the slum districts of Westminster, Bethnal Green, and Bermondsey, and worked out plans for installing sanitary facilities and running water in tenement houses; he established and superintended the Home at Shepherd's Bush for reforming prostitutes and then sending them abroad; he suggested plans for slum clearance and model housing projects and drew up detailed schemes for garden-surrounded community flats; and often, even while he was carrying on his own work, he took personal and active charge of many of these enterprises and devoted days to their details.

His insistence upon the need for free education was fierce and unfaltering. After his first visit to a Ragged School, "I have very seldom seen," he wrote, "in all the strange and dreadful things I have seen in London and elsewhere, anything so shocking as the dire neglect of soul and body exhibited in these children. And although I know; and am as sure as it is possible for one to be . . . that in the prodigious misery and ignorance of the swarming masses of mankind in England, the seeds of its certain ruin are sown, I never saw that Truth so staring out in hopeless characters, as it does from the walls of this place." Equally emphatic was his stress upon the principle that education must not be purely utilitarian and factual, but must appeal to the senses and the emotions. "Whether this effort will succeed, it is quite impossible to say. But that it is a great one, beginning at the right end, among thousands of immortal creatures, who cannot, in their present state, be held accountable for what they do, it is as impossible to doubt."

An identical insight illumines his plans for Urania Cottage, the Home at Shepherd's Bush. It is ridiculous, he points out, to talk to a prostitute of her duty to society. "Society has used her ill and turned away from her, and she cannot be expected to take much heed of its rights or wrongs." Instead, she must be "tempted to virtue" by kind-

ness; enabled to recover self-respect through acquiring control, neatness, and efficiency at an occupation. "Her pride, her emulation, her sense of shame, her heart, her reason, and her interest" must all be appealed to. There must be no emphasis upon a harsh and vindictive morality. There must be no suggestion that the work needed to carry on the Home was punishment. Everyone must be given hope that she could regain a decent position in society, perhaps some day even marry. The dresses must not be drab prisonlike uniforms, but have a variety of cheerful colors, striped and flowered. There must be recreational reading, not limited to the piously devotional, and group singing. (Mrs. Chisholm asked Dickens "if it were true that the girls at Shepherd's Bush 'had pianos'"; "I shall always regret," he gaily wrote Miss Coutts, "that I didn't say yes — each girl a grand, downstairs — and a cottage in her bedroom — besides a small guitar in the wash-house.") They must not be sent to bed at the absurdly early hours often imposed in other institutions. At the same time a discipline must be learned that would be useful both in strengthening the character and taking a place in the world.

No brief discussion can call attention to all of the other aspects of an enlightened social philosophy that are indicated in these letters on Urania Cottage and in those on the Westminster sanitary survey, the Columbia Square apartments, reform of the administrative agencies of government, and dozens of other topics. Without being in the slightest degree sentimentally deluded about what all the Circumlocution Offices in the country were in actuality, under a social system dominated by the power of wealth and privilege, Dickens was deterred by no fear of "centralization" or "creeping socialism" from demanding fiercely that the government reshape itself into an instrument for the welfare of the masses.

Nothing could be more remote from the flavor of these letters, however, than to imagine them as devoted largely to dealing with an abstract program of social reform. They are full of human interest, of dramatic episodes, and of vivid little pictures of people. There are, for example, the two matrons at Urania Cottage, feeling that it is beneath their dignity to arise early on washing days and superintend the laundering operations of the inmates; Mrs. Holdsworth tells Dickens "with a face of the most portentous woe and intensity, that 'she couldn't do it.' I informed her, in reply, that that was an answer which I could by no means give to you . . ." "I hope you will keep Mrs Graves and Mrs Holdsworth to their tether," he writes in his next letter. "It is intolerable to be met with such mincing nonsense from those toiling and all-enduring dowagers."

These two settled down into useful activity, but six months later one of the teachers, Miss Cunliffe, of whom Dickens had at first thought well, turned out to be "a woman of an atrocious temper," "hectoring and driving" her charges. Arriving at the Home on a Saturday, Dickens found her "looking like a stage maniac in a domestic drama." In addition, he learned that she had been satisfying her curiosity by cross-questioning one of the girls about her past life, a prying that had been strictly forbidden. Miss Cunliffe consequently had to go. Gradually, however, a reliable and smoothly functioning staff was built up.

Not infrequently, of course, the girls themselves created disturbances. Isabella Gordon, a repeated troublemaker, who had threatened and attacked some of the other girls, finally tried to start an insurrection. Ordered to her room, "she danced upstairs . . . holding her skirts like a lady at a ball." It was decided that she could be given no more chances, but must be expelled. The girls and even the matrons "all cried bitterly"; a girl she had attacked "implored us to let her stay and give her one more trial — sobbing and weeping terribly. The girl herself, now that it had really come to this, cried, and hung down her head, and when she got out at the door, stopped and leaned against the house for a minute or two before she went to the gate — in a most miserable and wretched state." But if Dickens could be kind, he could be firm — the welfare of all the rest must outweigh the transitory regret of a girl who had over and over again proved herself incorrigible.

"Last night," says another letter, "that very bad and false subject, Jemima Hiscock, forced open the door of the little beer cellar with knives, and drank until she was dead drunk; when she used the most horrible language and made a very repulsive exhibition of herself. She induced Mary Joynes (!) to drink the beer with her; and that young lady was also drunk, but stupidly and drowsily. Mrs Morson, with the gardener's assistance, wisely abstained from calling in the Police, got them both to bed, locked them up, and came to me this morning."

Still another girl, having behaved badly, had her marks taken away from her for a month, and asked to speak to Dickens about it. "I wish you could have seen her come in diplomatically to make terms with the establishment. 'O! Without her marks, she found she couldn't do her work agreeable to herself — 'If you do it agreeable to us,' said I, 'that'll do.' — 'O! But' she said 'I could wish not to have my marks took away.' — 'Exactly so,' said I. 'That's quite right; and the only way to get them back again, is to do as well as you can.' — 'Ho! But if she didn't have 'em giv' up at once, she could wish fur to go.' — 'Very well,' said I. 'You shall go tomorrow morning.'"

But it is not only in dealing with the inhabitants of Urania Cottage that these letters gleam with the creative vitality of the novelist. Electric flashes of observation, vivid bits of reporting, humorous perception, sensitive response to every nuance of emotion and atmosphere, all pour out with a profusion of exuberance. Going on an errand for Miss Coutts to the home of an elderly artist, Mrs. Brayne, he caused, he remarks, "the most frightful consternation" by his arrival. "A large young family fled from the back parlor . . . and took refuge (with their mother) at the top of the stairs — where they stood, as I saw from the passage, like so many Ostriches — with their heads hidden, but their legs plainly visible; and I think I never saw so many legs listening at once . . ."

Or, inspecting a slum called Hickman's Folly, he notes parenthetically, "a Folly it is much to be regretted that Hickman ever committed," and goes on to describe it: "No more road than in an American swamp — odious sheds for horses, and donkeys, and vagrants, and rubbish . . . wooden houses like horrible old packing cases full of fever for a countless number of years. In a broken down gallery at the back of a row of these, there was a wan child looking over at a starved old white horse who was making a meal of oyster shells. The sun was going down and flaring out like an angry fire at the child — and the child, and I, and the pale horse, stared at one another in silence for some five minutes as if we were so many figures in a dismal allegory."

V I

The quotations I have used will leave the reader in no doubt that Dickens takes shiningly high rank as a letter writer. He challenges comparison with England's acknowledged masters. If he does not display the range of Horace Walpole's acquaintance in diplomatic, political, and aristocratic circles, his observation extends down into humble levels of society that Walpole never knew. He does not have Walpole's *sharp feline wit, but he is often witty. And although it is easy to under-estimate Walpole's capacity for depth of feeling, here Dickens leaves him far surpassed. William Cowper exceeds Dickens in tenderness, playful charm, and intimacy of emotion, and sometimes in awful in-tensity, but does not approach him in breadth of canvas or thronging vitality of experience. Among those who came before him only the noble and beautiful letters of John Keats are richer, sparkling with a more prismatic variety, and more deeply suffused with the fullness of a powerful personality.*

Even the best of Dickens's contemporaries are not his equals in their letters. Many of them — Browning, Thackeray, Tennyson, George Eliot, and Matthew Arnold — do not shine as correspondents. Edward Fitzgerald is exquisite, but his range is circumscribed. Thomas Bab-ington Macaulay, tremulously sensitive and affectionate as he is with his family, delightful as he can be in schoolboyish humor, and absolute as he is in integrity, becomes in the outer world all complacent self-assurance, unimaginative rigidity, and loud intolerance. Jane Welsh Carlyle, though brilliant in wit and psychological penetration, is a waspish letter writer who never misses the opportunity for a lethal sting. No particle their inferior in color, vitality, and ease, Dickens's letters surpass those of all three in the health and balanced largeness of their vision of the world. And to health and balance they add power: they constitute a fascinating portrait of an intensely dynamic man.

With this high estimate Bernard Shaw did not altogether agree. Though Dickens towered like a giant, he proclaimed, over all other English novelists, the letters, though often fine, lay upon a lower slope. Discussing the subject with me at Ayot St. Lawrence in 1945, he characterized them as "roast beef and Yorkshire pudding letters," ex-plaining that what he meant by this was that they were all concerned with things done, places visited, what people looked like and how they acted, limited to the concrete, sensuous, and immediate, that Dickens had nothing to say about art, philosophy, sociology, religion — in short, no interest in what Shaw has elsewhere called "the great synthetic ideals."

Now, it is true that Dickens's letters never make any such nobly eloquent general affirmation of faith as Shaw's King Magnus in The Apple Cart: *"I stand for the great abstractions; for conscience and virtue; for the eternal against the expedient; for the evolutionary appe-*

*tite against the day's gluttony; for intellectual integrity, for humanity
. . ." Dickens gave little expression to abstract thought. He preferred
to think in concrete terms, with which he felt more at home. But even
in his letters there are many comments on precisely those great European developments of the nineteenth century in which Shaw says
Dickens took no interest. His ideals are implicit in the deeds he praises
and the specific evils he denounces; his principles are embodied in
the work for the welfare of others that his letters tell.*

*From the letters in this very volume one may plainly infer how
clearly Dickens realized the urgent need for popular education and
what he thought the aims of that education should be; how important
he realized art to be for the heart and the imagination; how vigorously
he insisted upon decent living conditions for the poor, the dissemination of opportunity, and the creation of renewed opportunities for those
who stumbled and fell; how powerfully he emphasized the evaded
responsibilities of government; how noble and all-embracing was his
demand for social justice. These ideal enthusiasms and hopes are precisely those in which Shaw thought the letters deficient. Their emer-
gence from the letters, to be sure, would not in itself justify the claim
of literary greatness. Letters may dwell entirely in a humble and
domestic backwater, leaving all the great outside world only implied,
and still be works of art. But the letters of Dickens clearly fuse both
the abstract and the personal, the lofty wing of the ideal and the warm
colors of the everyday.*

*Their achievement embraces more than vividness, charm, vitality,
stylistic brilliance and movement, variety of tone and feeling, more
even than scope of subject matter and intellectual range. It lies in the
organic wholeness with which they reflect every facet of Dickens's
personality, every shining ray of his interests, every crosscurrent of his
emotions, the whole man, and that man one of the profoundest depths
of character and the highest greatness. They image both the heights
and the depths, the sources of his joys and triumphs, and, no less, the
external defeats and the internal flaws that generated the darkest of
his griefs and unhappiness. "Sparkling, clear, and sunny," the letters
of Dickens are, as Carlyle said, in sum total an "auto-biography, un-
rivaled in clearness and credibility." They reveal Dickens as a warmhearted humanitarian indeed, but as more than that, an effective worker
in the world of action, an artist and a great man worthy of the tremendous literary achievement he left behind him. Carlyle may give*

the valedictory: "His bright and joyful sympathy with everything around him; his steady practicality, withal; the singularly solid business talent he continually had; and, deeper than all, if one has the eye to see deep enough, dark, fateful, silent elements, tragic to look upon, and hiding, amid dazzling radiances as of the sun, the elements of death itself."

I

Star Ascendant

*D*URING *the opening dozen years of Dickens's career his rise was rapid and dazzling. Almost every novel he wrote represented an advance over its predecessors in structural skill and intellectual grasp. With his glowing enjoyment of all the rich variety of existence, his delight in the varicolored aspects of human nature, and his zeal for the welfare of mankind, he developed as both a literary artist of brilliant genius and a social reformer of penetrating insight. In long explorations through London's slums and in repeated journeys through the manufacturing towns of England he learned how an industrial civilization was affecting the lives of the poor, and in innumerable parliamentary blue books he studied its consequences in child labor, conditions in mines and factories, filth and disease in people's homes, illiteracy, brutality, and crime in their lives.*

His knowledge made him both a compassionate advocate of social betterment in all his written works and a man of action, laboring persistently to help all victims of misfortune upon whom he came, seeking out still others, and tirelessly devising ways of dealing with specific evils to which he devoted hours of effort beyond those he spent at his desk. The letters of these years — and pre-eminently those here contained, which he wrote to Miss Coutts — reveal Dickens in action, moved by a most warmhearted social conscience to the most practical efforts, not only in behalf of individuals but in striking at the ignorance and dirt that degraded the lives of whole classes of the poor and fostered every social evil.

They reveal also the enormous vitality of a man responding vividly to every stimulus of his life: the love of his children, the companionship of his friends, the enthusiasm of his work, the development of his literary powers, and the excitement of his fame. There are traces, to be sure, even here, of the restlessness, the emotional dissatisfactions of his marriage, and the exasperation over the state of society that

*disturbed his later life. They are hinted in the quest for change that
rushed him off to America in 1842, that made him pull up stakes
again for a year in Italy in 1844 and brought him dashing back to
London that very winter merely to read* The Chimes *to his friends,
that took him away to Switzerland in 1846, and kept him shuttling
back and forth between London and Paris during the next two years.
But on the whole these years were not only vigorous — all Dickens's
life was that — they were happy ones as well, full of fruitful growth
and immeasurable gusto.*

*And outwardly he had attained a position of unequaled eminence.
By 1848 his fame was international. It had spread not only throughout
the British Empire and the United States; he was known everywhere
on the continent of Europe — in Germany, in France, in Italy, even in
Russia. During his incredible early years, a critic in the* Quarterly
Review *warned that he was writing too much and too fast; if he persisted his fate was certain: "he has risen like a rocket, and he will
come down like the stick." But he never did come down. What looked
like the ascent of a rocket — or the sweep of a comet — was in reality
the birth of a star.*

*The young man who dined with Miss Coutts at Mr. Marjoribanks's
table in 1835 was merely a clever reporter who had written a few
sketches. Collected into two volumes entitled* Sketches by Boz, *these
scored a modest success when they were published on February 6,
1836, the day before his twenty-fourth birthday. With the end of April
in that same year* Pickwick Papers *began coming out in green-covered
monthly installments. At the start the new venture languished, not
even selling the four hundred copies of its first printing. Suddenly,
after the introduction of Sam Weller in the fourth number, sales began to go with a rush; orders for back numbers swelled; before
the end, readers were snapping up forty thousand copies of every
number.*

*The enthusiasm of readers was echoed by a chorus of critical praise
loud and well-nigh unanimous. "Smollett never did anything better,"
said one reviewer. Another compared Mr. Pickwick and Sam Weller
to Don Quixote and Sancho Panza. Mary Russell Mitford compared
Dickens with Shakespeare. On every level, from Lord Chief Justice
Denman to street urchins, Pickwick became a mania. Never had there
been anything like it. There were Pickwick chintzes, Pickwick cigars,*

Pickwick hats and coats, Weller corduroys, Boz cabs. People named their dogs and cats "Sam," "Jingle," "Mrs. Bardell," and "Job Trotter." Hardly past twenty-five, Dickens was already famous, beaten upon by a limelight that bathed him for the remainder of his life.

He moved from the modest three rooms he had occupied at Furnival's Inn to a comfortable house in Doughty Street, and then, only two years later, to Devonshire Terrace, which was almost a miniature mansion, with a large walled garden at one side and a coach house in the rear. Reporting he gave up almost at once, became editor of Bentley's Miscellany, and — even while Pickwick was still in mid-career — began writing Oliver Twist and bringing it out in the pages of the new magazine. Before Oliver was ended he started publishing Nicholas Nickleby. He quarreled with Bentley, both about money and about the publisher's interferences in editing the magazine, and made still more advantageous arrangements with Chapman and Hall, his Pickwick publishers, who established a new weekly called Master Humphrey's Clock entirely for him and absolutely subject to his direction. In its pages he began The Old Curiosity Shop, which was to be followed there with Barnaby Rudge.

Dickens's first eight or nine surviving letters to Miss Coutts reflect neither this rising fame nor their growing intimacy. For the most part, these are brief notes responding to invitations to dinner, the opera, or the theater. But their friendship deepened quickly, as its first striking proof reveals. In April 1836 Dickens had married Catherine Hogarth. Their first child, Charles Dickens, Jr., was born on January 6, 1837 — Twelfth Night — and Miss Coutts became the baby's godmother. "We christen the living wonder," Dickens wrote his friend Thomas Beard, "on Saturday," December 9, 1837, "at 12, New Pancridge" — an early "Gampism" for New St. Pancras Church. The ties between the twenty-three-year-old heiress and the twenty-five-year-old writer were already fast knit.

In the course of the next three years Dickens's star continued its rapid rise. The first number of Master Humphrey's Clock appeared on April 4, 1840 and sold 70,000 copies. After a brief setback, when the public discovered that the new periodical was not a novel, but a miscellany, Dickens saved the day by dropping the other features and transforming the magazine into a vehicle for The Old Curiosity Shop, which he rapidly expanded from a short story into a serial. Before it ended as many as 100,000 copies of each weekly issue were being purchased: approximately one for every ten family groups in England.

As the story drew to its foreshadowed close – the death of Nell – readers were agonized by foreboding grief. Anxious crowds at a New York pier shouted to an incoming vessel, "Is little Nell dead?" Daniel O'Connell, the Irish M.P., reading the fateful chapters in a railway carriage, burst into tears, groaned, "He should not have killed her," and despairingly threw the pages out of the train window. Dickens's friend William Charles Macready, the famous actor, noted in his diary, "I have never read printed words that gave me so much pain." The famous critic, Lord Jeffrey, bowed his head upon the table of his library, his eyes wet with tears.

It is this deep emotional response of Dickens's readers that is the background to the first of his letters to Miss Coutts here printed:

~

1.   JANUARY 22 [1841], DEVONSHIRE TERRACE

It has occurred to me – this is a kind of vanity to which the meekest of authors are occasionally liable – that when you came to read this week's number of the clock, you might possibly desire to know what the next one contained, without waiting seven days. I therefore make bold to send you, inclosed, the two numbers together,[1] begging you not to be at the trouble of returning them, as I have always plenty by me.

Beseeching you to with-hold this mighty revelation from all the world – except Miss Meredith, who is free to share it to the utmost, I am always

~

2.   APRIL 8, 1841, DEVONSHIRE TERRACE [TO EDWARD MARJORIBANKS]

Twice a year – that is, at the end of each volume – I hold, not a solemn supper, but a solemn dinner, whereat all the Clock "Works," publishers, printers, artists, engravers, etc, etc assemble together in high festival. And we make wonderful speeches I assure you, and

---

[1] In the preceding installment of the story, No. 42, the malignant hunchback, Daniel Quilp, had been drowned. In the current number, January 22, 1841, old Mr. Trent's brother has started off with Mr. Garland on the coach journey to find Nell and her grandfather and restore them to loving care and prosperity. With his letter Dickens enclosed Nos. 43 and 44. The latter described the too-late arrival that finds the child lying dead upon her couch with strips of holly on her breast.

strange things happen — such as men in black who were never seen
to smile before, cutting jokes — and songs breaking out in unexpected
places — and many other moral Vesuviuses of that nature.
Unhappily next Saturday is the great day. Three white waistcoats
have been seen on lines in suburban districts under suspicious circumstances, and I have reason to suppose are preparing for the occasion;
a studious-looking man has been observed in Saint John's Wood mut-
tering such scraps as "Gentlemen I rise" — "on the present occasion" —
"more than I can express" and so forth — and the description tallies
exactly with a renowned engraver.[2] Under any other circumstances
(I am serious now) I would have a cold immediately, but in this
predicament I have nothing for it but to regret most heartily you didn't
say Monday or any other day, indeed, but this.

ono

3.   APRIL 20, 1841, DEVONSHIRE TERRACE
   I thank you very much for the order (which I intended calling for
today, to save you trouble) and as you are so good as to offer your box
at the German opera, I will avail myself of your kindness, if you please,
on Thursday night.
   I have at length been enabled to discover the benevolent Porkman.
His name is Edward Hurcomb; his address, 19 William Street Lissom

---

   [2] There were 194 woodcut illlustrations to *Master Humphrey's Clock*. Of this
total, 154 were drawn by Hablot Knight Browne (1815–1882), whose pseudonym
of "Phiz" was devised to parallel that of "Boz," 39 by George Cattermole (1800–
1868), and one by Daniel Maclise (1806–1870), the historical painter. The actual
engravings on wood were mostly done by C. Gray, E. Landells, and S. Williams,
but although in the first paragraph of this letter Dickens mentions the presence at
the dinner of both the artists and the engravers it seems more likely that in this
paragraph he is referring to one of the artists.
   Dickens had become acquainted with Browne when the artist drew three illustrations for his pamphlet, *Sunday Under Three Heads*, in 1836. On the death of
Robert Seymour, the illustrator of *Pickwick Papers*, in that same year, after a brief
unsatisfactory trial of R. W. Buss, Dickens chose Browne to do the steel engravings
for the remainder of the story. Browne continued to illustrate Dickens's novels
through *A Tale of Two Cities* in 1859. A shy and timorous eccentric, he adapted
himself with responsive docility to the exacting demands Dickens made of his
illustrators.
   Cattermole married a distant cousin of Dickens's, Clarissa Elderton, in 1839.
Water-colorist and painter in oils, mainly of Biblical subjects, he began his career
with considerable success, but gradually sank into poverty. Maclise became one
of Dickens's close friends. He spent most of the later part of his life on the decorations and frescoes of the new Houses of Parliament, begun in 1840 to replace
the old building destroyed by the fire of 1834.

Grove. The poor distracted creature who stole the pork (I think it *was* pork) lives, or did live then, at No 1 Carlisle Mews Paddington. Her name is Maria Robinson. The circumstances occurred in Monday December the Twenty Eighth, and was reported in the newspaper Police accounts of the following day.[3]

I have given my binder instructions to put up an Old Curiosity Shop in one volume, and when it is becomingly dressed, to send it to you. I hope I may venture to beg your acceptance of it, in this more pleasant shape, as a slight but very sincere tribute of my respect and esteem, and as conveying the author's most cordial and hearty regard.

I should add two more sentences in reference to this copy of the tale which I am proud to believe has added something to your stock of pleasant associations. The first is, that the binder to whom I have sent it, is the slowest man in England. The second, that as I have told him to weed out all the foreign matter that was mixed up with its earlier pages, in the Clock, it will have some blank sides here and there, and will be regularly irregular in the numbers at the top of the leaves. But it will be all together, and free from interruptions, and will serve you, I hope, until it comes to be printed in a more convenient form, some years hence.

The raven's body [4] was removed with every regard for my feelings, in a covered basket. It was taken off to be stuffed, but has not come home yet. He has left a considerable property (chiefly in cheese and halfpence) buried in different parts of the garden; and the new raven — for I have a successor — administers to the effects. He had buried in one place, a ~~brush brush~~ brush (which I have made two efforts to write plainly) a very large hammer, and several raw potatoes, which were discovered yesterday. He was very uneasy just before death, and wandering in his mind, talked amazing nonsense. My servant thinks the hammer troubled him. It is supposed to have been stolen from a carpenter of vindictive disposition. — He was heard to threaten, and I am not without suspicions of Poison.

---

[3] The story was in the London *Times*, December 29, 1840, and the details are as Dickens remembered. The woman's husband had been out of work a long time and there were six children with almost nothing to cover them. In court, the mother's "careworn countenance and attenuated frame excited the commiseration of all present." Convinced that she had committed the robbery through distress, the pork butcher refused to prosecute and she was discharged.

[4] The raven was a family pet that suggested the raven "Grip" in *Barnaby Rudge*. It died March 31, 1841.

[P.S.] I beg my compliments to Miss Meredith whose cold, I hope, is better.

❧

4.   MAY 23, 1841, DEVONSHIRE TERRACE
I return you the *Curiosity Shop* with the something inserted. I meant so much in asking you to accept the book, that I forgot to say anything. Pray forgive me.

I have not seen Rachel [5] yet, being unwilling to be forced to believe that anybody or anything could impart an interest to Racine. I mean to wait for Mary Stuart; I am told she is a wonder, and am prepared to think so.

If anybody should entreat you to go to the Polytechnic Institution and have a Photographic likeness done — don't be prevailed upon, on any terms. The Sun is a great fellow in his way, but portrait painting is not his line. I speak from experience, having suffered dreadfully.

❧

5.   AUGUST 16, 1841, BROADSTAIRS, KENT
A kind of daymare comes upon me sometimes, under the influence of which I have dismal visions of your supposing me careless of your kind Invitations — regardless of your notes — insensible to your friendship — and a species of moral monster with the usual number of legs and arms, a head, and so forth, but no heart at all.

This disorder, instead of diminishing within the cheerful influence of the Sea, is so much aggravated by distance from Stratton Street and the obstacles in the way of telling you about it by word of mouth, that I am fairly driven to the desperate step of writing to you, to tell you how notes and cards of Invitation from you have reached me in Scotland, in Yorkshire, in Kent — in every place but London, and how I have reason to suppose that some others are still taking sportive flights among the Post Offices, and getting very brown from change of air in various parts of the United Kingdom.[6]

---

[5] Rachel, the famous actress Élisa Félix (1820/1821?–1858), who was appearing in London in 1841. Her finest roles were in the tragedies of Corneille and Racine, and, later, in Scribe and Legouvé's *Adrienne Lecouvreur*.

[6] Dickens was in Scotland from June 22, 1841, to the middle of July, was given a public banquet in Edinburgh, received the freedom of the city, visited Lord Jeffrey, and then made a brief tour of the Highlands. After returning to London, he spent August and September at the small Kentish fishing village of Broadstairs,

I have too much pleasure and gratification in the sympathy you have expressed, with my visionary friends, to let you forget me if I can help it. In duty to myself therefore — this is a description of moral obligation which most men discharge with the utmost punctuality — I raise my still small voice from the ocean's brink, and humbly desire to live in your recollection as an innocent, and not erring Individual, until next October.

If Miss Meredith should remember a fair young man with whom she had a community of feeling in reference to the impossibility of getting up in the morning during the Great Frost of eighteen hundred and forty-one, — I beg to say that I am the person, and that I send my compliments.

Let me add that I am always with high regard and esteem

ᴄᴡ

6.   OCTOBER 27, 1841, DEVONSHIRE TERRACE

Let me thank you for your kind recollection of me yesterday. I was greatly pleased to hear from you once more, I assure you.

I should have called in Stratton Street immediately on my return to town, but I have been exceedingly unwell. It is scarcely three weeks since I was obliged to submit to a painful surgical operation (for which agreeable change I left the seaside) and although I have recovered with a rapidity whereat the Doctors are astounded, I have only just begun to feel my legs at all steady under my diminished weight. I almost thought, at first, that I was about to go through life on two pillars of jelly, or tremulous Italian cream, — but I am happy to say that I am again conscious of floors and pavements.[7]

They tell me that in two or three days I may go to Windsor, and set up for myself as one who has no need of the Faculty. I shall not be there, I hope, more than a fortnight at the utmost, and on my return

---

where the Macreadys also spent their vacations, and where Dickens had been summering since 1837. Dickens had visited Yorkshire in 1838 to gather local color for the Dotheboys Hall scenes of *Nicholas Nickleby*, and he was already on friendly terms with Charles Smithson (the partner of his solicitor Thomas Mitton), who had a residence at Easthorpe Hall, Malton, Yorkshire, but I can find no record of Dickens's visiting Yorkshire in 1841.

[7] The operation was for a fistula October 8, 1841 (surgery had not yet developed the use of anesthetics), and for almost ten days afterward Dickens was so weak that he had to lie on a sofa all day. By the beginning of November, however, he was off to Richmond and then to Windsor, where he speedily recovered his health and spirits.

I shall be only too well pleased to present myself at Roehampton, or, if you should have left there, at your house in town.[8] I defer all particulars about America, until then.[9]

Some friends in Yorkshire have sent me a raven, before whom *the* raven (the dead one) sinks into insignificance. He can say anything — and he has a power of swallowing doorkeys and reproducing them at pleasure, which fills all beholders with mingled sensations of horror and satisfaction — if I may [say] so; with a kind of awful delight. His infancy and youth have been passed at a country public house, and I am told that the sight of a drunken man calls forth his utmost powers. My groom is unfortunately sober, and I have had no opportunity of testing this effect, but I have told him to "provide himself" elsewhere, and am looking out for another who can have a dissolute character from his last master.

With best regards to Miss Meredith, I am always Dear Miss Coutts

7.   NOVEMBER 24, 1841, DEVONSHIRE TERRACE

I beg to report myself quite well, and contemplating a descent upon Roehampton, where — I learn on enquiring at your house in town — you still are.

My domestic peace is so disturbed by rumours of Adelaide Kemble,[1] and my hearth is rendered so very desolate by the incursions of those who have heard her, that I can never hope for peace of mind until I have carried Mrs Dickens to Covent Garden Theatre. If, to this end, you can let me have your box any night next week, you will eternally oblige me, and do much to smooth my passage from my native shores.

I heartily wish I had been to America and had come home again. I am told that getting up in the morning *there* in the winter time, is beyond Miss Meredith's conception.

I beg my compliments to her, and am with sincerity

---

[8] Miss Coutts had a summer residence at Roehampton, just east of Richmond Park, and south of London, in Surrey. Her town house was at 1 Stratton Street, just off Piccadilly.

[9] The last installment of *Barnaby Rudge* was to be published in early December, and Dickens had determined to take a year's rest from novel-writing, travel in the United States in the first half of 1842, and gather material for a volume of travel impressions of America. He planned to sail on the *Britannia* on January 4.

[1] Adelaide Kemble (1814–1879), the opera singer, niece of Mrs. Siddons, sister of Fanny Kemble, and daughter of Charles Kemble. She had made her reputation in *Norma* at Venice in 1839.

8.   December 14, 1841, Devonshire Terrace

I am sincerely obliged to you for your kind Invitation, but I am obliged, most reluctantly, to deny myself the pleasure of accepting it. Every day this week I am engaged. As I shall have only a fortnight more when next Sunday comes, I have "registered a vow" (in imitation of Mr O'Connell) [2] to pass those fourteen days at home, and not to be tempted forth. Having withstood your note and acted so manfully in this trying situation, which is a kind of reversal of Eve and the Serpent, I feel that I can be adamant to everybody else. This is the only comfort I have in the penmanship of these words.

You will allow me, notwithstanding, to call upon you one morning before I go, to say good bye, and to take your orders for any article of a portable nature in my new line of business — such as a phial of Niagara water, a neat tomahawk, or a few scales of the celebrated sea serpent, which would perhaps be an improvement on writing paper, for Miss Meredith's pillows.[3]

I beg my compliments to her, and am sincerely

∾

Dickens landed in Boston on Saturday, January 22, 1842, was greeted with wild enthusiasm, sat for his portrait to Francis Alexander and for a bust by Henry Dexter, visited jails, poorhouses, hospitals, institutions for the blind, and the mills of Lowell, Massachusetts, met Henry Wadsworth Longfellow, Richard Henry Dana, Charles Sumner, and all the other notabilities of Boston, was given a grandiose ball and a banquet with interminable speeches, visited Cambridge and Harvard, and left the city on February 5. He proceeded by rail to Worcester, where he was entertained by Governor Davis, and thence to Hartford and New Haven, where further mobs of people pumped his hands. By steamer down the Connecticut River and Long Island Sound he went on to New York, arriving there February 13 and attending a fantastic "Boz Ball" the following evening. Next he moved on to Philadelphia and

---

[2] Daniel O'Connell (1775–1847), orator and politician, the leader of the agitation for Catholic emancipation, elected to Parliament 1828, and the leader of the "repeal" agitation in 1840.

[3] Miss Meredith stuffed pillows with finely cut up bits of paper and sent them to hospitals and other institutions in the East. Miss Coutts also made these pillows, and often puzzled her guests by asking for old envelopes that they were about to throw into wastebaskets and refusing to explain what she wanted them for. "But they are only old envelopes," they would exclaim, to which she replied only, "I know, but I like old envelopes."

*Baltimore, where no less frenzied welcomes awaited him. After that
came Baltimore, and Washington, where he was received by President
Tyler, and then a return to Baltimore, preparatory to setting off for
St. Louis, the westernmost point of his journeys.*

1895938

9.   MARCH 22, 1842, BALTIMORE
    You have long ago discharged from your mind any favorable opinion
you may ever have entertained of me — and have set me down, I know,
as a neglectful, erratic, promise-breaking, and most unworthy person.
    And yet I have not forgotten the book you asked me to bring home
for you — nor the pebble I am to gather for Lady Burdett [4] at Niagara —
nor the something unstipulated, which I am to put in my portmanteau
for Miss Meredith. The truth is that they give me everything here, but
Time. That they never will leave me alone. That I shake hands every
day when I am not travelling, with five or six hundred people. That
Mrs Dickens and I hold a formal Levee in every town we come to, and
usually faint away (from fatigue) every day while dressing for dinner.
— In a word, that we devoutly long for Home, and look forward to the
seventh of next June when we sail, please God, from New York — most
ardently.
    I have sent you some newspapers; and I hope they have reached you.
They gave me a ball at New York, at which Three Thousand people
were present — and a public dinner besides — and another in Boston —
and another in a place called Hartford. Others were projected, literally
all through the States, but I gave public notice that I couldn't accept
them: being of mere flesh and blood, and having only mortal powers of
digestion. But I have made an exception in favor of one body of readers at St Louis — a town in the Far West, on the confines of the Indian
territory. I am going there to dinner — it's only two thousand miles from
here — and start the day after tomorrow.
    I look forward to making such an impression on you with the store
of anecdote and description with which I shall return, that I can't find
it in my Heart to open it — on paper. I don't see how I shall ever get
rid of my gatherings. It seems to me, at present, that when I come
home I must take a cottage on Putney Heath, or Richmond Green, or
some other wild and desolate place, and talk to myself for a month

---

[4] Lady Burdett — Miss Coutts's mother.

or two, until I have sobered down a little, and am quiet again. A prophetic feeling comes upon me sometimes, and hints that I shall return, a bore — :

We had a terrible passage out, and mean to return in a sailing ship. Can you think of anything I can bring back for you? If you can possibly commission me to bring you any article whatever from the new country, I need scarcely say how proud and glad you will make me. Any letter addressed to me to the care of David Colden Esquire [5] 28 Laight Street Hudson Square New York, would be forwarded to me wheresoever I might chance to be at the time of its receipt.

May I ask you when you next see Mr Majoribanks to tell him, with my best regards, that I thank him very much for his letters, and have received the greatest attention from all his correspondents — except the poor gentleman at Washington — who has been dead six years. Not finding him readily (no wonder!) I went into a bank to ask for him. I happened to make the enquiry of a very old clerk, who staggered to a stool and fell into a cold perspiration, as if he had seen a spectre. Being feeble, and the shock being very great, he took to his bed — but he has since recovered: to the great joy of his wife and family.

With every good and cordial wish for your health and happiness — many messages of regard to Miss Meredith — and very many scruples of conscience in sending you so poor a letter from so long a distance — I am always, Dear Miss Coutts

P.S. I forgot to say that I have been at Washington (which is beyond here) and as far beyond that, again, as Richmond in Virginia. But the prematurely hot weather, and the sight of slaves, turned me back.

∽

While Dickens was making this semiroyal progress across America, his father, back in England, was behaving with the same grandiloquent improvidence that in earlier years had brought about his imprisonment

---

[5] David Cadwallader Colden (1797–1850), son of Cadwallader D. Colden (1769–1834), who had been mayor of New York 1818–1820. David Colden, deeply interested in promoting the growth and prosperity of the fine arts in the United States, was a member of the New York Committee in charge of the Boz Ball. His wife, Frances née Wilkes (1796–1877), was a younger sister of Lord Jeffrey's wife. Dickens had met the Coldens at the home of Macready when they were in England a few years earlier. The renewal of their acquaintance in New York developed into a warm friendship, continued in letters after Dickens's return to England. After her husband's death Mrs. Colden traveled in Europe with her brother Dr. Wilkes in 1853–1854, and Dickens entertained the two in London.

for debt in the Marshalsea and condemned twelve-year-old Charles to despairing drudgery in the blacking warehouse. More than once after that John Dickens had been arrested; and on each of these later occasions had been rescued by his son. No sooner had Pickwick *become a success than, like Micawber, he began cadging sums of increasing size from Chapman and Hall, begging them not to tell Charles, and getting more and more deeply involved in other debts. His son Alfred, following in his footsteps, also dunned the publishers for small loans, and in later years Dickens was to find his brothers Frederick and Augustus shameless in their reiterated demands for financial aid. In 1839 John Dickens had again been in danger of arrest. Charles had stepped in and paid his debts, but to get him away from temptation had rented for his parents a pretty little white cottage with a garden and orchard, in the village of Alphington, a mile out of Exeter. Plaintively asking what he should do in such a little place, John Dickens was nevertheless unable to defy his son's will. But it was beyond the powers of a country village to change either his improvident nature or the flowery effusiveness of language that his son later borrowed in the portrayal of Micawber:*

⌁

10. MARCH 24, 1842, ALPHINGTON [FROM JOHN DICKENS TO COUTTS & COMPANY [6]]

I really know not what apology to offer for presuming to trouble you, other than the plea of necessity arising out of the position in which I find myself placed. Previously to my son, Mr Charles Dickens's leaving this country for America, it was settled between us, — but rather more hastily, in consequence of his then numerous engagements, than was consistent with a systematic arrangement, that I was as far as possible to rid myself of all obligations binding myself to this place, preparatory to my returning to London, in furtherance of other objects, on my youngest boy's leaving school finally in July. My term in my present residence expiring on the 31st instant, I was authorized to dispose of what furniture there was, and apply the proceeds towards the liquidation of outstanding obligations, though, as will be the case, my son

---

[6] Addressed by John Dickens to "Miss Coutts & Co." I have found no other evidence to confirm the statement in this letter that Dickens had agreed to his parents' giving up the Alphington cottage and returning to London at this time, although by the following December he was offering £70 a year for a little house on Blackheath for them to occupy.

anticipated, they would not realize a sufficient sum fully to accomplish that object, while my preparatory demonstrations of migration, have led to what may be considered a vote of "want of confidence," which tends very much to the embarassment of my financial arrangements. Contemporaneous events of this nature place me in a difficulty, from which without some anticipatory pecuniary effort I cannot extricate myself, and my good or evil genius, as the case may be, has prompted me to state my case to Miss Coutts & Co. — to this effect, whether they will advance me £25, on my own security for six months from the first Proximo, — I say on my own security because I know how indignant my son would be, if he were aware of this application, I make it not on his responsibility further than to the extent, that I should take the necessary step to guard them against loss, should my death occur, although now, as I have ever been, in excellent health, — in the interval. I might urge some circumstances in extenuation of this, — as I am fully aware irregular application, — but I refrain, consoling myself with the hope, that if inadmissible, — feeling as I do that it is not so much the smallness of the amount as the principle, which decides a question of this nature, — that it will be confidential.

∽

11. MARCH 26, 1842, STRAND [TO JOHN DICKENS FROM COUTTS & COMPANY]

We beg to acknowledge the receipt of your letter of the 24th Inst. and to mention that (as you seem to have anticipated) no directions were left with us by Mr Charles Dickens for any Payment to you on his account, and for the reasons to which you allude towards the conclusion of your letter we regret that in our capacity of Bankers we feel precluded from complying with the request you have made us.

∽

12. JULY 2, 1842, DEVONSHIRE TERRACE

I beg to report myself arrived and well — and in proof of the fact, to send you the rocking chair. Let me also ask your acceptance of some specimens of American Poetry, which I forward at the same time.

I send for Miss Meredith, an Eagle's feather. Its rightful owner fell over the great fall at Niagara last Winter (or, I should rather say, was carried over by the strong current) and was picked up, dead, some miles down the river.

I did not forget Lady Burdett's request. A piece of rock from the cave behind the great sheet of water is slumbering ignominiously in the custom House, among some other contraband articles. As soon as the chest comes to hand, I shall have the pleasure of redeeming my vow.

∽

13.   NOVEMBER 12, 1842, DEVONSHIRE TERRACE

Your most kind note found me in the agonies of plotting and contriving a new book; [7] in which stage of the tremendous process, I am accustomed to walk up and down the house, smiting my forehead dejectedly; and to be so horribly cross and surly, that the boldest fly at my approach. At such times, even the Postman knocks at the door with a mild feebleness, and my publishers always come two together, lest I should fall upon a single invader and do murder on his intrusive body.

I am afraid if I came to see you under such circumstances, you would be very glad to be rid of me in two hours at the most; but I would risk even that disgrace, in my desire to accept your kind Invitation, if it were not indispensable just now, that I should be always in the way. In starting a work which is to last for twenty months, there are so many little things to attend to, which require my personal superintendence, that I am obliged to be constantly on the watch; and I may add, seriously, that unless I were to shut myself up, obstinately and sullenly in my own room for a great many days without writing a word, I don't think I ever should make a beginning.

For these reasons, I am fain to be resolute and virtuous, and to deny myself and Mrs Dickens the great pleasure you offer us. I have not answered your letter until now, because I have really been tempted and hesitating. But the lapse of every new day, only gives me a stronger reason for being perseveringly uncomfortable, that out of my gloom and solitude something comical (or meant to be) may straightway grow up.

If you should still be in your present retreat when I have got my first number written (after which, I go on with great nonchalance) we shall be more than glad to come to you for one or two days. In the meantime Mrs Dickens begs me to add her best remembrances to my own; and to say that if you can oblige her with your box at

---

[7] *American Notes*, the record of Dickens's travels, had been entirely written in the three months between July and September, and was published before the end of October. The "new book" was *Martin Chuzzlewit*, which was to begin, in January 1843, its career as a serial in twenty monthly installments.

Covent Garden on any of Miss Kemble's nights, she will be very thankful.

[P.S.] It is impossible for me to say how I should argue with Miss Meredith, under existing circumstances.

∾

14.   JANUARY 13, 1843, DEVONSHIRE TERRACE [TO MISS MEREDITH]
    Pray thank Miss Coutts from me, for her kindness in respect of the box.

I am sorry I was not at home, and able to answer your note yesterday. I was ploughing at a tremendous pace through the snow near Harrow, with Mr Pinch on my right hand and the Pecksniffs on my left.[8]

Today I have sent Lady Burdett a piece (a very small one) of Niagara, and also a tiny scrap of Virginia Marble. As ill-luck would have it, I was already engaged for Monday.

Mrs Dickens begs me to add her compliments.

Always Believe me (with the firm conviction that you will shortly dote (dramatically speaking) on Anderson) [9] Faithfully yours

∾

15.   FEBRUARY 28, 1843, DEVONSHIRE TERRACE
    I don't know whether you may happen to remember that there was a Public Subscription some two or three years ago, for the purchase of a Testimonial to Macready, in honor of his exertions to elevate the National Drama. However, there was: a handsome piece of plate was designed and made; and is at last to be presented by the Duke of Sussex in the course of the ensuing month.

But the failure of Hammersley's Bank, and the consequent loss of a part of the money, has rendered a second subscription necessary. Being a member of the committee, and casting about to whom it would be right to apply, I have naturally though of you. Firstly, because I know you are attached to the most rational of all amusements. And secondly, because in the horrible indifference to it which prevails among people of influence and station, any support from you cannot fail to be at once most valuable to the cause, and most gratifying and cheering to Macready himself.

Therefore, if you see no objection to aiding the object (a much

---

[8] Tom Pinch and Seth Pecksniff, two of the principal characters in *Martin Chuzzlewit*: Dickens's way of saying he was thinking about the novel as he walked.
[9] Unidentified.

higher one than the froth of the world suppose) I shall be most proud and glad to act as your Secretary or steward in the matter. Lord Lansdowne [1] is one of the very few men in high places, who have dealt with it as they should. There be some (whose titles would startle you) who have put down their names with round sums attached, but have not put down their money; in consequence of which, I am in danger of turning misanthropical, Byronic, and devilish.

I hope you liked the Much ado — and the Comus — and that you will go to see Virginius next Monday.[2] If you were not pleased last Friday, I shall certainly carry my misanthropical impulses into effect, and leave off my neck cloth without further notice.

∾

16. MARCH 21, 1843, DEVONSHIRE TERRACE

I hope you have by this time got the better of your cold. I speak feelingly, having had a tremendous one of my own, besides the pleasure of six weeks contemplation of another in my wife. I have discovered a lonely Farm House at Finchley; and am going to bury myself there for at least a month to come; visiting this city at rare Intervals — and immersing myself in my story. But it is not so far off that I shall have any difficulty in reaching this place "for a consideration" — and if you will give me that kind of valuable one which will lie in a favorable answer to the enclosed, I shall be delighted.

Macready has been so much pleased by your approval and support; and is a man who while he courts nobody, feels such encouragement with great keenness; that I shall be glad to present him to you, if you will dine here. I know you will like him, as a private gentleman, exceedingly.

With best regards to Miss Meredith

P.S. I returned the enclosed with many thanks, and I need hardly say that it was most gratifying to all of us — but especially so to the party chiefly interested.

---

[1] Lord Lansdowne (1780–1863) became the third Marquis of Lansdowne in 1809. He supported the abolition of the slave trade, and brought about a coalition between a group of the Whigs and the followers of Canning. He had several times been a member of the Cabinet.

[2] Miss Coutts gave generously to the testimonial for Macready — see the following letter. In the benefit performances Macready played Benedick in *Much Ado About Nothing* and the title roles in *Comus* and James Sheridan Knowles's *Virginius*.

17.   APRIL 24, 1843, DEVONSHIRE TERRACE

Mr Marjoribanks was with me this morning; and I really cannot tell you how very much I feel your great kindness and interest in my behalf. I wrote him, and not to you, in the first instance; because, feeling assured of your friendship, I was the more sensitive and delicate in troubling you, if I could help it.

I enclose such a note to you as Mr Marjoribanks told me you wished to have.[3] Nor do I know that I can add anything to it, further than that I am prepared to catch thankfully at anything which promises a reasonable opening, no matter where.

We are much concerned to hear of Miss Meredith's illness. I am myself kept within doors by the doctor for a kind of rheumatism in the face, which penetrates into the depths of my ears, and makes me feel at times as if a beehive had been upset in the intricacies of my brain. But as divers small tortures are to be inflicted on me this morning, I look for a release into the open air tomorrow; and whenever I *do* get out, I shall walk straight to your door, and make my personal enquiries.

Pray let me recommend the Dragon in the Easter Piece to your particular regards. I look upon him as the most comic animal of modern times. When he gets drunk at the Fountain, he is sublime — the Learned Pig turns pale before him, in his dullest moments.

ᵒᴬᵒ

18.   APRIL 24, 1843, DEVONSHIRE TERRACE

I have it very much at heart at this time to obtain some suitable and worthy employment for a brother of mine [4] — just now of age — who has been bred a civil engineer, and has for the last four years been constantly employed on one of the great main lines of railway, performing all the duties of assistant engineer — drawing plans and

---

[3] Evidently Miss Coutts had offered through Mr. Marjoribanks to be of assistance to Dickens's brother Alfred, and the letter immediately following is the enclosure mentioned here.

[4] Alfred Lamert Dickens (1822–1860) had been a student engineer at Tamworth since 1840. In 1845 he obtained a post — whether or not through Miss Coutts's influence I do not know — with John Cass Birkinshaw of York. In December of that year he was one of the party of engineers that surveyed and laid out the Hull and Birmingham Railway. The following year he became local resident engineer on the Malton and Driffield Junction Railway. He married Helen Dobson, daughter of a stationmaster at Strensall near York, and in later life resided in Manchester.

executing them — levelling — constructing bridges — and so forth; all of which from the beginning of the work to its close, he has done to the great satisfaction of those above him, as his testimonials fully shew, and as I can most honestly avouch.

The work on which he was engaged, being completed; and the Profession being, as I dare say you know, most horribly overstocked; he has applied to me to exert any interest or influence I may possess in his behalf. And knowing the kind interest you take in any application or design of mine, I have determined to write to you to ask you if it is possible that you can assist me in this. I know him to be possessed of great energy, industry, and ability; and I am more anxious than I can tell you to procure him the means of exercising these qualities, either at home or abroad.

I will not ask you to forgive my troubling you on such a subject; for if I were not sure you had already done that, I could never have made up my mind to trouble you at all.

∽

19. JUNE 2, 1843, DEVONSHIRE TERRACE

I will not weary you, at present, by saying anything more in the way of Thanks. I enclose a note, written according to Mr Marjoribank's suggestion. It is quite needless, I am sure, for me to add that I am fully sensible of its value, and of his kindness.

Lady Sale, I renounce for ever. And I here register a vow to look upon her henceforth with an eye, colder and duller than a Fish's. Nor will I ever envy her Husband — her dog — her maid — nor anything that is her's, except the memory of her departed Son in Law.[5] He must have had a blessed release; and I have no doubt is in an uncommon state of Peace. If his wife took after her mother, I believe more implicitly than I ever did, that every bullet has its billet, and that there is a special Providence in the Fall of a Sparrow.

If Miss Meredith will receive me in that Poet's apartment you write of, on Sunday next; there will I be. I have pondered and reflected about the best time. Something seems to point in my mind to 3. But if

---

[5] Lady Sale was Florentia, wife of the distinguished soldier Sir Robert Henry Sale (1782–1845), who served in India and Afghanistan and died of wounds suffered at the battle of Mudki. In 1843 she published a journal describing her capture, sufferings, and escape in Afghanistan. Her son-in-law, Lieutenant J. D. L. Sturt of the Engineers, died of wounds in 1842 during the British retreat from Kabul. She was evidently a woman of a strong and perhaps aggressive personality, which may have been the reason for Dickens's antipathy.

that something be wrong by the Horse Guards, all times are alike to me in such a pleasant case, and an anonymous figure received per post in the course of tomorrow, will be perfectly understood and gratefully attended to.

There is a terrible paper on Theodore Hook, in the last Quarterly — admirably written — as I think, from its internal evidence, by Lockhart.[6] — I have not seen anything for a long time so very moving. It fills me with grief and sorrow. Men have been chained to hideous prison walls and other strange anchors 'ere now, but few have known such suffering and bitterness at one time or other, as those who have been bound to Pens. A pleasant thought for one who has been using this very quill all day!

ᘐ

20.   JULY 26, 1843, DEVONSHIRE TERRACE

I don't know whether you have seen an advertisement in the papers of this morning, signed by me, and having reference to the family of Mr Elton the actor, who was drowned in the Pegasus.[7] I consented last night to act as chairman of a committee for the assistance of his children; and I assure you that their condition is melancholy and desolate beyond all painting.

He was a struggling man through his whole existence — always very poor, and never extravagant. His wife died mad, Three Years ago, and he was left a widower with seven children — who were expecting his knock at the door, when a friend arrived with the terrible news of his Death.

If in the great extent of your charities, you have a niche left to fill

---

[6] The article in the *Quarterly Review* on Theodore Hook (1788–1841), the novelist and wit, was indeed, as Dickens had inferred, by its editor, John Gibson Lockhart (1794–1854). An appreciative and discriminating analysis of Hook's brilliant talents, it is also a painful study of the waste and prodigality of his career.

[7] Edward William Elton (1794–1843), the original Beauséant in Bulwer Lytton's *The Lady of Lyons,* and noted for his performance of Edgar in *King Lear.* He was drowned when the *Pegasus* struck a rock near the Holy Island and went down with a loss of forty-seven out of the fifty-three on board. Dickens, Marjoribanks, and Thomas Noon Talfourd (1795–1854) became trustees of the Elton Fund. Talfourd as a member of Parliament had worked hard to bring about an international copyright bill, and became a close friend of Dickens; *Pickwick Papers* was dedicated to him. He was himself a dramatist, author of *Ion, The Athenian Captives,* and *Glencoe,* all produced by Macready, and was the author of a biography of Charles Lamb. He was made serjeant in 1833 and Judge of Common Pleas in 1849.

up, I believe in my heart this is as sad a case as could possibly be put into it. If you have not, I know you will not mind saying so to me.

Do not trouble yourself to answer this, as I will call upon you today between one and two. I called on Sunday last, to enquire after Miss Meredith; but seeing your carriage at the door, I left my card. — By the way — lingering at the street corner, was a very strange looking fellow, watching your house intently. I hope it was not Mr Dunn.[8]

∞

21. JULY 28, 1843, DEVONSHIRE TERRACE

I will not attempt to tell you what I felt, when I received your noble letter last night.

---

[8] Richard Dunn was an unsavory character who harassed Miss Coutts with lawsuits claiming that she had written him love letters and promised him large sums of money. It is not clear whether he was an unscrupulous blackmailer or suffered from delusions. In 1838 he began annoying her with letters to which she did not reply, and following her about; in 1840 he was prosecuted, lost the case, and was confined to the Fleet Prison for the costs. He was still in jail at the time Dickens wrote this letter. There he remained till 1845, writing Miss Coutts constant appeals to be discharged, demanding money, and protesting affection.

In April of that year he was released through taking advantage of bankruptcy proceedings. It then occurred to him, so he said, that a doggerel composition in verse that he had received through the post must have been sent by Miss Coutts. This communication addressed him as "My dear pet," "my lover," "my sweet dove," and "my jewel," and contained stanzas that he professed to interpret as an invitation to draw on Coutts's Bank for whatever sums he wished:

> Send to Coutts's your bill,
> There's lots in the till;
> I'll give the clerks orders to do it,

and

> Fill a good round sum in,
> I've plenty of tin
> To make you a good compensation.

These sentiments he read as a sign that Miss Coutts, "growing tender," was

> Disposed to turn lender
> Of cash your sweet body to free.

It is not certain whether this effusion was sent him by a joker playing on a delusion or Dunn's own work, but he modestly demanded £100,000 from Coutts's Bank, and when it was refused brought action for payment. He was convicted of perjury, sentenced to jail, and not released again till August 1851. In November he again brought suit, claiming he had witnesses, but that Miss Coutts had constantly suborned them and sent them out of the way. In April 1853, having failed to proceed to trial, he was again arrested for costs. The London *Times*, August 4, 1853, has a résumé of the entire case. Without mentioning either Dunn or his victim by name, Dickens tells the story in an article entitled "Things That Cannot Be Done," in *Household Words*, October 8, 1853.

Trust me that I will be a faithful steward of your bounty; and that there is no charge in the wide World I would accept with so much pride and happiness as any such from you.

I should be uneasy if I did not let you know that your letter being put in my hands at the Freemasons' last night where the committee were sitting, I told them what it contained, *before* I arrived at your injunction of secrecy.[9] But the gentlemen who were there, were far too much impressed by what I had conveyed to them to betray your confidence, I am sure. I can answer for that.

Charley[1] will be ready at the appointed time, and is counting the clock already.

∽

22.   AUGUST 7, 1843, BROADSTAIRS, KENT

I went up to town last Thursday to preside at a Meeting of the Committee for poor Mr Elton's children; but as I came back here next morning, I had no opportunity of calling on you.

Owing to the offensive conduct of Mr Charles Mathews[2] and his estimable lady, we were unable to use either Harley, the Keeleys, Mrs Nisbett, or Mrs Stirling, at the Haymarket, although they had all been previously announced with Mr Webster's full consent. The conse-

---

[9] The occasion was a dinner meeting of the Committee arranging a subscription and benefit for the Elton children. Dickens had evidently failed to see Miss Coutts on the afternoon of July 26, and the letter promising her aid asked that her generosity be left anonymous.

[1] Charley — Dickens's eldest son, Charles Culliford Boz Dickens (1837–1896), and only six years old at this time.

[2] Charles James Mathews (1803–1878), actor, dramatist, theatrical manager; all the others are also actors and actresses under his management. John Pritt Harley (1786–1858), actor and singer, played at the St. James's Theatre under Braham's management 1837–1840, when the latter produced Dickens's *The Village Coquettes*, *The Strange Gentleman*, and *Is She His Wife?*, and had roles in all three. Robert Keeley (1793–1869) played the part of Mantalini in a stage adaptation of *Nicholas Nickleby*; his wife played Smike in the same performance; both played in stage versions of still other Dickens fictions. Louisa Cranstoun Nisbett (1812?–1858), née Macnamara, first acted under the name of Miss Mordaunt, married John Alexander Nisbett 1831, was charming in comedy. Mary Ann Stirling (1815–1895), née Kell, married Edward Stirling, a prolific adapter of novels to the stage; she made a hit as Sally Snow with Macready at Drury Lane in 1842, was Cordelia to his Lear in 1845, and later played Peg Woffington in *Masks and Faces*, Lady Bountiful in *The Beaux' Stratagem*, Mrs. Hardcastle, Mrs. Malaprop, and the Nurse in *Romeo and Juliet*. Benjamin Webster (1797–1882) was a leading comedian at the Haymarket, Drury Lane, and Covent Garden from 1829 on, and long manager at the Haymarket and the Adelphi.

quence was, that we were obliged at the last moment to alter an excellent bill; and the entertainments were very trash. You will be glad to hear, however, that the receipts were £280; a very large sum in that Theatre, which when crammed to the very utmost will not hold more than £300. Including this sum, we had in hand on Thursday night, hard upon a thousand pounds: since which time the benefit at the Surrey (the only return I have yet had) has produced a hundred and forty pounds more, and some additional private subscriptions have also come in.

Finding it exceedingly difficult in the midst of their trouble to arrive with anything like tolerable certainty at the weekly expenses of the family; last Thursday, I placed £10 – the ten you sent me – in the hands of a lady who knows them, and can be trusted to make a careful report: and begged her to account to me for it, and to get me an estimate by the time we meet again (next Monday) of their average bills. Before I see you on that head, I will visit the children myself. For I wish particularly to speak to the eldest girl about it, and to be very careful that your assistance, is free from the controul of any relation or friend, but such as she knows can be thoroughly trusted, and is kindly disposed towards them. I fancy I have observed some slight signs and tokens, which render this precaution indispensable.

This little place is very bright and beautiful – and I wish you and your Patient could see it this morning. I have been here six years, and have never had a Piano next door; but this fortune was too good to last, and now there is one close to the little bay window of the room I write in, which has six years' agony in every note it utters. I have been already obliged to take refuge on the other side of the house, but that looks into a street where the "Flies" stand, and where there are donkeys and drivers out of number. Their music is almost as bad as the other, and between the two, I was driven into such a state of desperation on Saturday, that I thought I must have run away and deserted my family. The matter was not mended when the paper came down, with Mr Thomas Duncombe's tribute to the character and acquirements of Mr Bunn:[3] which so exasperated me (though the

---

[3] Thomas Slingsby Duncombe (1796–1861) was a radical politician; he presented the Chartist petition in 1842. Alfred Bunn (1796–1860) was in 1843 manager of Drury Lane and Covent Garden. As the author of various doggerel productions in verse he was satirically known as "Poet Bunn"; he was the model of Thackeray's Mr. Dolphin in *Pendennis*.

two gentlemen are well worthy of each other's friendship) that I walked ten miles over burning chalk, before I could resume the least composure.

Charley and two hundred and fifty other children, are making fortifications in the sand with wooden spades, and picking up shells and sea weed. He is still full of his last visit to you, and brightened up like burnished copper at breakfast when I asked him if he had any message to send. If I thought his love would *do* (he said) he should like to forward it. So I promised to convey it to you, in due form. I have some idea of writing him a child's History of England, to the end that he may have tender-hearted notions of War and Murder, and may not fix his affections on wrong heroes, or see the bright side of Glory's sword and know nothing of the rusty one. If I should carry it out, I shall live in the hope that you will read it one wet day.[4]

I fear the weather has been sorely against Miss Meredith; as indeed it has been against all invalids, Mrs Dickens included, who begs me to send her best remembrances. It would give us great pleasure to hear that Miss Meredith had left her room, though individually I must say that if I once knew of her eating two thirds of a roast chicken, and drinking three glasses of Wine, I would be content to leave all the rest to Herself and Good Fortune. I beg to be heartily remembered to her, and am ever dear Miss Coutts with high regard Faithfully yours

〜

23.   SEPTEMBER 5, 1843, BROADSTAIRS, KENT
All of a sudden it occurred to me the other day that if I went to Liverpool with Macready they would bowstring his throat in New York, so tightly that not a word should come out of it upon the stage — and drive him out of the country, straightway.[5] While I was deliber-

---

[4] Dickens did not actually carry out this intention till considerably later. As *A Child's History of England* the narrative appeared in *Household Words* in irregular installments between January 25, 1851 and December 10, 1853.

[5] Though the mild criticisms in *American Notes* were mingled with a great deal of praise, they provoked a fantastic outbreak of indignation in the United States. "Don't burst — keep cool," the New York *Herald* warned its readers, and went on to say that Dickens had "the most coarse, vulgar, impudent, and superficial" mind "that had ever had the courage to write about . . . this original and remarkable country." His view "of the fermentative character of this land" was that of "a narrow-minded, conceited cockney"; of all its visitors he was "the most flimsy — the most childish — the most trashy — the most contemptible." Another newspaper said he was a "flash Reporter" with the feelings of a "low-bred scullion unexpectedly advanced from the kitchen to the parlour." An angry reader from St.

ating whether this was probable in the abstract, or I was like Dennis [6] (who after writing a satire on the French Nation, fled from the English coast on catching sight of a French ship in the distance: thinking it must be despatched to seize and bear him off) the Postman brought me a note from Marryatt,[7] adjuring me not to go, or Macready was "done for". As he knows the virtuous americans pretty well and as I think I do too, I immediately abandoned my intention. And so it came to pass that I sat down to Chuzzlewit quietly, and am now in the heart of it. Under other circumstances I should have been reporting to you this week, touching the Ragged Schools.[8]

I find that they are only open on Sundays and Thursdays. Next Thursday *week*, in the evening, I will take my seat among the fluttering rags of Saffron Hill. If I have finished my number, and can remain in town next day, I will come out to Putney. If I should be obliged to return on Friday morning, I will punctually write you a full account of the School, the pupils and the masters; and all concerning them.

Charley and his sisters desire their loves to be faithfully conveyed to you. The piano is gone, and the flute is out of hearing — at Dover. But a barrel organ, a monkey, a punch, a Jim Crow, and a man who plays twenty instruments at once and doesn't get the right sound out of any one of them, are hovering in the neighbourhood. Also a blind man who was in a Sea Fight in his youth; and after playing the hundredth psalm on a flageolet, recites a description of the Engagement.

Louis said he had spent his life "in the stews of London" and was "fit to associate only with the dancing monkeys and mulatto girls of Five Points." The sharp satire of the American scenes in *Martin Chuzzlewit* stimulated an even more violent fury. "All Yankee-Doodledom," wrote Carlyle, blazed "like one universal soda bottle"; on the stage of a New York theater, to the savage delight of the audience, a copy of the book was destroyed by being thrown into the witches' cauldron in a burlesque of *Macbeth*. Since Dickens had proclaimed his intimacy with Macready by dedicating *Nicholas Nickleby* to him, his concern for the effects of his own unpopularity in America on the success of Macready's theatrical tour there was understandable.

[6] John Dennis? (1657–1734), critic, one of the victims of Pope's *Dunciad*.
[7] Captain Frederick Marryat (1792–1848) was the well-known writer of sea tales. He had been in the United States.
[8] The Ragged Schools were volunteer organizations for giving free evening instruction to poor children in the slums. Founded some twenty years before by a shoemaker of Portsmouth and a chimney sweep of Windsor, they had been slowly spreading throughout England. The school in the neighborhood of Field Lane and Saffron Hill, Holborn, that Dickens describes in the next letter was under the guidance of a young lawyer's clerk named Samuel Starey, who had appealed to Miss Coutts for aid.

Charley is so popular with the boatmen, that I begin to think of Robinson Crusoe, and the propriety of living in-land. I saw him yesterday through a telescope, miles out at sea, steering an enormous fishing-smack, to the unspeakable delight of seven gigantic companions, clad in oilskin. Katey [9] is supposed to be secretly betrothed, inasmuch as a very young gentleman (so young, that being unable to reach the knocker, he called attention to the door by kicking it) called the other evening, and being gratified in a mysterious, I may say quite a melodramatic, request, to speak with the nurse, produced a live crab, which he said he had "promised her."

I hope Miss Meredith is past the fowl stage, and getting on towards beef. I beg to be cordially remembered to her.

ᖰᖰ

24.   SEPTEMBER 16, 1843, BROADSTAIRS, KENT

I wished very much to have had the pleasure of coming to Putney on Friday, and to have remained there that night, in compliance with your kind Invitation. But when I got to town on Thursday, I had still an unfinished number on my hands and mind. So I came back here again yesterday — too late for the post, or I would have saved it, and written to you. Pray tell Miss Meredith, with my best regards, that I have written the second chapter in the next number, with an eye to her experiences.[1] It is specially addressed to them, indeed.

On Thursday night, went to the Ragged School; and an awful sight it is. I blush to quote Oliver Twist for an authority, but it stands on that ground, and is precisely such a place as the Jew lived in. The school is held in three most wretched rooms on the first floor of a rotten house: every plank, and timber, and brick, and lath, and piece of plaster in which shakes as you walk. One room is devoted to the girls: two to the boys. The former are much the better-looking — I cannot say better dressed, for there is no such thing as dress among the seventy pupils; certainly not the elements of a whole suit of clothes, among them all. I have very seldom seen, in all the strange

---

[9] Charley's sister Katey was almost four.

[1] Chapter XXV, in the October number of *Martin Chuzzlewit*, has the following descriptive title: "Is in part Professional; and furnishes the Reader with some Valuable Hints in relationship to the Management of a Sick Chamber." It describes Mrs. Gamp dividing her nursing time between daytime care of old Chuffey in Anthony Chuzzlewit's house and night watching over the sick man at the Bull in Holborn. The original of Mrs. Gamp was a nurse whom Miss Coutts had employed to minister to Miss Meredith during a period of illness.

and dreadful things I have seen in London and elsewhere, anything so shocking as the dire neglect of soul and body exhibited in these children. And although I know; and am as sure as it is possible for one to be of anything which has not happened, that in the prodigious misery and ignorance of the swarming masses of mankind in England, the seeds of its certain ruin are sown, I never saw that Truth so staring out in hopeless characters, as it does from the walls of this place. The children in the Jails are almost as common sights to me as my own; but these are worse, for they have not arrived there yet, but are as plainly and certainly traveling there, as they are to their graves.

The Masters are extremely quiet, honest, good men. You may suppose they are, to be there at all. It is enough to break one's heart to get at the place: to say nothing of getting at the childrens' minds afterwards. They are well-grounded in the Scotch — the Glasgow — system of elementary instruction, which is an excellent one; [2] and they try to reach the boys by kindness. To gain their attention in any way, is a difficulty, quite gigantic. To impress them, even with the idea of a God, when their own condition is so desolate, becomes a monstrous task. To find anything within them — who know nothing of affection, care, love, or kindness of any sort — to which it is possible to appeal, is, at first, like a search for the philosopher's stone. And here it is that the viciousness of insisting on creeds and forms in educating such miserable beings, is most apparent. To talk of catechisms, outward and visible signs, and inward and spiritual graces, to these children is a thing no Bedlamite would do, who saw them. To get them, whose whole lives from the moment of their birth, are one continued punishment, to believe even in the Judgment of the Dead and a future state of punishment for their sins, requires a System in itself.

The Masters examined them, however, on these points, and they answered very well — sometimes in a shout all at once, sometimes only one boy, sometimes half a dozen. I put a great many questions to them upon their answers which they also answered very well. There was one boy, who had been selling Lucifer matches all day in the streets — not much older than Charley — clad in a bit of a sack — really

---

[2] Scottish elementary education taught reading mainly as an instrument of Calvinist moral training, but I have been able to discover no evidence that there was any pedagogical method formally identified as "the Glasgow system." Dr. I. L. Kandel, the editor of *School and Society*, a distinguished authority on the history of education, doubts there having been one recognized as such, and writes, "Dickens probably referred to the Scottish system as seen in Glasgow."

a clever child, and handsome too, who gave some excellent replies, though, of course, in language that would be very strange in your ears. Hardly any of them can read yet. For the Masters think it most important to impress them at first with some distinction (communicated in dialogue) between right and wrong, and I quite agree with them. They sell trifles in the streets, or beg (or some, I dare say, steal) all day; and coming tired to this place at night, are very slow to pick up any knowledge. That they *do* come at all, is, *I* think, a Victory.

They knew about the Saviour & the Day of Judgment. The little match boy told me that God was no respecter of persons, and that if he (the match boy) prayed "as if he meant it," and didn't keep company with bad boys, and didn't swear, and didn't drink, he would be as readily forgiven in Heaven, as the Queen would. They understood that the Deity was everywhere and had a knowledge of everything; and that there was something in them which they couldn't see or lay their hands on, which would have to account to him after they were dead.[3] They were very quiet and orderly, while the Master said a little prayer; and sang a short hymn before they broke up. The singing was evidently a great treat, and the match boy came out very strong, with a Shake, and a Second.

I am happy to say I afforded great amusement at first — in particular by having a pair of white trousers on, and very bright boots. The lat-

---

[3] The ignorance and illiteracy of the poor were indeed appalling. There had been no national appropriation for secular education whatsoever until 1833, when Parliament made an annual grant of £20,000, increased to £30,000 in 1839 — a sum that represented about one tenth of one per cent of the yearly budget, less than half the appropriation for building the Queen's stables. The Sunday schools, which alone reached large masses of the poor, usually neglected writing and arithmetic and concentrated on the Scriptures, the Catechism, and the Thirty-nine Articles. How well they achieved even these ends can be judged from a few quotations from the Report of the Children's Employment Commission in 1843:

"One child went to Sunday school regularly for five years; does not know who Jesus Christ is: had never heard of the twelve Apostles, Samson, Moses, Aaron, etc." Another "attended Sunday school regularly for six years; knows who Jesus Christ was: he died on the cross to save our Saviour; had never heard of St Peter or St Paul." A third "attended different Sunday schools seven years: can read only the thin, easy books with simple words of one syllable." To the question who Christ was, Horne received the following answers among others: "He was Adam." "He was an Apostle." "He was the Saviour's Lord's Son," and from a youth of sixteen; "He was a king of London long ago." Few knew where America was, or France.

In comparison with these the scholars at the Field Lane Ragged School come off brilliantly well.

ter articles of dress gave immense satisfaction, and were loudly laughed at. Mr Stanfield,[4] who was with me, — in consequence of looking rather burly and fat in the small room — was received with a perfect cheer; and his sudden retirement in consequence of being overcome by the closeness of the atmosphere, and the dread of Typhus Fever, was much regretted. When they saw that I was quite serious, and had interest in their answers, they became quiet, and took pains. They are still better-behaved on seeing that I stood with my hat off, before the Master (though I heard one boy express his opinion that I certainly wasn't a barber, or I should have cut my hair);[5] and so far as their behaviour is concerned, I should not have the least doubt of my ability or that of anybody else who went the right way to work — to reduce them to order in five minutes at any time.

The school is miserably poor, you may believe, and is almost entirely supported by the teachers themselves. If they could get a better room (the house they are in, is like an ugly dream); above all, if they could provide some convenience for washing; it would be an immense advantage. The moral courage of the teachers is beyond all praise. They are surrounded by every possible adversity, and every disheartening circumstance that can be imagined. Their office is worthy of the apostles.

My heart so sinks within me when I go into these scenes, that I almost lose the hope of ever seeing them changed. Whether this effort will succeed, it is quite impossible to say. But that it is a great one, beginning at the right end, among thousands of immortal creatures, who cannot, in their present state, be held accountable for what they do, it is *as* impossible to doubt. That it is much too squalid and ter-

---

[4] William Clarkson Stanfield (1793–1867), noted marine painter. A sailor in his youth, in 1818 he began painting the scenery for the Old Royalty, a sailors' theater in London; by 1826 he was painting at Drury Lane. In 1827 he exhibited his first important picture, "Wreckers Off Fort Rouge," at the British Institute. He was made A.R.A. in 1832 and R.A. 1835. Dickens met him through Douglas Jerrold, one of the leading contributors to *Punch*, who had been a midshipman in the Navy, and a warmly affectionate friendship rapidly developed between the younger man and the already middle-aged artist. Stanfield painted scenery for almost all Dickens's amateur theatricals; for *Every Man in His Humour* in 1845, for *Not So Bad as We Seem* in 1851, *The Lighthouse* in 1855, and *The Frozen Deep* in 1857. "Noble old Stanny," Dickens called him.

[5] At this time Dickens wore his hair, as numbers of other men still did, in long wavy locks descending almost to his shoulders. Its richly curling profusion can be seen in the Maclise portrait of 1839 and the Alexander portrait, painted while Dickens was in Boston in 1842.

rible to meet with any wide encouragement, I greatly fear. There is a kind of delicacy which is not at all shocked by the existence of such things, but is excessively shocked to know of them; and I am afraid it will shut its eyes on Ragged Schools until the Ragged Scholars are perfect in their learning out of doors, when woe to whole garments.[6]

I need not say, I am sure, that I deem it an experiment most worthy of your charitable hand. The reasons I have, for doubting its being generally assisted, all assure me that it will have an interest for you. For I know you to be very, very far-removed, from all the Givers in all the Court Guides between this, and China.

If you will let me know whether there is anything you would like me to do in the matter, I shall be truly rejoiced to do it — I shall certainly visit the School again;[7] for some important topics have occurred to me, in reference to which, I want to offer strong suggestions to the Masters.

We return to town on the second of next month. I am going down to Manchester for a couple of days, on the fifth, to preside at the re-opening of their Athenaeum, whereat some couple of thousand people are to be assembled. If you are at Putney on the Third or Fourth, perhaps you will let me come to see you.

With best regards to Miss Meredith — and Mr Young[8] if the bird of passage known by that name be still with you — I am always Dear Miss Coutts

　　Yours faithfully and obliged

ରୁଷ

25.　　　　　　　　SEPTEMBER 24, 1843, BROADSTAIRS, KENT

I shall be most glad to confer with you, about Little Nell;[9] and I will come out to Putney on Tuesday afternoon, the Third, which will be the day after I return to town. But I solemnly protest against the

---

[6] A prophecy to which Dickens returns again and again, in *The Old Curiosity Shop*, in *Barnaby Rudge*, in *Bleak House*, in *Hard Times*, and *A Tale of Two Cities*: let the upper and middle classes but neglect long enough their duty of fostering the welfare of their poorer brothers, and when these have sunk deep into ignorance, disease, crime, and hatred they will turn and rend those who gave no thought to them.

[7] Dickens did return, many times, to the Ragged School described in this letter, and visited many others as well, including that in the slum district of Westminster in which Miss Coutts was also interested.

[8] Unidentified.

[9] One of the orphaned Elton girls, Esther Elton, who three years later, March 13, 1846, was found a position as mistress of a school at Matcham.

number being read out of its proper course — especially as the first chapter is not mortally long.[1] If Miss Meredith resorts to any such improper and unjustifiable courses, Pinch is a dead man from that moment.

I will endeavour between this time and when I have the pleasure of seeing you, to ascertain what you so kindly desire to know, in reference to the Ragged Schools. There are fewer girls than boys; but the girls are more numerous than you would suppose, and much better behaved — although they are the wretchedest of the wretched. But there is much more good in Women than in Men, however ragged they are. People are apt to think otherwise, because the outward degradation of a woman strikes them more forcibly than any amount of hideousness in a man. They have no better reason.

Mr Rogers [2] is down here, with an old Schoolfellow, Mr Maltby. We have had some mutual tea-drinkings of a rather forlorn description: the same stories being related over and over again, at each festivity. But really Rogers walks about in a most surprising manner. I find him, with a little cane under his arm, airing himself on the top of inaccessible cliffs, and trotting, with his head on one side and his chin on his waistcoat, down gulfs and chasms where few middle-aged Visitors penetrate. Sometimes I see him on the sand, hustled by beggars, and defending himself manfully against a host of Vagrants. And his occupation within doors is to make perpetual alterations in the Pleasures of Memory, and blot them out again. "Everybody writes too fast," he says. It's the great pleasure of his life to think so.

Charley sends his best love, and so do his sisters. The unknown (who like a greater Unknown is called Walter)[3] does the like, on the faith of their representations. Mrs Dickens begs to add her best regards.

I don't wonder that Miss Meredith, in her weak state, has suffered from the heat. Everybody here has been ill from the same cause.

---

[1] Probably the October number of *Martin Chuzzlewit*, not yet published, in Chapter XXIV of which Tom Pinch administers a beating to Jonas Chuzzlewit.

[2] Samuel Rogers (1763–1855), banker and poet, author of *Italy* and *The Pleasures of Memory*, who gave famous "literary breakfasts" at his home in St. James's Place, facing the Green Park.

[3] Walter Landor Dickens (1841–1863), born February 8 and named after Walter Savage Landor, who was his godfather. "The Great Unknown" was Sir Walter Scott, whose identity as the author of the Waverley novels was not revealed till 1827. Although Walter was now over two and a half, Miss Coutts had evidently not yet seen him.

26. OCTOBER 13, 1843, DEVONSHIRE TERRACE

The "Ragged" Masters are really very honest men. I infer from the enclosed, that they fear they may not succeed in the long run, and are delicate of availing themselves of individual kindness, beyond the temporary help of a subscription. But I may be wrong in this; and when I have done my month's work (with which I am now in spasms) I will see the writer, and talk to him more fully. This will be, very early, I hope, in the week after next.

I have been thinking very much about Nell.[4] Will you tell me whether you wish her to *learn* anything? I am not quite clear about that. — I mean, to learn a trade, or learn what is popularly called "her book."

A hideous cold has taken possession of me to an almost unprecedented extent. I am not exactly, like Miss Squeers,[5] screaming out loud all the time I write; but I am executing another kind of performance beginning with an s and ending with a g; perpetually.

The Manchester Meeting,[6] composed of men of all parties, was very brilliant I assure you. A thousand tickets were sold, and most of them admitted two, — many three, — persons. I am strongly tempted to send you a local paper, containing all the speeches. But modesty (a besetting sin with authors) prevents me.

It will be a comfort to Miss Meredith to know that my other rheumatic friend who got well long before her — that is to say too soon — is turning all wrong again, just as she is turning all right. May I trouble you to tell her that my hair is growing, and I'll never do so any more?

Charley and his sisters, entrust me with messages full of partially unintelligible enthusiasm. Mrs Dickens begs me to say that if you can oblige her with your Drury Lane Box for any performing night next week, she will take it as a great favor.

[P.S.] I was greatly pleased with Mr. Morier.[7]

---

[4] Again Esther Elton.

[5] An allusion to the famous letter of Fanny Squeers in Chapter XV of *Nicholas Nickleby*.

[6] Dickens presided and spoke at a meeting of the Manchester Athenaeum October 5, 1843.

[7] Possibly, although not certainly, James Morier (1780?–1849), novelist and travel writer, author of *The Adventures of Hajji Baba of Ispahan,* who was a contributor to *Bentley's Miscellany,* but there is no means of telling what pleased Dickens about him.

27. October 18, 1843, 17 Ampton Street [to Charles Dickens from Samuel Roberts Starey]

I have to thank you most cordially for your kind interest on behalf of the Field Lane Schools both in procuring the £10. from Miss Burdett Coutts to whom I beg that you will express my grateful acknowledgments on behalf of the Committee and for laying the subject before the Council on Education which I sincerely trust will be attended with a favorable result — I beg to enclose a Receipt as requested —

With yourself I much regret that your excellent proposal with regard to washing and removal of the School to some more commodious and convenient premises cannot *at present* be carried into effect but since I last wrote you I have seen the Landlord of a large shed in West Street and am using my best endeavours to prevail on him to let it us to convert into a School room which will accomodate 3 or 400 pupils, this could be done for about £90. — besides the yearly Rent —

If I should be successful in obtaining a proposition from him I trust you will not consider me intruding on your valuable time by communicating the same

∞

28. November 2, 1843, Devonshire Terrace

On going out to Putney yesterday, I was perfectly amazed to find that Miss Meredith had gone direct to Brighton in the Garden chair. I trust she is better; and that your ague has gone over to Holland, to settle there.

I enclose you a note I have had from the Ragged School master. I don't know what you may have said to Lord Sandon,[8] or whether you would desire to shew it him. But I send it to you, on the chance.

Nell distracts me. It unfortunately happens that there is no Institution (that I know of, or can find out, at least) where such a girl could learn a trade. This throws one on a choice of trades. Then I think of tambour-working — then of stay-making — then of shoe-binding — then of ready made Linening — then of Millinery — then of Straw

---

[8] Dudley Ryder (1798–1882), son of the first Earl of Harrowby, known as Viscount Sandon till his father's death in 1847. He was married to Miss Coutts's cousin Lady Frances Stuart, a granddaughter of Thomas Coutts and daughter of John Stuart, fourth Earl and first Marquis of Bute. Lord Sandon vigorously aided the philanthropic activities of Lord Ashley (afterward Earl of Shaftesbury), and was an advocate of Negro emancipation and shorter factory hours.

Bonnet making — then of Mrs Brownrigge — then of surplus labor — and then I give it up, with a headache.[9]

Would it not be a good plan — first, to find out what the child thinks herself, and then to cast about among your servants for instance, whether they have not some friend or relation who is, or who knows some other friend or relation who is, in a respectable little way of business that would do for her? I could very easily find out, by personal inspection, whether it promised well. None of our former handmaidens are settled in any trade, except a most respectable cook, who married from us (in a cab — No 74) and keeps a thriving shop, I am told, "in the general line." But there seems to be nothing to learn, in the general line, except making up infinitessimal parcels of pepper, and chopping soap into little blocks — and she can do that now, I dare say.

There's half a bonnet-shop in Tottenham Court road, with an Inscription in the window in these words — "Wonted a feamail Prentis with a premum." *That* wouldn't do, perhaps?

This day week, I shall have paid the Eltons, the full amount you gave me. One of the poor girls is very ill, I am sorry to say, and seems consumptive. Did you see the cruel hoax of the bottle? We have the slip of paper which was shut up in it, and it is not (they tell me) in his handwriting, or at all like it. What strange minds those must be, which can find delight in such intolerable cruelties — for which, and which only, if I had my will, I would flog at the church-doors. After the President went down, Mrs Power had some new letter, almost every day, saying that he had landed in Ireland, and was staying at the Writer's house![1]

◌↝◌

29.   DECEMBER 27, 1843, DEVONSHIRE TERRACE

If every Christmas that comes to you, only makes you, or finds you, one half as happy and merry as I wish you to be, you will be the hap-

---

[9] Elizabeth Brownrigge was a midwife living in Fleur de Lys Court, Fleet Street, who in 1765 was appointed midwife to the parish workhouse of St. Dunstan's in the West. She had three apprentices whom she treated with such cruelty that one of them, Mary Clifford, died. Mrs. Brownrigge was tried, found guilty, and hanged at Tyburn, September 14, 1767. Her skeleton was exposed in a niche in the Surgeons' Hall in the Old Bailey.

[1] The *President*, an American steamer, sailed from New York for Liverpool March 21, 1841. She was sighted on March 24, but never seen or heard of again. Tyrone Power, an Irish comedian, was one of the passengers.

piest and merriest person in all the world. I should have sent you my seasonable wishes; but I feared (from not having heard from you) that Lady Burdett was still very ill; and am exceedingly sorry to have the apprehension confirmed by your note.

Mrs Dickens begs me to thank you for your kind remembrance of her, and to say that she will use the box *tonight*. She is not very well, and I am glad of a pantomime or anything else that is likely to amuse her.

Charley is in great force, and, with his sisters, desires his hearty love. They all went, with us, last night to a juvenile party at Mrs Macreadys, and came out very strong — especially Charley who called diverse small boys by their christian names (after the manner of a young nobleman on the Stage) and indulged in numerous phases of genteel dissipation. I have made a tremendous hit with a conjuring apparatus, which includes some of Döebler's best tricks, and was more popular last evening after cooking a plum pudding in a hat, and producing a pocket handkerchief from a Wine Bottle, than ever I have been in my life. I shall hope to raise myself in your esteem by these means.[2]

Macready still continues as successful as it is possible to be.[3] He is very well, and likes the people — which must be a great comfort to him.

We are getting on steadily with the Elton's. The sick one is quite restored to health.

I am very glad to hear that Miss Meredith has left that corner she was so long in turning, quite out of sight. Will you remember me, kindly and cordially to her?

I shall have a request — a petition I ought to say — to make to you before I finish the Chuzzlewit, which is very selfish, for it will give the book a new interest in my eyes.[4] But I will defer it, and all ques-

---

[2] The Christmas festivities were a wild Bohemian success, rising almost to a Bacchic rout. "Such dinings, such dancings, such conjurings, such blind-man's-buffings, such theatre-goings, such kissings-out of old years and kissings-in of new," Dickens wrote an American friend. With "the drinking of champagne," said Jane Welsh Carlyle, and dancing in which "the gigantic Thackeray" and the other guests were "all capering like *Maenades*," by midnight the scene was "something not unlike *the rape of the Sabines!*" Jane doubted that there was as much fun "in all the aristocratic, conventional drawing rooms" in London "as among us little knot of blackguardist literary people who felt ourselves above all rules, and independent of the universe!" Truly, "the pleasantest company . . . *are* the *blackguards!*"

[3] Macready was still on his theatrical tour in America.

[4] The request, which was that he be allowed to dedicate *Martin Chuzzlewit* to Miss Coutts, was of course granted.

tions concerning the charities into which I have made enquiry for you, until you have more leisure for such subjects. I am sure this ancient year must have been a very arduous one to you; and but for such occupations being their own reward, would have wearied you to a serious extent.

With every good wish

[P.S.] You will be glad to hear, I know — that my Carol is a prodigious success.[5]

ↄ⅄ↄ

30.   JANUARY 13, 1844, DEVONSHIRE TERRACE [TO MISS MEREDITH]

I am truly grieved (though not surprised) to hear of Lady Burdett's death. I have very often thought of Miss Coutts in her long and arduous attendance upon her poor mother; and but that I know how such hearts as hers are sustained in such duties, should have feared for her health. For her peace of mind in this and every trial, and for her gentle fortitude always, no one who knows her truly, can be anxious in the least. If she has not the materials of comfort and consolation within herself, there are no such things in any creature's nature.

I am much concerned for Sir Francis; but he has a strong mind and a young spirit; and I hope will rally soon.[6]

Let me thank you for your kind remembrance of me at such a time. I value it very much, and am exceedingly grateful to you.

Mrs. Dickens sends her best regards. She is in hourly expectation of her confinement,[7] but I trust is pretty well. Charley and his sisters are in rude health, and beg to add their loves.

Believe me Dear Miss Meredith

---

[5] *A Christmas Carol*, written at a white heat between early October and the end of November. Over it, Dickens said, he "wept and laughed, and wept again, and excited himself in a most extraordinary manner in the composition; and thinking whereof he walked about the black streets of London fifteen and twenty miles many a night when all sober folks had gone to bed." Six thousand copies of the first edition were sold on the very day of publication. The first of his five Christmas books, its tremendous success paved the way for the popularity of those that followed it.

[6] Sir Francis Burdett survived his wife less than a fortnight, dying January 23, 1844. The husband and wife were buried in a double funeral, in the village church of Ramsbury, Wiltshire, which was part of the Burdett family property in that county.

[7] Francis Jeffrey, Dickens's fifth child, (1844–1886), named after Lord Jeffrey, was born January 15. Francis, Lord Jeffrey (1773–1850), Scottish judge and critic, was one of the founders of the *Edinburgh Review* in 1802 and its editor 1803–

Despite the spectacular popularity of the Christmas Carol, *its expensive format — hand-colored plates, tinted end papers, and two-color title page — had made its profits disappointingly small. Convinced that Chapman and Hall had mismanaged it, Dickens angrily severed publishing relations with them and made new arrangements with Bradbury and Evans, who had previously been only his printers. Worried about the expenses of his growing family, he felt that he must economize. In the spring of 1844, therefore, he decided to spend a year abroad in Italy, living modestly and writing his next story there.*

On July 2 he started out with his family and the servants in an enormous traveling carriage and arrived in Genoa on the evening of the fifteenth. In the suburb of Albaro they had taken sight unseen the Villa di Bella Vista, which turned out to be a "lonely, rusty, stagnant old staggerer" of a rose-colored stucco house that Dickens soon christened the "Pink Jail." Unable to write there, he looked around for another residence available at a moderate rent, and within two and a half months moved to the first floor of the Palazzo Peschiere, the Palace of the Fishponds, a famous building with beautiful gardens and frescoes designed by Michelangelo. Here in the course of October he wrote his second Christmas story, The Chimes. *No sooner was it completed than he was wild to read it aloud to his friend Forster and a circle of intimates, and dashed back to London, arriving there in the wintry dark of November 30. The reading took place in Forster's chambers in Lincoln's Inn Fields on December 3, where it moved to tears an audience that included Thomas Carlyle, Daniel Maclise, and Douglas Jerrold.*

∽

31.   DECEMBER 8, 1844, PIAZZA COFFEE HOUSE, COVENT GARDEN

I have been in town a very few days; and leave it again, and start for Italy, tonight. I hoped to have seen you as a matter of course; but when I had disposed of the business part of my Christmas Book (which mainly brought me here, and imprisoned me at the Printer's two days) I had some arrangements to make for the extrication of some unhappy people from circumstances of great distress and perplexity, which have occupied my whole time. So that I have seen no one, and gone nowhere.[8]

1829. He was Lord Advocate 1830–1834 and Judge of the Court of Session 1834–1850. He became an early admirer and friend of Dickens.

[8] The family of John Overs, also mentioned three paragraphs below. Overs was

I had the greatest pleasure some months ago, in the receipt of your interesting letter from Germany. I was going to answer it with some account of my Italian adventures; but as soon as I had any to narrate, the time had come for my sitting down to my little book; and when I got up again, it was to come here. I hope you will like those Chimes which will be published on the 16th and though I am not malicious, I am bent on making you cry, or being most horribly disappointed.

The Sanatorium Committee have informed me of your munificent donation to that Establishment.[9] There is not in England an Institution whose design is more noble, useful, and excellent. I know some little histories connected with that place, and the blessing it has proved in sickness and Death, which are among the most affecting incidents that have ever come within my observation.

You may possibly have seen a Preface I wrote, before leaving England, to a little book by a Working Man; and may have learned from the newspapers that he is dead: leaving a destitute wife and six children, of whom one is a cripple. I have addressed a letter to the Governors of the Orphan Working School in behalf of the Eldest boy: and they tell me he has a good chance of being elected into that Institution in April next. It has occurred to me that at some time or other you might have an opportunity of presenting one of the girls to some other school or charity, and as I know full well that in such an event you would rather thank than blame me for making a real and strong case known to you, I send you the childrens' names and ages.

---

a poor carpenter, who worked for a manufacturer of medicine cabinets, and who had sent Dickens some poems during the last months he was editor of *Bentley's Miscellany* in 1839. Dickens passed on the poems to his friend and successor, Harrison Ainsworth (1805–1882), helped Overs find publication for some of his songs in *Tait's Magazine* in Edinburgh, and aided him in the composition of a number of short stories with historical backgrounds. In 1841 Overs learned that he had tuberculosis and was told that he could not live very long if he continued to work at his trade. Dickens put him in the hands of Dr. John Elliotson (1791–1868), the famous physician who had been Professor of the Practice of Medicine in London University 1831–1838, who had procured the foundation of University College Hospital, made investigations in the curative value of mesmerism, founded the Phrenological Society, and been the first to use the stethoscope. Dickens also enabled Overs to obtain lighter work as a doorkeeper in Macready's theater. It was through Dickens's aid, too, that Overs's stories, collected into *Evenings of a Working Man*, were published by Newby.

[9] The Sanatorium, the first "Nursing Home," in Devonshire Place, near Dickens's residence, had been founded in 1841 by Dr. Thomas Southwood Smith (1788–1861). Macready and Talfourd were both members of the committee.

Amelia Overs — 11 years old
John Richard — 9
Harriett   — 7
Geraldine   — 6
Editha   — 4
John   — 4 months

They live, at present, at 55 Vauxhall Street Lambeth.

My head quarters in Italy are at Genoa: where we live in a Palace (the Palazzo Peschiere) something larger than Whitehall multiplied by four; and where Charley and his Giant sisters play among orange Trees and Fountains all day long.[1] They were particularly anxious when I came away, that I should give their loves to you, and they entrusted me with the Private commission that I should ascertain whether "That Lady"[2] was still in bed upstairs. In pursuing my enquiries on this head, I have received information in reference to that lady, which has quite delighted me, and not at all surprised me. I hope I may still live in her memory; and that I may venture to send her my regards and congratulations.

I have been to Modena, Parma, Bologna, Ferrara, Cremona, Venice, and a hundred other places. Florence, Rome, Naples, and Palermo lie before me. I never could have believed in, and never did imagine, the full splendour and glory of Venice. That wonderful dream! The three days that I passed there, were like a Thousand and One Arabian Nights, wildly exaggerated a thousand and one times. I read Romeo and Juliet in Verona too, and bought some tooth-ache mixture of an apothecary in Mantua, lean enough and poor enough to "go on" in the Tragedy. I came to England by the Simplon — sledging through the snow upon the top — and through Switzerland, which was cool. But beautiful and grand, beyond expression. I shall remain in Paris — at the Hotel Brighton — until Friday Evening next; and if at that place or at any other, you could give me any commission to execute for you, I need not say how happy it would make me.

Mrs Dickens begged me to present her best regards, if I saw you. I do so with a very ill will, in this miserable substitute for the pleasure I had anticipated in doing so, after so long an interval.

I am Ever Dear Miss Coutts

---

[1] Charley was now almost eight, his sisters Mamey and Katey six and five.
[2] Miss Meredith, whose health was still poor. Dickens's "information" was of her approaching marriage to Dr. William Brown,

32.   MARCH 18, 1845, ROME

I am very much afraid that the date of this letter will contrast, to my disadvantage, with the date of Twelfth Night, which you made a proud night for Charley in Genoa, and a happy night to me in the more secret quarter of my own breast, by your kind and generous remembrance.[3] But I have been so constantly and incessantly on the wing since that great finale of the Christmas Holidays; and have been so cold, and so wet, and so muddy, and so everything which is currently supposed to be incompatible with Italy — and have been into such extraordinary places, and have eaten such unaccountable meals, and have slept in such incredible beds, and have led altogether, such a wildly preposterous life — that I have not had the heart to write to you, lest my letter, partaking in some degree of the character of my existence, should be of too vagabond a nature for delivery at your door.

Before I left Genoa, I had all the knives locked up: fearing that Charley would otherwise, in the excitement of his feelings, lay hands upon a sharp one, and do himself a mischief — I don't mean with any evil design upon his life, but in the endeavour to make a pen wherewith to write a note to you. The intention was so very active within him that I should have allowed him to gratify it, but for his writing being something large for the Foreign Post, which, at his rate of penmanship, would hardly carry more than his name. But I gave him a solemn promise that I would thank you twenty thousand times. That I would report him tolerant of Italian life and manners, but not attached to them: yielding a strong preference to those of his own country. That I would say he never could forget his ride with you to Hampstead. That I would tell you that such a thing as a Twelfth Cake was never seen in Genoa before; and that when it went to a Swiss Pastry-Cook's in that city, to have the sugar repaired (it was a very little chipped at one corner) it was *exhibited* to the principal Inhabitants, as a wonder and marvel. That I would give his love and his sisters' loves to "that lady", and would add that I had at length succeeded in impressing on their minds the great truth that she didn't always live in bed. That I would say that he looked forward to coming with me to see and thank you, on our return to England. And that I would be sure to tell you a great deal more, which I will not inflict upon you on any account.

---

[3] A large Twelfth Cake weighing ninety pounds, with magnificent sugar decorations, which Miss Coutts had sent Charley for his birthday.

The weather has been atrocious, ever since I returned from England at Christmas. I do not think I ever felt it so cold as between this place and Naples, about a month ago. Between Naples and Paestum too, three weeks ago; with a cold North Wind blowing over mountains covered with snow; it was quite intolerable. Within the last three days, there have been glimpses of Spring. I will not say more, in the fulness of my heart; for experience has taught me that tomorrow may be deep Winter again. I have certainly seen more Sun in England, between the end of December and the middle of March, than I have seen in Italy in that time. And for violent and sudden changes, there is surely no country in the world more remarkable than this. When it *is* fine (as people say) it is very fine — so beautiful, that the really good days blot out the recollection of the bad ones. But I do honestly believe that it is not oftener fine here, than it is elsewhere; and that we are far better off at home in that respect, than anything short of the rack, would induce most people to confess.

In the mass, I like the common people of Italy very much — the Neapolitans least of all: the Romans next, for they are fierce and brutal. Not falling on very good specimens of the higher orders, in the beginning, I have not pursued that Enquiry. I have had no leisure to do so, if I had had the inclination, so I have avoided them as much as possible, and have kept the greater part of my letters of introduction in my own desk. Florence I have not yet seen: intending to take it, next week, on my way back to Genoa. But of all the places I *have* seen, I like Venice, Genoa, and Verona, most. The Bay of Genoa has charms, in my eyes, which the Bay of Naples wants. The city of Genoa is very picturesque and beautiful. And the house we live in, is really like a Palace in a Fairy Tale.

I cannot remember, to my satisfaction, whether you were ever at Herculaneum and Pompeii. Though my impression is, that I have heard you speak of them. The interest and wonder of those ruined places, far exceeded my utmost expectations. Venice was such a splendid Dream to me, that I can never speak of it, — from sheer inability to describe its effect upon my mind. The ancient parts of Rome, and a portion of the Campagna, are *what I meant* when I came here; the rest a little below my imaginary mark, and very unlike it. The Coliseum by daylight, moonlight, torchlight, and every sort of light, most stupendous and awful. Saint Peters not so impressive within, as many Cathedrals I have seen at home. The great altar, and the state entrance to the Subterranean church might be Rundell and Bridge's show-room. And the canopies, hangings, and carpets (of all sorts of reds and greens) now hung up: and put down, for the Holy-Week ceremonies, have the effect of an enormous Bon-bon. Before which, and round which, and in and out of which, they are perpetually carrying the poor old Pope about on men's shoulders, like a Gorgeous Guy Faux.

The drollest thing I have seen, is a daily gathering of artists' "Models" on the steps of a church near the house (Meloni's Hotel) in which we live: where they dispose themselves in conventionally picturesque attitudes, and wait to be hired as sitters. The first time I went up there, I could *not* conceive how their faces were familiar to me — how they seemed to have bored me, for many years, in every variety of action and costume — and to come back upon my sight as perfect nightmares. At last it flashed upon me all at once that we had made acquaintance, and improved it, on the walls of the Royal Academy. So we had indeed. And there is not one among them whom you wouldn't know, at first sight, as well as the Statue at Charing Cross. The most aggravating of the party is a dismal old patriarch, with very long white hair and beard, who carries a great staff in his hand: which staff has been faithfully copied at the Exhibition in all its twists and knots, at least once through the catalogue. He is the venerable model. Another man in a sheepskin, who always lies asleep in the sun (when there is any) is the Pastorial Model. Another man in a brown cloak who leans against a wall with his arms folded, is the assassin model. Another man who looks over his shoulder and always seems to be going away, but never goes, is the haughty model. Several women and children form the family models. And the cream of the whole is, that they are one and all the falsest rascals in Rome or out of it: being specially made up for their trade, and having no likeness among the whole population. It is a good illustration of the Student life as it is, that young men should go on copying these people elaborately time after time and time out of mind, and find nothing fresh or suggestive in the actual world about them.

My English papers tell me of the death of Sydney Smith,[4] whom

---

[4] Sydney Smith (1771–1845), clergyman, wit, and essayist, one of the founders of the *Edinburgh Review* and its first editor, prebend of Bristol, rector of Combe-Flory, Canon of St. Paul's, a brilliant critic and conversationalist. Dickens greatly admired his lectures on moral philosophy, and in 1847 named his seventh child Sydney Smith Haldimand Dickens.

I deeply regret. I also hear, privately, that Hood,[5] the author, is past all chance of recovery. He was (I have a sad presentiment that even now I may speak of him as something past) a man of great power — of prodigious force and genius as a poet — and not generally known, perhaps, by his best credentials. Personally, he had a most noble and generous spirit. When he was under the pressure of severe misfortune and illness, and I had never seen him, he went far out of his way to praise me; and wrote (in the Athenaeum) a paper on The Curiosity Shop; so full of enthusiasm and high appreciation, and so free from any taint of envy or reluctance to acknowledge me, a young man far more fortunate than himself, that I can hardly bear to think of it.

I hope to be in Genoa again, before the middle of next month; and have arranged to leave there and turn homeward, in the middle of June. Whether we may linger on the way in France or Switzerland, I do not yet quite know. But in that case it is probable that I may run over to London for two or three days, to preside at a Public Dinner in aid of the Sanatorium. I shall hope to see you then, at latest, unless (I wish there were any hope of it!) you should be coming Genoa-way, and would give me a chance of shewing you the Peschiere orange trees.

In any case, when I am among them again, I shall trouble you with at least one more of Charley's messages, and a few words of my own. For I fear that I may otherwise (not undeservedly) pass out of your remembrance; and believe me dear Miss Coutts there are not many memories from which it would give me so much pain to fade, as from yours. I rate its worth too highly.

P.S. Mrs Dickens begs to unite in best regards to yourself, and "the lady" — who is well, I hope — and happy, I know. I hope you cried when you read the Chimes?

๛

In June 1845 Dickens returned from Italy to England. During his visit to London the preceding winter he and Forster had planned some amateur theatricals as an amusement for the fall, and Dickens now plunged busily into this enterprise. He also began to make arrangements for the founding of a great liberal newspaper, an idea that had fascinated him since his return from America. Energetically

---

[5] Thomas Hood (1799–1845), the poet and humorist.

throughout the fall, even as rehearsals were going on, he worked out its details, and on January 20, 1846, the Daily News *was born, with Dickens as its first editor.*

His connection with the paper, however, was brief. Some of its financial backers who were heavily involved in railway investments revealed an ominous desire to influence its policies, and Dickens soon felt cause to fear that the newspaper would become tarred with the brush of railway corruption. In addition, he found his own authority as editor — which he regarded as tantamount to an entire control of its management — checked and thwarted by the proprietors, who constantly countermanded his orders and sometimes refused to honor his commitments. These frictions rapidly led to an explosion. On February 9 Dickens resigned, after having edited just seventeen numbers. In later years, however, the Daily News *came to justify Dickens's hopes, growing into one of London's most powerful newspapers and consistently standing as a champion of liberal causes.*

∽

33. AUGUST 21, 1845, DEVONSHIRE TERRACE

It is most extraordinary. There seems to be a fatality in my not seeing you.

I was at Broadstairs, when your last kind note arrived. It was past ten before I returned home last night, and found your hand-writing on my table. Mrs Dickens was with me. And Charley and his sisters we have left behind, on the Seashore, for a month.

Under more fortunate circumstances, we should have been delighted to have come to you last night. I cannot tell you how much I have wished to see you.

I hope you are not going so far, or intend being absent so long, that you will be out of town on Saturday the 20th of September. I am Stage Manager of a company of amateurs who are going to have a Play at Miss Kelly's little Theatre that night. And I don't know what I shall do, if you are not "in front" — as we say, professionally. Mr Stanfield makes his first appearance on any stage, that night. Mr Stone, the artist, also.[6]

---

[6] Frank Stone (1800–1859), artist, A.R.A. 1851, whom Dickens had met as a member of the Shakespeare Society, of which Stone was secretary. When Dickens moved from Devonshire Terrace to Tavistock House in 1851, Stone became his next-door neighbor. Other members of the cast of the Ben Jonson play included Dickens's brothers, Frederick and Augustus, Mark Lemon, the editor of *Punch*, and the caricaturist John Leech. Frances Maria Kelly (1790–1882), at whose pri-

And some of the "Punch" people are also to appear before an admiring and delighted audience. The comedy is Every Man in his Humour. There will be one man very much out of humour, if you are out of town.

To ease my mind on this head, I have marked this letter to be forwarded. If I should hear in reply that you will not be in town that night — and further that Mrs Brown [7] will be away likewise — I shall take to drinking, immediately.

∽

34. SEPTEMBER 10, 1845, DEVONSHIRE TERRACE

I am deeply sensible, believe me, of your kind interest in my dear boy.[8] I feel it as much as it is possible to feel anything. Far too much to thank you in written words like these. I am so painfully happy in your thoughtful remembrance of him, that I can only thank you from my inmost heart; and say that I am proud to place my trust in your considerate friendship.

I could do nothing better for him than to accept — I could do nothing half so good for him as to accept — your generous offer. My object is, to make him a good man and a wise one; and to place him in the best position I can help him to, for the exercise of his abilities and acquirements. Your help towards such an end is priceless to me, and to him. You could not (but you know it, I am sure) have done me a more tender service.

He will be nine years old next Twelfth Day. He had a Governess at home originally; and used to go to school, for half a year before we went to Italy, at a Mr King's at St John's Wood. The gentleman is a good scholar, and has sons of Macready and some other friends of ours. Charley has returned to him, as a Day Boarder, since we came home;

---

vate theater in Dean Street, Soho, the performances took place, had been a famous Ophelia with Kean and played in other Shakespearean parts, and after her retirement had founded a dramatic school which used the theater in the rear of her house. Once beloved by Charles Lamb, she was now aging into a fussy eccentricity.

[7] On December 19, 1844, Miss Meredith had married Dr. William Brown, a junior partner in the medical firm of Tupper, Chilvers, and Brown, in Old Burlington Street, London. The couple resided at 80 Piccadilly, a house adjoining Miss Coutts's town house on Stratton Street, with an opening cut between the two residences on the ground floor. Both places belonged to Miss Coutts.

[8] Miss Coutts had asked to be allowed to defray the expenses of Charley's education, beginning with his entry in a public school.

and while we were abroad, he had lessons at home in English and French, and so forth. I should not say that in small scholarship, he is very far advanced as yet, for I have been more solicitous in the first instance, about his health than his study. But he is a child of a very uncommon capacity indeed; and I have no doubt (neither has his present Master) of his rapidly winning his way upward, in any school whatever. His natural talent is quite remarkable.

If you will let me know at what age he is presentable at Marlborough,[9] and whether it is desirable that his attention should be directed in the meantime to any particular books or branches of learning — or if you can put me in the way of ascertaining these things from the Head Master by going down there, myself — or if you can, at your leisure, tell me anything that it is advisable or necessary to do — I need not say how vigilantly I shall set about it. But do not trouble yourself to write to me, unnecessarily. I shall be quite easy until I hear from you.

I was both surprised and grieved to find, by your preceding letter, that you were at all an Invalid; of which I had not the least idea. I hope that the repose and freshness of the Devonshire Coast, have done you good already; and that your eyes have found many beautiful objects to refresh them.

When your letter reached me yesterday, I was on the point of writing to tell you (for I knew you would be gratified to hear) that Esther Elton, the eldest, in her training at the Normal School has uniformly conducted herself in a manner for which no praise could be too high; and has now the choice of two large schools in the country — to one of which she will go, as Mistress, early in the Spring. I never in my life saw such gentle perseverance and steady goodness as this girl has displayed, from the first. Going into the establishment, a woman grown — with her character already formed, and her habits adapted, as one would have thought, to the easy kind of life she had led, as her poor father's poor housekeeper — she settled herself at once, resolutely, to the discipline and hard-work of the place; and has never turned from it, for one moment, though it has involved her separation from her little sisters, to whom she feels as a mother — her resignation of all her old society — her self-denial in a hundred ways — in all the ways of her previous life. I regard it, really as an instance of patient womanly devo-

---

[9] Marlborough College, in Marlborough, Wiltshire, originally intended for the education of the sons of clergymen, was opened in 1843.

tion; a little piece of quiet, unpretending, domestic heroism; of a most affecting and interesting kind. And if you could see her, with her pleasant face, and her neat, composed, agreeable manner, you would recollect that time when you gave me a commission in behalf of herself and the others, with such an emotion as very few people can ever know.

My Dear Miss Coutts I will not thank you again; nor will I say for Charley's Mama, all that she wants me to say. No one can imagine it, better than you.

P.S. I beg my best regards to Miss Meredith — by which name I always call her, whether I will or no. I am quite sorry you and she are not in town to see the Play on Saturday Week; being pretty sure it would have amused you.

∽

35.   September 17, 1845, Devonshire Terrace

Immediately on the receipt of your letter, I set about enquiring into the reputation of Mr Tolfrey,[1] and as I knew nothing of him myself, and was even unacquainted with his name, I went away to the office of the Literary Fund (I am one of its Managing Committee); where I knew I should hear the Truth about him, if he had ever applied for assistance there; and where I knew my enquiry, in any case, would be strictly confidential; secresy being one of the main principles of the Establishment.

I found, to my disappointment, that it being vacation time, the Secretary (an excellent and charitable gentleman) was out of town. But I wrote to him straightway: and here is his letter in reply. I should decidedly say, on such evidence, that Mr Tolfrey is *not* a fit subject for your generous aid. If his story be true, his bookseller will certainly purchase a second Edition of his book from him. If his story be untrue, a Second Edition (supposing him to apply the money, if he got it from you, in its publication) would be mere wastepaper. The second Edition being all sold, would, certainly, be much more profitable to him if he published it on his own account, than if he made a bargain with

---

[1] I have not been able to identify Mr. Tolfrey, but it is evident from this letter itself that he had presented himself with some request for charity from Miss Coutts, and was only dubiously a literary man. As early as 1837 Dickens was associated with the Royal Literary Fund, an organization to give financial aid to deserving writers in embarrassed circumstances and sometimes to help the families of those who died penniless. It had an executive committee, a secretary, and a headquarters in Bloomsbury.

Bentley, Colburn,[2] or any other Shark of those waters. But I can hear nothing of the book. And I do not believe its success warrants any such presumption.

A slight thing may turn the scale when the balance is going very plainly one way. I did not like his mention of his "revered and lamented father," and his "beloved mother" in his letter to you. A man who is quite in earnest, can afford to leave his estimation of his parents, I think, to the understanding of his reader.

At the same time, if you be inclined to advance him the money, I need not say that I will give it him with the greatest caution, and in the most considerate manner. All I wish to say against it, is, that I think I would not give it to him, if I were you.

With a smaller sum, my dear Miss Coutts, I think I can do, on your behalf, an infinitely greater service. George Cruikshank [3] came to me some weeks ago, and told me the facts of the melancholy little history I am going to state to you. He asked me if I thought I could influence any rich friend in the sufferer's behalf. You were not in the way. I do not know that I should have had the courage to come to you, if you had been. And I told him No; I could not then; but if I ever could, I would. I should premise that Cruikshank is one of the best creatures in the World in his own odd way (he is a live caricature himself);

---

[2] Richard Bentley (1794–1871), publisher, and Henry Colburn (d. 1855), publisher, the Bacon and Bungay of Thackeray's *Pendennis*. They had been partners, but separated shortly before 1836, when Bentley founded *Bentley's Miscellany* and asked Dickens to be its editor. Dickens edited the magazine from January 1837 to February 1839, and *Oliver Twist* was published in serial form in its pages, but he and Bentley had friction with each other from the start, and Dickens at last resigned his editorship after prolonged and acrimonious struggles with Bentley. Even after this they wrangled bitterly till June 1840 over a remaining agreement for the publication of *Barnaby Rudge*. Dickens called Bentley "the Burlington Street brigand," and said he looked like a "fraudulent butler." With Colburn, also, Dickens quarreled, about the publication of a miscellaneous work entitled *The Pic-Nic Papers*, which he had agreed to edit for the benefit of Mrs. Macrone, the widow of his first publisher, who had been left indigent at her husband's death. Various authors donated contributions, and to Dickens's indignation "this sneaking vagabond," as he called Colburn, insultingly rejected that offered by the distinguished old poet Walter Savage Landor. Dickens regarded both Bentley and Colburn as unscrupulous — and Bentley, at least, certainly had a reciprocal opinion of Dickens.

[3] George Cruikshank (1792–1878), artist and caricaturist, who began his career as an illustrator of children's books and became a powerful radical cartoonist. He did the etchings for Dickens's first book, *Sketches by Boz*, in 1836, and for *Oliver Twist* both in *Bentley's Miscellany* and in book form. He continued to produce etchings in rapid succession until his eighty-third year.

and that to the extent of his means, he has rendered assistance here, already, from his own purse.

I don't know if you ever saw a book called "Mornings at Bow Street." It is a collection of Bow Street reports that appeared, years and years ago, in the Morning Herald; and did the paper immense service at that time. The writer is a Mr White, who from that time until very recently, has been connected with the Herald as one of its Sub-Editors. The paper changed hands within this Year and a Half, or so — he was not wanted in the new arrangements — and at 60 years of age was suddenly discharged, with a month's salary, from the establishment that had not only been his income but his whole prospect; for he thought himself (quite naturally) a leaf of the tree, and believed he would never be shaken off until he died. He had lived upon his salary, but had done no more — I really don't see how he could have done more — and this was a blow, as if his Bank had failed, or he had become paralyzed.

His daughter had been engaged to be married, *Fourteen Years.* Her lover was not rich — was fighting his way, very slowly, to the Bar — and they had always said they would be married, when he was 'called.' After all these many years, he was called, at last; and her wedding clothes were being made, when one night (just at the time of this discharge), after they had been to the opera together, he went home to his chambers and was seized with congestion of the Brain. In a very few hours she was sent for. If she wished to see him before he died, the message said, she must come without delay. She was taken down to the Adelphi (where the chambers were) by her mother; and they arrived in the Bedroom, just in time to see him die. Quite frantic, she ran out of the chamber; opened a window, four tall stories high; and plunged herself, head-foremost from it! By a kind of miracle, she fell into a tank of water at the back of one of the neighbouring houses; and was taken out, insensible, but unhurt. Since that time, she has been watched, day and night. Her mother has never been told the Truth, but her father knows it. The poor girl sits all day in a sort of dream, repeating little scraps of comfort from the Bible. She has never shed a tear.

The wretched father is oppressed with some small debts. But they are very small; and if he could release his plate, which he has pawned for Thirty Pounds, I have no doubt Cruikshank could compound for every one of them with the produce of its Sale; and then he could, with an easier mind, seek some employment; or at the worst, go away to live with his son who is a poor curate – I think – in Wales. My dear Miss Coutts, these are all miserable facts within my knowledge. Thirty Pounds here, will be like Help from Heaven. There is no possibility of imposition; Cruikshank has known the parties twenty years at least; and the circumstances surely are peculiarly affecting and distressful.

My letter is so long already, that I will tell you of the other Eltons in my next. We have never had the least trouble with them; and they are all as well, as happy, and as full of promise – thank God for it! – as we could possibly desire.

With best regards to Miss Meredith

∽

36.   [ENVELOPE POSTMARKED SEPTEMBER 24, 1845] DEVONSHIRE TER-RACE

I return you Mr Tolfrey's letter.

A thousand thanks on behalf of Mr White. I have rigidly observed your injunctions; and will write you fully about that poor girl, when I have setted the adjustment of the Fifty Pounds. Suffice it to say at this moment that I hope to be able to make such lasting use of it, as will delight your generous Heart. She is much better.

Where shall I write to you? I shall be glad to know at your perfect leisure.

∽

37.   DECEMBER 1, 1845, DEVONSHIRE TERRACE

I have delayed answering your last kind note until now, because I wished, previously, to have a long talk with Charley's Mama on the subject to which it refers; and I could not very well do that, until she was quite well and down-stairs again.

We have no reason to think that Charley has anything but a vigorous constitution, and good sound health. But when he is in full school employment, there is a strange kind of *fading* comes over him sometimes: the like of which, I don't think I ever saw. Whether the child is anxious at his book, or excited at his Play, or what, I cannot make out. But I see it occasionally, in a very remarkable degree – more plainly, I think, than his mother does, although I am by no means open to such impressions in general, and am not at all fearful for him, except as I know him to be very quick and sensitive.

But I fear if it were to continue, and he were at school at a distance from home, I should have real cause for anxiety; and as you leave the choice to me, I would, solely on this account, prefer King's College,[4] if you think well of it too. I have taken a long time to think of this, because I feel that such kindness as yours *should* be thought of and deliberated upon. And I have come to the conclusion that this is the best course for him.

Bertha White is quite restored. She is depressed of course, but perfectly rational, composed, and resigned. I am trying to keep back a part of your gift for her own sole use in after-life. Whether the necessities of her father will admit of this, I cannot, as yet, say. But I hope they may. She is living with him just now in Wales, and is endeavouring to obtain a situation as companion to a Lady.

I have just finished my little Christmas Book,[5] which I hope will please you. It is very quiet and domestic. I trust it is interesting and pretty. At all events I think so. If you have any fancy for reading a book before it is published, I shall be more than delighted to send you the Proofs by post, if you will let me know in one line that you are still at the place whither I address this letter.

Mrs Overs succeeded the other day in getting one of her children into the Orphan School. It is a great thing for her.

I cannot help wondering when I shall see you again: remembering how long it is since I had that pleasure. I shall be at Liverpool for a day or two towards the end of next week; and at Paris for a week or two, immediately after Christmas Day. If there be anything I can do for you in either place (especially the last) I need not tell you how glad I shall be, to do it.

Charley sends his love, and his sisters beg to add their small remembrances. Mrs Dickens again adds messages which I do *not* send: and I have a very touching letter from Miss White, in which she expresses her gratitude to an unknown person, with as much sincerity and earnestness as ever I saw expressed in words, in my life.

Kindly keep me in "Miss Meredith's" recollection, and ever believe me Dear Miss Coutts,

Your most obliged and faithful friend

---

[4] King's College School, a preparatory school maintained by King's College, University of London.

[5] *The Cricket on the Hearth.* It was immensely popular, doubling the circulation of its predecessors. In 1847, when its publishers were issuing the tenth edition of *A Christmas Carol* and the twelfth edition of *The Chimes,* they were advertising the twenty-second edition of *The Cricket.*

38.   JANUARY 7, 1846, DEVONSHIRE TERRACE

I am sure I need not say to you that it would give me the truest pleasure to be of the least help to anyone in whom you have an interest; and that I should esteem myself most fortunate in having the power. But the courier rumor has not the least foundation. The man who served me in that capacity abroad (one of the best servants in the World) [6] I recommended to some employment only the other day. He is constantly backwards and forwards here, to play with the children: who are his most intimate friends. And if I were to want any other courier, I think it would break his heart. I cannot conceive how your man got such information — unless he derived it from a newspaper. I see almost daily, in those sources of intelligence, the most prodigious accounts of my occupations, intentions, etc etc, which are all so new to me that they make my hair stand on end.

I saw Dr Self [7] the other morning, (yesterday morning) and received the greatest courtesy and attention from him. As he thinks I had best see Dr Major,[8] who is the Head Master of the *School*, I contemplate an inroad on that gentleman tomorrow morning. When I have seen him, and know all that is to be done, I will bring my large son to Stratton Street. He has been writing a play lately. There are four acts in it; two scenes in each; and about twelve words in each scene. The Hero of the piece is a certain "Boy" (it is a nautical subject) who, by reason of his always having to introduce the other characters by asking them where they come from, and having to get them off by proposing to "come along" (which he invariably does, at the end of every scene) has a part, in proportion, longer than Hamlet.

∽

39.   APRIL 22, 1846, DEVONSHIRE TERRACE

I call with Charley this morning to see you. But in case you should be out, or not yet returned, I write this to bring with me.

I saw Dr Self some months ago; and then Dr Major, into whose department of King's College Charley would fall. He seemed to think Charley rather young for the purpose (though he has some scholars not older) and suggested that it would certainly be better for him not to begin until the May term, when the mornings would be lighter and

---

[6] Louis Roche, who accompanied Dickens during his journeyings through France, Italy, and Switzerland in 1844, and who is often called "The Brave Courier" in *Pictures from Italy* and in Dickens's letters.
[7] Unidentified.   [8] Unidentified.

finer for his daily Progresses down the Strand. Very much obliged to him for his consideration, I agreed to defer the business until May, and settled that shortly before that time I would see Dr Major again. He knew Charley's present Master by the bye — spoke highly of him — and said he couldn't be in better preparation.

Until within a fortnight or three weeks ago, I have retained the intention of entering Charley in May. But since then, I have conceived the idea of going to Switzerland for a year. Firstly, because I am most desirous to separate myself in a marked way from the Daily News (with which I have long since ceased to have any connexion, and in connecting myself with which at all, I have no doubt I made a mistake). Secondly, because I have a long book to write, which I could write better in retirement. Thirdly, because I want to get up some mountain knowledge in all the four seasons of the year, for purposes of fiction. Now I think that if I go to Lausanne or some such place, where there are English clergymen who take pupils, and keep Charley in good training under such auspices, he will enter King's College at greater advantage and with a better prestige about him, than if he began as I originally designed. I have not said anything to Dr Major or to Charley yet, as I wished to tell you what I had in my mind, first. But I have a very strong belief that I shall be all the better for acting on this resolution, and I should be glad if you thought with me that Charley would be none the worse.

ᕽᕽ

40.   MAY 26, 1846, DEVONSHIRE TERRACE

I find those who are best acquainted with the subject and the class of persons to be addressed, decidedly in favor of the School and the Church being Free.[9] You may remember this to have been my impression at first, but I have not expressed any opinion of my own to those whom I have sounded on the subject.

In reference to the asylum,[1] it seems to me very expedient that you should know, if possible, whether the Government would assist you to the extent of informing you from time to time into what distant

---

[9] Probably St. Stephen's and its associated school, which Miss Coutts endowed and built in Westminster in 1847.

[1] This is the first reference to the project of establishing a home for the rehabilitation of prostitutes who wished to reform and start a new life. It materialized the following year as Urania Cottage, in Shepherd's Bush. As subsequent letters reveal, Dickens not only outlined the entire organization of the institution, but chose the house in which it was lodged, superintended the modification of the

parts of the World, women could be sent for marriage, with the greatest hope for their future families, and with the greatest service to the existing male population, whether expatriated from England or born there. If these poor women *could* be sent abroad with the distinct recognition and aid of the Government, it would be a service to the effort. But I have (with reason) a doubt of all Governments in England considering such a question in the light, in which men undertaking that immense responsibility, are bound, before God, to consider it. And therefore I would suggest this appeal to you, merely as something which you owe to yourself and to the experiment: the failure of which, does not at all affect the immeasurable goodness and hopefulness of the project itself.

I do not think it would be necessary, in the first instance at all events, to build a house for the Asylum. There are many houses, either in London or in the immediate neighbourhood, that could be altered for the purpose. It would be necessary to limit the number of inmates, but I would make the reception of them as easy as possible to themselves. I would put in the power of any Governor of a London Prison to send an unhappy creature of this kind (by her own choice of course) straight from his prison, when her term expired, to the asylum. I would put it in the power of any penitent creature to knock at the door, and say For God's sake, take me in. But I would divide the interior into two portions; and into the first portion I would put all new-comers without exception, as a place of probation, whence they should pass, by their own good-conduct and self-denial alone, into what I may call the Society of the house. I do not know of any plan, so well conceived, or so firmly grounded in a knowledge of human nature, or so judiciously addressed to it, for observance in this place, as what is called Captain Maconnochie's Mark System,[2] which I will try, very roughly and generally, to describe to you.

A woman or girl coming to the asylum, it is explained to her that

building for its purposes, chose the matrons and teachers placed in charge, and administered it for years, visiting it once a month, checking its accounts, and settling its disciplinary problems. Although not the first enterprise of its kind, it was among the pioneers. The enlightenment of the principles and of the regimen Dickens devised speak for themselves.

[2] Captain Alexander Maconnochie (1787–1860), whose *Crime and Punishments* was announced in the *Publishers' Circular* of July 15, 1846, as just published by Hatchard and Son. Dickens must have obtained an advance copy. Maconnochie was also the author of various later works on prison reform and discipline.

she has come there for *useful* repentance and reform, and because her past way of life has been dreadful in its nature and consequences, and full of affliction, misery, and despair *to herself.* Never mind society while she is at that pass. Society has used her ill and turned away from her, and she cannot be expected to take much heed of its rights or wrongs. It is destructive to *herself,* and there is no hope in it, or in her, as long as she pursues it. It is explained to her that she is degraded and fallen, but not lost, having this shelter; and that the means of return to Happiness are now about to be put into her own hands, and trusted to her own keeping. That with this view, she is, instead of being placed in this probationary class for a month, or two months, or three months, or any specified *time* whatever, required to earn there, a certain number of *marks* (they are mere scratches in a book) so that she may make her probation a very short one, or a very long one, according to her own conduct. For so much work, she has so many marks; for a day's good conduct, so many more. For every instance of ill-temper, disrespect, bad language, any outbreak of any sort or kind, so many — a very large number in proportion to her receipts — are deducted. A perfect Debtor and Creditor account is kept between her and the Superintendent, for every day; and the state of that account, it is in her own power and nobody else's, to adjust to her advantage. It is expressly pointed out to her, that before she can be considered qualified to return to any kind of society — even to the Society of the asylum — she must give proofs of her power of self-restraint and her sincerity, and her determination to try to shew that she deserves the confidence it is proposed to place in her. Her pride, her emulation, her sense of shame, her heart, her reason, and her interest, are all appealed to at once, and if she pass through this trial, she *must* (I believe it to be in the eternal nature of things) rise somewhat in her own self-respect, and give the managers a power of appeal to her, in future, which nothing else could invest them with. I would carry a modification of this mark system through the whole establishment; for it is its great philosophy and its chief excellence that it is not a mere form or course of training adapted to the life within the house, but is a preparation — which is a much higher consideration — for the right performance of duty outside, and for the formation of habits of firmness and self-restraint. And the more these unfortunate persons were educated in their duty towards Heaven and Earth, and the more they were tried on this plan, the more they would feel that to dream of returning to society, or of becoming Virtuous Wives, until they had earned a certain gross number of marks required of everyone without the least exception, would be to prove that they were not worthy of restoration to the place they had lost. It is a part of this system, even to put at last, some temptation within their reach, as enabling them to go out, putting them in possession of some money, and the like; for it is clear that unless they are used to some temptation and used to resist it, within the walls, their capacity of resisting it, without, cannot be considered as fairly tested.

What they would be taught in the house, would be grounded in religion, most unquestionably. It must be the basis of the whole system. But it is very essential in dealing with this class of persons to have a system of training established, which, while it is steady and firm, is cheerful and hopeful. Order, punctuality, cleanliness, the whole routine of household duties — as washing, mending, cooking — the establishment itself would supply the means of teaching practically, to everyone. But then I would have it understood by all — I would have it written up in every room — that they were not going through a monotonous round of occupation and self-denial which began and ended there, but which began, or was resumed, under that roof, and would end, by God's blessing, in happy homes of their own.

I have said that I would put it in the power of Governors of Prisons to recommend Inmates. I think this most important, because such gentlemen as Mr Chesterton of the Middlesex House of Correction, and Lieutenant Tracey of Cold Bath Fields, Bridewell, (both of whom I know very well) [3] are well acquainted with the good that is in the bottom of the hearts, of many of these poor creatures, and with the whole history of their past lives; and frequently have deplored to me the not having any such place as the proposed establishment, to which to send them, when they are set free from Prison. It is necessary to observe that very many of these unfortunate women are constantly in and out of the Prisons, for no other fault or crime than their original one of having fallen from virtue. Policemen can take them up, almost when they choose, for being of that class, and being in the streets; and the magistrates commit them to jail for short terms. When they come out, they can but return to their old occupation, and so come in again. It is well known that many of them fee the Police to remain un-

---

[3] G. L. Chesterton was the governor of the Middlesex House of Correction, Lieutenant Augustus Tracey the Governor of Bridewell Prison, Tothill Fields.

molested; and being too poor to pay the fee, or dissipating the money in some other way, are taken up again, forthwith. Very many of them are good, excellent, steady characters when under restraint — even without the advantage of systematic training, which they would have in this Institution — and are tender nurses to the sick, and are as kind and gentle as the best of women.

There is no doubt that many of them would go on well for some time, and would then be seized with a violent fit of the most extraordinary passion, apparently quite motiveless, and insist on going away. There seems to be something inherent in their course of life, which engenders and awakens a sudden restlessness and recklessness which may be long suppressed, but breaks out like madness; and which all people who have had opportunities of observation in Penitentiaries and elsewhere, must have contemplated with astonishment and pity. I would have some rule to the effect that no request to be allowed to go away would be received for at least four and twenty hours, and that in the interval the person should be kindly reasoned with, if possible, and implored to consider well what she was doing. This sudden dashing down of all the building up of months upon months, is, to my thinking, so distinctly a Disease with the persons under consideration that I would pay particular attention to it, and treat it with particular gentleness and anxiety; *and I would not make one, or two, or three, or four, or six departures from the Establishment a binding reason against the re-admission of that person being again penitent,* but would leave it to the managers to decide upon the merits of the case: giving very great weight to general good conduct within the house.

I would begin with some comparatively small number — say thirty — and I would have it impressed upon them, from day to day, that the success of the experiment rested with them, and that on their conduct depended the rescue and salvation, of hundreds and thousands of women yet unborn. In what proportion this experiment would be successful, it is very difficult to predict; but I think that if the Establishment were founded on a well-considered system, and were well managed, one half of the Inmates would be reclaimed from the very beginning, and that after a time the proportion would be very much larger. I believe this estimate to be within very reasonable bounds.

The main question that arises, is, if the co-operation of the Government — beginning at that point when they are supposed to be reclaimed — cannot be secured, how are they to be provided for, permanently? Supposing the mark system and the training to be very successful, and gradually to acquire a great share of public confidence and respect, I think it not too sanguine to suppose that many good people would be glad to take them into situations. But the power of beginning life anew, in a world perfectly untried by them, would be so important in many cases, as an effectual detaching of them from old associates, and from the chances of recognition and challenge, that it is most desirable to be, somehow or other, attained.

I do not know whether you would be disposed to entrust me with any share in the supervision and direction of the Institution. But I need not say that I should enter on such a task with my whole heart and soul; and that in this respect, as in all others, I have but one sincere and zealous wish to assist you, by any humble means in my power, in carrying out your benevolent intentions.

And at all events it would be necessary for you to have, in the first instance, on paper, all the results of previous experience in this way, as regards scheme, plan, management, and expence. These I think I could procure, and render plain, as quietly and satisfactorily as anyone. And I would suggest to you, this course of action.

That, the School and Church proceeding — this Design remain in abeyance for the present. That when I go to Paris (whither I shall remove, please God, before Christmas) I examine every Institution of this sort existing there, and gather together all the information I possibly can. I believe more valuable knowledge is to be got there, on such a subject, than anywhere else; and this, combined with the results of our English experience, I would digest into the plainest and clearest form; so that you could see it, as if it were a map. And in the meantime you would have these advantages.

1. That in the establishment of your School and Dispensary, you might find or make some Instruments that would be very important and useful in the working out of this scheme.

2. That there will then have been matured, and probably tried, certain partial schemes going a very little way on this same road, which are now on foot in the City of London, and the success or failure of which will be alike instructive.

3. That there is a very great probability of the whole Transportation system [4] being shortly brought under the consideration of the

---

[4] It will be recalled that during the nineteenth century many criminals were transported to penal colonies in Australia.

Legislature; and it is particularly worthy of consideration that the various preliminary reports on the subject, (which I have lately been reading) recognize the question of sending out women to the different settlements, as one of very great importance.

I have that deep sense, dear Miss Coutts, of the value of your confidence in such a matter, and of the pure, exalted, and generous motives by which you are impelled, that I feel a most earnest anxiety that such an effort as you contemplate in behalf of your Sex, should have every advantage in the outset it can possibly receive, and should, if undertaken at all, be undertaken to the lasting honor of your name and country. In this feeling, I make the suggestion I think best calculated to promote that end. Trust me, if you agree in it, I will not lose sight of the subject, or grow cold to it, or fail to bestow upon it my best exertions and reflection. But, if there be any other course you would prefer to take; and you will tell me so; I shall be as devoted to you in that as in this, and as much honored by being asked to render you the least assistance.

~

Subletting Devonshire Terrace, Dickens departed for Switzerland at the end of May 1846, with his family and servants, and with the faithful Roche again as courier. After a few days at the Hotel Gibbon, a large ugly structure facing the Lake of Geneva, he rented Rosemont, a little villa with a sufficiency of bedrooms, a hall, a dining room, and two drawing rooms with mirrors and shining inlaid floors, one furnished in red velvet and the other in green. Six French windows under a balcony looked across the blue waters toward the prodigious mountain gorges rising to the Simplon Pass.

~

41. JUNE 25, 1846, ROSEMONT, LAUSANNE, SWITZERLAND
The enclosed sheets of paper are dated on the day on which — and at the place where — they were begun. When you have read and considered them, I shall hope to have the pleasure of receiving a letter from you.

This is an odd little house, which I think might be easily put into the great sala of our old Genoese Palazzo — bodily. It stands in the midst of beautiful grounds, on the slope of the Hill going down to the Lake — and the blue waters thereof, and the whole range of mountains, lie in front of the windows. Between it, and Ouchy, is a School, very famous in these parts, kept by a German gentleman; and in that School, Charley is imprisoned as a weekly Boarder. As there are only three other English boys, I hope he will soon be a proficient in the French language. He went, last Monday. It was rather a trial for him, and indeed for all of us, that first departure from home in a strange place. But he went with a gallant heart; and when I saw him sitting at the Garden Gate last night as I walked by, though I had an idea that he was counting the hours until Saturday at noon, yet he looked happy and very brown. His sisters have a little French Governess at home, who can't speak a word of English.

The heat as we came here, was more intense than any I have ever felt, and so it has been here, until the day before yesterday, when there was a violent thunderstorm of some hours' duration, which I hope has cleared the air for good and all, as it is now quite cool and windy. I have a study, something larger than a Plate Warmer,[5] opening into a Balcony and commanding a lovely view. I am contemplating terrific and tremendous industry — am mightily resolved to begin the book in numbers without delay — and have already begun to look the little Christmas Volume in its small red face; though I hardly know it by sight yet.

As my handwriting always becomes very hideous under such circumstances (as I fear I need hardly mention to you, who have so much of it to read) I will only add that Mrs Dickens unites with me in cordial remembrances to you, and that we desire to add our best regards to Mr and Mrs Brown. Ever Faithfully yours — Charles Dickens. I am much distressed by having no room for the flourish.[6]

∽

42.   JULY 25, 1846, ROSEMONT, LAUSANNE, SWITZERLAND
I think I recollect to have seen a former appeal of that Pentonville

---

[5] Nineteenth-century plate-warmers were large wooden cupboards placed in front of kitchen ranges.

[6] Dickens usually signed his name with an elaborate flourish beneath it, as:

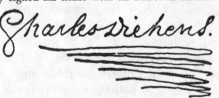

Society,[7] and to have regarded it in exactly the same light as that in which you view this recent one. I certainly think that if it be well managed, it might form, *in part*, a model for your Institution, but I think it would be inexpedient for you to found yours, until you have a general knowledge of the management of many similar Institutions. Very little has yet been done in this respect; and if you could do no better than has been done already I really doubt the expediency of founding an entirely new establishment in preference to assisting in the endowment of an existing one. I fear you would be disappointed in the result, and that you would spend your money to but little purpose.

Have you considered the practical difficulty of confining such an Institution to a single Parish? What would be the qualification (so to speak) for admission? Must the person have been born there, or must she have resided there, a certain time? If the latter, I fear the opposition of the Parish itself, and its perpetual hunting down of these unhappy objects lest they should be establishing themselves there, with some kind of faint view to the asylum, would entail upon them a frightful persecution. If the former, I fear that some of the most pitiable, and truly distressing, and hopeful cases (those of young people coming from the Country, and sinking down into the vice of London) would be without any relief from you.

Your two objections to my sketch of a plan, I wish to offer half a dozen words upon.

1st. As to marriage. I do not propose to put that before them as the immediate end and object to be gained, but assuredly to keep it in view as the possible consequence of a sincere, true, practical repentance, and an altered life. A kind of penitence is bred in our prisons and purgatories just now, which is a very pretty penitence inside the walls, but fades into nothing when it comes into contact with worldly realities. In the generality of cases, it is almost impossible to produce a penitence which shall stand the wear and tear of this rough world, without Hope — worldly hope — the hope of at one time or other recovering something like the lost station. I would make this Hope, however faint and afar off it might be, exactly the one that out of the asylum and without its aid, seemed (and was) impossible of attainment.

2ndly. With regard to Temptation. I would simply ask you to con-

---

[7] An organization having similar aims to those Miss Coutts proposed for Urania Cottage.

sider whether we do not, all of us, in our stations, tempt our fellow creatures at every turn. Whether there is a merchant in London who does not hourly expose his servants to strong temptation. Whether a night or morning ever comes, when you do not tempt your butler with a hundred times the worth of his year's wages. Whether there are not at the Banking House in the Strand, many young men whose lives are one exposure to, and resistance of, temptation. And whether it is not a Christian act to say to such unfortunate creatures as you propose, by God's blessing, to reclaim "Test for yourselves the reality of your repentance and your power of resisting temptation, while you are *here,* and before you are in the World outside, to fall before it!"

Now about Punch. I have no influence whatever, with that Potentate save such as may lie in its being owned by my printers, and in my having a personal knowledge of some of its principal contributors. You may guess how powerful my influence is, when I tell you that during my Stage Management of the amateur Play, I spoke to the gentleman most prominent among them, about that very Duke [8] — more than once — and said that I believed him to be an excellent creature. That I had myself received the most remarkable courtesy from him, and that I knew that in his treatment of his Governess, and of others about him, he was a bright example to three fourths of the middle classes. The gentleman to whom I spoke, laughed about it, and said that there was no ill nature in their jokes at his expence, and that they merely jested at peculiarities of speech and manner that were generally notorious. After this conversation, or about the same time, however, the Duke happened to make a very unfortunate and apparently unfeeling speech, about the diseased potatoes. This, Punch resented and took in great dudgeon. Between ourselves, I really hardly

---

[8] Charles Gordon Lennox (1791–1860), fifth Duke of Richmond, president of the Royal Agricultural Society, 1845–1860. He served with Wellington in Portugal 1810–1814, and was Postmaster-General 1830–1834. The *Greville Memoirs* characterize him as "prejudiced, narrow-minded, illiterate, and ignorant, good-looking, good-humoured, and unaffected, tedious, prolix, unassuming, and a duke." The blight that ruined the potato crop of 1846 caused great suffering among the poor. I have not traced the Duke's "unfeeling speech, about the diseased potatoes," but *Punch* resented it bitterly and maintained throughout the year a running fire of angry satire and caricature against the heartlessness of Richmond and others of ducal rank: "The Richmond War-Trump," "Richmond in Sussex," "Sussex Arcadias," "What to Do with the Dukes," "Ducal Dummies," "Mark Antony Richmond on the Body of Protection," "The Duke of Richmond's Oratory," and so on, and cartoons entitled "I Think There Be Six Richmonds in the Field," "Actaeon Worried by His Own Dogs," and "Richmond's 'Black-Draught.'"

know how they could have done otherwise, for it was especially ill-timed and ill-chosen. But both on the occasions to which I have referred, and since, I have championed him strongly, in the same quarter. And, as I have already said, you may guess from this, how great my influence is. I thoroughly agree with you in all you say about him; but I never wrote, or stayed the writing, of, a word in Punch, and am not in the least degree in his confidence or councils.

Mrs Dickens, Charley, and his sisters, beg, with me, to be earnestly remembered in those two corners.

᷇

43. OCTOBER 5, 1846, ROSEMONT, LAUSANNE, SWITZERLAND
I have made one or two attempts, in the midst of my other occupations to note down (as you asked me) the heads of what I had previously written to you. But I found it so difficult to collect them, while my attention was loaded with all sorts of imaginary baggage, and I was so afraid of bewildering you by putting down twenty after-ideas that I have not yet mentioned to you, and leaving out twenty I had mentioned — that I thought it best not to try any more — feeling assured that your kindness and consideration would attribute my silence, just now, to the right cause.

I will take care as soon as I am well set down in Paris (I hope to be there, by the middle of next month) to make some careful enquiries on the essential particular to which you call my attention — which I can also make, I think, without much difficulty, when I come to London. I shall have the greatest satisfaction at the same time in putting you in communication with two or three gentlemen who I am sure will be most valuable, willing, and suggestive advisers. The clergyman of that Westminster Prison I think a very good man, and I know he has great experience of these objects. [I] have no doubt whatever of the feasibility of finding such inmates of the asylum in the beginning, as would afford a most interesting and worthy trial of such a work.

The locality you suggest is a central and good one. But you would require to have a place attached, for exercise. Have you thought of that? The cultivation of little gardens, if they be no bigger than graves, is a great resource and a great reward. It has always been found to be productive of good effects wherever it has been tried; and I earnestly hope you will be able to make it a part of your training.

When I know at what time I can come to London, I will write from

Paris, and tell you beforehand. After that visit, I shall never be further away than Paris, and can constantly and frequently return, if I can be of service. I may mention that I saw in the newspaper some weeks ago, an advertisement to the effect that a pamphlet descriptive of Captain Macconochie's plan: *some modification* of which, I am so strongly inclined to recommend for adoption: is published, either by Hatchard or Ridgway in Piccadilly. I think the latter. It may be bought for two or three shillings. It will certainly interest you if you will read it — I am sure of that — and we should then be able to talk it over on equal terms.

I am only half through my Christmas Book,[9] for which I have a little notion that I should have been very glad indeed to have retained for a longer story, as it is necessarily very much contracted in its development in so small a space. I hear that the Dombey has been launched with great success, and was out of print on the first night.[1]

Mrs Dickens sends her kind remembrances. Charley has won a Geneva watch by speaking French in three months. I rashly pledged myself to make that desperate present in the event of his succeeding — and as he *has* succeeded, I mean to go over to Geneva with him in great state, and endow him with his prize in as solemn a manner as I can possibly confer it. I think of enclosing it in a pathetic epistle. He sends his love, and says he means to distinguish himself at King's College.

Mr and Mrs Brown are well, I hope. I don't wish Mrs Brown would be ill again, but I wish she would do something, which would lead to her suggesting another character to me, as serviceable as Mrs Gamp.

*

44.   JANUARY 12, 1847, 48, RUE DE COURCELLES, PARIS

I have been casting about, in reference to the blind machine. No way of recommending it occurs to me at this moment, or has yet presented itself, but I will not forget it, if I can find one, depend upon me. Do

---

[9] *The Battle of Life,* completed October 17, 1846, and published December 19, just two days before the appearance of a dramatic version at the Lyceum Theater, adapted by Albert Smith and produced by the Keeleys.

[1] Dickens had begun writing *Dombey and Son* on June 28; its opening number was published October 1. On the eleventh he exultantly wrote his friend Forster: "The Dombey sale is BRILLIANT! I had put before me thirty thousand as the limit of the most extreme success, saying that if we should reach that, I should be more than satisfied and more than happy; you will judge how happy I am!" Evidently the sale was well above thirty thousand.

you know there are many inventions for the same purpose already in use?

I am very glad you have seen Mr Chesterton. He may be implicitly relied upon. His experience is as great as any man's alive, on such subjects, and his humanity and good sense are equal to it. I know nothing of him but what is good.

Do you know, I question the laying down of that rule though, which he recommends, in reference to those who have contracted habits of intoxication? I more than question it, and shall venture to make a great stand with him and you for no such principle being established. Remind him, or Mr Tracey, when you see them both, that it would exclude such a case as "Wilton's." And I believe that girl was, of all others, exactly the object for such an Institution as yours. It would be very difficult indeed to know what should be called habits of intoxication. No poor creature is likely to be ever in the place, at any time, of whose previous life intoxication has not been a continual incident. From all modes of existence that are precarious, miserable, degrading, and suggestive of self-reproach — but most especially from theirs — drunkenness, to a greater or less extent, is well nigh inseparable.

As to there being no hope of drunkards, we mustn't start from that point. If we can't find hope ready-made (but I believe we can) we must try to make it. I am not friendly to total abstinence societies, nor have I ever promoted one, but I do not doubt that they have set this question at rest, and have demonstrated the possibility.

I would make the decision between trying or rejecting, dependent in every case of which Chesterton and Tracey gave us any knowledge, on the woman herself, and her apparent earnestness, and the best judgment that could be formed from what she said. The Saviour laid down no rules that kept the wretched at a distance from Him; and a noble effort like this should be, in that respect I think, as accessible and free.

The Schools of which I spoke to you are at Limehouse. They were established through the exertions of the chairman of the Board of Guardians, Mr G. F. Young of that place — a shipowner who acquired the character of a prodigious bore, in Parliament, by speaking immediately before every Division, great or small, to the anguish and horror of all parties; but he is a worthy man, and you will think so, if he accompany you over these schools. He lives close to the church, at the corner of Church Row; and I enclose a note of introduction to him in case you should care to use it.

Let me thank you my dear Miss Coutts for Toby's [2] magnificent cake, and for that best of wishes (for it includes all other good ones) that you send him in your letter to me. He will present himself in Stratton Street, with a King's College paper for you to sign, a day or two before the end of the month. I have arranged that he shall board at Dr Major's in Bloomsbury Square — coming home from Saturday to Monday when we return to England.

I feel it a kind of common honesty to say, that from some of the public opinions and proceedings of the Bishop of London, [3] I most strongly dissent — holding them to be ungenerous and inconsiderate towards the multitude who work hard for their bread — and by no means conceived in the true spirit of Christianity. But I desire to say this to *you* — not to *him* — and I will willingly call on him when I come back: trusting in the unlikelihood of such questions arising out of any conversation between us.

Charley and his brothers and sisters, and his mama join with me in cordial remembrances and fervent wishes, seasonable and unseasonable. And I am, as ever,

NB I would make an appointment with Mr Young, to make sure of his being there.

∽

45.   JANUARY 18, 1847, 48, RUE DE COURCELLES, PARIS

I cannot help sending you a hasty note to explain what must appear rather an extraordinary omission on my part. — I should have thanked you for the print of Sir Francis Burdett, but that it did not get to the

---

[2] A nickname for Charley, who had received another Twelfth Cake, sent as a birthday present.

[3] Charles James Blomfield (1786–1857), Bishop of London 1826–1856, editor of plays of Aeschylus and others. He had aroused Dickens's indignation as early as 1836 by supporting Sir Andrew Agnew's Sabbath Observances Bill, which was intended to close all shops and places of amusement, including libraries and museums, on Sunday, forbid the operation of public conveyances, stagecoaches, and excursion steamers, and curtail all except the barest minimum of necessary occupations from being carried on during that day. Dickens angrily regarded this as a vicious piece of class legislation designed to prevent the poor from having any pleasures on their only day of leisure, and had written a pamphlet against it, entitled *Sunday Under Three Heads,* 1836, which he caustically dedicated to the bishop.

Piazza Coffee House until I had left,[4] and I had not the least idea of your having sent it to me, until I heard so from a friend last Saturday, who had received it from the Hotel, together with some letters and papers. Let me thank you for it now, and assure you sincerely, that I shall value it highly, and shall place it, on my return, in that work-room which I hope you and Mrs Brown *will* see, one of these days, after all.

I have had a long letter from Mr Chesterton, full of interest and earnestness in reference to the project. He tells me of having brought Tracey to you on the previous day.

Charley expects to leave here, this day fortnight. His movments depend on the gentleman who is to bring him over, but they are not likely to be longer delayed.

Between ourselves — Paul is dead.[5] He died on Friday night about 10 o'clock; and as I had no hope of getting to sleep afterwards, I went out, and walked about Paris until breakfast-time next morning.

∾

Dickens was brought unexpectedly back to London at the end of February by Charley's falling ill with scarlet fever. Devonshire Terrace was still rented, so he and his wife, leaving the other children with her sister Georgina in Paris, stayed at the Victoria Hotel, while Dickens looked for a temporary residence. This he found at Chester Place. Here on April 18 their seventh child was born, Sydney Smith Haldimand Dickens (1847–1872). The last of these names was for William Haldimand, a Lausanne friend who became the baby's godfather.

∾

46.   MAY 16, 1847, 1 CHESTER PLACE, REGENT'S PARK

I cannot help thinking there must have been some mistake in the delivery of a letter I wrote to you more than three weeks ago, wherein I appointed a certain day for calling on you. I called on that day — heard you were out of town — and that the letter had been forwarded — but have not heard anything more. My object was (and is) to con-

---

[4] Dickens had run over to London from Paris for a few days just before Christmas to arrange with Chapman and Hall, who still had the publication rights to his earlier books, for a cheap edition of all his writings, and to help the Keeleys with the staging of *The Battle of Life*.

[5] Little Paul Dombey, who dies in Chapter XVI, in the fifth monthly installment of *Dombey and Son*.

sult you about a house Mr Chesterton and I had seen, which is not dear, and we think would suit your project better than almost any other, not built for the purpose.[6] I prevented the owner from advertizing it, as he had intended to do; and he has been to me since, but I could say nothing to him.

I have been so very unwell from an accident, that I have not been able to write, and we are going to Brighton tomorrow (148 King's Road) for change.[7] If you will let me hear from you there, I will send you full particulars of this house. Or maybe you *are* at Brighton, and I can see you there?

⁓

47. MAY 23, 1847, 148 KING'S ROAD, BRIGHTON

I am glad my letter did not miscarry. That was all I cared about. I thought it possible, because it happens curiously that the letter you wrote to Macready at Manchester has never, to this hour, reached him: though various letters have gone there for him since he left, and been forwarded to town.

Some little interval has passed since I received your note here; but I know you will excuse it when I tell you that I was so very unwell before I left town, that I had not the heart to sit down to the current Dombey. Ever since I have been here, I have been hard at work. And I wish you may even be half as much interested in the story as I am — or think it half as good as I do!!!

I return to town next Saturday, and will come to you this day week at about 2, unless you say no. In the meantime, these are, in brief, the particulars of the house.

It is on the Acton Road. Less than two miles, I should say, from Hyde Park in Oxford Street. I have not the particulars here, but it may be got, I think for sixty or sixty five pounds a year, on lease for 7, 14, or 21 years. It is retired, but cheerful. There is a garden, and a little Lawn. The taxes are very low.

A stable would have to be changed into a wash-house, and I would decidedly fence the garden all round. It seems to me to want only that.

---

[6] The house in Shepherd's Bush, on the Acton Road, mentioned in the next letter, which became Urania Cottage, the headquarters of the Home for Women.

[7] Dickens's arm had been severely bitten by a horse, who made a sudden attack on him in the stable and tore off his coat sleeve and shirt sleeve. The trip to Brighton was partly for the purpose, too, of helping his wife recuperate from her recent confinement.

I do not know the expence of such a thing, but I should say that an expenditure of fifty pounds or seventy five pounds may-be, in addition to Chesterton's estimate, would amply cover the whole. I have no doubt this is the outside.

Chesterton thinks he has found an unexceptionable matron. I am sure the house would please you. I told the owners it was designed for an Institution, and they did not object. I did not say what the objects were, or would be, or had been, because it seems to me a great point of usefulness and merit that this should never be told. I wouldn't label them among the neighbours.

Charley, who came down yesterday for the Whitsun holidays, sends his love. Mr King reports him rather weak still, but I mean to tumble him into the sea, tomorrow, and I hope that will freshen him up.

ᕋᕗ

48. JUNE 3, 1847, 1 CHESTER PLACE, REGENTS PARK

The terms of the house are to be sixty guineas a year, for seven, fourteen, or twenty one years. The proprietor's name and address — it is the address of *our* house too, for that is close to it — is "Mrs Scott, near the White Horse, Shepherd's Bush." The Solicitors are Messrs Hawkins, Bloxam, Stocker, & Co, New Boswell Court. I have appointed to be there (at Boswell Court, I mean) between 2 and 3 on Saturday, to give instructions for the lease. I will then tell them to send the draft to your Solicitor's for revision. Will you (I forgot to make a note of it on Sunday) send me that gentleman's name and address?

ᕋᕗ

49. JUNE 27, 1847, ATHENAEUM [8]

Last Thursday week, Mrs Dickens and I (in great state) repaired to Stratton Street, in accordance with an invitation still producible in any court in Christendom, and not being able to get in, withdrew in melancholy splendor. I should have reported this fact long ago, but I have been so extremely busy, that I have not had an hour by day (and not many by night) to call my own.

Tomorrow morning we are going down to Broadstairs, where we

---

[8] The Athenaeum Club had been founded in 1824 as a gathering place for England's men of achievement. It was a mark of Dickens's rapid success that he was elected a member at the age of twenty-six in 1838, after the publication of his first two novels. Thackeray had to wait until he was forty, and Browning until he was fifty-six.

propose remaining until the end of September — though of course I shall be continually coming backwards and forwards. Our children have all got the whooping cough, and the change is recommended for them. They never cry, but go into corners to be convulsed, and come out cheerful.

May I impress upon you, that it would be an immense thing for the Institution, to begin before it is winter weather, and while the garden is green and sunny. Your solicitor places Chesterton and myself in the awkward position of seeming to have acted in the matter of the lease, without authority; he is so very tardy.

A line from you addressed to Broadstairs, telling me where you will be through July will be very welcome, as I shall make a point of seeing Chesterton often, as soon as we have the power of proceeding.

With best regards to Mr and Mrs Brown, I am ever dear Miss Coutts

ᴄᴡ

50. JULY [1847] STRATTON STREET

I seem fated to miss you. Having been detained in Liverpool [9] a day longer than I had expected, I did not reach Town until 9 o'clock last night. Today I fear it will be impossible for me to get to Finchley; and I have promised the children that I will be at Broadstairs tomorrow, to dine with them.

I shall see Mr Chesterton today, and learn from him how the business of the Lease is progressing. I can easily come to town in a few hours, whenever you wish to see me, and by taking the Express train can easily reach here any day by 12 o'clock. Supposing nothing arises to produce a summons from you (for which, however, I shall always be in readiness, as I can return on the same day, in case I should be busy at the time) I will write to you some few days before my next visit to town, which I think will be on this day fortnight, and make an ap-

---

[9] In June Dickens had gathered together the company that had acted *Every Man in His Humour* two years before, to give a series of benefit performances for the veteran writer Leigh Hunt (1784–1859), the friend of Shelley and Keats, who was in desperate financial straits. New members of his cast included the essayist and dramatic critic George Henry Lewes (1817–1878) and the artist Augustus Egg (1816–1863). While they were rehearsing at Miss Kelly's theater, the Government granted Hunt a pension. But Hunt still had many debts, so Dickens modified his plans only by dropping the London performances he had scheduled and adding as a second beneficiary the aging and now impoverished dramatist John Poole (1786–1872), author of the successful farces *Paul Pry* and *Turning the Tables*. The benefit performances were given in Manchester on July 26 and in Liverpool on July 28, and took in receipts of over £900.

pointment for bringing the matron. All the initiative proceedings in the way of alteration and adaptation are quite understood between Mr Chesterton and myself, and ready to be entered upon, as soon as the Lease is settled. I understand from him that the delay is not attributable in any way to your solicitor, but to the determination of *our* side that you are not to be taken advantage of, because of your position — which is sound sense and justice.

You will be glad to hear that our nurse writes great news of the disappearance of the whooping cough, and that Charley is every day more robust and hearty.

∞

51. AUGUST 26, 1847, "AT YOUR HOUSE IN TOWN"

I have missed you — of course. But before coming here, I went to Mr Chesterton, and from him heard what you had done this morning. I am going to see the matron tomorrow, and we are afterwards going to the house. Several of the proposed inmates have passed in review before me this morning, at Mr Chesterton's prison; and though they necessarily present a most distressing subject for contemplation, it is still a most hopeful and encouraging one. The matron of that place, who is very intelligent and has (as you may suppose) great experience, told me this morning (not knowing my strong conviction on that head) that she was sure it was of great importance to the design, to hold before them, as prominently as possible, their final restoration to society, and their hope of becoming wives, in another country. Nothing would touch them so much, she said, and nothing else would give them such earnest emotions of gratitude, or inspire them with such a desire to do well. To observe the effect of this upon them, is one of the most touching things you can imagine.

I hope we shall be ready, very early in October, to shew you the Institution in perfect order. If you would not dislike it, I should particularly like you — you can sit in the room perfectly unnoticed and unknown — to see, at Mr Chesterton's House of Correction, the young women who are coming from there, as they are, and in their prison dresses. You will feel so much more, afterwards, the change that, with God's leave, will be worked in them.

I am going back to Broadstairs on Saturday morning, and shall remain there, until the end of September, when I return to my own house in Devonshire Terrace, which my tenant has, at last, deserted.

I heard that someone on your behalf had been looking at a house at Broadstairs. Some faint hope was lingering within me that you might be coming there after all, until I read in your letter that you were going to Sandgate.

Will you tell Mrs Brown that I hope she will soon see that mysterious inside of my house, which has been a Blue Chamber [1] for so many years. It looks almost strange to me now; it is so long since I have seen it.

∞

52. OCTOBER 28, 1847, DEVONSHIRE TERRACE

I am in a state of great anxiety to talk to you about your "Home" (that is the name I propose to give it) with which I have been very busy for some time, and which will be ready for the reception of its inmates, please God, on Saturday fortnight. I have a perfect confidence in your approving of the details, but it would be most interesting to me to talk them over with you.

You have so long overstayed your time, that I begin to think you must be keeping out of the way to preserve that spell unbroken. I send this to Stratton Street by the post, on the chance of its finding you somewhere.

I cannot tell you how much cause I have seen, and see daily, during the preparation of this place, to admire the goodness and devotion of Mr Chesterton, whose time is always at our command, and whose interest in the design cannot be surpassed.

There are two objects (promising, I hope) recently discharged from his prison, who are giving the best proof of the sincerity of their desire to come to us, by remaining in the prison — prison clothed and fed — until we are enabled to take them, which I think is an affecting and encouraging circumstance, as they knew on the evening when their time was up, that some of their old companions were waiting at the gate to bear them away. There is another girl — only seventeen — born of drunken parents, ill used from her cradle, plundered of her clothes that they might be sold for liquor, and sent to evil courses for their gain, to whom we are giving a few shillings now and then (her discharge took place some weeks ago, and they could not keep her in the prison too) until we are ready to take her. She comes to Mr

---

[1] Evidently until this time chance had prevented Mrs. Brown from ever having been in Devonshire Terrace; the reference is of course to Bluebeard's forbidden cabinet.

Chesterton at stated times clean, decent, and quiet, and apparently quite altered. We have now eight, and I have as much confidence in five of them, as one *can* have in the beginning of anything so new. As we go on, I sincerely trust and believe you will do more good than your most sanguine expectations picture now.

We were at Mr Tracey's today to look for some others. There is a young woman there, who has more feeling — who shews more at least — than I have seen in any of them, but some points in her wretched history remain to be examined. I have taken some pains to find out the dispositions and natures of every individual we take; and I think I know them pretty well, and may be able to give the matron some useful foreknowledge of them, and to exercise some personal influence with them in case of need. A most extraordinary and mysterious study it is, but interesting and touching in the extreme.

I think it well to say to you that I have avoided Macconochie's ideas, as they hardly seemed (or I fancied so) to meet with your full approval, and as they were perhaps unsuited to so small an establishment. The design is simply, as you and I agreed, to appeal to them by means of affectionate kindness and trustfulness, — but firmly too. To improve them by education and example — establish habits of the most rigid order, punctuality, and neatness — but to make as great a variety in their daily lives as their daily lives will admit of — and to render them an innocently cheerful Family while they live together there. On the cheerfulness and kindness all our hopes rest.

I am very anxious about Mr Tracey's chaplain. But if I go on entering into all my points of anxiety and interest, I shall never leave off. Therefore I will only say that I hope you will write to me as soon as you come home, and give me an opportunity of unburdening my mind.

You must not see the house until it is quite ready. The bedsteads will not be put up for ten days, and there will be some trifling matters to get in after that. The dresses and linen are bought and making. The Superintendent's rooms are furnished, and she is living there.

I still remain in the hope that you will come with me to Mr Chesterton's, where there is nothing to shock you but the sight of women in captivity — and where there is very much to gratify you in the humanity with which they are treated — for unless you see them now, you never can sufficiently feel what you will have done for those who turn out well.

We found it necessary that there should be some appeal for Mr Chesterton to read to them, and then give them to read in their cells. I wrote the enclosed for the purpose, and he found it affects them very heartily indeed.

P.S. I forgot to mention in reference to the Bishop of London that I shall be happy to call upon him when he is in town, if you please.

∽

ENCLOSURE WITH PRECEDING LETTER

AN APPEAL TO FALLEN WOMEN

You will see, on beginning to read this letter, that it is not addressed to you by name. But I address it to a woman — a very young woman still — who was born to be happy and has lived miserably; who has no prospect before her but sorrow, or behind her but a wasted youth; who, if she has ever been a mother, has felt shame instead of pride in her own unhappy child.

You are such a person, or this letter would not have been put into your hands. If you have ever wished (I know you must have done so at some time) for a chance of rising out of your sad life, and having friends, a quiet home, means of being useful to yourself and others, peace of mind, self-respect, everything you have lost, pray read it attentively and reflect upon it afterwards.

I am going to offer you, not the chance but the *certainty* of all these blessings, if you will exert yourself to deserve them. And do not think that I write you as if I felt myself very much above you, or wished to hurt your feelings by reminding you of the situation in which you are placed. God forbid! I mean nothing but kindness to you, and I write as if you were my sister.

Think for a moment what your present situation is. Think how impossible it is that it can ever be better if you continue to live as you have lived, and how certain it is that it must be worse. You know what the streets are; you know how cruel the companions you find there are; you know the vices practised there, and to what wretched consequences they bring you, even while you are young. Shunned by decent people, marked out from all other kinds of women as you walk along, avoided by the very children, hunted by the police, imprisoned, and only set free to be imprisoned, over and over again — reading this very letter in a common jail you have already dismal experience of the truth.

But to grow old in such a way of life, and among such company — to escape an early death from terrible disease, or your own maddened hand, and arrive at old age in such a course — will be an aggravation of every misery that you know now, which words cannot describe. Imagine for yourself the bed on which you, then an object terrible to look at, will lie down to die. Imagine all the long, long years of shame, want, crime, and ruin that will arise before you. And by that dreadful day, and by the judgment that will follow it, and by the recollections you are certain to have then, when it is too late, of the offer that is made to you now, when it is NOT too late, I implore you to think of it and weigh it well.

There is a lady in this town who from the window of her house has seen such as you going past at night, and has felt her heart bleed at the sight. She is what is called a great lady, but she has looked after you with compassion as being of her own sex and nature, and the thought of such fallen women has troubled her in her bed.

She has resolved to open at her own expense a place of refuge near London for a small number of females, who without such hope are lost forever, and to make a HOME for them. In this home they will be taught all household work that would be useful to them in a home of their own and enable them to make it comfortable and happy. In this home, which stands in a pleasant country lane and where each may have her little flower-garden if she pleases, they will be treated with the greatest kindness: will lead an active, cheerful, healthy life: will learn many things it is profitable and good to know, and being entirely removed from all who have any knowledge of their past career will begin life afresh and be able to win a good name and character.

And because it is not this lady's wish that these young women should be shut out from the world after they have repented and learned to do their duty there, and because it is her wish and object that they may be restored to society — a comfort to themselves and it — they will be supplied with every means, when some time shall have elapsed and their conduct shall have fully proved their earnestness and reformation, to go abroad, where in a distant country they may become the faithful wives of honest men, and live and die in peace.

I have been told that those who see you daily in this place believe that there are virtuous inclinations lingering within you, and that you may be reclaimed. I offer the Home I have described in these few words, to you.

But, consider well before you accept it. As you are to pass from the gate of this Prison to a perfectly new life, where all the means of happiness, from which you are now shut out, are opened brightly to you, so remember on the other hand that you must have the strength to leave behind you all old habits. You must resolve to set a watch upon yourself, and be firm in your control over yourself, and restrain yourself; to be gentle, patient, persevering, and good-tempered. Above all things, to be truthful in every word you speak. Do this, and all the rest is easy. But you must solemnly remember that if you enter this Home without such constant resolutions, you will occupy, unworthily and uselessly, the place of some other unhappy girl, now wandering and lost; and that her ruin, no less than your own, will be upon your head, before Almighty God, who knows the secrets of our breasts; and Christ, who died upon the Cross to save us.

In case there should be anything you wish to know, or any question you would like to ask about this Home, you have only to say so, and every information shall be given to you. Whether you accept it or reject it, think of it. If you awake in the silence and solitude of the night, think of it then. If any remembrance ever comes into your mind of any time when you were innocent and very different, think of it then. If you should be softened by a moment's recollection of any tenderness or affection you have ever felt, or that has ever been shown to you, think of it then. If ever your poor heart is moved to feel truly, what you might have been, and what you are, oh think of it then, and consider what you may yet become.

Believe me that I am indeed,
YOUR FRIEND

ow

In the course of time, Urania Cottage came to take in a considerably wider range of women than it had originally been designed for. Dickens lists, some six years later, some classes of women who had taken refuge there: "Starving needlewomen of good character, poor needlewomen who have robbed their furnished lodgings, violent girls committed to prison for disturbances in ill-conducted workhouses, poor girls from Ragged Schools, destitute girls who have applied at Police Offices for relief, young women from the streets: young women of the same class taken from the prisons after undergoing punishment there as disorderly characters, or for shoplifting, or for thefts from the person:

domestic servants who have been seduced, and two young women held to bail for attempting suicide."

Between 1847 and 1853 the Home received fifty-six inmates, of ages from about fourteen to twenty-six. Seven left of their own desire during their probation; ten were expelled for incorrigible misconduct; seven ran away. Of those who passed its requirements and were enabled to go abroad to Australia or elsewhere only three relapsed — all three on the passage out — the others acquired good characters and did well. It is clear that most of the failures were discovered in the Home itself and that there were remarkably few after emigration. Figures for the later success of the Home are not available, but Dickens's connection with it continued for years, and its affairs will often recur in future letters.

∽

53. NOVEMBER 3, 1847, DEVONSHIRE TERRACE

I will answer the points you mention — if the slight means of a note like this may be dignified with the name of answer — in the order in which you mention them, and without any preparatory matter.

I had no idea of concluding the question of the chaplain, until you return. But I was very anxious about Mr Tracey's, as I knew him to possess remarkable qualifications for the post — exercised daily among that class of persons — and was morally certain of your approval, when you should come to know him. My anxiety was to ascertain whether he was free to accept the trust. And I am very sorry to find (his own engaging him from morning until night) that he is *not*.

I have great faith in the soundness of your opinions in reference to the religious instruction; knowing you to be full of that enlarged consideration for the special circumstances under which it is to be administered in this case, without which nothing hopeful or useful can be done. I trust that those enlightenments to which you refer, are to be found in the *New* Testament? I am confident that harm is done to this class of minds by the injudicious use of the Old — and I am hardly less confident that I could shew you how, in talking the subject over.

The expediency of explaining to them that the rules of the Establishment may alter, I greatly doubt. For this reason. — If we did so, they would immediately conceive that we did not know what we were about, and that we were experimentalizing, which would desperately shake their trust in us. Such rules as we agree upon in the outset will be known only to the Superintendents and ourselves. They will not be told to the Inmates. There will be a certain daily routine which they will be called upon to observe. If we see fit to alter it, it will be altered as a matter of course, I should say — explaining to them beforehand, the why and wherefore. But if the establishment worked well, I would strongly counsel you not to try experiments. My belief is that nothing would unsettle them so much, or render their staying with us so doubtful. — Recollect that we address a peculiar and strangely-made character.

There is this objection to the address of the chaplain to each person individually. — It would decidedly involve the risk of their refusing to come to us. The extraordinary monotony of the refuges and asylums now existing, and the almost insupportable extent to which they carry the words and forms of religion, is known to no order of people so well as to these women; and they have that exaggerated dread of it, and that preconceived sense of their inability to bear it, which the reports of those who have refused to stay in them, have bred in their minds. I am afraid if they were thus taken to task, and especially by a clergyman, they would be alarmed — would say "it's the old story after all, and we have mistaken the sort of place. It's better to say at once that we are not fit for it" — and that so we should lose them. That they are sensible of the sinfulness and degradation of their lives — that nothing else but that, has been impressed upon them by society since they began those lives — is, to say the least, reasonably probable. And he must be a very remarkably discreet and gentle man indeed, who could execute this difficult task, without rendering them apprehensive of what was to follow. — (I should add here that Mr Chesterton has addressed them on this head, repeatedly, and very sensibly.)

That their past lives should never be referred to, at the Home, there can be no doubt. I should say that any such reference on the part of the Superintendent would be an instance of blind mistake that in itself would render her dismissal necessary.

The temptation that has occurred to you, in pursuance of Macconnochie's idea, suggests this consideration — that it is one to which, in all probability, they will never be exposed abroad, and that it is a very severe one. If a girl goes out by herself, where is she to go? Every one she knows now is, to a greater or less extent, an infamous associate; and suffering her to go out by herself would be to expose her to the arts and temptations and recognitions of fifty such. Even supposing that her old habits and her new freedom didn't lead her among them, it is likely some of them would come in her way; and her very decency might give them the advantage, as by inducing her to go away with them in the first instance, rather than be jeered and mocked in the open streets. I propose that, in the country, about the house, they shall constantly go out in twos or threes with Mrs Holdsworth.[2] I would, as they advanced in their training and shewed decided improvement, trust them with keys, and with many little offices withindoors that would test their self-denial. But the streets of London, I confess I view with very great apprehension. We shall have ample leisure to discuss this point, and could easily take the opinion of Macconnochie (who, I am happy to say, is appointed by Government to exercise his system on a number of convicts employed in the construction of a Harbor at Weymouth) but I mention it in this passing manner, because you mention it.

One great point that I try to bear in mind continually, and which I hope the clergyman will steadily remember, is, that these unfortunate creatures are to be *tempted* to virtue. They cannot be dragged, driven, or frightened. You originate this great work for the salvation of the women who come into that Home; and I hold it to be the sacred duty of every one who assists you in it, *first to consider how best to get them there, and how best to keep them there.* Every other consideration should fade before these two, because every other consideration follows upon them, and is included in them, and is impracticable without them. It is for this vital reason that a knowledge of human nature as it shews itself in these tarnished and battered images of God — and a patient consideration for it — and a determined putting of the question to one's self, not on whether this or that piece of instruction or correction be in itself good and true, but how it can be best adapted to the state in which we find these people, and the necessity we are under of dealing gently with them, lest they should run headlong back on their own destruction — are the great, merciful, Christian thoughts for such an enterprise, and form the only spirit in which it can be successfully undertaken. Do you not feel with me, that this must be kept steadily in view, and that a chaplain imbued with this feeling in the outset, is the only minister for this place?

I forgot to mention in its right place, about the temptation, that I saw, at Mr Tracey's prison the other day, a girl who was there, some

---

[2] Mrs. Holdsworth was the matron in charge at the Home.

time ago (merely, if I remember right, for being in the streets, or, if for felony, for some offence arising out of that life) whose appearance and behaviour had so interested some lady or other, living hard by, that when her term was over, she took her for a servant. That girl, although she had the reputation of being a drunkard, worked hard and honestly in this employment for seven or eight months, and had wine and spirits constantly in her keeping, which she never touched. But in an evil hour her mistress gave her a holiday. She fell among her old companions — her removal from whom had been the main cause of her reformation, poor creature — never went back again, fell into her old way of life, and is in prison now. I saw her with Mr Chesterton, and talked to her, but thought it best to decline her: for besides the danger of her attachment to liquor (though I do not, like Mr Chesterton: neither does Mr Tracey, attach overwhelming importance to that in a *young* woman of that way of life, who drinks because she is utterly miserable — a middle aged woman who drinks, is another thing, and is always hopeless) she had a singularly bad head, and looked discouragingly secret and moody.

I must tell you of one of the two young women who were remaining in Prison voluntarily, until we could take them. When I first went there, about your home, she was produced to me by Mr Chesterton, before I saw any of the others, as a model. She was the matron's model, and the head female turnkey's model, and the peculiar pet and protegée of Mr Rotch [3] the magistrate who is a very good man, and takes infinite pains in the prisons — though I doubt his understanding of the company he finds there. She was much better educated than any of the others (some of whom are extremely ignorant), had a very intelligent face, and a remarkably good voice; but she impressed me as being something too grateful, and too voluble in her earnestness, and she seemed, in a vague, indescribable, uneasy way, to be doubtful of me, which I suppose made me doubtful of her. However this was, I observed her as closely as I could, and when they had all gone, told Chesterton that he would be amazed at what I was going to say, but that I doubted the model more than any of them, and believed that if we failed with anybody, we should fail with her. This made such a rebellion among the matrons and turnkeys that I was almost ashamed of myself, and heartily wished I had kept my opinion quiet. But we

---

[3] Probably Benjamin Rotch, barrister, whose address is given in the Post Office Directory of 1849 as 1 Furnival's Inn, Holborn.

have always talked about her since, naturally; and when she stayed in prison on her own accord, I gave way altogether, and became quite abject. Last Saturday, Chesterton and I were at the Home together, and the model was still in great force. Last Sunday, I went to him by appointment on this same theme, and the model was gone! —

The other girl, remaining in prison voluntarily, who had an affection for her, cried all day, and had cried ever since she went. But she made no effort to go too, though the parting was very bitter to her — for she really had hoped to reform, with this companion, and had thought they would become like sisters. I sent a dress down to the Prison yesterday, to be made for her to come to Shepherd's Bush in when we are ready, thinking that the knowledge of our actually preparing for her, would keep her in her good resolutions. If she remain, I have no doubt of her, and hope we may count upon her reclamation as almost certain.

This brings me to the day of opening. I hope you do not contemplate our postponing it beyond Saturday week, if we should be ready then? Otherwise we shall be in this difficulty — that more of these unfortunate creatures' terms will have expired, and we shall not know what to do with them. There is a certain Emma Lea, of whom I am disposed to be hopeful, who is released next Sunday, and there are others who will be released this week and next week. These girls have been continually spoken to and have had the address in their hands for days upon days together; and it would be a deplorable thing, if they really are in the improved state of mind they profess (and they seem sincerely anxious to come) to let them fall back again, which they cannot help doing — it is the literal truth — can not help — unless we take them. I shall be very glad to receive a few lines from you on this point. We are at present not certain of the assistant, and that *may* retard us. But I hope not, and shall make every exertion to prevent it.

The poor girl out of prison continues to do well. I have sent for her today. I am afraid of every hour, in her case, because she is constantly exposed to the hazard of going among old companions. But she certainly has done well as yet, and on a very, very, little money. And hers is, like some other cases that we have, a case in which it was next to impossible but that she must have gone, in youth, the way she has gone. It is dreadful to think how some of these doomed women have no chance or choice. It is impossible to disguise from one's self the horrible truth that it would have been a social marvel and miracle if some of them had been anything else than what they are.

I have laid in all the dresses and linen of every sort for the whole house — purchasing the materials at Shoolbred's in Tottenham Court Road, at the wholesale prices. I have made them as cheerful in appearance as they reasonably could be — at the same time very neat and modest. Three of them will be dressed alike, so that there are four colors of dresses in the Home at once; and those who go out together, with Mrs Holdsworth, will not attract attention, or feel themselves marked out, by being dressed alike. In their living room I have put up two little inscriptions selected from the sermons of Jeremy Taylor and Barrow [4] — both very simple and beautiful in themselves, and remarkably appropriate (as I hope you will think) to the purpose. Also a little inscription of my own, referring to the advantages of order, punctuality, and good temper; and another setting forth the Saviour's exposition of our duty towards God, and our duty towards our neighbour. In each bedroom is another Inscription, admonishing them against every lying down to rest, without being affectionate and reconciled among themselves. And I am now writing a little address which Mrs Holdsworth shall read to each, alone, when she comes in. The enclosed paper is for that lady and ourselves. I shall be glad if you will read it, and tell me whether you have any objection to anything it contains. You will see that I speak of the "Governors," for want of any better word. I have provided a form of book, in which we shall keep the history of each case, and which has certain printed enquiries to be filled up by us, before each comes in, and a final blank headed its "Subsequent History," which will remain to be filled up, by degrees, as we shall hear of them, and from them, abroad. I hope there is nothing whatever, in the business arrangement, which is not in working order.

The arrangements in the printed paper I send with this, for the domestic duties and their allotment, I have taken from the Normal School for Governesses at Whitelands. I am also getting their books of instruction, with some other reading of my own selection. The arrangements (not mentioned in the paper) for washing and dressing, and putting away of clothes, and everything of that kind, I have endeavoured to form with a view to every chance and mischance to which we are exposed — and something that escaped from the Model

---

[4] Jeremy Taylor (1613–1667), English divine, author of *Holy Living* and *Holy Dying;* Isaac Barrow (1630–1677), theologian, classical scholar, and mathematician, chaplain to Charles II, Master of Trinity College 1672.

before she went away — or from a friend of hers — I forget which — shewed, in a remarkable manner, that one of them was right. In short, I believe that nothing has been done without a reason; and I must again say, that I cannot tell you how efficient and devoted Mr Chesterton has been.

You will see, in the printed paper I send you, an allusion to Music, as a means towards our end. If you will authorize me, I will see Mr Hullah,[5] (who is an old friend of mine) and consult with him about the times and forms of instruction. I think it extremely important that the assistant should at least be able to play simple tunes on the Piano; and I am looking about, high and low, for a cheap second-hand one, to stand in Mrs Holdsworth's room. The fondness for music among these people generally, is most remarkable; and I can imagine nothing more likely to impress or soften a new-comer, than finding them with this art among them, and hearing them sing their evening Hymn before they go to bed. — Treating of bed, by the bye, Mr Chesterton, Mr Tracey, and I, have proposed ten o'clock as the time for their being in bed, from our common knowledge of the terrible mistake that is sometimes made in this regard, and the danger of shutting them up, with unoccupied minds, at preposterously early hours.

Mrs Holdsworth promises very well indeed, I think, and improves greatly on acquaintance. We have already had some Rehearsals of the routine of each day's life (not set forth in the regulations), and we shall have some more on Saturday, and next week. I hope the Furniture will be completed on Saturday. It is all promised.

I was vexed to see a stupid account of the Home in the newspapers some time ago. If they blunder upon anything else, the design can be easily explained, as you wish, either by my writing a letter on the subject, or an account of the Institution: selecting any channel of publication that is within reach, and that you may think most desirable. It is possible that there may be nothing more written about it; but if there be, it is easily set right.

We are trying now, whether we can find two or three sufficiently hopeful cases that have not been in Prison at all. I cannot say — yet,

---

[5] John Pyke Hullah (1812–1884), musician, a fellow pupil of Dickens's sister Fanny at the Royal Academy of Music in 1833, the composer of *The Village Coquettes*, of which Dickens wrote the libretto. He taught singing classes at Battersea beginning in 1840 and popularized choral singing groups; later, 1858–1884, he was organist at Charterhouse.

with what success. The advantage of selecting from Prisons in the infancy of such a design, is, firstly that we know more about them, and secondly, that there is an important break in old habits and associations.

I most entirely agree with you that it is right they should feel perfectly free before going abroad. If this system hold (and I have a faith in its doing so, simply because it is the system of Christianity, and nothing more or less) I believe they *will* feel perfectly free, when that times comes. But we can examine into this, and devise for it, leisurely. It has occurred to me that it would be an admirable means of promoting friendly and affectionate feelings among them, to give them to understand that no one should ever be sent abroad alone. It would be a beautiful thing, and would give us a wonderful power over them, if they would form strong attachments among themselves. To say nothing of the encouragement and support they would be to one another in a foreign country.

My dear Miss Coutts, you will attribute my earnestness to the true cause — the unspeakable interest I have in a design fraught with such great consequences, and the knowledge I have (if I have any knowledge at all) of these sad aspects of humanity, and their workings — when I again refer to that indispensable necessity of remembering the formed character that is to be addressed, and of considering everything that is addressed to it, not with reference to itself alone, but in connexion with its adaptability to the nature, sufferings, and whole experiences of the objects of your benevolence. In proportion as the details of any one of these young lives would be strange and difficult to a good man who had kept away from such knowledge, so the best man in the world could never make his way to the truth of these people, unless he were content to win it very slowly, and with the nicest perception always present to him, of the results engendered in them by what they have gone through. Wrongly addressed, they are certain to deceive. The greatest anxiety I feel, in connexion with this scheme — it is a greater one than any that arises out of my sense of responsibility to you, though that is not slight — is, that the clergyman with whom I hope I am to act as one confiding in him and perfectly confided in, should be not only a well-intentioned man, as I believe most clergymen would be, but one of the kindest, most considerate, most judicious, and least exacting of his order. Kind regards to Mr and Mrs Brown. Mrs Dickens desires the same.

54.   NOVEMBER 9, 1847, DEVONSHIRE TERRACE

I write a last line to say that I have marked some prayers in the book
of Common Prayer, for Mrs Holdsworth's temporary use, morning and
night. If the assistant is engaged by Saturday (I am now in communication with her) I would propose to open on that day. One of the girls,
who has remained in prison three weeks voluntarily, is now there, with
Mrs Holdsworth, and is making her own clothes. Her remaining in confinement so long, seemed to dispirit the others rather; and we therefore
thought it best (as she seemed oppressed herself, too, by the con-
tinuance of the heavy discipline of the jail) to take her out yesterday,
and carry her to the Home. I went out to see her last evening at 9
o'Clock, and she expressed herself as being very happy and grateful.

∽

55.   NOVEMBER 20, 1847, DEVONSHIRE TERRACE

I received your letter today. I am going, next Saturday, into Northamptonshire for five or six days.[6] If you don't come home before then,
I shall think the spell impossible to be broken, until I can find a Hermit
sitting on the road to a mountain, unable to speak in consequence of
the length of his white beard; having cut off which, with a pair of
scissors, I shall receive his instructions where to find the talisman that
will do it. To this talisman I shall be conducted by a bowl (given me
by the Hermit) which will roll on of itself before the Horse's feet, until
it arrives at mountain which I shall ascend on foot until I descry, amidst
the tumult of threatening voices around me — etc etc etc

Mary Anne Stonnell, the little girl in whom you were interested as
being allowed a trifle out of doors, goes into the Home *tonight*. Also
another girl of the name of Rosina Gale. There will then be four — and
more are coming next week, and more the week after. All these girls
I have seen repeatedly, and know very well, and I believe they have the
strongest disposition to be confiding and faithful. The two at present in
the Home (both of whom stayed voluntarily in prison three weeks)
are wonderfully happy and grateful, and have altered in appearance
in a most extraordinary manner. Not with eating, certainly, for they
have had no appetite yet — being much troubled (so to speak) by their
thankful feelings. I don't know whether I told you that the first girl
cried very much when she saw her Bed. There is a vast deal to do, of

---

[6] On December 1, 1847, Dickens presided at a soiree of the Leeds Mechanics'
Institute, where he made a speech eloquently defending education for the masses
against those who feared putting the power of knowledge into their hands.

course, in the making of clothes and so forth, and their industry is beyond all praise. Indeed, I have told Mrs Holdsworth not to let that be carried too far.

I have had great anxiety in endeavours to obtain an eligible second lady. I thought it (so did Mr Chesterton) of vital importance to the plan that she should be young — and many ladies were afraid of it, and evidently shrunk from the association. Mrs Fisher, the lady at last secured and now there, is a widow of six and twenty — very youthful looking — vitally interested in the project — of mild sweet manners — accustomed to teaching young people — and who has known great sorrow. I have been out there, on alternate evenings, since I wrote to you last. I wish you could have seen them at work, on the first night of this lady's engagement — with a pet canary of hers walking about the table, and the two girls deep in my account of the lesson books, and all the knowledge that was to be got out of them, as we were putting them away on the shelves.

I will not say any more until you come home, or I shall sacrifice a quire of paper. Divers schemes in connexion with the secular education have occurred to me, to be developed (if you approve) as we go on — including a series of small evening lectures which I should like to deliver to them in April when Dombey is done.

P.S. Pray let me know as soon as you are in town.

ᴄᴡᴄ

56.   December 29, 1847, Glasgow
I am very much obliged to you for writing to me so soon, on the subject of Mrs Fisher. I cannot but say that I greatly regret her departure, and that the cause of it, is extremely painful to me, as it involves a point, on which, though I have no sympathy whatever with her private opinions, I have a very strong feeling indeed — which is not yours. At the same time I have no doubt whatever, that she ought to have stated the fact of her being a Dissenter, to me, before she was engaged; and I should then, before engaging her, have most certainly stated it to you. With these few words, and with the fullest sense of your very kind and considerate manner of making this change, I leave it.

After leaving Jeffrey [7] (to whom I go tomorrow) I shall have to pay

_____

[7] Dickens was on a holiday visit to Scotland with his wife, seeing old friends, sightseeing, and going over Scott's home at Abbotsford, on the Tweed.

a visit of a few hours at Malton in Yorkshire.⁸ It being doubtful, therefore, whether I shall be able to get home before Tuesday morning, I will write to Mr Chesterton and Lieutenant Tracey, and appoint that day for our meeting, instead of Monday.

My presidency ⁹ went off with great success last night, and was a very grand scene indeed, attended by nearly four thousand people. I would send you a newspaper of this morning with an account of the proceedings, but my speech is so dismally done in the report, that I can't make up my mind to send it.

I have been over the prison this morning, and see exactly the same things here, that we are dealing with at Shepherd's Bush.

Mrs Dickens (who was taken ill on the railroad,¹ and couldn't go last night, after coming all this way) sends her kindest regards.

ᴖ

57.   JANUARY 7, 1848, DEVONSHIRE TERRACE

I enclose you a list of all the expences of Shepherd's Bush, from the date of the lease to the present time. The amount is greatly swelled by the builder's account for necessary repairs, fence-making, and so forth; but you will find that everything that has been bought, has been bought at the lowest ready-money prices for good things, and at the most respectable wholesale warehouses.

I have numbered every bill, for the greater convenience of your reference. You will see that receipts are not attached to some of them. In those cases, they have been paid by Mr Chesterton, and the receipts have not yet come in to me. But I have paid everything.

I shall be glad if you will tell me when you can see me. I wish to explain to you how the case stands about the gas. I have been much dismayed by what I have heard about the books (I mean the reading books) at the Home, and imagine there is some mistake, but it makes me very unquiet, and extremely anxious to speak with you on the sub-

---

⁸ Probably to visit Mrs. Smithson. Her husband, the partner of Dickens's old friend Thomas Mitton, had died in 1844, but Dickens remained a warm friend both to Mrs. Smithson and her brother T. J. Thompson.

⁹ Dickens presided on December 28 over the first anniversary of the Glasgow Athenaeum.

¹ Catherine Dickens had a miscarriage on the train between Edinburgh and Glasgow, was hurriedly conveyed to the home of Sheriff Alison, where they were staying in Glasgow, put to bed, and a famous doctor called in. Two days later she felt well enough to accompany Dickens back to Edinburgh, but there fell violently ill again, and was unable to return home to London for several days.

ject. There is also a point in reference to the acceptance or rejection of one new Inmate that I deem it necessary to submit to you for your decision. The straw-plaiting, and one or two other questions, also occur to me as requiring mention.

Charley has just brought me in a document which looks so like a begging-letter that I am afraid to send it by itself lest it should not be taken in — and therefore enclose it.

∾

58. JANUARY 10, 1848, DEVONSHIRE TERRACE

I am concerned to hear there is anything wrong at Shepherd's Bush. I should have been there yesterday or today, but am perfectly over-powered with a cold that seems like a second edition of my former one, and is most ridiculously intense. But I shall be at my post tomorrow, and will not fail to let you know through Mr Brown all that has been done.

Julia Moreley's letter was immediately forwarded to its destination. It will happen no doubt, in many of these cases, that the friends are not disposed to renew the broken intercourse. It is a most extraordinary circumstance that the girls themselves seem to have no idea of this. She can write again, I will tell her tomorrow, if she likes.

Mrs Dickens is down stairs again, and wishes me to thank you for your kind remembrance of her.

59. JANUARY 11, 1847 [1848], DEVONSHIRE TERRACE [TO DR. WILLIAM BROWN]

Miss Coutts begged me to let you know what was done at Shepherd's Bush today.

Only Archdeacon Sinclair and Mr Tennant [2] were there, besides myself; Lieutenant Tracey being ill, and Mr Chesterton suddenly called away on business.

It appears that Mrs Holdsworth was led to suspect that Julia Morley might be secretly holding communication with some person, over or through the garden fence, in consequence of her regularly absenting herself from the long room, for the last ten evenings or so, immediately

---

[2] The Reverend William Tennant was vicar of the Church of St. Stephen, West-minster, which Miss Coutts had erected and endowed in memory of her father, Sir Francis Burdett. John Sinclair (1797–1875), educated at Edinburgh University and Pembroke College, Oxford, became Vicar of Kensington 1843 and Arch-deacon of Middlesex 1844.

after tea, and remaining absent, a quarter of an hour or twenty minutes — sometimes alone, and sometimes (that might naturally happen) with one or other of the other girls. That in consequence of this, she begged the gardener to watch, last Sunday night, outside the fence, on the side near the wash-house. That the gardener did watch accordingly, and a man soon came by him, going along the fence towards that corner. That the gardener "happening," as he says "to have the influenza" (as if it were a strange event!) coughed prematurely, and the man came back. That the gardener caught him by the coat, to detain and question him, and tore his coat, and so he ran away. But not before the gardener recognized him for a young man of 17 or 18, who is a brickmaker out of work. This morning or yesterday (I forget which) the gardener encountered this person again, elsewhere, and by chance: who seemed ill at ease at having been caught there — told him he needn't have been so sharp upon him, as he was about no harm — and gave a reason for being there, which might possibly be true. On that Sunday night, Julia Morley's manner was observed to change, and she has been low-spirited, silent, and churlish ever since. It should be observed, however, that she is not well. On being told today that we had reason to believe some communication had been held with some person outside, she most strenuously denied any such proceeding on her part, and asseverated over and over again that nothing was farther from her thoughts. She also said that she knew of no such communication on the part of anybody else, and was very staunch indeed in her defence, though I did not think she shewed the least surprise on the subject being mentioned to her; and on my saying beforehand, "You seem changed in your manner. Is there anything the matter with you?" she replied "Not as I knows on."

You will understand that the gardener did not see her, and that the man did not communicate, or try to communicate, with anybody inside, while he was there. We agreed that if we could, beyond all doubt, connect her with the man, that would be a sufficient reason for immediately dismissing her; but there is no such proof at all. The suspicious circumstances against her, are 1stly the coincidence between Mrs Holdsworth's suspicion and the man's appearance and 2ndly the alteration in her manner from the time of his encountering the gardener, as if she divined that he had been caught and prevented from coming any more. That her manner is greatly altered, there seems no doubt.

But, as I said before, she is not well; and that, and the consciousness of being suspected, *may* sufficiently account for the change.

The main circumstance against the man, is his running away. But he is a brickmaker; and all brickmakers are supposed to be prowling vagabonds with more or less reason to run away, arising in petty-larceny recollections.

We admonished her about her temper, and said if she resumed her old manner, we hoped we should have no reason to revert to this topic. In the present unsatisfactory state of the matter, we did not feel justi-fied in doing any more. But I gave the gardener a charge to resume his watch, and a sovereign (by way of Christmas Box) to sharpen it; and I begged Mrs Holdsworth, in the event of her noting the least demon-stration in the girl of increased sullenness, or determination to resort to that place or any other, to let me know immediately.

My own impression is, that she is in the restless state which pre-cedes the determination to go away. I think it possible that she may have got this man to go to some other man with whom she was formerly acquainted, and that this other man has returned some message im-porting that he has no desire to renew the acquaintance, which would depress and irritate her. But supposing she resumes her old demeanour, I shall think this is not the case, and that there really has been no communication at all. My reason for desiring to know accurately what she is about, is, that we may be beforehand with her, and, if we have any new reason to believe she is going, that we may — for the general example — discharge her. I will go out on Thursday night, and see her again. And if I should be summoned in the meantime, will go there immediately.

I should have called to tell you all this in a few words, but did not leave the Home until after five o'clock. All the rest appear to be doing very well, and are looking very well, and everything is in perfect order. [P.S.] She is to have some medicine, and some application to her throat tonight. Mrs Holdsworth thinks nothing of her indisposition.

∽

60.   JANUARY 14, 1848, DEVONSHIRE TERRACE

Mr Wardley [3] (in a most amusing letter, which I must save to shew you) writes to inform me that he has discovered one Mrs Leslie, aged thirty-six, whom he recommends for the vacant post of Instructress. Would you like to see her, first, or shall I?

---

[3] William Wardley, otherwise unidentified.

I was out at Shepherd's Bush last night, and spoke very kindly to Julia Morley. Her manner of replying, in the presence of the rest, was so very sullen and insolent that I fear some strong notice of it must be taken on Tuesday. In observance of the principle laid down for the other governing powers, I did not take the least notice of it to anybody, at the time, but it will not do to let it pass.

P.S. I have sent out the Carpenter to make the alteration of the upper bedroom door, this morning.

◦◦◦

61. JANUARY 16, 1848 [TO DR. WILLIAM BROWN]

Of the cases I saw yesterday, I would greatly desire, with Miss Coutts's sanction, to take in one — Adelaide Thomas, aged 17 — ignorant — poor in the last degree — her history most awful — and her fall, in its beginning, impossible to be attributed to herself. Mr Chesterton, his matron, and I, saw the girl's mother (her father went mad, in his grief for this child) and are acquainted with her whole story from her cradle. We strongly believe she may be saved without much difficulty. If we reject her, nothing on earth can stop her in her course to destruction.

Her appearance is pleasant, and her disposition, we are assured, patient and good humoured. She is very anxious to go abroad. She has never been in any Institution.

Among the applicants (who, for various sufficient reasons, I cannot recommend) is one whose case Miss Coutts may perhaps like to reconsider — Martha Goldsmith, aged 21; the girl who was a year in the Magdalen [4] and discharged yesterday. It appears that they are only kept in the Magdalen one year, and are then discharged. Supposing that situations are not to be got (as at this time) they are discharged at the twelvemonths' end, to make room for new inmates. This girl was sent away yesterday, with an excellent testimonial from the matron, a change of clothing, and three shillings. She has no relatives but sisters who are in service, or poor, and cannot take her in. It appears to me that the Magdalen is an absurdity (the public statement of such a case as this, would do it grievous damage) and that this girl is positively worse off, than if she had never been there. She is terribly depressed at finding herself again in the world, with a horror of her old life, and no means of taking to a better. One of her sisters was with her, crying

---

[4] A reformatory for prostitutes.

bitterly, and implored me so earnestly to make another appeal to Miss Coutts (though I explained the general objection to her, which she very reasonably received) that I feel obliged to state these facts. She is a good plain needlewoman — having worked at her needle, through her year — ordinary looking, though not ugly — and with a discreet quiet manner.

I shall be glad to have your answer relative to these two cases, without loss of time, to avoid keeping the people in a state of painful anxiety.

I may also repeat that Mr Chesterton, Mrs Meriton (his matron) and Lieutenant Tracey, all most decidedly recommend that we should now take in some girls who have not been tried and imprisoned. It would be next to impossible to have stronger authorities in such a case, and they all consider this infusion necessary to the welfare of the Home.

∽

62.   JANUARY 31, 1848, DEVONSHIRE TERRACE
I am very glad indeed to hear that there is a prospect of our soon filling up that gap at the Home. It is very important that it should not remain vacant, longer than is absolutely necessary.

Mrs Brown's report is also extremely cheering. I am quite confident that she is right. I never go there, but the same feeling impresses me, strongly.

I was there on Friday afternoon, and wrote Martha Goldsmith's history into the book. Her manner pleased me greatly. She answered all I asked her very well indeed, and (I have no doubt) truly.

Mr Hullah is going out with me this week, to begin his course.

My own impression is, — No Shutters! I will explain why, to Mr Brown tomorrow. Of course if you should still think them necessary, I will take care that they are immediately made.

I was in the Prisons today. One girl of the Rubina Waller class — that is, who has never committed any theft — may possibly turn out sufficiently promising to be enquired about, but there are other cases also, out of doors.

I hope Dr Skey [5] will find himself better of that disorder he thought

---

[5] Frederick William Skey (1798–1872), surgeon, pupil of Abernethy; taught in Aldersgate Street School of Medicine as lecturer on anatomy, 1843–1865; professor of human anatomy to College of Surgeons 1852, and president 1863; sur-

I had given him, this month. Tortures should not have elicited a word from me when I was reproached in Stratton Street.

⁓

63. MARCH 24, 1848, DEVONSHIRE TERRACE

It occurred to me in walking home from Stratton Street today, that you might have some interest in hearing all about Dombey[6] before everybody knows about him; and if we could manage it, I should be delighted to read it to you and Mr and Mrs Brown. The only evening that would seem to answer the purpose — with reference to my Salisbury trip, and the time of publication — would be next Wednesday. Mrs Dickens would be greatly pleased if you and Mr and Mrs Brown could dine with us on that day at half past six. We would not ask anybody else, except perhaps the Kay-Shuttleworths,[7] and we should see the end of our (of course immortal) acquaintance, after dinner.

⁓

64. [EARLY APRIL, 1848] DEVONSHIRE TERRACE

Your note was answered by Mrs Dickens this morning; but I find, on enquiry, that it was posted instead of sent. Which I hope will explain your not having received an earlier reply.

Mrs Dickens, I am sorry to say, is in her own room, and likely to be there for two or three days. I am not without some idea that the indisposition of my intended host of tomorrow, may release me. In that case, I shall present myself in Stratton Street, however informal the circumstances of my coming there.

I was at the Home today, where all appears to be progressing with

geon at St. Bartholomew's Hospital 1854–1864; received C.B. for services as chairman of a committee on contagious diseases; author of *Operative Surgery*, 1851, and *Hysteria*, 1867.

[6] This was the last number of *Dombey and Son*, to be published at the end of the month, in which Mr. Dombey, ruined and deserted, is reconciled with his daughter. On its completion, Dickens took a short holiday trip to Salisbury with Mark Lemon, John Leech, and John Forster. The Wednesday he was proposing (March 29) was immediately after this vacation. But the postscript of the following letter makes it clear Miss Coutts could not have been present at the reading, even if it took place.

[7] Sir James Kay-Shuttleworth (1804–1877), first baronet 1849, founder of English popular education, first secretary of the Council on Education 1839–1849, joint founder of Battersea training college for pupil-teachers 1839–1840, vice-chairman of the central relief committee in the Lancashire cotton famine 1861–1865.

perfect comfort and promise. Archdeacon Sinclair was there, and seemed much pleased, I thought, with what he saw and heard.

Our friend Mrs Graves is rather of a delicate gentility, I fear; and her aspect is sombre. She will enter on her duties on Saturday week. Mrs Fisher will retire on the same day.

I will endeavour to make out the accounts tomorrow morning. Whatever has occured to me to say to you on any little point, I will say when I shall have the pleasure of seeing you.

[P.S.] I hope you liked the little loves of Florence and Walter? If you had seen Jeffrey crying over them the other night, you would have been charmed with *him* at all events.[8]

෮

65.   MAY 20, 1848, DEVONSHIRE TERRACE

Every enquiry that Mr Tracey's matron has made, personally, about the girl Godfrey, substantiates her statement in the minutest particular. While I was at the Prison today, the School-mistress was gone to Mile End, to make one additional enquiry. Assuming that to be equally satisfactory, all the evidence is clearly and distinctly in the girl's favor; and with that reservation, I have made arrangements for her admission on Wednesday Evening.

I afterwards proceeded to call on Miss Cunliffe; [9] but she had gone out, to call on you. I therefore enclosed a card in your note, informing her that I should be at home here, on Monday, between 11 and 1 o'clock.

෮

66.   MAY 22, 1848, DEVONSHIRE TERRACE

I brought away the references by mistake. Here they are.

In case you should, by any evil chance, in visiting Stonnell, encounter a magistrate of the name of Rotch, let me advise you to say nothing to him, either about her, or the Home. For whatever is said to him, he is as certain to pervert, if it should suit his purpose, as the Sun is to rise tomorrow morning.

I am expecting Miss Cunliffe. Godfrey's references turned out quite

---

[8] The lyrical conclusion of *Dombey and Son*, over which Lord Jeffrey wept, pictures the married life of Florence Dombey and Walter Gay, and Mr. Dombey's almost anguished tenderness for the children of the daughter to whom, in her childhood, he had been cold.

[9] Miss Cunliffe was an applicant for a post on the staff of Urania Cottage.

satisfactory. The materials for her clothes, have gone down to Mr Tracey's this morning. I had a note from Mrs Holdsworth last night, reporting Rubina Waller gouty, Martha Goldsmith ricketty, and the rest of the family "charming."

∽

67.   MAY 23, 1848, DEVONSHIRE TERRACE

Nothing can be better, I think, than the letter to Sally.[1] I am sorry for her, but I must say I think she is less adapted to the situation than anything else in the human form of which I have any idea.

It strikes me that Mrs Graves must walk without knowing why, and that everybody else must walk after her.

Miss Cunliffe was here, yesterday. I like her very much. There is something in her face, exceedingly agreeable and promising, and she improves greatly on being talked to. She seems to have a little conscientious timidity, in reference to the task before her, for which I like her none the worse. Whether she has any susceptible gentility, I don't quite know, but I think she promises very well indeed, and I feel an interest in her.

∽

68.   MAY 24, 1848, DEVONSHIRE TERRACE

I thought there was something in my way. — Talfourd and I are under a compact to Miss Kelly to shed the refulgence of our presence upon a private reading she is going to hold tomorrow night, as a feeler for getting a livelihood through the provincial Literary Societies and Mechanics' Institutions. It is really a question of existence to her, and we have both endeavoured, for some time past, to keep her creditors away from her. Consequently, I *must* go; and Mrs Dickens (who don't want to go) is pledged, through me, any time these two months, to make a similar bright example of herself.

On Friday morning, I am going to Birmingham;[2] and I think I shall

---

[1] Unidentified, but probably an applicant for admission to the Home.

[2] To make arrangements for the Birmingham performance in a new series of his amateur theatrical performances, this time for the benefit of James Sheridan Knowles (1784–1862), dramatist, the author of numerous plays, including *Virginius, William Tell, The Hunchback*, and *The Love Chase*. In 1844 Knowles became a Baptist and preached at Exeter Hall and other places against Roman Catholicism and Cardinal Wiseman. When Dickens was in Edinburgh the previous winter, he had learned from Lord Jeffrey on New Year's Day that Knowles had just signed a petition of bankruptcy, and had immediately begun cudgeling his

be away, ten or twelve days. I have set my heart on seeing Sheridan Knowles installed at Stratford on Avon, as the Curator of Shakespeare's House — the only and the best resource I know for him — and am going, in advance of my troupe, to interest the sympathies of his friends in that town, and in Liverpool, and Manchester — at the same time pursuing those other observations I have in my mind, and mentioned to you yesterday. If you should have anything to write to me about the Home, and will send it here, it will be immediately forwarded to me.

The blind-maker and I, held a great council yesterday. And the blind-maker shewed me such good reasons for the common outside Venetian blinds, drawing up into cases, being at once the most enduring, the neatest, and cheapest, for our purpose, that I unhesitatingly concluded to order that kind. They will be done in about nine days.

I send you back the little pamphlet. Apropos of which — I have a tempting offer just now, to be returned, free of expence, for one of the largest metropolitan boroughs, and I believe I could be brought in, very triumphantly. But considerations of the greater peace and happiness of my own pursuits — to say nothing of the butcher and baker — hold me back, gently, as they have done twice before.[3] To which I add the reflection, if I *did* come out in that way, what a frightful radical you would think me!

---

brains for a means of helping him. A project was under way for the Government to acquire Shakespeare House in Stratford as a national museum; Dickens combined the aim of getting Knowles appointed curator with that of raising money for him by another series of dramatic benefits.

At the time of this letter, his company had already given *The Merry Wives of Windsor* at the Haymarket Theater on May 15 and *Every Man in His Humour* on May 17; still other performances of the two plays were given in Manchester, Liverpool, and Birmingham in the course of June, and in Edinburgh and Glasgow in July. The gross receipts were over £2500. In the end, the Government granted Knowles a pension, and the Shakespeare house was acquired by the town of Stratford. The profits of the theatricals were placed directly in Knowles's hands.

[3] Dickens had refused to stand as a candidate to represent the town of Reading in 1841 and, a little later in the same year, had refused an appeal to represent a Scottish county. On the first occasion he was half tempted by the hope that he might help bring about some measures for the public welfare, and was mainly deterred by the difficulties of retaining his independence of action as a member of Parliament and the loss of income that would result from dividing his time between writing and public office. But as his contempt for the chicaneries and corruptions of politics deepened, he formed a fixed resolve never to stand for office. When he was asked to do so in later years he invariably replied, "I believe no consideration would induce me to become a Member of that amazing institution."

69.   JULY 25, 1848, DEVONSHIRE TERRACE

I am afraid I cannot come to Shepherd's Bush today, as I want to go to Broadstairs to see my children, and have been unable to do so, on account of certain sad daily visits to a sister at Hornsey, who is dying.[4] In case of your going yourself, and entering on any accounts, I enclose you some outstanding bills. Also Mr Walesby's[5] acknowledgment for the £5.

Will you let me know on what days and at what hours you will probably be at home this week, after tomorrow?

∽

70.   AUGUST 10, 1848, BROADSTAIRS, KENT

I enclose the two accounts of Mr King, relative to Charley. I will have a long talk with him, as to the expediency of Charley's removal at Christmas, and will let you know what his opinion is, in good time. I am going to bring him back to town to school, tomorrow.

Before receiving this, I dare say you will have seen Mrs Holdsworth. I told her, in the course of the committee proceedings the other day, that you wished her to get up on every alternate washing-day; Mrs Graves taking the other. She did not object then, but afterwards — when I was going, and the rest were gone — informed me, with a face of most portentous woe and intensity, that "she couldn't do it." I informed her, in reply, that that was an answer which I could by no means give to you, in so easy a matter, and that she must make that communication to you herself.

We had an accident here yesterday, which might have been a very bad one. I have a pretty little pony, nearly thorough-bred, who is not vicious, but requires great care in the driving. Mrs Dickens, in a little phaeton which this animal draws, set off for Margate to meet me, under the coachmanship of our footman. At the top of a hill the pony made a sudden start, and the man instantly jumped out (he says he was thrown out, but it could not have been so) leaving her gallopping down a steep hill, with the reins wound round the wheel, and his mistress astounding the whole Isle of Thanet with her screams. However, she kept her seat and the pony plunging over a steep bank, broke

---

[4] Dickens's eldest sister Fanny (1810–1848), who had been living in Manchester with her husband Henry Burnett, but who was now in London under the care of specialists there. She died of tuberculosis September 2, 1848.

[5] Unidentified.

the shafts and tumbled down on her side, without upsetting the carriage! A lady and gentleman living near, who were driving by in their carriage, got Mrs Dickens out, and sent for some wine and so forth, and took her home to their house, where the man was carried too, and where (to my unspeakable astonishment) I was borne off to see them, when I landed from the boat. She is none the worse, I hope, for the fright, but the man is greatly cut and bruised from head to heel, and the surgeon is afraid he may be lamed, from the injury done to some leading sinews of his legs. I am going to take the pony to the scene of the disaster this morning, where I shall try to cure her of such freaks for the future.

∞

71.   AUGUST 13, 1848, BROADSTAIRS, KENT

I brought Charley to town on Friday evening; but coming against tide, and having a long detention in the river, we did not arrive until 6 o'clock. As I knew that would be a very inconvenient time for our calling on you, I carried him direct to school, and came back here myself early next morning.

I found, at home, your kind present, and its accompanying note. Believe me, I accept the picture with feelings of the truest gratification, and shall ever attach a value to it which can only belong to a gift from such a friend.

Mrs Holdsworth's balance of duties, I enclose. Miss Cunliffe's sketch I gave back to her, last Tuesday, requesting her to have the goodness to give it to you.

Captain Macconnochie's paper, I will forward to you in a day or two.

I hope you will keep Mrs Graves and Mrs Holdsworth to their tether. It is intolerable to be met with such mincing nonsense from those toiling and all-enduring dowagers. I wish I could draw Mrs Holdsworth's face for you, as she appeared when she opened her objection to me.

Mrs Dickens is very much obliged by your kind solicitude. I hope she is none the worse, but have cautioned her to keep quiet for some days. It was a very great alarm; and I assure you, on looking at the place, I cannot imagine how she escaped. The man is still disabled, but I don't think myself that he has received any permanent injury. The pony made two or three similar attempts with me, but we are pretty well acquainted, and in the course of five and twenty miles' trot, she seemed to begin to think a quiet life the best.

Whenever you will like to have a conference on the proposed arrangements, I will come to Stratton Street or elsewhere at 11 o'clock, if you will give me a day or two's notice.

With regards to Mr and Mrs Brown

&

72.   AUGUST 20, 1848, BROADSTAIRS, KENT

I will come up on *Wednesday* morning, as that is one of the two convenient days you mention, and shall hope to be in Stratton Street by eleven o'clock. I will bring Captain Macconnochie's paper with me, and your rules also. Generally, I quite concur in them all. I mean your rules. There are one or two little points on which we can say a word or two when we meet. They are merely slight matters which occur to me as being practically difficult of incorporation with the Mark System.

I should have written sooner, but I have been considering the subject and thinking about something for Christmas besides.[6]

I am happy to say that Mrs Dickens seems quite well, and has been out with me behind the identical pony, whom I drove to Dover and back yesterday. The servant is getting on very well, and will certainly not be lame, though he is still invalided.

&

73.   AUGUST 28, 1848, BROADSTAIRS, KENT [TO MRS. BROWN]

Will you tell Miss Coutts that I have read her suggestions several times, and think I quite understand them. I will immediately set about drawing up the different papers she refers to, for her revision. The Mark tables I believe are perfectly clear and simple as I have sketched them, but I will keep them a day or so, to look at again with a fresh eye, before I send a copy to Miss Coutts. I do not propose to encumber them with any explanations, but to make all explanatory matter a part of the other printed papers.

I will write to Miss Coutts either tomorrow or Wednesday, proposing a day, either at the end of this week or the very beginning of next, for our talk — and for that day I shall hold myself entirely at her disposal. I am waiting for a note from Macready to whom I have given a choice of days for a farewell Confabulation before he goes to America — and one journey to town will thus answer both purposes. I am greatly obliged by your kind offer of a bed, but I can sleep at home quite com-

---

[6] His Christmas story for 1848, *The Haunted Man.*

fortably. I will bring all the papers Miss Coutts suggests, with me. The Mark table itself, I will send her when I write to propose our day of meeting.

Mrs Dickens is not very well, but I don't think the pony is to blame. She sends her kindest regards.

I am beginning to think about Christmas, when I hope we may have another little reading in Devonshire Terrace.

∽

74.   AUGUST 29, 1848, BROADSTAIRS, KENT
If Friday next will suit you, I and the large box will appear, with drafts of all the documents you have suggested.

I infer from Mrs Brown's note, that if you should be disengaged on that day, you mean to ask me to dinner. Would you not wish to see me in the morning also? I intended yesterday, to have sent you the Mark Table with this, but I think it will be better for me to reserve it, until I am by, to give all needful explanation.

Will you write me a word to say at what time I shall come? All times between eleven in the morning and ten at night (when I will make another engagement) will be alike to me.

I have heard from Mr Chesterton this morning, and he is evidently a little hurt and mortified by the impression that the "Committee" are rather summarily discharged of their duties, and have no very powerful existence but in name. I have written to give him another aspect of the case; but as he has always been greatly interested in the design, and is a very sincere and zealous man, perhaps, if you should see him again, you would not object to set him right yourself. I merely mention this, because I think you ought to know it, and because no one else can so gracefully reassure him. Looking at the matter from his point of view too, I don't think he sees it in an unreasonable light.

∽

ENCLOSURE WITH PRECEDING LETTER

Explanation of The Mark Table.

This has been limited to as few heads as possible, in order that it may be rendered the plainer to the comprehension of the young women themselves. I think it will be found, in practice, that the heads are sufficiently numerous for all purposes.

The highest number of Good Marks capable of being earned on any one day under any one head, is 4; the lowest, 1. Thus, average desert, under any one head, or every head, would be marked as 2; something below that, 1; something above that, 3. According to this mode of proceeding, 1 may be considered to mean pretty well; 2, well; 3, very well; 4, excellent. Where there is really no desert, and yet no tangible and positive misconduct, no mark will be given. A bad mark is to be entered cautiously, as it destroys the fruits of one whole day's irreproachable conduct; but when it is deserved under the head of "truthfulness," by any wilful falsehood, no matter what, it is never to be foregone.

I propose to attach to the marks, the money-value of three pence pr score. It is *possible* (but not at all probable) that an Inmate may earn four marks under every head, in one day. This would give a day's total of forty; the value of which would be six pence.

I should think, myself, that the money-earnings would rarely exceed half a crown pr week for one person.

I propose to limit the reward for "Voluntary self denial", to abstinence from beer, on the part of those employed in the laundry on Washing-days (to whom, alone, it is to be issued, unless medically prescribed) and to abstinence on other days, on the part of any one otherwise employed, from tea and sugar. For either of these acts of self-denial, four good marks are to be entered (with the exception of the case presently to be stated). I assume that the two examples of abstinence cannot occur together, as I would not allow the washers to deprive themselves, both of beer and tea.

My reason for suggesting this limitation of the voluntary self-denial, to two kinds of abstinence in the first instance, is, that distrust or discontent may not be awakened in the young women by this means, before they have a practical understanding of the system. It would be comparatively easy to extend the list of things they may deny themselves if they please, after it had been some little time in operation; and it is not at all unlikely that some suggestion to that effect, may come from among themselves.

The excepted case I have referred to, is this. — It is not unlikely that some young woman may now and then deny herself her beer or tea, because she is sulky. In that case, I would either not mark it as "Voluntary Self Denial" at all, or would mark it at the reduced amount of 2, — according to circumstances.

My reason for this proposal and for not giving a larger number of marks under this head, is, that they may understand it as a Moral effort, and not as a distinct and certain saving, exactly proportioned to, or absurdedly exceeding, the mere money-value of what they abstain from.

Supposing a young woman has a bad mark on Thursday, under the head of Truthfulness, it is very likely that she may earn no good mark under that head, on Friday. The keeper of the Mark Tables may very reasonably say, "I have had no opportunity of seeing, since that bad mark, that you are disposed to tell the Truth, and therefore I cannot mark you for truthfulness." So, with temper. Supposing one young woman to be violent with another, on Monday. The lady may, with equally good reason, say on Tuesday, "I don't know that your temper has been tried since yesterday." But if this were properly received, she would say, on Wednesday, "you shewed so much good temper when I spoke to you last night, that I can now, with pleasure, mark you 4, and 4 for improvement too." A course like this, judiciously and carefully pursued, must be productive of very good and enduring results.

Of every Mark-paper I would have a duplicate, which should be kept, from day to day, by the young woman herself. Besides the probability of its producing some moral effect upon her, it would be a lesson in arithmetic, in which she could not fail to have a personal interest. When the lady who keeps the Mark table, enters Julia Morley's marks, for example, at night, I would have Julia Morley make corresponding entries in her own paper — add up the day's line — and submit her total to the lady. I would propose that the weekly balance be struck, in the same way, every Saturday evening, when a kind of Savings' Bank should be held for making the entries in the book-accounts of the young women. The daily columns in the Mark table, are added up at the end of each day, from the bottom. The weekly addition, which gives the number of marks under each separate head, is made across all the columns from left to right, and then added up from the bottom. I would have every young woman keep her own book in her own custody. The lady would keep each account, separately, in one large book provided for the purpose. I would issue the Mark Tables for the ensuing week, every Saturday night, after these accounts were made up; and those kept by the lady must be filed after they are balanced.

The expression, so many "odd good marks" or "good marks over," applies to any balance less than a score, after the weekly total has been divided by twenty. To prevent the confusion of fractional divisions of money, these are always to be carried to the next weeks account, and entered in it, then and there. Thus 190 good marks, divided by twenty are 9 score (2°/3d) — and 10 marks over, to be entered in the next account.

Supposing such a case as once occurred with Emma Lea, when she called another girl by opprobrious names, and threatened her, and was otherwise violent and defiant. Such an extreme case would involve, under this table, a bad mark for "temper", a bad mark for "propriety of deportment," a bad mark for "propriety of language," and a bad mark for "improvement" — every one of which, I would certainly have entered.

I have considered Mr Kay Shuttleworth's desire to introduce some greater *moral* stimulant into this system, and do not descry any means by which it can hopefully be done. But I submit this consideration for his reflection — whether incentives to good conduct, successfully addressed to the reason and prudence of people and obviously tending to their welfare, be not likely to become, imperceptibly, the awakeners of a real moral sentiment — suggesting, in the first instance, the wisdom of virtue and the folly of vice: and, afterwards, the inherent beauty of the former, and deformity of the latter? In this, my hope of the system as a moral influence, mainly lies.

⁊

The "heads" under which the inmates in the Home were marked totaled nine: Truthfulness, Industry, Temper, Propriety of Conduct and Conversation, Temperance, Order, Punctuality, Economy, Cleanliness. "The word Temperance," Dickens explained, "is not used in the modern slang acceptation, but in its enlarged meaning, as defined by Johnson from the English of Spenser: 'Moderation, patience, calmness, sedateness, moderation of passion.'"

The methods of fostering self-control he outlined naturally weighed with a certain heaviness upon girls who had previously led wild and irregular lives, although they were warmed and softened, as Dickens's previous letters show, by the enjoyments of flower gardening, music and group singing, and reading for pleasure. Not all the inmates of the Home were able to submit themselves to its discipline; some left and some were expelled for bad conduct. One of those departing was Mary Ann Stonnell, who had been admitted the preceding November,

*not long after the institution opened. She soon resumed her former way
of life, was jailed once more, and visited in prison by Miss Coutts. A
letter she then wrote Miss Coutts, and Dickens's comment on it, are
revealing:*

ᴄᴡ

75.   AUGUST 31, 1848 [TO MISS COUTTS FROM MARY ANN STONNELL]
I take the liberty of writing a few lines to thank you for the kindness
you have shown to such an unworthy creature as I have been to leave
such a good home and I thank you for taking the trouble you have to
come and see me who am not worthy of such a kind benefactress I
hope Madam that you will forgive me for I am very sorry for what I
have done

ᴄᴡ

76.   SEPTEMBER 8, 1848, DEVONSHIRE TERRACE
As I understand, on coming home, that your servant has only just
now been here, I write you this hasty note.

Stonnell, *in prison,* will always, I think, be tolerably good. Out of it,
until — perhaps — after great suffering, I have no hope of her. I have
no doubt she feels (as God knows she should) what she writes to you.
If she were free, she might feel it still, at odd times, but I firmly believe would feel it to no good end.

Miss Cunliffe misses one of my intentions, and an important one. I
will write to her from Broadstairs, and explain. I will send you a proof
of the proposed Mark Table, in three or four days, and convey the
same explanation to you.

The best Hotel at Liverpool is one of the very best in England — the
Adelphi. The Landlord, Mr Radley, is an excellent fellow, and much
respected. I have quite a regard for him. I will answer for your being
well pleased by his manner and face, and by everything he does for
you.

If you will give me, when you write, the name and address of your
solicitor (with whom I have never communicated directly) I will explain Mrs Scott's [7] case to him as her son explained it to me the other
day. It involves a little point of Property Tax-law (the right is quite
plain) which I think it would be best for a practical lawyer to decide.

I am afraid I write illegibly — but I have been at my sister's funeral
today, and my hand is not as steady as usual.

---

[7] Unidentified.

77.   SEPTEMBER 17, 1848, BROADSTAIRS, KENT

I send you a proof (only received this morning) of the Mark Table. It shall not be finally printed, until I have heard from you.

I have received no tidings from Mrs Holdsworth, and therefore have no doubt that all is going on well. I dare say I shall hear from her, in the course of tomorrow.

There is the finest weather here, I ever saw. It don't seem to agree with Rogers,[8] who is horribly cross.

∽

78.   OCTOBER 5, 1848, DEVONSHIRE TERRACE

On coming home the night before last, I found your two notes, and your MSS. I *think* I read the latter correctly, and that you will find the proof sheets pretty accurate. The explanation shall go to the printer's tomorrow (I am just now having the copy made from dictation) and I shall hope to send you the proofs by next day's post — including the amended Mark Table. Will you lose no time in returning them to me? They are all very anxious at the Home, to begin.

I was there, yesterday. Everything seemed comfortable and quiet. There were no complaints of any kind.

Mrs Holdsworth had, about a fortnight ago, fifteen pounds for petty cash. The bills paid yesterday were £32..12..6.

I have received from you	£50..0..0
I have paid	47.12..6

Consequently, I have in hand £ 2..7..6

The blind-maker's bill, in accordance with his estimate, has come in. It amounts to £19..6..0. There is also a bill for books of £19..7..6. But of this, I have some part (I think) in hand, out of a little balance you left with me when we first settled accounts, for printer and bookseller.

The field at the side, and the field at the bottom of the garden — in all about 2½ acres — can now be rented, if you wish, on reasonable terms. As you were thinking of a removal, one of these days, I suppose you will not take them? *But an answer must be given at once.* There-

---

[8] Samuel Rogers, always acid-tongued, and now, at the age of eighty-five, sharper than ever.

fore, will you empower me to decline, if that be your wish? Or to come to some decision?

I hope I have the name of your hotel right? I have been hammering again and again in the most ridiculous manner, at a *rather* illegible passage in one of your notes.[9] I read it "— could simplify it more." Who could, was the great question I had to solve. Proglyns? It looked like Proglyns. I began to think whether I had ever met any clear-headed gentleman of that name, at your house. Not remembering him, I looked at it again. "Judy's son" it was then, plainly. But I rejected that, as a manifest impossibility. Tennyson — July Sawyer — Wednesday night — p.n.d.y.s.g.n. (which looked like a Welsh name) until all at once I found it was "perhaps you" — and was very much relieved and complimented.

I think the explanation admirably calculated to supply what is otherwise wanting in the spirit of the system, and am really sanguine on the subject.

Best regards to Mr and Mrs Brown.

79. OCTOBER 14, 1848, DEVONSHIRE TERRACE

I have made the alterations and additions you suggested in those papers, and they are now finally printing.

Mr Tennant was so kind as to write to me on the subject of the enclosed, and give me the same explanation. I replied that of course we could do nothing, until we knew your own view of the matter. Mine, I will state now.

On the first head, I have very strong doubts indeed, of the policy of accepting Mrs Wharton's offer.[1] I cannot forget the strong emphatic exception that was made by the matron of the Magdalen as to the hopefulness of any disposal of Martha Goldsmith, *at home*. She knows

---

[9] This is one of Dickens's many jesting references to the illegibility of Miss Coutts's handwriting. Although it had every appearance of plainness, it was often almost completely unreadable, a fact from which Miss Coutts derived much quiet amusement. Not infrequently unable to read it herself, she was inclined to look with suspicion on any claims to decipher it with certainty.

[1] Evidently an offer to give employment in London to Martha Goldsmith, one of the girls in the Home, but I have not been able to identify Mrs. Wharton. For reasons outlined in earlier letters, Dickens thought it wiser that the girls should go abroad to new countries where they were not known. The same reasons prompt the rejection, in the following paragraph, of a similar offer from the Cambridge Heath Laundry.

her, much better than we do; and I do not think it fair to the girl, or to the Home, to put her into this association in London.

The second point, as to the Cambridge Heath Laundry, is also a very difficult one. I certainly don't know anybody, in the Home *now*, whom I could comfortably trust there. I can imagine its being a very desirable place for a comparatively trustworthy girl, and a very wholesome change; but I think that those who are in the Home now, are better *in* the Home than anywhere else in this country. Even supposing the head of this Laundry to be a 'very wise and discreet person — which women of that class very commonly are not, and which ought to be very distinctly shewn to be the case.

The third offer seems to me the most valuable of all. In reference to the Emigration Committee, I have received a letter from Mr Engelbach,[2] begging me to address an official kind of statement of your views and wants to them. But I cannot well do this (as I have told him, in answer) until you shall have returned, and I shall have been able to speak with you on the subject. It would be an excellent thing to have a steady young woman as Jane Westaway's (and, I suppose, Martha Goldsmith's?) companion on the voyage. But we don't yet know — which seems to be the difficulty at this moment, of settling the matter — where they are to go or how they are to go, or that they are going at all in this young woman's direction.

You know Miss Newton,[3] I presume? — I don't.

With best regards to Mr and Mrs Brown, dear Miss Coutts

ᴏᴧᴧ

80.   NOVEMBER 1, 1848, DEVONSHIRE TERRACE

I want to ask your kind assistance in getting a highly esteemed and valued old servant of mine, who went abroad with us — the Brave courier of my little Italian book[4] — into St George's Hospital.

His case, the surgeon says, is distinctly admissible there. It would be also admissible at the Brompton Hospital for diseases of the chest. That institution is under an old obligation to me, and they are very ready and willing to take him in; but the bed he is to occupy (if

---

[2] Alfred Harold Engelbach was clerk at the Colonial Land and Emigration Board, at 9 Park Street, Westminster, the co-operation of which Dickens intended to evoke in sending the girls to Australia, New Zealand, and Canada.

[3] Unidentified.

[4] Louis Roche, who had also accompanied Dickens to Switzerland in 1846, and who was now seriously ill of heart disease.

he should live to go there) is not likely to be vacant for the next two or three months.

I enclose the medical description of his case, on which I have it much at heart to get him into St George's forthwith. I don't know how to set about it. It has occurred to me that perhaps you may have some direct power of nominating him as a patient, and that if you have not, Mr Brown (on whose good-feeling I know I may rely) will help me with his advice.

Pray forgive my troubling you. I have the deepest interest in the matter. He is a most faithful, affectionate, and devoted man. He is dreadfully changed from a fine handsome fellow, in a very short time. His doctor urgently recommends his being got into a hospital where he will never be left alone (he is in a poor little lodging now), and I must accomplish it if it can be done.

⁂

81.   NOVEMBER 2, 1848, DEVONSHIRE TERRACE
I am exceedingly obliged to you for your prompt kindness, and I thank you heartily. Pray tell Mr Brown, with my best regards and acknowledgments, that I will not trouble him to endeavour to get the poor man in, before the next reception day. His case does not appear to be so very urgent, as to justify it. He shall go on Wednesday at the appointed time.

⁂

82.   NOVEMBER 15, 1848, DEVONSHIRE TERRACE
I kept the paper, until I had an opportunity of ascertaining whether the Chapman signature was *my* Chapman.[5] This house is cousin to *my* house. Having discovered so much, I return the document as you request.

I was at Shepherd's Bush yesterday evening, and went carefully over the Mark Papers already filled up, with Miss Cunliffe. She seems

---

[5] There were two Chapmans of Dickens's acquaintance, Edward Chapman (1804–1880), the burly senior partner in the firm of Chapman and Hall, his former publishers, and Thomas Chapman who was the senior proprietor of John Chapman and Company, merchants, of 2 Leadenhall Street, and chairman of Lloyd's Register of shipping. The two were not related to each other. Thomas Chapman in 1844 gave Dickens's youngest brother Augustus a clerical position in his firm. His character and importance in the business world are supposed to have suggested some of the traits of Mr. Dombey, in *Dombey and Son*. There is no way of telling which of the two Chapmans is referred to here.

to understand the system very well indeed, and I hope it will be productive of excellent results.

The great thing to avoid, and the danger towards which I certainly think we rather tend at present, is the being too grim and gloomy.

Miss Cunliffe thinks it would be well for her to select some little things from Wordsworth, and some from Crabbe, to read to them. Have you any objection to the introduction of these books, subject to her selection? I think the library might be extended, in this direction, with great advantage. All people who have led hazardous and forbidden lives are, in a certain sense, imaginative; and if their imaginations are not filled with good things, they will choke them, for themselves, with bad ones.

Mr Wardley came to me yesterday to say that Mr Duffy [6] (whom he represents as the impersonation of glowing disinterestedness) is anxious to "finish off" those young women who are likely to go soon; and that he would gladly, without any additional charge, extend *their* evening lessons by two or three hours a week. Will you let me know what I shall reply? I incline to the impression that it would interfere with other pursuits, without being attended with a counter-balancing advantage: but of course you only can decide.

The Haunted Man [7] says he thinks he will want a little fresh air shortly. I think of taking him down to Brighton next week for ten days or so, and putting an end to him.

∽

83.   NOVEMBER 18, 1848, DEVONSHIRE TERRACE

I return you the enclosed letter, which seems very promising and satisfactory. Between the Government and the Company, I hope we shall soon get this knot untied.

The poor courier is as comfortable and contented as it is possible for man to be. He recovered very considerably during the first two or three days, but, after that, began to go back a little.[8] These changes of weather, I imagine, are very much against that kind of complaint.

---

[6] Unidentified, but evidently a teacher employed to instruct the young women at the Home in some capacity.

[7] Dickens had begun *The Haunted Man* early in October, but had a good deal of difficulty in writing it. The third week in November, however, as the next letter announces, saw the end of these troubles, and the story was finished at Brighton on the last day of the month.

[8] The deterioration in Roche's health continued, and he died in 1849.

But better attention or greater kindness, he could not (thanks to you) by any possibility receive.

I had a very kind letter from Dr Wilson [9] who admitted him, and expressed warm interest in him — and I have no doubt I shall be told if he seem to grow much worse.

The haunted man won't do something I want him to do — or at least nothing would induce him to do it until this morning, when he suddenly seemed to become more tractable.

∽

84.   [NOVEMBER ? 1848] DEVONSHIRE TERRACE

I have seen Miss Coomes [1] this morning — she could hardly be called interesting, certainly, even in Newspaper reports, but she seems to understand her business.

She is to come out to Shepherd's Bush today, to see the place; and I impressed upon her, among other things, that she must try to come before next Monday week (the day she suggested) if possible.

I think we want a little more conciliation of manner and feeling, among our ladies. I doubt Mrs Holdsworth in that respect, but not Mrs Graves. Mrs Holdsworth always seems to me to have a secret idea that her charges are her natural enemies.

I think Ann Cattle (whom I have seen this morning) the best case we have yet taken. I should not have had the faintest idea from her appearance or manner that she was an applicant for admission.

---

[9] Otherwise unidentified.

[1] It can be inferred only that Miss Coomes (or Coombs as Dickens spells it in another letter) was a candidate for some position in the Home.

I I
Pinnacle of Fame

NEVER had Dickens's position been more unassailable or his renown more glittering than they were as the world approached the middle of the nineteenth century. He was not yet in his fortieth year. Though his novels were following one another less swiftly than in his amazing first five years, if there be thrown into the balance his acting and play producing, his enormous correspondence, the huge outlay of time and effort he gave to working with Miss Coutts, and the tremendous editorial labors that from 1850 on he devoted to conducting Household Words, *the weekly magazine that he then established, it is difficult to observe any slackening of his energies. And artistically he was at the height of his powers. Firmer in structure, deeper in intellectual grasp, sharper in social criticism, even imaginatively richer, his work assumed new dimensions of profound significance.*

And yet there is a nervous tension underlying all these vigorous activities that reflects a gnawing dissatisfaction. The dramatic productions followed one another in frenzies of distraction filled with galvanic euphoria, and as each came to an end Dickens subsided into black depths of gloom and despair. "I have no energy whatever, I am very miserable. I loathe domestic hearths. I yearn to be a vagabond." Both with his personal life and nineteenth-century society itself there was much that he found painfully amiss. He sought oblivion from his own distresses in furious feats of toil and play; he grappled with the state of society in constant criticism and constant efforts to repair its evils.

Something of what troubled his private life is symbolized in The Haunted Man, *the Christmas story he had just written for 1848. Like its hero, Redlaw, a distinguished chemist, Dickens is a famous and outwardly successful man. In the imaginative laboratory of his art, as in Redlaw's test tubes and retorts, there are hosts of spectral shapes* like those glass vessels with their chemicals, all subject to his power to uncombine and recombine. But like Redlaw he has known wrongs and sufferings from under the burden of which he cannot escape, until he wonders whether the years bring anything but "more figures in the lengthening sum of recollection that we work and work at to our torment."

"I am he," says Redlaw, "neglected in my youth, and miserably poor, who strove and suffered, until I hewed out knowledge from the mine where it was buried . . ." "No mother's self-denying love, no father's counsel aided me." It was unjust to Dickens's parents, but so he had always felt since the days in the blacking warehouse. "My parents," Redlaw continues, "at the best, were of that sort whose care soon ends, and whose duty is soon done; who cast their offspring loose, early, as birds do theirs; and, if they do well, claim the credit; and, if ill, the pity."

His experience has not made him hardhearted; he sympathizes with others and hastens to relieve those who are unfortunate. But would not both they and he be happier and better if they could lose their unfortunate weight of memories darkening every hour? Thus reflects Redlaw, taciturn, "shadowed by habitual reserve," a haunted figure, though still well-knit, with his "sunken brilliant eye" and "his grizzled hair." Thus, too, Dickens, so deeply reserved about his inmost feelings, despite the frank manner that seemed to reveal his every thought, and despite the vitality that flung itself with such gusto into every enjoyment. Even in physique he was no longer the almost girlishly beautiful figure he had been, but a mature man, coming to think of himself as middle-aged, with lines beneath the eyes, a glance that could be hard and unyielding, and hair beginning to recede above the brow.

In the story, Dickens has his hero realize that not oblivion, and not a corrosive brooding, but the strengthening and purifying influences of memory are the sources of self-conquest and peace of mind. It was a victory he did not find it so easy to achieve for himself. Perhaps only through a complete ventilation of his entire past and its conflicts, only by committing it to paper and as it were casting it out of himself, could he lay its unhappy ghost. He tried to write his autobiography, but found it too painful and gave it up. The part dealing with his childhood, through the blacking warehouse days and up to the time he was a schoolboy at Wellington House Academy, he did produce. But as

he came to the humiliations of his heartbroken love for Maria Bead-
nell, he found that he could not bear to go on.

Only in the disguised and fictional form of David Copperfield, *with*
many changes and omissions as significant as what he tells, could he
make confessional to the world. In that novel, however, one of his great-
est triumphs (and with Bleak House *one of the two peak achievements*
of this period of his life), he made a mighty and for the most part suc-
cessful effort at self-understanding. Into it he precipitated all the pain-
ful elements of his childhood and youth, facing the experiences that
had shaped him for good and ill, and striving to clarify his image of his
own character and fortune in life. David Copperfield *is Dickens tak-*
ing the measure of himself and of his world.

Marching no less vigorously than his self-analysis, his social insight
grew relentlessly deeper and more penetrating. He no longer saw the
problems of society as isolated from each other; they were all parts of
a dreadful pattern. Out of 61,000 offenders listed by the metropolitan
police statistics of 1847, he pointed out, 22,000 were totally illiterate,
and only a few hundred could do more than "blunder over a book like
a little child." "Side by side with Crime, Disease, and Misery in Eng-
land, Ignorance is always brooding, and is always certain to be found."
"Foul smells, disgusting habitations, bad workshops and workshop cus-
toms, want of light, air, and water, the absence of all easy means of
decency and health," were the causes of social evil. "To your tents, O
Israel! but see that they are your own tents! Set them in order; leave
nothing to be done there; and outpost will convey your lesson to out-
post . . ."

In Dombey and Son *he had for the first time portrayed society as a*
single interlinked system poisoned by the heartlessness of a money
ethic. In Bleak House, *which was immediately to follow* David Copperfield, *this same insight unifies the portrayal of the courts of chancery,*
the slum tenements of Tom-all-Alone's, Mrs. Jellyby's neglect of her
home for the natives of Borioboola-Gha, Mrs. Pardiggle's bullying of
the poor under the guise of concern for their welfare, Sir Leicester Ded-
lock's indignant surprise that there should be any question of the right
of his class to rule the country, and the parliamentary satire on Coodle
and Doodle. All of these details are simply symbolic devices for articu-
lating all the institutions of society, from government and law to phi-
lanthropy and religion, as a corrupt and entangled web of vested inter-
ests and power.

*The letters of this stage in Dickens's career reveal the growth of this
fierce preoccupation with the fundamental causes of society's problems at the same time that they show all the other activities of his life
continuing with unabated force. They record the vacations and the
theatricals — more frequent and more furiously indulged in than ever;
they reflect his ceaseless loving concern for his children; they reveal
the hurryings about England, the speeches before mechanics' institutes
and benevolent associations, the trips abroad; above all they detail the
constant collaboration with Miss Coutts on every variety of plan both
for helping the individual victims of misfortune and advancing the
social welfare. But under them spreads a steadily growing shadow of
angry disillusion with the social order itself that darkens the radiance
of success and fame.*

∽

85   [JANUARY 6, 1849] DEVONSHIRE TERRACE
    You are *perfectly right*, and I very much regret having given you
the trouble to convince me of it. I had a fixed idea that Mr Hullah's
account was £50; [1] and being just dull from a day's work, when your
kind enclosure came, could not get it out of my head. I have now referred to my memorandum, and find (as I might have known) not
only what it was intended for, but what it accurately tallies with.
    Charley's cake — a most splendid one — arrived an hour ago. He and
his two sisters instantly celebrated the event by putting it on a table
and dancing a polka round it.
    [P.S.] Maria Cridge will be back in a week. I begged Mrs. Morson [2] to
make some particular enquiries about her at the Hospital, and the
answers were *most satisfactory*.

∽

86.   JANUARY 11, 1849, DEVONSHIRE TERRACE
    I have been out of town since Sunday, or I would have answered
your letter sooner.
    I shall go to the Home on Saturday at 3. As that is often your day
for going there, perhaps I shall see you before I come away. I am very
glad that Jane Westaway and Martha Goldsmith are provided for, in

---

    [1] Hullah, it will be remembered, was providing music lessons at the Home.
    [2] Mrs. Morson will presently emerge as a new matron in the Home, but it is not
clear whether or not she was already employed there.

the Emigration regard. But I fear Julia Morley will become restless, if she be left behind.

I have thought, much and often, of that point in the little address, which encourages them with the *possibility* of marriage. I am quite satisfied and convinced that it is a powerful, and a justly powerful, incentive to patience and good conduct; and I can not, of my own deed, take it out of the paper. If they, or any of them, labor under any mistake on this point, I suppose it to be a part of Miss Cunliffe's business to set them right. You will not think me claiming much, if I claim to know much better than she does, or by any possibility can, what the force of that suggestion secretly is. I even think it — to say the truth — a little presumptuous in her, coming to the consideration of such things so freshly, to suggest the alteration — of its being an alteration enormously for the worse, I have no more doubt than I have of my writing this note with my right hand.

Charley had a very merry birthday [3] — I had the honor of conjuring for the party, in a Chinese dress and a very large mask — and his noble cake was the admiration and wonder of all beholders. We are at present engaged in getting up a play in a toy theatre. I am steeped to the very eyebrows in glue and paste.

∾

87. JANUARY 27, 1849, DEVONSHIRE TERRACE
I hope it was all well, yesterday. Nothing could have been better, more kindly, or more carefully arranged, I think.

Mr Illingworth [4] and I are to see the new girl No 2. today.

I am sorry to say that I have been brooding very gloomily over our Shepherd's Bush prospects. All possible deductions and allowances

---

[3] It was Charley's twelfth birthday and a festive one indeed. His two sisters, Mamey, who was almost eleven, and Katey, who had just turned nine, had taught their father how to dance the polka for the occasion. In the middle of the night before the party Dickens suddenly found himself afraid he had forgotten its steps, and leaped out of bed in the wintry darkness to practice on the cold floor. Numbers of "children of larger growth" had also been invited, including Captain Marryat, the author of sea tales, and Mrs. Macready, whose husband was again touring in America. Dickens wrote the actor a description of how they drank his health, "then dashed into a Sir Roger de Coverley—then into a reel—" and how, "for two mortal hours," he himself and Mrs. Macready "danced without ceasing . . . reducing to 'tarnal smash' (as we say in our country) all the other couples one by one. With grief and shame I own that at last I—I—gave in, when she was fresh and active still."

[4] Possibly Henry Stanhope Illingworth, surgeon, of the firm of Moore and Illingworth.

made, it is quite clear to me that Miss Cunliffe is a woman of an atrocious temper, and that she violently mistakes her office and its functions. I do not descry any prospect of our keeping the young women in the house, when she has the sole charge of them. The idea of hectoring and driving them, is the most ignorant and the most fatal that could be possibly entertained. I am quite confident she will bring about such an outbreak as we have not had there.[5]

∞

88.   FEBRUARY 5, 1849, DEVONSHIRE TERRACE

I was at the Home on Saturday, when I found Miss Cunliffe looking like a stage maniac in a domestic drama, or an illustration of "The Bottle" [6] on very bad paper. All that Mrs Holdsworth related of the three emigrants, interested and pleased me very much.

Will you not receive the new girl on Saturday?

What day in the week would you prefer for the single weekly lesson of Mr Hullah? I have promised to inform him.

Am I to pay the mark money into the Savings' Bank? If so, how much?

I think this is all I have to ask, touching Shepherd's Bush. I enclose Charley's memorandum to Christmas. Some time ago, you gave me a begging letter to make enquiry about, from one Mr Tolfrey, who represented himself as the author of a book, called The Sportsman in Canada. I am afraid it is not likely, in such an enormous correspondence as you have of that nature, that you can remember any more of it, or refer to it. But if you can, by any possible chance, do either, may I entreat you to do so, for a particular reason that I have.[7]

∞

89.   FEBRUARY 10, 1849, DEVONSHIRE TERRACE

I beg to report all quiet and comfortable at Shepherd's Bush this afternoon. Miss Cunliffe rigidly secluded in her own chamber — mak-

---

[5] Dickens's earlier favorable impression of Miss Cunliffe had become sharply modified.

[6] *The Bottle*, by George Cruikshank, 1847. During the earlier part of his career an enthusiastic drinker, climber of lampposts, and wallower in gutters, Cruikshank had by this time turned fanatical temperance reformer and was using the genius of his etching needle to serve that cause.

[7] Tolfrey is originally mentioned in Dickens's letter of September 17, 1845. His "particular reason" for recurring to the subject here remains unexplained.

ing a perfect Brougham [8] of herself in point of oratory, I have no doubt. In entering Isabella Gordon's case, by the bye, I incidentally found that the aforesaid Miss Cunliffe (but it is no matter, as she is going) had been already questioning her about her past life.[9]

∽

90.   MARCH 3, 1848, DEVONSHIRE TERRACE [1]
    I had gone to the Home when you called, and when I was very sorry to miss you — as was Mrs Dickens too, who was out walking.

Everything was orderly and comfortable; not the less so, by reason of Miss Cunliffe's taking herself off, very solemnly, in a fly while I was there.

I have a reasonably good little anecdote in reverse, of Rachael Bradley, whom I "booked" today. There was a simplicity in the circumstance that I thought a good omen.

In reference to Sir George Grey's [2] case, I have not the least doubt of the expediency of immediately taking it. His interest in it is very agreeable to observe. I know the Recorder of Birmingham (Mr Hill) and know him to be a man of good experience and discernment, and much kind feeling, in all these matters. I have no doubt he has well investigated the case.

---

[8] Henry Brougham (1778–1868), Baron Brougham and Vaux, celebrated statesman, jurist, scientist, and orator, defender of Queen Caroline 1820–1821, Lord Chancellor of England, 1830–1834.

[9] All such inquiries Dickens had strictly forbidden. See letter of November 3, 1847.

[1] Plainly so dated, as 1848, but it seems most probable that Dickens made a slip. March 3, 1849, was a Saturday, but March 3, 1848, a Friday, and the letter is also headed "Saturday evening." Furthermore, he and his wife spent the fortnight following February 29, 1848, in Brighton, from which there are letters showing that they were there on March 2 and 5, so that they would have been obliged to come up to London especially for the intervening two days if he were to go to the Home and she to be out walking when Miss Coutts called, as the first paragraph notes. The reference in the last paragraph to "the Coombses and the Cunliffes," with its suggestion that both these ladies had proved unsatisfactory, places the letter some time after the initial appearance of Miss Coombs in November 1848, and the reference in the second paragraph to "Miss Cunliffe's taking herself off" follows as the logical climax to the friction with her expressed in the letters of January 27, February 5, and February 10, 1849.

[2] Sir George Grey (1799–1882), who succeeded in 1828 to the baronetcy of his father, the third son of the first Earl Grey. Sir George Grey was prominent in Lord Melbourne's ministry, and worked for the emancipation of the slaves in the West Indies; he was Judge-Advocate General between 1839 and 1841, and in 1846 became Home Secretary under Lord John Russell, a post he held with only slight interruptions for the next twenty years.

The name of Mrs Tripp [3] is naturally a severe shock to me, but I try to bear it as I ought. I would suggest to you, seriously, that it would be most advisable for Mrs Holdsworth to remain in power for a fortnight after Mrs. T——p's arrival in London, and for Mrs T——p to go out there, three or four times a week, during that interval, to become acquainted with the place, and the young women. She and Mrs Holdsworth could not possibly clash then, and it would no doubt (from her own letter) meet Mrs T——p's convenience too. I think it scarcely probable that Mrs T——p could go into the place at once, suddenly deposing Mrs Holdsworth, and get on well. And this has now become such an important subject, after our experience of the Coombses and the Cunliffes, that I really should not be in any strength of hope, under less precautionary arrangements.

Will you think of this?

◦◦◦

91.   MARCH 13, 1849, DEVONSHIRE TERRACE

I think Mr Engelbach's idea of an Emigrant Ship in the Steerage Department, must be received with that amount of deduction which his connexion with an Emigration Company and his having become like the Dyer's hand, "subdued to what it works in", may properly warrant. I have no doubt myself that it is very bad, that Miss Morris [4] had no idea what it was, when she shipped herself with that order of passengers. I never was so much astonished in my life as when I saw the Steerage of an American Liner — *on the passage* — and I remember Mr Tracey's face assuming a most extraordinary appearance when I told him the young women were going in the Steerage of the Posthumous. [5] I mention this, as he is a naval officer of considerable experience, and universally respected.

At the same time I certainly am not at all agreeably impressed by

---

[3] Mrs. Tripp was being considered to replace Mrs. Holdsworth as the matron in chief authority, but this change did not occur. Dickens's "shock" was caused by the fact that "Tripp" or "Trip" was a nickname for Mrs. Brown — see his letter of June 1, 1852.

[4] Unidentified.

[5] So written, but surely a slip for *Posthumus* — "posthumous" would have strange and even ominous overtones as the name of a ship. Steerage conditions in the mid-nineteenth century were certainly horrible, but, as Dickens remarks, there were strong elements of discomfort for a passenger in any class, and young women from the Home who balked at the steerage might have a good deal of difficulty adjusting themselves to a raw pioneering life in Australia.

the letter the girls have written you. I doubt their delicacy very much indeed, and I think they should have undergone anything short of actual offence, before they dreamed of taking such a step. That about the washing is sheer nonsense. The best-provided passenger on board a passenger-ship, endures all kinds of inconveniences in that respect — and I question whether they will find themselves much better off at first, after they land.

No doubt the best course is that which you have taken.

The Bishop of London is a mystery I can't penetrate — unless they have got somebody else's books.

When I look at the style and orthography of these two letters, and call to mind Jane Westaway's too, I am emboldened to state to you an opinion I have been gradually forming of late, and which the abrupt disappearance of the estimable Trip has confirmed, that it would be sound and wise to *try* Mrs Holdsworth and a servant woman. I feel confident that under any more settled sort of administration there, she could teach the girls better than they have yet been taught, and enable them to do you and your great generosity and charity more credit than these results do. We are sure of her temper, sure of her good intentions, and sure of their (I mean the inmates) being prepared to like her. Moreover, she has a positive, practical, experience of the place. And I believe this combination to be more important, than any sort of flourish of trumpets with which anybody else could enter on the duty. For the plain, limited education that is required, I think she is competent; and in those other qualities without which the instruction of the best successor would be a dismal failure, I really consider her quite a remarkable person. Whatever my opinion is worth, it is worth so much the more for this — that I had no leaning towards her, at first, and have really come to like her without the least inclination to do so. Such restrictions upon the comings and goings of her children as you might think right, could be easily placed upon her, but I do not think it likely that — for the money — or for anything near the money — we shall ever find so unobjectionable a person again. And nobody would be more resolute against counselling you to spend more on this head, than I am; because I sincerely feel that it would be unjust and wrong.

I think with you that the habit of asking is a bad one, but I confess I would increase the quantity of writing paper. Some of them may have nobody to write to; but the separation even from so much Earth that they have been used to, is a tremendous one, and the feeling that they *can* connect themselves with England by a few pothooks, twenty times or thirty times instead of six or eight, is not an unwholesome one. Indeed I am inclined to believe it has its root in a sentiment that it is desirable, with a view to our future hopes of them, to encourage.

I am just going to bed with an abominable cold, and hope I may have written more intelligibly than I am able to speak.

∽

92.   MARCH 29, 1849, DEVONSHIRE TERRACE

As I believe you will give me credit for being very slow to intrude upon your generosity, I will say nothing more in defence of this application.

There has come to my knowledge a case, in which if you should feel disposed to render any assistance, I can answer for its being well bestowed. The object is, to help the family of the grandson of that Henry Goldsmith to whom Oliver dedicated the Traveller, and who is supposed to have been the original of some parts of Mr Primrose's character in the Vicar of Wakefield — a book of which I think it is not too much to say that it has perhaps done more good in the world, and instructed more kinds of people in virtue, than any other fiction ever written.

This grandson [6] has six sons and a daughter. On an income never exceeding two hundred a year, and for a great part of his life never exceeding a hundred and sixty, he has contrived to bring them up well (those that are grown) and to get two of them abroad as sailors, and another into the Naval School. He is a Lieutenant in the Navy himself, and now in command of a Revenue Cruiser; but the expences of his family, and in particular the having borrowed £50 for the outfit of one of his sons, have involved him in temporary distress; and unless he can clear himself, it is probable that he will be seriously damaged at the Admiralty.

I have a letter by me from his wife, which is very plainly and pathetically written, and which convinces me that lasting good may be done to a very deserving man, by a little money. A private subscription

---

[6] The grandson of Oliver Goldsmith's brother Henry was Lieutenant Charles Goldsmith (1795–1854), who later held the rank of commander in the navy. His elder brother Hugh Colvill Goldsmith (1789–1841) had also been a lieutenant in the Royal Navy, and had died at sea in the West Indies. A number of further letters, including that of July 21, 1849, make it clear that Miss Coutts responded generously to the story given here.

among some literary men is the only thing that occurs to me, as a way of raising the whole sum borrowed (the least amount, I take it, that would do him real service) and if you feel yourself justified in aiding it, I shall be very heartily sensible of your assistance.

Don't take the trouble to write, as I am to see you on Saturday. I think Mrs Morson *very promising.*

ক্ষ

93.   MAY 7, 1849, DEVONSHIRE TERRACE

Pending some further enquiries of Mr Tracey's, I have arranged to be at his prison on Wednesday at 12, to see a young girl of 16, whose case he hopes is a good one. The worst of it, is, that she is committed for six months, and has only been there three; but possibly we might get her sentence commuted, if the circumstances seem favorable. I will report to you after seeing her.

I want to ask you to give me your permission to put you down as a subscriber to a certain book of poetry price ten shillings. I have a horror of subscription-books in general, but the writer of this is Mr Charles Whitehead [7] (the author, some few years ago, of a very clever novel indeed, called Richard Savage). He has been struggling with poverty all his life, and resorts to this form of publication as a means of keeping his brother (a lunatic) another year in an asylum. I am much interested in helping him to good names.

ক্ষ

94.   MAY 16, 1849, DEVONSHIRE TERRACE

I send you, enclosed, a document relating to Mary Jones, which Mr Hill the recorder of Birmingham has sent me. I stated Mary Jones's case (as she puts it) in writing for him, that there might be no mistake, and at his request.

I am afraid her story is quite untrue. There is still a *possibility* of its being true, because there is a possibility of the neighbour represented to have seen her take money out of the till, being false. But the probabilities are very strong indeed against her.

---

[7] Charles Whitehead (1804–1862) was also the author of *The Solitary*, 1831, and *The Autobiography of Jack Ketch*, 1834. As editor of Chapman and Hall's "Library of Fiction" in 1836, he had invited Dickens to become a contributor and had published two of his sketches, "The Tuggses at Ramsgate" and "A Little Talk about Spring and Sweeps." Whitehead had been asked to provide the text for Seymour's etchings that developed into *Pickwick Papers*, but had feared himself unable to do the work and had suggested Dickens's name.

[P.S.] I have been at Shepherds Bush three times lately, and have seen a good deal of Mrs Morson and taken counsel with her in reference to a dispute between Isabella Gordon and Rachael Bradley. I have a very strong hope that she is exactly the person we have always wanted.

∽

95.   JULY 21, 1849, DEVONSHIRE TERRACE

When Mrs Goldsmith wrote that honorable letter about the money which you so generously sent her, I told her that if anything could ever be done for any of her children by speaking to anyone on her behalf, and she would tell me so, I would try my best to help to do it. Yesterday she wrote, emboldened by this, as follows:

"I most cordially desire to get our son William Burgess (who is now in the Royal Hospital School, Greenwich) into the Royal Naval School, New Cross, on the reduced or gratuitous list, as the instruction in this school is much superior to Greenwich. I enclose an abstract of the relative services of my husband's and my own family, to prove that we have some claim on the privileges of this excellent Institution."

That abstract, I send you with this.

"Or," she adds, "if we could succeed in securing a presentation to Christ's Hospital, for either of our younger boys — Hugh Colville, who was nine last February, or Edward, who will be seven next July, I believe the Travers foundation in Christ's Hospital is expressly for the sons of Lieutenants in the Royal Navy."

The last, I am afraid, is out of the question. But I have such an exalted opinion of this lady, founded upon the character her letters disclose, and the high sense of truth and honor she exhibited in that last transaction, that I venture to ask you whether, among the Powers that be, there is any one with whom you are on sufficiently friendly terms to ask the first favor from? I should conceive that it is a very slight one, and that the great name this lady bears, and her whole case altogether, would present a strong claim to any man of worth.

Will you write to me at Bonchurch? [8]

---

[8] On the Isle of Wight, where Dickens had rented, for this summer, a residence called Winterbourne, owned by the Reverend James White (1803–1862), a literary clergyman he had probably met through Macready, who had produced White's successful play *The King of the Commons* in 1846. Dickens and White had certainly been on cordial terms by that year, and when *Household Words* began its career in 1850, with Dickens as "Conductor," White became one of its regular contributors.

96. August 5, 1849, Winterbourne, Bonchurch, Isle of Wight

I sent up to town for the enclosed list (your note reaching me here, and not in Devonshire Terrace), and only received it this morning. I allude to the list of Vice Presidents etc of the Naval School.

Along with it, I send Mr King's opinion of Charley for the halfyear, and his usual memorandum. Charley is with us, of course. He did not seem to me to look at all well when we came down, and had a sort of faded air about him that made me think of taking him back again, for medical advice. But I think the place, and the being constantly in the open air, have done him a great deal of good. We have also discovered a small pony in the neighbourhood, which carries him about the Downs, very much to the improvement of his looks.

As I am at work on Copperfield,[9] and the going and coming between this and London is a work of time, I shall not come up to the next Committee; supposing (as I hear nothing from Shepherds Bush) that everything is going on well. Have you had any conversation with Mrs Morson about that unlucky Drain, which has resulted in her not writing to me, after seeing a workman on the subject, as I arranged with her that she should? I have been expecting, every day, to receive a letter from her, and cannot understand (except on this supposition) why she has not done as we distinctly arranged. I am very uneasy about its remaining in its present state (it is so extremely dangerous to health) if anything reasonable can be done with it.

I hope the troublesome affairs which keep you in town, may be progressing as favorably as such affairs ever can or do. I hope too that Mrs Brown's "temper" is better, in respect of that monthly trial to which it is unhappily subjected.

It is delightful here, though rather cold. You will be sorry to learn, for I think you know and like him, that I had a letter from Jeffrey[1] the day before yesterday, in which his description of his present state of health is such that I fear he will live but a short time longer. I have the greatest affection for him; and if I should receive any confirmation or aggravation of this account, should go away to Edinburgh, if it were only for an hour, to see him once more.

Is there any intelligence of any of our emigrants?

[P.S.] I find that Charley's documents have a most unaccountable smell of medicine about them, which I hope will evaporate in the Post office.

---

[9] Publication of *David Copperfield* in monthly installments had begun in May 1849 and continued till November 1850.   [1] Lord Jeffrey.

97. AUGUST 12, 1849, WINTERBOURNE, BONCHURCH, ISLE OF WIGHT

Very many thanks on Charley's behalf. He has quite recovered his good looks, I am happy to say, and is climbing about the whole neighbourhood all day long.

I am not guilty of the cherries. But I am so fond of that place,[2] that I almost wish I were. It will be quite an event in my life to see it from the inside after knowing it, outside, so long. Let me congratulate you on getting at last into your present Selkirkian position in reference to it.

I think with you about the Cape, and hold that nothing could be better or more to the purpose than the Bishop's letter (enclosed).[3] The letter from the girls (also enclosed) looks very well indeed.

I am sorry, but not surprised, to hear of Isabella Gordon. I should have come to town on Tuesday, but for my friend David,[4] who has a tight hold upon me at this distance, but will release it for the month (I hope) next day. Will you ask Mrs Morson, if she be expelled, to write and tell me exactly *how she goes away*. I have a particular reason, as a point of experience, for asking this, and for hoping that she will observe her behaviour particularly.

By a letter I have received from Mr Tracey this morning, I learn that he has a case of which he thinks very well, and which he is anxious we should take. I have written back to inform him that we shall be glad to receive the girl on his recommendation. Her term of imprisonment has expired, and she is now "staying back," with a view to the Home. I have also begged him, as Isabella Gordon came from his Prison, to attend on Tuesday if he possibly can.

I cannot recollect the exact pedigree of Mrs Goldsmith's family, in connexion with our dear friend. My impression, is, however, that her

---

[2] Holly Lodge, Highgate, the suburban residence north of Hampstead Heath that Thomas Coutts, Miss Coutts's grandfather, had purchased for his second wife, Harriot. She had willed it to her second husband, the Duke of St. Albans, for the duration of his life, but when he died on May 27, 1849, it became the property of Miss Coutts. Her "Selkirkian" retreat there is an allusion to Alexander Selkirk, the eighteenth-century sailor whose four-year solitude on the island of Juan Fernandez inspired Defoe's *Robinson Crusoe*. The reader can guess as well as I what Dickens means by being "guilty of the cherries" — A gift? A depredation?

[3] Robert Gray (1809–1872) became the first Bishop of Capetown when Miss Coutts endowed that diocese in 1847. His communication, clearly in connection with the Home, probably bore upon the possibility of South Africa as one of the colonial goals of its graduates.

[4] *David Copperfield.*

husband is the grandson of the brother to whom he dedicated the deserted Village.[5] But I have written home for a letter, in which the fact is stated — shall receive it here on Tuesday morning — and will write to you again, on Tuesday night.

The only point I should be particularly careful about, if I were at the Committee on Tuesday, would be to ascertain beyond all question that the charge against Isabella Gordon is an undoubted matter of fact, and does not originate in any league against her.

~

98.   AUGUST 15, 1849, WINTERBOURNE, BONCHURCH, ISLE OF WIGHT
Many thanks for your note. I answer it hastily, with the postman in waiting.

If I come to town at all before I return for good, I shall hope to be initiated into the beauties of Holly Lodge. But ever since I have been here, I have been quite unwell with a monstrous cold, which has now resolved itself (for a change) into a cough like "the faithful watchdog's honest bark."

Mrs Goldsmith's husband *is* the grandson of the brother to whom he dedicated the Traveller. My mind misgives me that I said "deserted Village" the other day. He is the Grandson of the identical clergyman "passing rich with forty pounds a year," [6] whom Oliver admired and loved.

[P.S.] I am all in suspense about the wretched Isabella Gordon.

~

99.   AUGUST 30, 1849, WINTERBOURNE, BONCHURCH, ISLE OF WIGHT
The sense of the question is so clearly stated in your letter received yesterday, that I have no doubt it will be best for Charley to go first to Eton, and then (for the professional conclusion of his education) to King's College. I know Dr Hawtrey,[7] who is head master at Eton.

---

[5] Dickens meant *The Traveller*, as he guiltily explains in the next letter.

[6] *The Traveller* was dedicated to the Reverend Henry Goldsmith, but the quotation is from *The Deserted Village*, 1.142, where it is part of the description of the poor clergyman.

[7] Edward Craven Hawtrey (1789–1862), scholar, educated at Eton and King's College, Cambridge, who edited Goethe's lyrics 1833–1834, made translations of Italian, German, and Greek verse, and published a translation of Homer into English hexameters 1843. He was assistant master at Eton under Keate 1814–1834; as headmaster 1834–1852 he nearly doubled the numbers of its students. He became provost in 1852, and was the last person buried in the college chapel.

I also know (and so does Mr King) Mr Evans [8] the water-color painter, who is drawing master at Eton; who is in great repute among the other masters, and very popular with the boys. He has, for some years, been one of the masters who receive boys in their houses; and I have no doubt that Charley will be happier and better watched in his house, than he could be at any Dame's. I should be quite at ease about him, if he could be placed there. Mr Chitty,[9] the special pleader, has had two sons with him, both much distinguished at Eton, and found him (I know from himself) everything that could be desired. Therefore, if you please, when I come to town, I will go down and see Dr Hawtrey, and Mr Evans, and ascertain every particular that we should desire to know. In the meantime I will write to Mr King, and beg him to prepare Charley specifically for Eton at Christmas. Mr King has a plan of his own, about the Latin Grammar, which will have to be departed from with a view to that school.

I hope you will tell Mrs Brown (as some claim upon her charitable consideration) that I have never forgiven my father and mother, and that my possession of those names [1] is a secret which I had thought Tortures would never extract from me. The superscription of your letter (though delicate and kind, as all you do is — being limited to the initials) greatly shocked me, and is supposed to have affected the Postman; who looked haggard this morning.

In the matter of that unfortunate young chartist, I have done what you kindly empower me to do. I quite agree with you as to the principle of such a subscription, and must add that while I feel for many working men who are chartists and mean no ill by it, I have no sympathy for the amateur members of that body.[2] But I have no doubt that in this instance the money will do good.

---

[8] William Evans (1798–1877), who frequently exhibited with the Society of Painters in Water-Colours; drawing master at Eton 1818–1827 and housemaster 1840–1877.

[9] Possibly a son of Joseph Chitty (1776–1841), the famous special pleader, author of many treatises on the law, with whom Dickens's friend Talfourd had studied.

[1] The awful "secret" was that Dickens's full name was Charles John Huffham Dickens — Charles for his grandfather, Charles Barrow; John for his father; and Huffham — so misspelled in the church register — for Christopher Huffam, his godfather. Dickens never used the additional names after his adolescence.

[2] Dickens had a good deal of sympathy even for the program of the Chartists: manhood suffrage, annual Parliaments, vote by ballot, abolition of property qualifications for election to Parliament, payment of its members, and division of the country into equal electoral districts. But he had no sympathy for the "physical

I hope Isabella Gordon is justifying the clemency that has been shewn her.

With many thanks for your excellent advice, believe me Dear Miss Coutts

~

100.   SEPTEMBER 7, 1849, WINTERBOURNE, BONCHURCH, ISLE OF WIGHT
    I am greatly mortified to hear from Mrs Morson of what has happened at Shepherd's Bush. Though it is a great comfort to me that the girl is a new girl and not one in whom we have trusted and been long deceived. I have told Mrs Morson that I hope she will lay stress, in speaking of it to the others, on her not having had the benefit of the Home's instruction and advice for any length of time.

I do not make out, from Mrs Morson's letter whether the wardrobe from which the girl took the bonnet and shawl, was locked *and the key taken away* — in short whether she forced it open. If she did anything *but* force it open, I think there was, so far, a little remissness on Mrs Morson's part. I have repeatedly cautioned her on that subject, and warned her to leave nothing open, or about. The always having some one or two of whom we know very little, is the best reason in the world to the general body for this.

I hope we have, generally, gone on so well since Sarah Wood, that you will not be much discouraged by this circumstance. I can hardly imagine how any one can be so wantonly and ungratefully wicked, but such things are, outside the Home, and will be, I am afraid, for many a long year.

I acknowledge the receipt of Lord Fitzroy Somerset's [3] letter, immediately.

[P.S.] What does Mrs Brown say? I must go (I think) and ask the Lime Burner [4] what *he* says to it.

---

force" Chartists who were ready to invoke violence to secure their demands, and although he could excuse laboring men who saw no other course open to them he felt impatient of gentlemanly "amateurs" who joined the movement. Who was the "unfortunate young chartist" mentioned in this letter I do not know, nor for what purpose the money was given him.

    [3] Lord Fitzroy Somerset (1788–1855), youngest son of the fifth Duke of Beaufort, who had been aide-de-camp to Wellington at Vimeira and was wounded at Waterloo. He was secretary at the Horse Guards 1827–1852, and then succeeded Wellington as commander of the forces, at which time he was made Baron Raglan. He commanded in Crimea, 1854–1855. There is no indication of what he was writing to Dickens about.
    [4] Unidentified.

101. NOVEMBER 6, 1849, DEVONSHIRE TERRACE [TO DR. WILLIAM
BROWN]

We had a Committee at the Home today, when we transacted the
usual business, and I paid all the bills. Mr Chesterton, Mr Illingworth,
and Mr Tennant were there with me.

I made them acquainted with the contents of the Bishop's letter
from Adelaide,[5] which made upon all of them, as it had previously
done upon me, an impression of heavy disappointment and great vexa-
tion. God send we may do better with some of the others! (I must
claim, once more, to have been never a believer in Goldsmith. And I
think the Bishop's emphasizing marriage as their only chance of reclamation, most important. That idea I have steadily had in view, always.)

We found that Isabella Gordon was endeavouring to make a party
in the house against Mrs Morson and Mrs Macartney [6] — was disturbing the general peace again — and intended coming to us with
complaints. We investigated them with the utmost care, confronted
her with Mrs Morson, and were convinced that her whole story was
utterly false and malicious. We ordered her to her room while we considered the subject, and she danced upstairs before Mrs Morson, holding her skirts like a lady at a ball.

We were all of opinion that the authority of the place *must* be up-
held — especially after the receipt of such news from abroad as the
bishop's letter put us in possession of — and that however repugnant
to our own feelings it might be, our duty to Miss Coutts and her be-
neficent undertaking *must* be discharged, and could only be discharged
in one way. We therefore had her down again some time afterwards,
and, to her utter bewilderment and amazement and that of the whole
house, dismissed her.

Hannah Myers, who was unquestionably in concert with her, we
spoke to in like manner, and confronted with both ladies. Her whole
statement was evidently false, and her malignity against them (for the
time) very intense and passionate. We informed her that after such
conduct she could have no marks whatever for a week, and that she

---

[5] Augustus Short (1802–1883), who was made the first Bishop of Adelaide, in
Australia, when it was endowed by Miss Coutts in 1847. "Goldsmith" refers to
Martha Goldsmith, one of the girls from the Home, mentioned in a number of
previous letters, and among those sent to Australia. The Bishop's letter must have
reported her as having fallen back into her former way of life.

[6] Mrs. Macartney was another matron at Urania Cottage.

would, on the first repetition of such behaviour, be inexorably dismissed. She was not in the least prepared for this, and was quite as much amazed as the other.

A girl of the name of Sesina, lately come from Mr Tracey's, and who I am persuaded is the pertest, vainest, (preposterous as the word seems in such a connexion) and most deceitful little minx in this town — I never saw such a draggled piece of fringe upon the skirts of all that is bad — was the third party. I gave this young lady to understand, in the plainest and most emphatic words, that she appeared to us to misunderstand the place — and its object. That she must thoroughly change her whole feelings and demeanour, and put on a very different character, and conduct herself towards both the superintendents as a new creature altogether, if she had the least hope of remaining. My impression is that she will *not* remain; and I have no doubt, after taking her history and observing her closely while she tried to gloze it, that it will be much better for us if she goes away.

It was five o'clock, and dark, when we had got to this. As it was quite impossible to say what Isabella Gordon might or might not do if she were left alone with them, Mr Chesterton and I remained there, until she went away. As she had no clothes she departed, of necessity, in those she had on, and in one of the rough shawls. We gave her half a crown to get a night's lodging, and directed her to a certain charity where she is *sure* to be taken in if she chooses, and if she means to work. Her going away, was a most pitiable sight. They all cried bitterly (Mrs Morson and Mrs Macartney included) and Rachael Bradley held to her skirts as she went out at the door, and implored us to let her stay and to give her one more trial — sobbing and weeping terribly. The girl herself, now that it had really come to this, cried, and hung down her head, and when she got out at the door, stopped and leaned against the house for a minute or two before she went to the gate — in a most miserable and wretched state. As it was impossible to relent, with any hope of doing good, we could not do so. We passed her in the lane, afterwards, going slowly away, and wiping her face with her shawl. A more forlorn and hopeless thing altogether, I never saw.

It has made a great impression on the rest, unquestionably. How long it may last, Heaven knows. As I know you will report this, all, to Miss Coutts I do not write to her about it, — the rather as I am in a dull state myself, just before going to bed, with the whole of the sad picture in my mind. Pray convey my best remembrances to Miss Coutts, and to Mrs Brown.

I am glad to receive your hopeful and interesting account of Paris. I have heard here that the Legitimist party *are* plotting darkly in the desperate hope of setting on the throne another of that ill-fated and incapable House. You see no signs of that, I suppose?

∽

102. NOVEMBER 7, 1849, DEVONSHIRE TERRACE [TO DR. WILLIAM BROWN]

As a sequel to my letter of last night, I write to let you know that at half past eight this morning Mrs Morson came here in a fly to tell me that little Sesina had been very insolent last night, and had been ordered to her own room; and that this morning she positively refused to get up, or to return any answer whatever, to any of the remonstrances that were made to her. In consequence of her behaviour they had kept the gardener in the house all night — a precaution at which I could not help laughing, when I thought of its object being a little dumpy atom of a girl whose head may be somewhere on a level with Mrs Macartney's waist.

I directed Mrs Morson to go back, give her her own clothes, and tell her she was to dress herself, and leave the place directly; or that when I came, in half an hour, if I found her still in bed, or found her there at all, I should send for a policeman and give her in custody for being there without our consent and making a disturbance. On receipt of this message she parleyed a little, and, after making a slight pretence of being ill, threw her nightcap to one end of the room and her nightgown to the other, and proceeded, very leisurely, to dress herself. On coming down stairs, she objected that she couldn't go away in the rain, on which she was told that she had better sit in the long room then, 'till I came. Declining this offer, she walked off. I met her in the lane, taking her departure. Before she went, she told Mrs Morson "that she know'd Miss Coutts's address, and would write her a good long letter, telling her what treatment was had there." I passed her afterwards, walking in a jaunty way up Notting Hill, and refreshing herself with an occasional contemplation of the shop windows.

All the rest were very quiet, and Hannah Myers was very much subdued. My belief is that this Sesina will join Isabella Gordon some-where, today. I think she would corrupt a Nunnery in a fortnight.

∽

103.   DECEMBER 6, 1849, DEVONSHIRE TERRACE
I trouble you with this note, to put you in possession of what I had not a suitable opportunity of saying today.

I have given the best consideration (as you may suppose) that I could possibly give, to the alternative you so kindly mentioned to me on Sunday, for Charley.[7] I hope my anxiety may not have obscured my judgment, but I think his first destination, better than the cadetship. I need not explain to you that my position is too public and prominent a one to leave me much hope of ever being rich. I cannot but consider, mainly, in what position Charley would be most likely to be of service to his sisters if I were dead. I think he would be far more likely to have a beneficial influence on them, and on all who might have to look up to him to sustain their name in honor and respect, if he took the chances of being within reach which a regiment of the line would give him, than if he went for so many years to India.

Again, I think your friendship and his own name would be of far greater service to him in our Army, than they could be in the Indian Army — where he must be, to some extent, lost to the great English World. If he should be a clever man, I think his ability would be likely to stand him in better stead here, than in India. His education and companions would be of more use to him, too, here, than there. Lastly, I think his life would be (under God) infinitely safer and more to be hoped for, — as he, and all our children, have shewn, so far, a peculiar sensitiveness to heat when the English summer has come round.

I am so sure of your generous interest understanding, on a mere hint, all I would say, that I say not a tithe of what I think. If I had any reason to believe that you have the least inclination towards the Cadetship in preference to the other idea, I should feel an uneasiness in coming to this conclusion, though I must still think it the right one. But I do not understand that to be the case.

---

[7] Miss Coutts, as the following paragraph indicates, must have suggested that she might use her influence to obtain Charley's nomination to a cadetship leading to a commission in the Indian Army, instead of one in a line regiment. Dickens, of course, was thinking of Charley's position as that of the eldest son, who would naturally become the head of the family. The younger sons might go into the Army, the Navy, or the law, or emigrate to the colonies — as Dickens's younger sons in fact did.

I shall be very, very, glad, if you, on consideration, think with me. [P.S.] In reference to Mrs Morson and the Mark Papers. — I think — if I took the latter home every week and looked into them at my leisure, I could form a pretty certain judgment — knowing their construction and intention — whether she was doing right, and, if not, where she was wrong. Do you see any objection to this? If not, perhaps when you speak to her you will suggest it.

ᢙ

104. DECEMBER 7, 1849, DEVONSHIRE TERRACE

I will not attempt to thank you for your most kind note; for no words I could use, would do it. I am sure it is because you know in some degree how much I feel the value of your inestimable friendship, and of what a load it lightens me, and what an accession it is to the happiness of my life, that you give me such extraordinary proofs of your goodness and regard.

For Charley's next brother, Walter Landor, now nine years old, I never could desire to do a better thing than you propose. He is a tougher subject than Charley, not so quick or sensitive, a hardworking, patient capable child, better fitted in all respects for such a life, and much more safely to be left to himself. I feel certain he would strive on and do well in India; and that Charley nearer home, as the eldest of so many children (to say nothing of his mother, who might live long after me) would have a good influence upon him, and upon himself, and upon all the rest.

He is at Mr King's, doing very well indeed. For a child of his age, he already knows a good deal. And I don't think I can do better than leave him there, until the Haileybury [8] time comes on?

I shall be very glad to have the talk that you propose about the marks. I thought about them a good deal, coming home yesterday, and I feel that they may be very much improved. Would this evening do? If I *don't* hear from you, I will come at 8. If I *do* hear from you that you are engaged, will you choose between next Tuesday, Wednesday, or Thursday?

---

[8] Haileybury College, near Hertford, one of the principal public schools, originally founded, in 1805, by the East India Company, for the education of civil service students. Dickens was confusing it, as is shown by his letter of January 10, 1850, with the Company's military college at Addiscombe, near Croydon.

105.   CHRISTMAS DAY 1849, DEVONSHIRE TERRACE
The best and truest wishes of the time, to you and all who are dear
to you!

I should have mentioned Hullah's account to you before, but was
unwilling to trouble you. It is five and twenty pounds (I think). I
will pay it tomorrow.

As I have engaged to go to Eton with Charley, to spend the day, on
Tuesday the first, I propose (if you have no objection) to hold our
Committee Meeting on Monday, the last day of the old year.

I was at the Home on Saturday for some time, making up the book
— and shall be there again tomorrow. Everything was going on well.
Mrs Morson has such a small son in blue coat boy's clothes, that he
looks like a toy. He ought to have a little wire handle just below his
shoes, to make dismal music when turned round.

Mr Cooksley,[9] Charley's tutor at Eton, has written a very handsome letter about him to Mr King. And Mr Hardisty the clergyman,
under whom he is learning to make those verses every day, has written to Mr Evans, praising Charley highly.

I hope your accounts of poor Mrs Otway Cave [1] may improve. When
I see you, I will give you the latest Mon cher intelligence. It has been
of a threatening character, but I hope has become pacific.

With best regards and wishes to Mr and Mrs Brown,
P.S. The man who alone executed the whole of the nefarious Howitt
imposition, is, I have ascertained, one Mr Youls.[2] He wrote a begging-
letter to you once, in his own name, and I made some enquiries about
him for you. I am afraid you gave him some money then. He is a
most abandoned and wicked thief, but he had not begun this career
at that time.

106.   JANUARY 1, 1850, DEVONSHIRE TERRACE
Many many happy years to you and all who are dear to you!

---

[9] William Gifford Cookesley (1802–1880), classical scholar, assistant master at
Eton, educated at Eton and King's College, Cambridge, who edited Pindar, Catul-
lus, Propertius, Ovid and Tibullus, and Caesar's *Gallic War,* and published a
translation of the New Testament.

[1] I cannot identify Mrs. Otway Cave or explain the meaning of "the latest Mon
cher intelligence."

[2] William Howitt (1792–1879) was a poet and miscellaneous writer who was
deeply interested in the supernatural, investigated haunted houses, and experi-
mented with table turning and thought transference. Mr. Youls's "nefarious imposition" may have been in these fields.

The enclosed note is indeed a delightful one to begin a new year with. Looking back on the history of your noble effort — especially with this added light — I sincerely think it has prospered as well as our most hopeful anticipations could have reasonably encouraged us to believe. — Don't you?

I was there, yesterday, alone in my glory. I enclose the bill book. I paid all the accounts set down in it, and there is a sum of twelve shillings to add to the total, for a Diary for the New Year for Mrs Morson. I saw all the girls as usual, and looked over the Mark Tables. In one or two instances where I thought them not perfectly correct, I told Mrs Morson so, and explained why. There were no complaints, and everything was quiet. The drain's in progress at last. Mrs Morson brisk, Mrs Macartney useful. Mrs Morson's hair in the old places, with reference to her eyebrows.

I went into the bonnet question with her — only with *her,* for I think she exercised a sound discretion at the time of the mysterious business, in affecting not to suspect. I have little doubt but that two among them contemplated a move — not that day, but before the following Sunday. I mistrust the smaller Glyn as having been one of the two. I have no reason for it, but her supernatural mildness — and a certain queer look that was trying to get back into her eyes before it came out.

I enclose Charley's "documents." His tutor writes me very highly of him, and he is first in his department. He is going to Rockingham [3] with us on Tuesday, for a country run of ten days or so. After which,

---

[3] Rockingham Castle, in Northamptonshire, was the residence of the Honorable Mr. and Mrs. Richard Watson, who had become Dickens's friends during his stay at Lausanne in 1846. Watson (1800–1852) had been a liberal Whig M.P. in 1832, and supported Earl Grey in bringing about the passage of the Reform Bill. His ancestral home was a thirteenth-century structure surrounding a great court entered by an archway between two bastion towers; its keep and terraces suggested Chesney Wold in *Bleak House.*

Dickens tremendously enjoyed this holiday. On the last night of his visit there were private theatricals, conjuring, and country dances in the great hall lasting until three in the morning. Dickens played Sir Peter Teazle in some scenes from *The School for Scandal* and the scene from *Nicholas Nickleby* in which the deranged old gentleman on the garden wall makes passionate declarations of love to Mrs. Nickleby. "To see . . . a blushing sleek-headed footman produce, for the watch-trick," he wrote his friend Forster, "a silver watch of the most portentous dimension, amidst the rapturous delight of his brethren and sisterhood; was a very pleasant spectacle. . . ."

his Mama will avail herself of your kindness, and write to ask for the box at Drury Lane.

I have sent your Copperfield to Stratton Street.

◦◦◦

107. JANUARY 10, 1850, DEVONSHIRE TERRACE

What you suggest to me to say to Mrs Gaskell [4] about the girls and the passage, I wrote to her yesterday. All the rest that you so kindly write, I will make known to her tonight.

Addiscombe is the military college – Haileybury, the civil. Walter Landor, as a cadet, will have to go, I take it, to the former.

Mr Hardisty is *not* Charley's Tutor at Eton. He is a clergyman here – one of the Curates of St Giles's in the Fields – to whom, as an old Etonian, his Eton tutor wished him to go, in the holidays.

I will be very particular to ascertain exactly how he goes on, and what he is doing, during the first three months. I will go down pretty often for the purpose. I do not think there is much fear of their *over-working* him, as it is not a very ferocious school.

If you should remain at Brighton after the twenty second or twenty third, and should encourage me to do so, (by a silence on the subject) I hope to call one morning.

Charley sends his love. And I, a thousand thanks.

◦◦◦

108. JANUARY 14, 1850, DEVONSHIRE TERRACE

I send you a letter I have received from Mrs Gaskell this morning (to whom, with your permission, I sent the first sheet of your letter) by which you will see what she has done. She is perfectly discreet and modest, and I knew would take no advantage of your kindness.

I left Charley at Eton, on Saturday evening. I dined with his tutor. Evans's boys had not come back, and he looked dull enough, in a big hall with an immense fireplace, by himself. But he made no sign

---

[4] Elizabeth Cleghorn Gaskell (1810–1865), novelist, author of *Mary Barton, Cranford, North and South,* and other novels dealing with the factory workers in the manufacturing districts, whose work made an enormous impression on Dickens. The latter two of these novels and many other stories of hers were first published in *Household Words,* the weekly periodical edited by Dickens, of which the first number appeared on March 30 of this year.

of shrinking, and left here, amidst a prodigious wailing from his brothers and sisters, like a man.

I hope this note may be intelligible. But I am in such a state of imbecility from a bad cold, and am so little able to see the paper on account of the enormous size of my own head, that I am not at all clear about it.

ᐁ

109. JANUARY 8 [1850], 121 UPPER RUMFORD STREET, MANCHESTER [FROM MRS. GASKELL TO CHARLES DICKENS]

In the first place I am going to give you some trouble, and I must make an apology for it; for I am very sorry to intrude upon you in your busy life. But I want some help, and I cannot think of any one who can give it to me so well as you. Some years since I asked Mr Burnett [5] to apply to you for a prospectus of Miss Coutts' refuge for female prisoners, and the answer I received was something to the effect that you did not think such an establishment could be carried out successfully anywhere, *unless connected with a scheme of emigration, as Miss Coutts was.* (As I have written it it seems like a cross question & crooked answer, but I believe Mr Burnett told you the report was required by people desirous of establishing a similar refuge in Manchester.)

I am just now very much interested in a young girl, who is in our New Bayley prison. She is the daughter of an Irish clergyman who died when she was two years old; but even before that her mother had shown most complete indifference to her; and soon after the husband's death, she married again, keeping her child out at nurse. The girl's uncle had her placed at 6 years old in the Dublin School for orphan daughters of the clergy; and when she was about 14, she was apprenticed to an Irish dress-maker here, of very great reputation for fashion. Last September but one this dress-maker failed, and had to dismiss all her apprentices; she placed this girl with a woman who occasionally worked for her, and who has since succeeded to her business; this woman was very profligate and connived at the girl's seduction by a surgeon in the neighbourhood who was called in when the poor creature was ill. Then she was in despair, & wrote to her mother, (*who had never corresponded with her all the time she was at school*

---

[5] Henry Burnett, the singer, who was married to Dickens's sister Fanny and who lived in Manchester.

and an apprentice;) and while awaiting the answer went into the penitentiary; she wrote 3 times but no answer came, and in desperation she listened to a woman, who had obtained admittance to the penitentiary, solely as it turned out to decoy girls into her mode of life, and left with her; & for four months she has led the most miserable life! in the hopes, as she tells me, of killing herself, for "no one had ever cared for her in this world;" — she drank, "wishing it might be poison," pawned every article of clothing — and at last stole. I have been to see her in prison at Mr. Wright's request, and she looks quite a young child (she is but 16,) with a wild wistful look in her eyes, as if searching for the kindness she has never known, — and she pines to redeem herself; her uncle (who won't see her, but confirms fully the account of the mother's cruel hardness,) says he has 30 £ of her father's money in his hands; and she agrees to emigrate to Australia, for which her expenses would be paid. But the account of common emigrant ships is so bad one would not like to expose her to such chances of corruption; and what I want you to tell me is, how Miss Coutts sends out *her* protegees? Under the charge of a matron? And might she be included among them? I want her to go out with as free and unbranded a character as she can; if possible, the very fact of her having been in prison etc to be unknown on her landing. I will try and procure her friends when she arrives; only, how am I to manage about the voyage? and how soon will a *creditable* ship sail; for she comes out of prison on Wednesday, & there are two of the worst women in the town who have been in prison with her, intending to way-lay her, and I want to keep her out of all temptation, and even chance of recognition. Please, will you help me? I think you know Miss Coutts. I can manage all except the voyage. She is a good reader, writer and a beautiful needle-woman; and we can pay all her expenses etc.

Pray don't say you can't help me for I don't know any one else to ask, and you see the message you sent about emigration some years ago has been the mother of all this mischief. Will you give my love to Mrs. Dickens & Miss Hogarth [6] & believe me

[P.S.] I have not told you one incident about the poor girl. Her seducer was lately appointed assistant surgeon to the New Bayley Prison; and as Pasley was not quite well she was sent for for him to see her. The matron told me when they came thus suddenly face to face, the girl just fainted dead away, and he was so affected he had to sit down, —

---

[6] Georgina Hogarth, Dickens's sister-in-law, who was a member of his household.

he said "Good God how did you come here." He has been dismissed
from his post in consequence. The chaplain will guarantee the truth
of all I have said. She is such a pretty sweet looking girl, I am sure
she will do well if we can but get her out in a *good* ship.

૦૪૭

110.   JANUARY 12 [1850], 121 UPPER RUMFORD STREET, MANCHESTER
       [FROM MRS. GASKELL TO CHARLES DICKENS]

   I am exceedingly obliged to you for what you have done about my
poor girl. I return you Miss Coutts' letter (which I only received late
last night). She is really and truly kind, for she has taken the trouble to
think of several plans, and her suggestions are very valuable. As she
is out of town, I have written off at once to the forewoman at Silvers',
choosing out the plan which seemed to me the most desirable, — i.e.
placing the girl under the charge of some respectable family (of the
working-class if possible). If Miss Kaye should not know of any one,
then, if you will allow me, I will write again to ask Miss Coutts,
through you, if she will kindly write to the Plymouth ladies, of whom
I never heard before — I have already received kind offices from Mrs.
Chisholm [7] in helping out a family of emigrants, but I thought she required those whom she assisted to be of unblemished character. Miss
Coutts is very, very kind — for she evidently thinks as she writes, of
what can be done. — My head & eyes ache so, with crying over the
loss of three dear little cousins, who have died of S. Fever since I last
wrote, leaving a childless mother, that I hardly know how or what I
write, but will you thank Miss Coutts as you know she will like best.
Of course I never named her name at Silvers'.

   The girl herself is in a Refuge — a literal refuge for any destitute female without enquiry as to her past life being made; — all are received, and not classified, so it is a bad place, but what can we do?

---

   [7] Mrs. Caroline Chisholm established the Family Colonization Loan Society in
May 1850, with the support of Lord Ashley, Sidney Herbert, and other influential
people. Its purpose was to aid poor persons desirous of emigrating to Australia.
In the same year she published her *A.B.C. of Colonization*. Dickens certainly vis-
ited the Chisholms' house at 3 Charlton Crescent, Islington, and he published in
Household Words a number of articles and stories about Australian emigration for
which Mrs. Chisholm supplied the material, as well as an article in the issue of
August 24, 1850, describing in some detail the operations of the Society and praising Mrs. Chisholm. Between 1850–1854 the Society sent 3000 emigrants to
Australia.

I am going to see her today to keep up & nurse her hopes & good resolutions.

My best love to Mrs. Dickens and Miss Hogarth.

ᛣ

111.   JANUARY 28, 1850, DEVONSHIRE TERRACE

I return you the two letters from the Cape (with which I have been greatly pleased and also M. Soyer's plan.[8] I send too, the Diary for Mrs Brown's eventful chronology, (which cannot now be got un-ruled) Sydney Smith's book,[9] the two emigrant books, the Shepherd's Bush red book, and a memorandum of what I have paid on the Home account. Likewise (what an enormous catalogue!) Charley's memo-randa in a separate envelope. You will see that Mr King proposes to make a deduction for the time (during the cholera) when I kept Charley in the Isle of Wight. I did not think it just to allow of this generosity in Walter's case, and perhaps you will think that the de-duction ought not to be allowed in Charley's either.

Soyer's scheme, like everything he does, has a certain amount of good sense and good purpose in it, with a considerable infusion of puffing and quackery. I think the scheme of teaching young ladies domestic economy, *admirable,* but to exclude the system of daily classes to which they could go, and from which they could come home, seems to me absurd. "The Mansion," and the musical instruments, and all that, is very well for the dignity and renown of the name of Soyer, but would make the thing ridiculous — and a failure besides. I conceive that the model of the thing should be, Mr Hullah's classes. Young ladies at such an hour, and on such terms. Servants, or improvers, or whatever he likes to call them, at such another hour on such other terms. For a couple of hours together, or whatever period he might

---

[8] Alexis Benoît Soyer (1809–1858), famous chef, the Mirobolant of Thackeray's *Pendennis,* who left Paris in 1830 for the service of the Duke of Cambridge and became chef at the Reform Club in 1837. In 1847 the Government asked him to take charge of the soup kitchens established in Dublin, and in 1851 he opened a restaurant, the Symposium, in Gore House, formerly the residence of Lady Bles-sington, to cater for the visitors to the Great Exhibition. During the Crimean War, in 1855, he went to Scutari, reorganized the victualing of hospitals, introduced cooking wagons, and became the leading authority on military and naval cooking. He was the author of several books on cooking, including a *History of Food in All Ages,* 1853. What the present plan was, Dickens's letter sufficiently explains.

[9] Sydney Smith's book was probably his *Lectures in Moral Philosophy,* published in 1850.

choose to make it, they could be practically shewn, in a sort of hall-kitchen made for the purpose, every useful household duty, in a regular course of exposition. There could be no harm in connecting with this, a residence for those young people who should come from the country, but the two branches (to make the scheme thoroughly useful) should be distinct. This learning could be very easily imparted to numbers at once. And I am sure I should send my own daughters to acquire it, if they were old enough.

All is well at the Home. I write in haste, having been there until nearly dinner-time.

With best regards to Mr and Mrs Brown

∽

112.   FEBRUARY 4, 1850, DEVONSHIRE TERRACE

I will immediately apply myself to getting all the information you want. It fortunately happens that I have already directed the gentleman of whom I spoke the other day (as the person to whom I had entrusted the active business management of the new design)[1] to see the writers of those pamphlets, and confer with them on the practicability of our doing something useful, in the Periodical, on the subject of emigration. In sending me those books, they wrote me a very earnest letter, expressive of their desires to become contributors on that subject. I will ascertain exactly what kind of man the brother now here is (for I fancy the Bushman brother has gone back again), and will take care, if there should seem to be the least doubt about him, to keep you in the background while the information is obtained. Everything connected with the expences of a vessel, I will have ascertained as if for the purposes of the work; and as this gentleman of mine is an extremely careful, methodical man, and a great part of his office is to get facts together, I have no doubt the result will be perfectly reliable.

The perusal of those books, and the knowledge they give me of a state of society of which one could have no previous understanding, and which would seem to be quite misunderstood, or very little known, even in the cities of New South Wales itself, leads me to much the same conclusion as it leads you. I am not quite sure that perfect peni-

---

[1] I do not know what the "new design" was, or to whom it was entrusted, although it clearly had something to do with Australian emigration. Nor can "the Bushman brother" be identified. The periodical is, of course, *Household Words*.

tence in these women — in the best of them I mean — would lead them in all cases not to marry; for I can certainly (I think) descry a kind of active repentance in their being faithful wives and the mothers of virtuous children; but in all other respects I most entirely concur with you.

To prevent your being committed in any way to new prison cases (of which Mr Tracey had one, the other day, while Mr Illingworth had, I believe, one or two in contemplation) I announced at our last meeting that you had decided to change the character and object of the Home.

I shall be very glad indeed to talk with you on the sad subject [2] to which you have — with a moral bravery which you must forgive my saying I cannot enough respect — directed your thoughts. It is difficult to approach, in pages that are intended for readers of all classes and all ages of life; but I have not the least misgiving about being able to bring people gently to its consideration. You will observe that I am endeavouring to turn their thoughts a little that way, in Copperfield. And I hope before I finish the story, to do something strongly suggestive, in that kind of preparation.

Will you tell "the General Objector," [3] with my best regards that I sent her that ruled Diary, because in consequence of the men of business (so inferior to the women of business!) objecting to plain Diaries, the Manufacturer now makes none of the last mentioned description? I knew she had a ruled one already, but I thought she wanted two volumes — one as a kind of day book, — for that eventful existence of hers, and the other as a Ledger, into which the entries were to be "posted." I wonder whether she would listen to any liberal proposal for a series of extracts from her journal, for my new Miscellany! We might call them "Passages in the life of a General Objector" — or "Scraps of my daily observation. By a shrewd Woman." If you think this literary adventure might be accomplished, perhaps you would use your influence!

I was going to consult you about names for the thing, the other day — but forgot it. What do you think of the proposed one, which I write

---

[2] Prostitution, in the character of Martha Endell, in *David Copperfield*, who had already been introduced and who was to recur again in the story. In the very next number of the book, too, Dickens was to deal with Steerforth's seduction of Little Em'ly and their flight from Yarmouth.

[3] A facetious nickname for Mrs. Brown, with whom Dickens frequently argued on all sorts of subjects.

underneath? It is the profoundest secret and most mighty mystery, except to you and Mrs and Mr Brown.

"Household Words"

A Weekly Journal

Designed for the instruction and entertainment of all classes of readers.

Conducted by Charles Dickens.

"Familiar in their mouths, as Household Words"

Shakspeare

∽

113.   MARCH 4, 1850, DEVONSHIRE TERRACE

The Colonial letters are certainly discouraging; but less so, having the girls here, than if we had sent them out.

I return Sir W Napier's letter.[4] It is a very good and characteristic one, and has interested me very much.

I dream of Mrs Chisholm, and her housekeeping. The dirty faces of her children are my continual companions.[5] I forgot to tell you that she asked me if it were true that the girls at Shepherd's Bush "had *Pianos.*" I shall always regret that I didn't answer yes — each girl a grand, downstairs — and a cottage in her bedroom — besides a small guitar in the wash-house.

∽

114.   MARCH 6, 1850, DEVONSHIRE TERRACE

I have been working away so hard, at these Household Words, that I am going to Brighton tomorrow for a fortnight, to pursue Copperfield in peace. My address is, 148 King's Road. I shall be at 16 Wellington Street North,[6] on Saturday at 3.

---

[4] Probably Sir William Francis Patrick Napier (1785–1860), military historian and general, who had been with Sir John Moore at Corunna, fought in the Peninsular campaign, and written *A History of the War in the Peninsula*, published 1828–1840, and *A History of the Conquest of Scinde*, 1844–1846. I have no information about his letter.

[5] Although Dickens supported Mrs. Chisholm's emigration projects, it is clear that her domestic arrangements suggested those of Mrs. Jellyby, in *Bleak House* two years later, a lady who neglected her family while she wrote innumerable letters devoted to furthering the colonization of the banks of the Borioboola-Gha in Africa.

[6] The offices of *Household Words*.

I mention these interesting particulars, in case you should want me for anything.

You will be pleased to hear, I know, that Mr Cooksly gave us, yesterday, a most brilliant account of Charley. He says he is a frank ingenuous boy, "who wears his heart upon his sleeve" — that work is no trouble to him, and he always does it admirably — that he has never had any pupil in whom he has been so warmly interested — and that he is fast becoming one of the most popular boys at Eton.

With kind regards to Mr and Mrs Brown

∽

115.   APRIL 1, 1850, DEVONSHIRE TERRACE

We held the Committee, last Tuesday. There were no complaints, and all was going on well.

The monthly book (including fire insurance, gardeners salary etc) was £44 . . 1 . . 11½, in addition to which I have given Mrs Morson, she having no money, £5 for petty cash. Her salary and Miss Macartney's being due, I should have paid them also, but that I was not sure whether you would prefer to pay them yourself. Shall I do so, now?

I enclose Mr Evans's account of Charley's expences at Eton, with the vouchers belonging to them. Some of the charges, you will see, belong to the commencement of his career there. I have a sort of half doubt whether I ought to send them all to you, but as they are all included in the one statement I decide to do so.

∽

116.   APRIL 12, 1850, DEVONSHIRE TERRACE

I return the Bishop's letter. It really puts one in heart again. I do not think *upon the whole,* after all, that we have been very unfortunate or have much reason to be discouraged.

Myers was tried the other day at the Middlessex Sessions for a felony, and found guilty. She begged very hard to be transported, and probably would have been gratified, but that Mr Chesterton, not thinking her gratification advisable under the circumstances, exerted himself against it with the Judge. She is at Mr Tracey's for twelve months.

I cannot think of any better plan for finding inmates for the Home, than getting a room near the Magdalen on their receiving-days, and seeing the girls whom they cannot take in. Will you think of this? In the course of my nightly wanderings into strange places, I have spoken to several women and girls, who are very thankful, but make a fatal and decisive confusion between emigration and transportation. In this, as in everything else, this country suffers frightfully, and will suffer more, from ignorance. It is astonishing and horrible to find how little education (worthy of the name in any respect) there has been among the common people.

The Household Words I hope (and have every reason to hope) will become a *good property*.[7] It is exceedingly well liked, and "goes", in the trade phrase, admirably. I daresay I shall be able to tell you, by the end of the month, what the steady sale is. It is quite as high now, as I ever anticipated; and although the expenses of such a venture are necessarily very great, the circulation much more than pays them, so far. The labor, in conjunction with Copperfield, is something rather ponderous; but to establish it firmly would be to gain such an immense point for the future (I mean my future) that I think nothing of that. It is playing havoc with the villainous literature.

What a stock of objections Mrs Brown must have got up against it by this time!

There is a Mr Forster on the Morning Post, but he is a very different man from my Forster.[8] My Forster distinguished himself a good deal in the Edinburgh Review, and wrote, for many years, the Literary and Dramatic criticisms in the Examiner. Since Mr Fon-

---

[7] *Household Words* did become a good property. In its first year of publication its clear profits were over £1700, rising the following two years to £2000 and £2200. Its average weekly sales came to be around 36,000 to 40,000. Its career came to an end only when, in 1858, Dickens merged it with the even more successful *All the Year Round*.

[8] John Forster (1812–1876), editor, historian, and biographer. From 1836 on, he was Dickens's closest friend. He studied at University College, London, and was called to the bar at the Inner Temple in 1843; meanwhile he had become dramatic critic of the *Examiner,* then under the editorship of Albany Fonblanque. Forster succeeded him in the editorship 1847, became secretary to the Lunacy Commission in 1855, and was made one of the commissioners in 1861. He wrote lives of Oliver Goldsmith, Walter Savage Landor, Sir John Eliot, and Dickens. As a critic he wielded an almost Johnsonian authority. Bulky, brassy-voiced, dictatorial, and touchy, his social demeanor inspired the character of Podsnap in *Our Mutual Friend;* but although he quarreled repeatedly with all his closest intimates he was also loyal, affectionate, and capable of unlimited services in their behalf. From the fifteenth number of *Pickwick* on there was no work of Dickens's that he did not see in manuscript or in proofs, making innumerable suggestions and often shouldering the labor of the proofreading. As both friend and critic, he did yeoman's work in helping and defending Browning, Carlyle, Landor, and Tennyson. His large and valuable collection of books, manuscripts, paintings, drawings, and engravings was bequeathed to the nation, and is housed in the Victoria and Albert Museum at South Kensington.

blanque [9] has held a place in the Board of Trade, Mr Forster has been the Editor of that Paper. He has no other connexion with that very uncomfortable Engine which is popularly called "The Press."
The Bush Salaries were £15 . . 4 . . 6

⌒

117.   APRIL 17, 1850, DEVONSHIRE TERRACE
Last night, Mrs Morson being out and Mrs Macartney at home, that very bad and false subject, Jemima Hiscock, forced opened the door of the little beer cellar with knives, and drank until she was dead drunk; when she used the most horrible language and made a very repulsive exhibition of herself. She induced *Mary Joynes* (!) to drink the beer with her; and that young lady was also drunk, but stupidly and drowsily. Mrs Morson, with the gardener's assistance, wisely abstained from calling in the Police, got them both to bed, locked them up, and came to me this morning.

Being obliged to write all day, I told her to go back straight, and immediately discharge Jemima Hiscock — to put her on her own clothes, however bad — and on no account to give her any money. As to Mary Joynes, to keep her in disgrace, until I should get out there this afternoon, and enquire further into the matter. They had both confessed to these particulars.

I have no doubt myself, that they had spirits from outside. I am perfectly sure that no woman of that Jemima Hiscock's habits could get so madly intoxicated with that weak beer. I am inclined to think, from the difference in the states of the two, that she had spirits and Mary Joynes had not. A woman was seen looking over the palings where Hannah Myers and Ellen Walsh broke out; and from certain circumstances and artifices recently observed in Jemima, I am strongly impressed with the belief that she was in communication with people outside, and wanted to lay hands upon the linen on the first convenient opportunity, after it was washed and ironed.

This same woman made the most pious pretences of any in the place,

---

[9] Albany Fonblanque (1793–1872), journalist, before twenty a successful contributor to the newspapers, and from 1826 the principal leader-writer for the *Examiner,* which was recognized as the chief organ of intellectual radicalism. He was intimate with Bentham, Mill, and Grote, and a contributor to the *Westminster Review* from the time of its establishment in 1823. From 1830 to 1847 he was editor of the *Examiner*. His best articles were collected in a volume entitled *England under Seven Administrations*. Dickens made over a score of contributions to the *Examiner* 1838–1849.

and wrote the most hypocritical letters. I am afraid Mr Illingworth makes grave mistakes, in attaching undue importance to this prostitution of Religion. He believed her when she made a pretence of having seen somebody she had known, in church, and wishing to stay away. I thought it (knowing the girl's antecedents) a piece of unmitigated falsehood. I have no doubt of her having had a design to make off, after robbing you. There are strong reasons to bear out this notion.

And now what on earth is to be done with Mary Joynes? I really think Sir George Grey [1] ought to know this. And I would most strongly suggest to you that nothing ought to induce us ever to retain a woman whom we have seen reason to discharge. In every case in which we have shewn this vacillation (Ellen Walsh and this Jemima Hiscock being the two last) the end has been failure. And God knows how they infect the rest.

∽

118.   APRIL 25, 1850, DEVONSHIRE TERRACE

I am sincerely concerned to find from your note that you have been so much troubled and annoyed of late, and I confess I feel a selfish kind of dissatisfaction, that you should be in a difficulty, and one of your most attached and zealous friends unable to be of any use to you in it. I hope it is past and gone. In that case, I shall be interested in the story, whenever you will tell it to me.

Mr Brown will have told you what we did today. I am more indignant with that Mary Joynes, than I have ever been with any of them. For I now believe Matthew Hill, and utterly discredit her story about her case. I had already made the enquiries you suggest, into the Beer question, and asked the girl if she supposed we were such Idiots as to deem it possible — I would not say probable, but possible — that they could have taken beer enough to produce that effect. I have not the least doubt that spirits were handed over the wall.

What do you think of a very big dog in a barrel, at that part of the garden? Mrs Morson would always know, then, of a stranger on the other side.

I have let the field for five months, for cows and a pony to graze in, to a very respectable neighbour — at least he appears so. He is a

---

[1] The Home Secretary. But why he should be told of Mary Joynes's beery intoxication, unless perhaps he had recommended her admission to the Home, cannot be explained.

married gentleman of steady aspect, and has what he calls "a Milk Walk," in the vicinity.

My best regards to Mrs Brown, whose better health I was very glad to hear of, from her (of course) worser half, today.

Household Words I shall report of, when I see you in peace and quiet again.

[P.S.] I administered a mild dose of dissatisfaction to Miss Templin to-day. I am afraid she is deceitful.

თა

119. AUGUST 1, 1850, DEVONSHIRE TERRACE

It is extraordinary to me, — but I cannot find anyone who knows Mr De Lara.² I have enquired among artists, great and small — among theatrical people — among the gentlemen engaged at Household Words, who I should have thought almost certain to have some trace of such a man — but quite unsuccessfully.

Of course I have been careful to give no clue to my reason for asking about him.

I cannot say that I think his second letter very good, yet there is something in his first that looks real. I need not say, of course, that I will see him with pleasure if you wish it. But I have not thought it right to do so, without your instructions — or to ask Ackermans, or Moon,³ to whom he refers, and both of whom I know. I have abstained, because of the reference being in his letter. Shall I make enquiry in one of those two quarters? If you say yes, I can do so in a morning. Will you let me know?

Yesterday, I went to the Westminster Ragged School, but, though I went by appointment, the Master was not there. It is an awful place, in a maze of filth and squalor, so dense and deserted by all decency, that my apparition in those streets in whose heart it lies, brought out the people in a crowd. We were on a very good understanding, however, and some people to whom I talked, took occasion to admire my diamond ring. I left word for the master to come to me, but I greatly doubt our finding any cases there, that will do. They are so low and wretched.

I went to look at the church, and I cannot tell you how pleased I

---

² A begging-letter writer who represented himself as a lithographer and artist.

³ Ackermans I have not identified, but J. G. Moon was a magistrate at the Guild-hall, and later, in 1853, an alderman.

was with the little garden. I am confident of the humanizing influence of a few leaves and flowers in that place. They will suggest to the commonest mind that you wish to please the poor, and will make a thousand people think about you, who might not be addressed otherwise.

I return Mr De Lara's letters, but have made a note — like Captain Cuttle [4] — of his address.

120.   AUGUST 14, 1850, DEVONSHIRE TERRACE

I was about to come down last night, agreeably to your kind remembrance of me, to be delighted by the genius of that matchless actress whom you so much admire, when I was waylaid by a parcel, in dimensions like a spare bed, containing "doubtful articles" for Household Words, on which decision was necessary to the peace of mind of the writers. As my days are taken possession of by Copperfield, I had no alternative but to sit down and have them read to me. And extremely dreary they were — all with a drone of imitation of myself in them, which pervaded the whole parcel, as the Anabaptist strain does the opera.

I believe Mr Elliot is not known by name to Bentley's Miscellany. That would not invalidate his story, of itself, as he might have written something in an assumed name. But I am quite confident that I know his handwriting; and I have a strong impression, either that it is the writing of a man who wrote begging letters for years under the name of Collins, or that it is the writing of another man, and a great Impostor, against whom I once appeared at a Police Office. I feel certain that I know the character, well; and the contents are quite in the regular style. I would not answer the letter, if I were you.

I retain it for a day or so, that I may ask my printers (whom I shall probably see today) about the two references. Even supposing them to have authorized that use of their names, I believe they are of doubtful weight.

I enclose Charley's accounts.

There are two suggestions I wish you would consider, relative to Shepherd's Bush. If they cannot, with that small number, do the washing of themselves, then, I think a woman should be hired to come and help — which would teach the girls. To put the washing out,

---

[4] Captain Cuttle, in *Dombey and Son,* one of whose favorite observations was, "When found, make a note of."

seems to me a great mistake of Mrs Morson's. If they cannot bake, somebody should come and help (and teach) in that work too, I think. But I would not let them buy bread, with that oven there.

∽

121. AUGUST 23, 1850, 16 WELLINGTON STREET NORTH – STRAND; OFFICE OF *Household Words*

I am at Broadstairs with my various children – real and imaginary – and only got your kind note there, yesterday. Today I am here on business – and shall go back, tomorrow.

Reverting in my mind to the Ragged Schools before I left town, and reviewing the mental portrait I brought away with me of the only girl I saw, at all likely to suit us, I *could not* make up my mind to take her, as the matter stands. I feel sure you would agree with me, if you saw the case and all its accompaniments. I have thought it best to write to the Secretary (who is out of town) and gravely point out to him the immense importance of what you propose to do, and of their trying to take advantage of it in a proper manner. The teachers at those schools, though devoted to their uninviting work, are so narrow-minded and odd – and the whole thing (which might be so good) is such a scramble [5] – that unless they exert themselves and interest themselves zealously in a case, I really think we ought not to take it, even if we could find it. They seem to have no idea of the value of such help as your taking one or two would be.

Do you recollect promising me a note to the Librarian at the India House? And will you send it to me at Broadstairs?

I am happy to say that Mrs Dickens is in a noble condition,[6] and that Household Words is taking its ground vigorously.

With regards to Mr and Mrs Brown, believe me ever

[P.S.] There are several cases (which I have gone into) preparing, from Mr. Chesterton; and I dare say Mr Tracy will be heard from soon.

∽

122. AUGUST 31, 1850, DEVONSHIRE TERRACE

I this afternoon saw four girls – attendant at the Field Lane Ragged School – whom I think we may try. I am not sanguine about them all

---

[5] Compare with the opinion of the Field Lane Ragged School and its teachers that Dickens expressed in his letter of September 16, 1843.

[6] Catherine Dickens had given birth, on August 16, to their ninth child, Dora Annie (1850–1851).

(if I am, in any strong sense of the word, about any of them) but I think they represent a class, fairly, and are worth the experiment. They all appear pretty strong and healthy. The youngest is 15; the oldest "going on," as she says, "for 19."

I promised to take two, Ellen Glyn and Emma Spencer; and have sent the necessary instructions to Mrs Morson about the clothes etc, with the tidings that she may expect them on Wednesday afternoon. They have all been in the Clerkenwell Workhouse. Both are terribly destitute and wretched. Each assured me, separately, that she in no sense belonged to the class from whom the greater part of our inmates have been taken. I cannot say that I quite believe this, but I have no other reason to doubt it, than the suspicion which their faces awaken within me. One is 17; the other 15. I don't know, from their stories, how they very well could have been less wretched than they are. Neither has been in prison.

I thought it best — that they might attach due value to the Home — not to *promise* the two of whom I am now going to write, that they would be taken. I said I would represent their cases to you, and I hoped you might think it well to try them, but could not answer for it. One of these, is Charlotte Glyn, the sister of Ellen, long in attendance on a dying mother (the teacher has constantly seen her there) and now occupied in waiting for this mother's release by Death from a most forlorn and abject state. I did not think it well to ask this girl the question I usually put. It is probable that what I doubt in the other cases, may be true in hers.

The last of these unpromised two, is Mary Anne Wilson: a desolate creature without father or mother. This is she who is "going on for 19." She answered me plainly, and said she had been about the streets for a year. I believe she told me the whole truth. I should like to give her a trial, in consequence. She would be a robust strong girl, after a little regular food and shelter.

I arranged with the teacher that in taking the two accepted ones to the Home on Wednesday, she should ask Mrs Morson if the other two were to be received; and, if Mrs Morson said "Yes," she should bring back their clothes. Therefore, if you object to them for any reason, perhaps you will tell Mrs Morson so, *before Wednesday*. If you try these two, as well as the two first, I think you will give the Ragged-School class of objects, a very reasonable trial indeed.

As I am going back to Broadstairs tomorrow morning, I write all this long rigmarole in order that the business may be all arranged as if I were here.

The Raven sends you his duty. He says (with a respectful croak) that if all the people who were attentive to the Nepaulese were like you, he should have nothing to remark upon. But he must take the liberty (he adds) of considering you as a very different person indeed, in all things, from the crowd of their admirers. He hopes you may have read an article called The Paper Mill.[7]

My regards to Mr and Mrs Brown.

[P.S.] I trust I shall be able to get to Shepherd's Bush next Thursday, about mid-day.

∽

123.   SEPTEMBER 6, 1850, BROADSTAIRS, KENT

I was in town yesterday, or I should have written to you.

Anticipating the possibility of your being away from home, I had told Mrs Morson that if she did *not* hear from you to the contrary, she should inform the Ragged School teacher when she brought the two promised girls, that the two unpromised were accepted. Therefore there was no hitch in the matter, in any case.

I shall now be obliged to remain here without going to town, until I shall have got through the next Copperfield. I have written to Sir Robert Campbell [8] to thank him for his kindness, and to say that I shall have the honor of calling on him in a fortnight. I have thanked him, of course, for his courtesy expressed through you. — I never thank *you* for all your recollections of me; they are so many.

It would be a great thing for all of us, if more who are powerfully concerned with Education, thought as you do, of the imaginative faculty.[9] Precisely what you say in your note, is always in my mind

---

[7] Neither the first nor the second of Dickens's ravens — the first died in 1841 and the second in 1845 — but a purely fictitious bird whom Dickens sometimes used as an imaginary satiric commentator on affairs. See "Perfect Felicity in a Bird's-Eye View," "From the Raven in the Happy Family," *Household Words*, April 6, May 11, and June 8, 1850. I cannot explain the reference to "the Nepaulese." "The Paper Mill," in *Household Words*, August 31, 1850, is merely a lively account of the process of manufacturing rags into paper.

[8] Unidentified.

[9] The neglect of feeling and imagination, as readers of *Hard Times* will recall, was one of Dickens's chief criticisms of both the theory and the practice of the educational reformers who were creating English popular education. He approved of Kay-Shuttleworth's efforts to build a school system and train teachers, but Mr. Gradgrind conveys his judgment on Kay-Shuttleworth's idea of the nature of edu-

in that connexion. The three best houses for childrens' books, are Arthur Hall, Paternoster Row — Grant and Griffiths Saint Paul's Churchyard — Darton & Co Holborn Hill. Tegg of Cheapside, also published a charming collection of stories, called The Child's Fairy Library — in which I had great delight on the Voyage to America. I have begged my printers to see whether the Houses I have mentioned, publish catalogues. They doubt whether the usages of "The Trade" apply to these little books; but if there be such things, they will get them for me, and I will immediately send them on to you.

Charley has grown two inches since the receipt of your message relative to his commander in chief. He is as brown as any boatman here, and goes back to Eton tomorrow week.

Will you tell me, at your leisure, whether I shall try to get a number of little books for you to select from — and when?

∽

124. Sᴇᴘᴛᴇᴍʙᴇʀ 13, 1850, Bʀᴏᴀᴅsᴛᴀɪʀs, Kᴇɴᴛ
Not being able (on account of my work) to go to town when the last Committee Day came round, and knowing you to be away too, I told Mrs Morson not to call the usual meeting, but to write to me, and send me the papers. I enclose the book. I have added (at her request) £5 for petty cash, to the total, and paid it. I am sorry to say that the Ragged School girls seem (on her report) desperately unpromising. If they fail, we shall have tried 'em — and made an end of 'em!

Miss Payne, their teacher, addresses the enclosed to you, and sends it to me to forward. I am afraid you will not find it agreeably expressed — she seems to me to be always blowing a shrill set of spiritual Pan's pipes — but she is earnest, though bitterly in want of sound teaching for the office of teacher.

I have requested Bradbury and Evans, if they can get a quantity of those little books from "the Trade", to send them, for your inspection, to Stratton Street.

In about a week or so, when I hope to have finished the current Copperfield, I shall come to town for a day, and carry a severe countenance into the Bush.

---

cation; and Mr. M'Choakumchild was drawn directly from the Educational Board's questions for the examination of teachers. Dickens's letter to Miss Coutts, July 11, 1856, has another expression of his objections to a purely utilitarian and factual education.

125. SEPTEMBER 22, 1850, BROADSTAIRS, KENT

I have told Mr Brown how I came not to answer his kind note on your behalf, in due course.

I went to Shepherd's Bush yesterday, where I found Mrs Morson very hopeful — the Ragged School Girls apparently improving — and decidedly much changed for the better, in their appearance. Before going out there, I went to the Office of the Commissioners of Sewers in Greek Street, and delivered a most pathetic and moving address on the subject of the Drains — at which the Surveyor was so much touched, that he engaged to go out there, immediately, and then "communicate with" me, here. Notwithstanding the vague nature of this repentant promise, I have hopes that we shall shortly (though not, I am afraid, without incurring some expence) remove that nuisance. At any rate, as the affected Surveyor said, "The premises must be relieved." And what kind of relief is proposed, I will let you know, after I have been "communicated with."

As I shall soon be sitting down to my final wrestle with Copperfield, and as it takes some time, I am afraid I shall not be able to attend at Shepherd's Bush, on the next regular Committee Day. Would you wish the Committee to be holden on that day? Perhaps you will let me know. Mrs Morson asked me, yesterday, and I told her I would ask you.

Mr Charles Knight [1] considered it expedient to withhold the greater part of your gift to that Mr Devlin [2] (after consulting with me) until he was sure of its doing him some good: otherwise, he had made up his mind to return it to me. But Mr Devlin is now going to America; and (although I find it difficult to understand how *that* can do anybody good) we have descried hopefulness in giving him the rest. I mention this, in case he should write to thank you, and you should wonder why he does so, now, instead of long since.

---

[1] Charles Knight (1791–1873), author and publisher of various cheap series of books condensing the information in voluminous works, editor and part proprietor of *The Guardian* 1820–1822, publisher for the Society for the Diffusion of Useful Knowledge, produced the *Penny Magazine* 1832–1845, the *Penny Cyclopaedia* 1833–1844, the *Pictorial History of England* in parts 1837–1844, and the *Pictorial Shakespeare* in parts 1838–1841. In 1844 he began a "weekly volume" series, and in 1847 a series of "half hours with the best authors." His *History of the Thirty Years' Peace,* completed by Harriet Martineau, was published in 1851, and his autobiography, *Passages of a Working Life,* in 1864–1865.

[2] Unidentified.

OCTOBER 23, 1850, BROADSTAIRS, KENT

...ished Copperfield, and don't know whether to laugh

Will you look at these two letters (No 2, in answer to an enquiry of mine, after the receipt of No 1) and tell me whether it shall be done? If you will write to me, at home in town, I shall probably get your letter the sooner. I have an idea of wandering somewhere for a day or two — to Rochester, I think, where I was a small boy — to get all this fortnight's work out of my head, but I shall be at home soon. [P.S.] I beg my regards to Mr and Mrs Brown. I hope "She" will like the close of the story — to say nothing of *You!*

∽

127. NOVEMBER 8, 1850, 16 WELLINGTON STREET NORTH — STRAND [OFFICE OF *Household Words*]

I have come here from Shepherds Bush, just in time for Post.

Mrs Morson tells me she has written you an account of the disaster — very unexpected; for I was there on Tuesday, when all seemed prosperous and thriving. I found, in addition to what she had told me, a purse of Mrs Macartney's gone, containing half a crown. It seems that it may have been taken out of her drawer at any time since Sunday (when she saw it last) but how, remains a mystery; for she declares it has been always locked, and that the key has been always, as it is now, attached to the key of the gate. I have directed all the beds to be narrowly and secretly examined this evening while the girls are in the long room — in case it should have been taken and secreted by any one but the runaways.

I find this curious circumstance in the case, which makes me a little suspicious of some one — I don't know whom — still in the house. Davis slept by herself; Humphrys in the room on the first floor. It is remarkable that the key which happened to fit Mrs Morson's Wardrobe, was not taken out of that little press in that bedroom, but out of the other press in the upstairs bedroom — and yet, when I bethought myself of trying if the key in Humphries first floor room, would open the same wardrobe too, I found it would! — From which I rather conclude that some one sleeping in the top-room must have found out that use for the key there, and told Humphries. Because, if Humphries had been prowling about, to make that discovery for herself, it is reasonable to suppose that she would have begun with the key most ready to her hand and eye.

I will write to you on Monday, in reply to your kind note received yesterday. At present I am in a mighty state of indignation — and the Post presses. I have instructed the Police to take the girls up, if they can find them, as I am confident that the example would be better than any precept. I ought to tell you that I have narrowly investigated everything, and that I cannot conclude that any blame attaches, either to Mrs Morson or Mrs Macartney.

∽

128. NOVEMBER 24, 1850, DEVONSHIRE TERRACE

Those wretched girls who robbed the Home, *gave themselves up, last night,* at a Police Station in the City. Going to Shepherds Bush just now, I found that the Police had just been there, requiring Mrs Morson to be at the Mansion House at 12 tomorrow.

After thinking about it, I have adopted the following course, which I hope you will deem the best that such circumstances will admit of. I think you may desire, if possible, to give the case no additional notoriety, by the introduction into it of my very notorious name. I have therefore possessed my Solicitor (who is a very shrewd, intelligent person) with the facts of the case, and requested him to send some one from his office with Mrs Morson tomorrow, to ensure its being properly and concisely stated. I have made him acquainted with my part in the business, and explained to him why it may be best not to refer to me unless there should be some positive necessity — which I consider most unlikely; *all the property stolen being Mrs Morson's.* No unnecessary sensation will be made, and I have made him perfectly understand the bearings of the circumstances all through.

I write hastily, and will write again by tomorrow night's post. I enclose a short note for Mr Brown

∽

129. NOVEMBER 25, 1850, DEVONSHIRE TERRACE

Mr Loaden [3] (the solicitor I mentioned) went himself with Mrs Morson today, and stated everything as quietly as possible. The girls neither spoke nor looked up, and were committed for trial. Mrs

---

[3] There is a note addressed to Dickens from William J. Loaden, November 29, 1850, announcing that the two girls — whose names Loaden gives as Anne Davies and Mary Humphreys — were convicted and sentenced. Under the disagreeable necessity of attending at the Mansion House and the Old Bailey, Mrs. Morson, he commented, "acted very steadily and much like a lady in every stage of the business."

Morson will be taken before the Grand Jury at the Old Bailey, next Wednesday. I have just time to write this.

∽

130.   JANUARY 18, 1851, DEVONSHIRE TERRACE
I receive (you will readily believe) a good many letters intended for your eye, which I put in the fire.

But the enclosed commendation of *its* enclosure to me, is so extraordinarily French and out of the way, that I have thought it might afford you a laugh. Hence, I send it.

Your note about Charley gave his Mama and me the greatest delight. It came most opportunely, for I am not so happy with some of my other relations, who are millstones round my neck. One of my brothers [4] is rasping my very heart just now, by trading on my name. However, when I think of you and all your attendant phenomena, I have the consolation of good company!

With kind regards to Mr and Mrs Brown
P.S. Are you ever coming home any more?

∽

131.   MARCH 20, 1851, KNUTSFORD LODGE, GREAT MALVERN
I can find no reprints in English, or in any language but German, of Strauss's Life of Christ (that are known in this country at least) but a 2 vol 8° English Edition, printed in America, price 36/ — and one published by John Chapman of the Strand [5] — and one published by "Taylor Birmingham, and Hetherington London." The prices of the two latter, which it is important to know — especially the last — I have not got yet, but I will have them by Tuesday, when I hope to be at Shepherd's Bush at 3 — not ½ past.

I have no reliable Clerkenwell information either, but hope to have that too, at the same time, and have little doubt I shall.

I send you enclosed, the first proof of the design which Bulwer and

---

[4] Probably his brother Augustus at the moment, for, although Fred was quite as improvident and quite as likely to use Dickens's name for the purpose of obtaining credit if he could, a letter from Dickens to Fred on January 12 — only six days earlier than this — is written in casual and chatty terms that preclude the possibility of any tension between these two. In later years, after repeated trials of his generosity, Dickens was brought to the point of refusing to give any further aid or have any further dealings with either Augustus or Fred.

[5] The edition of Strauss's *Life of Jesus* published by John Chapman was the translation by George Eliot.

I have projected, and for which he has written the Comedy.[6] It is still susceptible of many little improvements and explanations which we are gradually getting into it. The Duke of Devonshire [7] has taken it up (on my shewing it to him) in a most generous and noble manner, and we are going to play the Comedy for the first time, at his House, in the last week in April. On which occasion the Queen is to be invited, and I don't know how much money made.

The maze of bewilderment into which I have got myself with carpenters, painters, tailors, machinists, and others, in consequence —

---

[6] Edward George Earle Lytton Bulwer Lytton (1803–1873), first Baron Lytton, the well-known dramatist and novelist. When Dickens was a journalist in the reporters' gallery of the House of Commons he had taken down Edward Bulwer's speeches in shorthand (it was not until after the death of Bulwer's mother that the son assumed her surname of Lytton); when *Pickwick* burst upon the world Bulwer was already one of the most popular novelists of the day, with the successes of *Pelham, Paul Clifford, Eugene Aram, Last Days of Pompeii,* and *Rienzi* already behind him. Far from resenting Dickens's triumph, Bulwer greeted his rival only with the heartiest praise, and the two men became friends. Meanwhile, Bulwer Lytton carved out a new popularity in the theater, with Macready's productions of *The Lady of Lyons, Richelieu,* and *Cromwell,* and continued to be a prolific and popular novelist.

For three successive nights in November 1850, Dickens and his amateur players had been Lytton's guests at his Hertfordshire estate of Knebworth, and entertained a series of invited audiences there. From this episode grew the enterprise Dickens here describes to Miss Coutts. Lytton proposed creating an endowment that could be used to aid deserving artists and men of letters; he himself would write a comedy, all the earnings of which should be devoted to the purpose, and Dickens's amateurs, with their tremendous reputation, would act it. The foundation was called "The Guild of Literature and Art," and in addition to presenting it with the earnings of his play Lytton gave it a freehold site of some three acres at Stevenage, a short distance from Knebworth, upon which were subsequently erected three buildings designed by Alfred Darbyshire. Lytton's comedy, entitled *Not So Bad as We Seem,* was a costume piece set in the reign of George II.

[7] The play was first presented before the Queen and the Prince Consort and a distinguished audience whose members paid five guineas a ticket, at Devonshire House, the Duke of Devonshire's palatial residence on Piccadilly, on May 16, 1851, and again on May 27. Later performances for the general public were given at the Hanover Square Rooms, and many additional performances, during the next year, on tour throughout the country.

William George Spencer Cavendish (1790–1858), sixth Duke of Devonshire, to whom Dickens addressed an appeal for the use of his mansion, was a Whig of enormous wealth — in 1883 the ducal properties brought an annual income of £180,750 — a gentle and modest spirit, a lover of antiquities, and a patron of art and literature. To Dickens's letter, the Duke replied within two hours: "My services, my house, and my subscription will be at your orders. And I beg you to let me see you before long, not merely to converse upon this subject, but because I have long had the greatest wish to improve our acquaintance, which has, as yet, been only one of crowded rooms."

to say nothing of two nights every week when the whole company are drilled for five hours, the undersigned presiding — or of this trifling addition to my usual occupations — is of the most entangled description; but, if I could help to set right what is wrong here and what I see every day to be so unhappily wrong, I should be munificently recompensed. Mrs Dickens has derived great advantage, I am glad to say, from this place.[8] Charley has been "out of school," laid up with Influenza, but is much better.

ᔄ

132.   MARCH 23, 1851, KNUTSFORD LODGE, GREAT MALVERN

We always intended to have the controul over the subjects and treatment of those Lectures.[9] But I think your suggestion so sound, that I have written to Bulwer to say I shall add a provision in the Prospectus to that effect, and elucidatory of their wholesome purpose.

We know among ourselves, of course, whether a man would really want one of those places or not.[1] But all such assistance hitherto, has been so much in the way of alms-giving that we purposely make the *merit,* rather than the *means* of the applicant, our test. In addition to our own professional knowledge, we assume that no man would ask for such a thing, unless he wanted it. But we consider it so important that a man of character and ability should set the example of accepting that aid, that we would rather at first get a man who did *not* actually want it, to take it, than bestow it on any man who has held out his hat in any way, before.

I have perceived a dim shadow of your mysterious objection to my acting, before now.[2] Yet I hope you will go to this Play, consoling your

---

[8] Since the birth of Dora Annie, the previous August, Catherine Dickens had been in nervous ill health, and was now at Great Malvern for "the waters."

[9] It was proposed that the beneficiaries of the Guild of Literature and Art should give a certain number of stated lectures during each year.

[1] The Guild houses at Stevenage were to provide accommodations for a resident warden, with an income of £200 a year, a number of resident members, with £170 a year; in addition there were to be nonresident members, with £200 a year, and a number of associates, young men of promise, with one-year grants of £100.

[2] Miss Coutts either felt that public play-acting was undignified for a man of letters, or that Dickens was overdoing it, both of which opinions were held by other friends. Certainly since 1845 he had been resorting to it more and more often upon various pretexts, using it as an anodyne for his restlessness and as a device for blowing off steam.

mind with the belief that we have on former occasions done a great deal of good by it, and that no such thing would ever be done but for me, and that there is no one else whom these men would allow to hold them together, or to whose direction they would good-humouredly and with perfect confidence yield themselves. It was in the circumstance of Bulwer's being so much struck and surprised by this union when we played at his house a few months ago, that this scheme originated. For he said, "this is a great power that has grown up about you, out of a winter-night's amusement, and do let us try to use it for the lasting service of our order."

You will not find it like any other amateur Plays, I think. You will be impressed by the general intelligence and good sense. And you will find a certain neatness in it which I should compare with the French stage, if you were not so profoundly English!

As to the mournful spectacle of your friend upon the boards, I can only ask you to do your best to forget him. If I thought that deeply-anchored objection were capable of being argued down, I should press you, darkly to reveal it. But I have no such belief, for I think you are in your way as obstinate as ——— Mrs Brown ——— I can't say more.

[P.S.] Charley is better. The influenza there, is beyond precedent. Five and twenty boys laid up, in Evans's house alone.

&

133.   APRIL 17, 1851, DEVONSHIRE TERRACE

Our poor little Dora! — I had just been playing with her, and went to preside at a Public Dinner to which I was pledged. Before it was over — even before they sang the Grace — she was dead.[3] I had left her well and gay. My servant came down with the sad news, but they kept it from me until the meeting was over.

Mrs Dickens was at Malvern. By bringing her to town on a pretence of the poor little pet's being hopelessly ill, we made the shock as gradual as we could. She is as well as I could hope, and begs me to say so to you and to thank you earnestly.

We laid the child in her grave today. And it is a part of the goodness and mercy of God that if we could call her back to life, now, with a wish, we would not do it.

[P.S.] Our kind regards to Mr and Mrs Brown.

---

[3] Dickens presided at the annual dinner of the General Theatrical Fund on the evening of April 14, and his friend Forster tenderly kept the news of the death

134.   AUGUST 17, 1851, BROADSTAIRS, KENT

I don't see anything to distrust *much*, in Rachael Bradley's letter — which I retain for the present, to note it in our book.[4] How she got the "ladies' old clothes" is inscrutable to us, but the state of society is strange and unsettled where she is, and there may be ways and means of proceeding there, that look unlikely to old-world eyes.

After I left Highgate the other day, intending to write to the Australian merchant I spoke of, it suddenly occurred to me (I cannot conceive how it comes to pass that I never thought of it before) that I knew a certain Commodore Brown who is officially "The Registrar of Merchant Seamen",[5] and who I thought *must* know all about the Emigrant Ships. I accordingly wrote to him, and he sends me this reply.

"I am able and most willing to give exactly the sort of information you want. Whenever you will let me know where you wish to send — when — and how many — I will ascertain at any time which is the best ship, and who is the best Captain, and all other particulars."

I really hope this will relieve you of one of the most troublesome and anxious of the details. He is (as you may suppose from his office) a thoroughly practical man, well acquainted with the whole mercantile service.

Perhaps you will have the kindness, in the matter of Charley, to do just what is most convenient to you.

I begin to be pondering afar off, a new book.[6] Violent restlessness, and vague ideas of going I don't know where, I don't know why, are the present symptoms of the disorder.

I understand Lord Granville is to be made the next President of the French Republic. Have you heard it? Also that Lady Granville is to

---

from him until after he had made his speech. The child had lived a little short of nine months.

[4] Rachael Bradley, who had been an inmate of Urania Cottage in 1849, was now evidently in one of the colonies — probably Australia.

[5] Lieutenant John Hoskyns Brown, R.N., was the registrar of the Seamen's General Register and Record Office, in the customhouse.

[6] Dickens did not actually begin writing the new book, however, until the end of November, after the first provincial performances of *Not So Bad as We Seem* at Clifton and Bristol. Throughout most of the spring and summer all the attention he could spare from *Household Words* and Guild affairs was devoted to finding a larger house than Devonshire Terrace for his large family and, when he had taken it, having it altered and decorated. He moved into Tavistock House, Tavistock Square, near the end of October, and was still busied in settling down for the next four weeks. Thereafter *Bleak House* was started; the first number was published in March.

go into the French Chamber of Peers, as the first representative of the Rights of Women — and that the Lord Mayor wants to be naturalized as a French Subject. This looks bad for England.[7]

I have not heard again from Mr Dunn [8]

೧೪೨

135.   AUGUST 22, 1851, BROADSTAIRS, KENT

The gentleman to whom the enclosed letter is addressed (I mention this to explain its being addressed to a name you don't know) is my Secretary and Sub Editor at The Household Words,[9] whom the Commodore (who is the writer) supposes to represent all my affairs in my absence. Will you read it? The Ship mentioned sails, I fear, too soon, and leaves too short an interval for your preparations? I will write to the Commodore again, on the other points of his note, after hearing from you.

Many thanks for the Hieroglyphic suggestion.[1] It is an excellent subject, but the difficulty in treating it for so large an audience is to find anyone well acquainted with it, who has the power of sufficiently popularizing it. I hope, however, that I can discover the man.

The Government will do with those Irish ruffians, exactly what it did with Puseyism — interfere, feebly, when the mischief is done. I feel quite certain that but for the laisser-aller dealing with the candlestick and confessional matters, we never should have got to this pass — for

---

[7] Granville George Leveson-Gower (1815–1891), second Earl Granville, who had been Undersecretary of State for Foreign Affairs 1840–1841, was one of a deputation of commissioners who visited France in August 1851 on the invitation of the municipality of Paris. "He spoke French like a Parisian, with a slight court accent, recalling the *ancien régime,* and his personal influence did much to promote the entente cordiale." Lady Granville was the only child and heiress of Emeric Joseph, Duc de Dalberg, the widow of Sir Ferdinand Acton, and mother of the first Lord Acton, the historian. "There was probably no one more unlikely," writes C. C. Osborne, "to enter the French Chamber of Peers as the first representative of the rights of women." The effusive exchange of cordialities between the English delegation and the French on this occasion amused Dickens immoderately.

[8] Miss Coutts's old persecutor Richard Dunn, who had again been before the Insolvent Debtors' Court earlier that month.

[9] William Henry Wills (1810–1880), writer, a member of the original staff of *Punch,* subeditor of the *Daily News* 1846, editor of *Chambers's Journal,* and from 1850 to 1868 subeditor first of *Household Words* and then of *All the Year Round* under Dickens. In 1856 he became Miss Coutts's private secretary as well. The Commodore is Lieutenant Brown, mentioned in the preceding letter.

[1] Probably a suggested subject for an article in *Household Words.*

the Pope was made, through that medium, to believe that there was a tendency towards him in England which does not exist — and presumed upon it — and went too far to retract.[2] *Now,* a war between the Roman Catholic Religion — that curse upon the world — and Freedom, is inevitable. And numbers of people of the better order of sense and spirit are so indignant with the Protestant Church for its indolent temporizing and its miserable internal squabbles, that they have lost their natural interest in the struggle. I cannot tell you how strongly I am confirmed, when I reflect upon all this, in my unvarying faith that Reform is the only true Preservation. If we had had a bold Government, boldly setting right the abuses in the Church, twenty years ago, its strength at this moment would have been Sampson's to General Tom Thumb's — and if the Universities had been forced to adjust themselves to the character of the times, we never should have had to bless Oxford for the intolerable enormity it has dug out of the mire.[3]

Terrible things will be done and suffered, before we get out of *this* trouble. I believe it will produce the last, great, long, direful war of the world.

Charley is down at Watson's in Northamptonshire, for a fortnight. If you should not have gone abroad when he comes back, I will present him. He is very much grown [4] — an excellent boy at home, and as good to his brothers and sisters as if he had never been away. All he wants, is a habit of perseverance. With that, he could do anything. He wants it as a fixed purpose and habit of his nature. He gets on at Eton, with credit, so easily that he merely takes short rides on his Pegasus and jumps off again, when he ought to be putting him at great leaps.

I am going to send Walter [5] (the Cadet) at Christmas, to a Mr

---

[2] Dickens is referring to the papal bull of September 30, 1850, setting up a hierarchy of Catholic bishops in England, who were to derive their titles from English sees created by the bull. The step aroused violent alarm and indignation among English Protestants, who interpreted it as an aggressive endeavor to reassert papal supremacy. England countered with the Ecclesiastical Titles Bill, February, 1851, which forbade the Catholic clergy to assume titles derived from any territory or place in the United Kingdom. The "Irish ruffians" were probably members of the "Young Ireland" party, radical Irish nationalists who were resorting to violence to enforce their demands.

[3] Dickens's reaction to the Oxford movement, as it had developed under Keble, Hurrel Froude, W. G. Ward, and Newman.

[4] Charley was now almost fifteen.

[5] Walter was ten the preceding February and was preparing for the Indian Army.

Trimmer at Putney who educates expressly for Addiscombe and India. I don't think he is so clever as Charley, but he is a very steady amiable boy, of a good reliable capacity, and brings exalted certificates from Mr King.

You will write to me about the ship? I presume you will prefer the next good one after this mentioned in the note?

∽

136.   OCTOBER 9, 1851, BROADSTAIRS, KENT

Until within these few days, I have heard nothing in the way of ship-recommendation from my friend the Registrar of Merchant Seamen. But at last I am happy to say I have his strongest possible recommendation of a ship that sails on the 25th. As she was beset by gold-seekers, mad to get a passage on any terms, he caused three berths to be reserved, as soon as he knew of her certainly going. I have now paid for them — £45 — and I hope we shall export these lingering three in safety.

There has been some small commotion — but not much — at Shepherds Bush; Mr Tracey's last girl demanding to go; and the Irish girl shewing a very national incapability of getting on with anybody on any subject — accompanied with expressions of a violent desire to "do for" the establishment in general. The Irish girl is accordingly discharged as incurable; but Mr Tracey's girl being extremely penitent, and most earnestly imploring (when it came to the point) not to be sent away, remains on her good behaviour. I have taken a new case from the Field Lane Ragged School, and have rejected another, in which it was quite clear to me that the girl would never go abroad. I have also (I hope) paved the way for the supply of more cases from that source, when we want them. Mrs Morson and Mrs Macartney go on zealously, and in a business-like way.

I have no news — except that I am three parts distracted and the fourth part wretched, in the agonies of getting into a new house — Tavistock House, Tavistock Square. Pending which desirable consummation of my troubles, I *can not* work at my new book — having all my notions of order turned completely topsy-turvy. I hope when you come back you will find us settled, and me hard at work — and will approve, both the tangible house and the less substantial Edifice.

I have excellent accounts of Charley at Eton, who was the best of boys at home here all the holidays through. I think of leaving here for town about the 20th of this month, and shall then go down and see him.

As for you, I suppose you are full of the change, novelty, and delight of travelling, and feel an elevated pity for the captives on a poor cliff like this. Mrs Brown, I take it for granted, agrees with Dr Skey,[6] in reference to all the Institutions you examine. I wish I were with you, to help the general unanimity! Pray remember me kindly to both of them and to Mr Brown, and believe me Dear Miss Coutts

ᕫᕬᕬ

137.   NOVEMBER 17, 1851, TAVISTOCK HOUSE

As I was sitting down this morning to write to you, I received a letter from Mr Brown dated Berlin, in which he gives me an account of the missing trio that fills me with pleasure on your account.

You may perhaps have seen in the Times how one of our girls has given us a little trouble. She came from Mr Tracey's. On a certain morning not long ago, Mrs Morson appeared here with a report that the said girl had contrived (behind Mrs Macartney's back) to secrete a bonnet and some clothes out of the Wardrobe room, with which she had intended to decamp — that being singled out by Mrs Morson, and taxed as the delinquent (and I think her penetration does her great credit) she admitted her guilt, but implored not to be turned away as she was utterly destitute — etc etc. I immediately went out, and decided in my own mind, on the road, that I would act, as to this last punishment of expulsion, according to the girl's appearance and manner; and that if they inspired the least belief in her repentance, I would give her one more trial. I had her into the parlor the instant I arrived at the Home, in order that she might have no time for preparation; and, finding no extenuating circumstance in the case, but all sorts of aggravating circumstances instead — and being perfectly convinced, that she was altogether imposing upon me, or trying to do it — told Mrs Morson in her presence, that she must put her old clothes upon her and discharge her at 12 next day. But I privately added instructions to Mrs Morson not to discharge her in rags. At six next morning, she robbed the place and made off, but was taken in the lane by a policeman, brought back, and locked up in a bedroom while Mrs Morson once more came to me. I felt an example so indispensable that I immediately transferred her to Mr Loaden, with instructions to

---

[6] Previously mentioned in Dickens's letter of January 31, 1848.

Mr L to give the girl into custody directly, take her before the Magistrate, and beg the Magistrate quietly, to convict her summarily and so prevent trouble and noise at the Old Bailey. All this was done, and she is now undergoing two months of Mr Tracey's severest discipline.

I hope you approve of these proceedings?

Mr A Beckett [7] the Magistrate wrote to me on the very same day, about a girl who had been brought before him for trying to get admission into the workhouse at an unseasonable hour. I went over to his court, immediately, and found her to be a little country girl of 17 — rather pretty — who had been deserted by her father, and had been tramping and hop-picking and vagabondizing generally, all her life. She told me the truth about herself, and I took her. She is profoundly ignorant, but very quiet, and much gentler (so far) than we could have supposed. If she can be brought to learn, I think it may turn out a strong case. At any rate, it is decidedly worth the trial.

I saw, on the same day at the same court, as applicants for relief from the Poor box two sisters — daughters of a deceased harbor master at Ramsgate — one 30, the other 40 — both young for their years, strong, stout-hearted, full of courage though unable to live by shop needlework, and horribly reduced — of great natural cheerfulness in the midst of their misery — of excellent manners and unblemished character. All they desired was to be got abroad, and to live by their own hard work. I was so very much impressed by these women, and so deeply sensible of the pathetic contrast between their ardent desire to have such charitable aid as the other pestilent wretch had thanklessly flung away, that I was strongly impelled to take them into the Home, and try the influence of two such inmates on the rest. I did not, however, feel myself justified in making that departure from your usual plan, in your absence and without your concurrence. As I could not bear to leave them in that state without an effort, I wrote to Sidney Herbert about them, and have great hopes from the reply I have received, that his committee will accept them, though they are not strictly within their rules. But in case they should not, would you wish me to do anything with them?

If I were profoundly confident in your English sympathies, I should be tempted to believe that you were by this time forgetting this small Island, and debating whether it would be worth while ever to come

---

[7] Gilbert Abbott à Beckett (1811–1856), lawyer and writer, a member of the staff of *Punch*, author of the *Comic History of England, Comic History of Rome,* and *Comic Blackstone.*

back to it. It has fallen into a pleasant dulness since the closing of the Great Exhibition — an event for which I am fervently thankful.

I saw Charley a little while ago, who was very well and strongly praised by his tutor. He wrote home this morning for — a pound of tea (!) — and dwelt, with some enthusiasm, on the circumstance that the holidays will commence in three weeks. We are beginning to be settled in our new house (which I hope you will think a pretty one, when you *do* come back) and I am beginning to find my papers, and to know where the pen and ink are. For the last month, I have been drearily watching Cubitt's [8] workmen, in strong draughts, all day. They have fled at last (thank God) from the miserable expression of my face, and order is re-established.

I will not inflict a longer letter upon you; being already very doubtful whether you will ever get to this point. For of course you carry that Secretarial table, covered all over with correspondence and other documents, wherever you go. I always picture you as having it set up, the instant you arrive in a town, and falling to work on the spot.

Mrs Dickens and her sister beg me to send their kind regards to you and your fellow travellers

∞

138.   DECEMBER 22, 1851, TAVISTOCK HOUSE
I found Mrs Morson on Saturday, full of sympathy for the widow. Whose curtsey is certainly low, but is meant to be very respectful, and who is exceedingly humble and grateful.

Finding her very different from the rest of our people — able to work and embroider, and a much better "scholar" than we are ever able to make — I thought it right to give her some encouragement. I told her that as she already knew what we usually taught, I had no doubt you would be disposed to send her abroad much sooner than usual, *if* you were satisfied with her general conduct and behaviour. That of course she must understand that whatever she was required to do in the

[8] Thomas Cubitt (1788–1855) and William Cubitt (1791–1863) were well-known builders, who erected the London Institution, Finsbury Circus, villas at Highbury and rows of houses near Newington Green, developed six acres at Barnsbury Park, and were responsible for upper Woburn Square, Woburn Buildings, Gordon Square, Tavistock Square, Euston Square, Belgrave Square, and numbers of other residential areas. William Cubitt, who retired from business in 1851, had been Sheriff of London and Middlesex 1847–1849 and alderman in 1851, and became Lord Mayor of London 1860–1861. Their firm was employed in the extensive alteration of Tavistock House.

Home, she was to do with the rest on all occasions. And that she could not too thoroughly understand that everything done there would be necessary to be done, and useful to be known, in a new country. I said I would represent to you what I had mentioned to her, and that we should rely on her setting a good example, and going hopefully and cheerfully to work. She expressed a most earnest desire to do so, but had been in much distress of mind. Mrs Morson had discreetly told Matilda Thompson (as the most civilized of our young friends) to give her any little help and support that she could.

I notice a most singular lie in Charlotte Glyn, who persists in representing herself as 13 years old, and whose mother (whether originating or imitating the absurdity I don't know) makes the same representation. It is needless to say that it's ridiculous impossibility is self evident. And referring to the memorandum I made of her case when I first saw her at the Ragged School Teacher's in Newgate Street, I find that she stated herself to be then 15. I have no doubt it was her real age.

I considered it necessary to caution Mrs Morson respecting Mary Anne Church, whose pilfering propensities (I find on her own shewing) to have been very strong, and exercised under no pressure of necessity; and whom I greatly doubt. Little Elizabeth Hogg is quite a phenomenon of slyness, I think. I was there some hours making up the Case Book which I want to leave in no arrear at the close of the year — and made these remarks in the course of that operation which is still unfinished.

I enclose Charley's papers, and a testimonial that Mr Evans sent me from one of the Masters.

⤷

139. JANUARY 13, 1852, TAVISTOCK HOUSE
I think the Leads you have sent me, and which I have read with the greatest interest, *admirable*. In general, I do not think their wisdom to be questioned. Some minor points occur to me from time to time, which I jot down and will mention when we talk the subject over. But I believe it to be *certain* that a scheme like yours is the only hopeful way of doing lasting good, and raising up the wretched.

I saw Inspector Field [9] last night. I could only approach the subject

---

[9] Inspector Charles F. Field, who was promoted to inspector in the R Division, Greenwich, and became a well-known member of the detective police. He appears

afar off, in consequence of his horrible sharpness, but I am disposed to doubt the efficacy of his peculiar sort of knowledge and sagacity in this stage of the matter. A locality chosen, I have no doubt that, at a small expence, his assistance in the beginning would be of immense service; or, a locality suggested, that his observations upon it would also be very important — for, if there were a serious objection, he would be certain to know it. But the habits of his mind hardly lead him (I think I observe) to the present point before us.

I have been thinking a good deal about it, and it seems to me that Dr Southwood Smith [1] is the man, of all others, to consult first. His fever-practice has made him, for many years, well acquainted with all the poor parts of London; he is in possession of all the reports made to the Board of Health in the late Survey; and he knows what work there is in this or that place; and how the people live; and how their tenements are held; and all about them. I am well acquainted with him — have both advised him and advised with him in many delicate matters — and can implicitly trust him. Not that I should think it necessary to mention you, or to proceed beyond generalities, but I mean, I can trust his interest in such a subject and his giving an opinion on sound knowledge and careful consideration and well regulated humanity. I do not go to him straightway, because I would rather get your concurrence first, but if you will write me "Yes," I will see him

---

as Inspector Wield in three of Dickens's articles for *Household Words* (August 10, August 24, and September 14, 1850) and under his own name in "On Duty with Inspector Field," June 14, 1851. In collected editions of Dickens's work these appear in *Reprinted Pieces*. Dickens denied, however, that Field was the original of Inspector Bucket in *Bleak House*.

[1] Thomas Southwood Smith (1788–1861), sanitary reformer, one of the founders of the *Westminster Review* in 1824, the Useful Knowledge Society, the Health of Towns Association, and other similar bodies, and the author of valuable works on epidemics and sanitary improvements. He was also the founder of the sanatorium in Devonshire Place and medical adviser to Sir Edwin Chadwick's Poor Law Commission. It was he who put into Dickens's hands in 1841 the horrifying report of the Children's Employment Commission on the ways in which small children were worked in the mines, and the later report on conditions in the factories and iron foundries: two documents that Dickens read with a burning fury reflected in all his later judgments on the relations of capital and labor.

The project on which Dickens suggested consulting him was one of buying up waste ground in the slums and building model dwellings. It developed into the purchase of the squalid area in the East End of London known as Nova Scotia Gardens and the erection of the Columbia Square apartments, four buildings accommodating two hundred families, or about one thousand persons. Dickens outlined the guiding principles of the entire enterprise in a later letter to Miss Coutts, April 18, 1852. She carried out the plan, and the buildings were opened in 1862.

without delay, and afterwards see Field again. I have no doubt of our opening the way as clearly as it can be opened, by such means.

In reference to the Shower Bath (by the bye, I suppose the baths for the Infants are not to be Showery?) I am really and truly affected by your solicitude. But I do sincerely believe that it does me unspeakable service. I take but a very small part of the shock, on the head; and I have quite a remarkable power of enduring fatigue for which I believe I am very much indebted to this treatment, as the power has certainly increased since I have pursued it. It is because my cut-out way in life obliges me to be so much upon the strain, that I think it is of service to me as a refresher — not as a taker out, but as a putter in of energy. However, I shall certainly not observe its influence from day to day, the less narrowly, because of your kind caution. For which, and for much more, my heartiest thanks.

You have not seen the dreadful instrument yet, as it is set up here!

I shall be delighted to dine with you on Friday — when I hope Wheatstone [2] in the exposition of those marvels will not be too shrill.

Sydney,[3] my peculiar protegé among the smaller fry, is in a dreadful state of anticipation at this moment; the eventful occasion (of which I am going to be a spectator) of his first appearance in your box or any Theatre being so near at hand. Of the many wonderful contrasts that one sees, I can hardly imagine a greater one than being with little children at the play tonight, and sitting last night, for hours, with that grim Inspector in a world of villainy and punishment.

It is dreadfully difficult to work at the new book on these dull days.

☙

140.   FEBRUARY 8, 1852, TAVISTOCK HOUSE

The indisposition of my fellow-counsellor in the matter of the Bethnal Green Survey, has obliged me to postpone our appointment and take it out of this last week. I am further obliged to put it into next

---

[2] Probably Sir Charles Wheatstone (1802–1875), physicist and inventor, professor in King's College, London, one of the inventors of the electric telegraph and inventor of the stereoscope and the concertina; carried on researches in electricity, sound, and light.

[3] Sydney Smith Haldimand Dickens (1847–1872), Dickens's seventh child, not yet five years old, whom Dickens nicknamed "the Ocean Spectre" from a strange faraway look in his eyes when he gazed out over the waves at Broadstairs. He became a lieutenant in the Navy, and died and was buried at sea.

week now, instead of this present one, as I am going to Manchester and Liverpool tomorrow, and shall be absent five or six days.[4]

I have communicated with Mr Tracey about Mary Anne Church, and I am sorry to say he gives no encouragement at all. He says, as to communicating with that aunt, "it's all moonshine" – and he has exactly that opinion of her which I mentioned to you I had formed myself – I ought to add that I have expressed none to him. He says that he could not press his own opinion of the girl against the united opinions of his two chaplains that she was a proper subject for the Home; but that her conduct in the Home, and her previous history, deprive him of any faith in her. He has evidently my apprehension that she will get the better of us at last; and he has been looking freshly into her story. She seems not to have had a second "place" (as she told me, and, as I entered in the book, I believed falsely) but to have been taken in, out of charity, by a poor woman whom she basely robbed. She had a great capacity for taking in the chaplains, and would take in most people who had any thing to do with teaching her. It is hopeless to expect the least assistance from her relations, – and, if she do not most thoroughly and entirely amend, she is not a girl with whom it will be possible to hold any lenient terms. I make this report without in the least thinking that it ought to prejudice her if she should do well in future – but, if she do not, it becomes a case of self-defence, and there will be nothing for it but to turn her out.

I propose being back in town, at latest, this day week. In the meantime any letter addressed to me at Liverpool would find me.

[P.S.] Would you care to hear my first Number [5] before it comes out? If you would (though it is reading at a disadvantage to read an incomplete thing) I should be delighted to read it to you – though I needn't say *that!*

༺༻

141.   FEBRUARY 19, 1852, TAVISTOCK HOUSE

I have appointed to go to the House of Detention today at 2 o'Clock to see the girl recommended by Mr Hardwick [6] the Magistrate (brother

---

[4] Part of the theatrical tour of *Not So Bad as We Seem* for the Guild of Literature and Art.

[5] The opening number of *Bleak House*, published in March.

[6] John Hardwick (1791–1875), barrister, magistrate at Lambeth 1821, and at Marlborough Street 1841–1856. His brother Philip Hardwick (1792–1870) was the architect to Bridewell and Bethlehem Hospitals 1816, of the St. Catherine's Docks

to the architect); whom I shall take, in accordance with your wish, if her case seem a good one.

I return the Dens of London. It is perfectly true in the main, though the accounts which such people give of themselves are perhaps as little to be trusted as anything that can be put into human speech. However, it is done (to my thinking) with such an excruciating flatness and insipidity that it is hard labor to read it.

Mr Austin [7] having only just gone on his Board of Health expedition, and Mr Hardwick having found that piece of ground (which promises capitally) what do you think of Mr Brown and I making an expedition to the spot in the first instance? Such questions as suggest themselves to us, we can then refer to Dr Southwood Smith and Mr Austin, with whom I will then make another expedition. I think we shall get at everything desirable to be known, in this way, without losing time. Or I will ask Dr Southwood Smith to go with Mr Brown and me on the first voyage of discovery, if he can.

I am going down to have a holiday with Charley next Tuesday; and on Wednesday evening I must present myself at Lady John's.[8] I have no other engagement (except Work) next week, and should be happy to dine with you any day. If you will arrange with Mr Brown, I will be at his disposal, for exploring purposes, any afternoon he likes to name in the next week, subject to these two engagements.

The idea of the wooden building is an excellent one, — but I fear the Building Act, which (like most other acts) is full of preposterous stipulations.

With kindest regards to Mrs Brown

1825, Goldsmiths' Company 1828, the Euston and Victoria Hotels and Stations 1834–1839, and the Lincoln's Inn Hall and Library 1845. He became F.S.A. 1824, F.R.S. 1831, R.A. 1841, was vice-president of the Institute of British Architects in 1839 and 1841, and treasurer of the Royal Academy 1850–1861.

[7] Henry Austin (d. 1861), architect and sanitary engineer, married Dickens's sister Letitia in 1837, was for years secretary to the Sanitary Commission. He was Dickens's architectural adviser on the alterations of Tavistock House and, later, on his country house at Gad's Hill, near Rochester.

[8] Probably Lady Russell, wife of Lord John Russell (1792–1878), third son of the sixth Duke of Bedford, created Earl Russell in 1861. This distinguished statesman became leader of the Whig party in 1834, Home Secretary 1833–1839, Secretary for War and the Colonies 1839–1841, and Prime Minister and First Lord of the Treasury 1846–1852, Foreign Secretary 1852–1855, Colonial Secretary 1855, and Foreign Secretary again in the Russell-Palmerston administration 1859–1865. Dickens was a friend of the Russells and often visited them at Pembroke Lodge.

142.   MARCH 2, 1852, TAVISTOCK HOUSE
This was the Committee Day at Shepherds Bush. Mr Chesterton and
Mr Tracey attended. The girls were all looking very well, and everything was satisfactory. As Mary Anne Church is, in a manner, out of
our hands, I thought it best not to have her in. There being a complaint of Watts in Mrs Morson's Diary, Mr Tracey (from whose place
she came) spoke very gravely to her.

I send you the book, for 5 weeks. As Mrs Morson had no money for
petty cash, I gave her, in all, a cheque for fifty Pounds.

Mr Hardwick and I paid a visit to the ground yesterday, and went
minutely over it, and the immediate neighbourhood. I mentioned something to him in reference to the position of such houses as you may
build which I will mention to you, and which I think you will quite
agree with. We afterwards went to "The Model Buildings" — a collection of small houses which I visited when they were first erected by a
Society, and which I should greatly like you to see one day.

I enclose the plan.

The chip shall be duly presented. We were obliged to go to Press
again with Bleak House No 1, last night.

P.S. Mamey and Katey are in ecstacies, as I write, with Mrs Brown's
kind notes and presents.

ᙡ

143.   MARCH 3, 1852, TAVISTOCK HOUSE
I have received the money, safely.

The "Model Buildings" are close to Bagnigge Wells. They lie between it and Calthorpe Street Grey's Inn Road. Drive to either place,
and anyone will shew you where they are, close at hand. Don't be
alarmed by the apparent size of the little houses, because every house
is in reality two complete houses. Knock at any door, and ask the
people to let you see their rooms. There are houses of two sizes. Pray
see both. The people are very civil and obliging, and will explain anything to you.

One house (I think No 17) is a large one, let in single rooms to
widows and old women. It is capital. For eighteen pence a week, an
old creature lives healthily, peacefully, and in perfect comfort — as far
as her lodging and washing go.

144.   MARCH 7, 1852, TAVISTOCK HOUSE

I went to Mr Hardwick's court, yesterday, by appointment, and saw the girl. Her name is Almina (!) Holgate, and she is twenty-seven years of age, but looks younger. She is of exceedingly respectable appearance, and is a good Milliner and Dress Maker.

It appears that she has no idea of abandoning her child. The poor people who take care of it for her are so persuaded of that, that they have not the least objection to retain it if she goes to Australia; knowing very well (she says) that she will surely remit money for its support from her earnings. Mr Hardwick has seen it (it is a little boy aged nine months) and says it is very clean and healthy, and evidently well cared for. She looks forward to having it sent out to her in good time. There was an idea on Mr Hardwick's part before he wrote to me of sending her down to Lincoln where she knows some poor people. But she said it was of no use; she had better try to begin afresh, and get over all this, and go abroad. It was her only chance of recovering herself.

She is to present herself to him again, on Tuesday afternoon. How would you wish me to proceed? It seems to be a good case; and if you should think it well to send her out, without passing her through the Home, it occurs to me that it would not be a bad experience for Mrs Morson if she were to see the girl (as she might do here) and manage the details along with her — throwing the girl upon herself to help herself, but taking care that all you might desire to be done, was thoroughly and faithfully done. Shall I come round to you at a quarter past three on Tuesday, before I go to Mr Hardwick's court again? Bleak House will probably hold me until the afternoon.

ↄﻭ

145.   MARCH 16, 1852, TAVISTOCK HOUSE

I shall be delighted to dine with you, this day week.

The enclosed Nova Scotian [9] proposals seem to me to be fair enough. I had previously gone over the plan carefully, with Mr Hardwick, on the ground. Before you sanction any plan of building, decidedly, I hope you will take Dr Southwood Smith and Mr Austin into consultation. I think you would save a great deal of money by doing so, and

---

[9] The plan to acquire this waste ground and erect model flats upon it. At the time it was a place of foul, slimy pools and mounds of refuse, decaying garbage, and cinders, pervaded by an intolerable stench.

would get good sanitary arrangements on the most efficient and simple terms. The knowledge that the Board of Health has acquired of all these things, founded upon their personal inspection of the abodes of the poor in all parts of the country, is very important in such a work. I should not like to say this to Mr Hardwick (knowing what tender corns architects usually have) but I have no doubt that your noble design would benefit by such a course. They know little (but most important) things, beforehand, which an architect would only find out, probably, by your experiencing the want of them when the building was done.

I am happy to say that Mrs Dickens and the seventh son [1] — whom I cannot afford to receive with perfect cordiality, as on the whole I could have dispensed with him — are as well as possible, and in a most blooming state. I had been in an unsettled and anxious condition for a week or so, but may now shut myself up in Bleak House again.

The Wonderful Lamp [2] does its duty in the most splendid manner.

∞

146.   APRIL 18, 1852, TAVISTOCK HOUSE

Two points occur to me in reference to this paper. In the first place, it is indispensable to the specification of the plans required, that the size and shape of the piece of ground should be accurately stated. In the second place, it seems to me very important that the request for plans should be kept altogether separate from the request for suggestions. I would therefore have two papers instead of one, and I would *print* both of them; it being very difficult to get people to read writing, or to read it without confusion if they read it at all.

Should you think with me, I will measure the ground (Mr Austin could do it by walking over it), and go through these notes to render them as plain as possible, and then have them printed. I enclose them now, in case you should think of anything to add.

It is a very good thing to try several descriptions of houses, but I have no doubt myself (after long consideration of the subject) that the large houses are best. You never can, for the same money, offer

---

[1] Edward Bulwer Lytton Dickens was born March 13, 1852, Dickens's tenth and last child. Despite his father's unenthusiastic welcome, he became a favorite child. He emigrated to Australia and died in New South Wales in 1902.

[2] Probably a gift from Miss Coutts.

anything like the same advantages in small houses. It is *not* desirable to encourage any small carpenter or builder who has a few pounds to invest, to run up small dwelling houses. If they had been discouraged long ago, London would be an immeasurably healthier place than it can be made in scores of years to come. If you go into any common outskirts of the town, now, and see the advancing army of brick and mortar laying waste the country fields and shutting out the air, you cannot fail to be struck by the consideration that if large buildings had been erected for the working people, instead of the absurd and expensive separate walnut shells in which they live, London would have been about a third of its present size, and every family would have had a country walk, miles nearer to their own door. Besides this, men would have been nearer to their work — would not have had to dine at public houses — there would have been thicker walls of separation and better means of separation than you can ever give (except at a preposterous cost) in small tenements — and they would have had gas, water, drainage, and a variety of other humanizing things which you *can't* give them so well in little houses. Further, in little houses, you must keep them near the ground, and you cannot by any possibility afford such sound and wholesome foundations (remedying this objection) in little houses as in large ones. The example of large houses appears to me, in all respects, (always supposing their locality to be a great place like London) far better than any example you can set by small houses; and the compensation you give for any overgrown shadow they may cast upon a street at certain hours of the day, is out of all proportion to that drawback.

I know everybody at Manchester, and in most of those places. But I think the people for the suggestion-paper are people connected with Railways passing through remote Yorkshire Moors, where they have had to frame schools and churches, and establish an orderly system of society out of the strangest disorder — as in one case in Yorkshire, now, where a Tunnel has been making for some years. Also large ironmasters — of whom there are some notable cases — who have proceeded on the self-supporting principle, and have done wonders with their workpeople. Also other manufacturers in isolated places who have awakened to find themselves in the midst of a mass of workpeople going headlong to destruction, and have stopped the current and quite turned it by establishing decent houses, paying schools, savings banks, little libraries etc. Several of these instances come into my mind as

I write this, and I have no doubt we could get the results of such experience by merely asking for them.[3]

I enclose Charley's papers. I am having some grave councils with him in reference to the future, and I will report the result to you very soon. On second thoughts I have considered it best *not* to advise with Mr Cookesley. He is very fond of Charley, and has a high opinion of his abilities, and would like nothing better than to keep him making Latin verses for the next five years. Quite natural to a man of his pursuits, but not quite rational in such a case.

Many thanks for the Polling Paper.

I hope you have recovered [from?] Doctor Smith's extreme rapidity and rush of words? He reminds me in that respect of Charles Matthews. He is a very sound man indeed, notwithstanding — but he is too voluble and dashing.

∽

147.   APRIL 20, 1852, TAVISTOCK HOUSE

After some trouble (in consequence of her being too late for her appointments) I have at last seen the Sidney Herbert[4] girl. I cannot say I am at all confident of success in the case, but I think it one it is quite right to try. The two best things I observed in her were, her trembling very much while I was talking to her, and her being extremely grateful when I gave her hope. In manner, dress, etc she is above the general run of our girls, but she can't write. I doubted one expression in her letter to you as not being what the girl herself would be likely to use; and, on pressing her, I found that the letter had been written for her by someone. I am not at all clear of the innocent nature of her knowledge of the Mr Vernon whose letter you gave me.

Nevertheless, she seems quite earnest in her application; and if you can save her, you will save a very good average representative of a large class. *I would most certainly try her.* If you will reply "yes", I will send Mrs Morson for her, tomorrow.

---

[3] Doubtless the reader has noted the remarkable perception of these proposals for making each such group of dwellings a model community, composed of a large number of flats under one roof rather than of separate houses, with the advantages of economy in making water supply, drainage, and lighting therefore cheaply available to all, and having open spaces, schools, shops, savings banks, and libraries all near at hand. In essence it is the animating principle of all subsequent enlightened town planning.

[4] Possibly Sidney Herbert (1810–1861), first Baron Herbert, statesman. He was primarily responsible for enabling Florence Nightingale to go to the Crimea.

P.S. She says she wants to be sent to Port Philip if possible "because she has been told she has an uncle there, who is rich."

∞

148. JUNE 1, 1852, TAVISTOCK HOUSE

I am delighted to welcome you home again.

Mr Sidney (referred to in the letter you have sent me) is, I presume, a gentleman connected with the Government Emigration Office who has written various stories arising out of Australian life which have appeared in Household Words. Before seeing the girl referred to (which I will gladly do) I will write him one line of enquiry respecting this Mr Crookenden — to make sure that he is what he represents himself.[5]

I think the case described, a very possible one as to its present history — *not* as to its past history. I very much doubt that part of the statement. However, to arrest such a course in the beginning, would be to do immense good. Whether the girl's character be what it is represented, or anything near it, can only be found out (I think) by seeing her.

Pursuing the enquiry I had begun when I last wrote to you, about the Australian Newspaper, I did *not* find that it seemed a promising affair.

The most bewildering doubts beset me concerning "Trip" — or "Flip" — I can't make out which it is. I hardly think you would propose Flip to me (which is a strong drink) at Noon; and unless the word is "Trip", and means Mrs Brown, I am on a Wide Ocean of conjecture. (Since writing the above, I have looked at your note again, in a sudden burst of hope that it might be "Tripe" — but there is no e). It *must* be Mrs Brown!

I am afraid I cannot get out in the middle of the day on Thursday, for I am hard at work with No 5, and anxious to get it done. And if I let myself out of my room under such circumstances, I have lost my power over myself for the day. But I will try. If I don't succeed, and you will ask me to come and see you any day next week at 5 or 6 o'clock, I shall be truly glad. Not that I quite give up Thursday yet.

I thought you were coming back to Highgate, instead of Stratton Street?

With my kindest regards to
T.R.I.P

---

[5] I have not identified either Mr. Sidney or Mr. Crookenden.

149. JULY 25, 1852, 10 CAMDEN CRESCENT, DOVER

We hope Mrs Brown is better? Any bulletin will be thankfully received.

I hear from Mrs Morson [6] that she is not elected, and that you have given her great joy by consenting to retain her. You have given me scarcely less, for I feel how kind and how right it is, and am sure she will prove worthy of it.

The Bishop of Capetown [7] has written me a note, proposing to call on me at Tavistock House at 2 on Wednesday next.

I *must* send you the enclosed (received yesterday evening) from Charley. Not only because he has done so well, but because it is such a brilliant boy's-letter. The immense and overweening importance of the boat race, and the necessity of returning to it with that tabular statement, amused me very much.

I am sure you will be glad to hear that Mr Stone (who is one of the Examiners at the East India College, and volunteers an examination periodically, at Mr Trimmer's at Putney [8]) writes me that he had occasion just now, to mention Walter with special commendation. I am much pleased to hear it, as I have always thought him a little slow — though I have never made the mistake of attempting to quicken him, I must add in self defence.

We are very pleasantly situated here in a very cool house.[9] I suppose there is no chance of your coming this way?

[P.S.] I have two girls ready, and am to see another on Wednesday.

☙

150. AUGUST 1, 1852, 10 CAMDEN CRESCENT, DOVER

I have instituted — through my Sub Editor Mr Wills, who is a most conscientious gentleman, and well accustomed to my sort of enquiry

---

[6] Mrs. Morson had been seeking appointment in another position, but, failing to obtain it, was kept on in her post at the Home.

[7] See note 3 to letter of August 12, 1849. Robert Gray had been educated at University College, Oxford, receiving his B.A. with an honorary fourth class in classics, was ordained deacon in 1833 and priest the following year, and held the livings of Whitworth, Durham, and then of Stockton, before becoming Bishop of Capetown.

[8] Mr. Trimmer, mentioned in Dickens's letter of August 22, 1851, was a coach who prepared students especially for admission to the East India Company's military college at Addiscombe and the Indian service.

[9] Dickens and his family were at Dover from July through October. He praised its sea air and country walks, but found the place "too bandy (I mean musical, no reference to its legs) and infinitely too genteel."

— the most searching examination into the case of the clergyman Mr Richards. He has produced a number of letters (a very affecting one from his wife among the number) and a quantity of references, principally to clergyman. One of them being a clergyman at Ham, of whom we had some knowledge Mr Wills went down and saw him, among several others. The representations made in Mr Richard's letter, he fully and entirely corroborated; adding that he had the highest opinion of him and confidence in him. He also said that he was a sensible and moderate clergyman — *not* tractarian — and that he was a man of ability, and that his preaching was far above the averge. So much so, that this Ham gentleman had great hopes for him of some good to himself finally resulting from his having a license to preach in London.

I do not think there is any room whatever to doubt that he has faithfully described his case. I need not observe that we have made all these enquiries with as much delicacy as care, and that no one has any idea of your being in any way connected with them.

Will you let me know by return of post what you will do for him, and whether I shall come to you for the money on Wednesday forenoon when I come to town? I am sorry that I cannot be at the Committee tomorrow, but I am steeped in work.

I write a few lines to Mr Brown by this post, in answer to a kind note of his, referring to the death of my dear friend Watson.[1] Poor dear fellow he was with us this day three weeks, so happy, and so full of Christmas plans for Rockingham!

∽

151.   AUGUST 3, 1852, 10 CAMDEN CRESCENT, DOVER

The sum named in the Clergyman's letter as the extent of the embarrassments which have placed him in a condition of so much suffering is a hundred pounds. Your recollection is quite accurate.

Since I wrote to you, I have made some further enquiries (at his request), and they fully establish the results of the former examination.

Perhaps you will send to me at the Household Words office tomorrow forenoon, instead of Tavistock House, as I am likely to be kept at the office some hours.

---

[1] The Honorable Richard Watson, at whose home at Rockingham there had been amateur theatricals in 1849 and 1851. Dickens was deeply grieved. "When I think of that bright house," he wrote, "and his fine simple honest heart, both so open to me, the blank and loss are like a dream."

We sincerely hope that Mrs Brown will begin to move in good sound earnest now. I should think nothing so likely to do her good as change. The country about Streatham is very pretty.

Our kindest regards to her.

P.S. In giving the clergyman the money, may I tell him from whom it comes?

ぐ

152. AUGUST 5, 1852, 10 CAMDEN CRESCENT, DOVER. N.B. NOT 32 CAMDEN TERRACE

I have safely received the one hundred pounds — your noble gift to Mr Richards — and have myself placed it in his hands. As he assumed that the friend whom I did not mention was a gentleman, and spoke of the friend as "him," I acted on that suggestion and did the same. He hopes that he has obtained a curacy in Regent Street. This will bring him to London; and he seems sincerely anxious that I should know all about his proceedings after he comes here. I shall hear of him again, I have no doubt.

You remember Mrs Goldsmith of Oliver's family, to whom you were very kind sometime ago, and who behaved so exceedingly well in foregoing half the sum she might have had, when she found it was not actually wanted for the purpose she had supposed it would be necessary for? Enclosed is a letter from her, which I think I ought to shew you, though I am very much indisposed to do so. I can give her half the money she wants, from a little sum I have in hand for such purposes.

Poor Watson was buried yesterday, in his own church. She is a woman of great courage and understanding, and of a well disciplined though very affectionate nature. I hope she will find comfort and resignation in sources that she has not been accustomed to neglect while happy. She has four children (the eldest eleven years old) and expects to be confined sometime hence — which is very sad. She has come home, her brother writes me, far more tranquilly than they could have hoped, and has her children about her, and means, from the first, to live with them at Rockingham — whither she went, straight. I am so glad to think that she can associate her home with his grace.

Our best regards to Mrs Brown, of whom we are extremely glad to hear such hopeful tidings.

153. AUGUST 8, 1852, 10 CAMDEN CRESCENT, DOVER

I have safely received the £10 note, your kind donation to Mrs Goldsmith, and have remitted it to her. I am glad you think so well of the case. It certainly *is* helping those who help themselves.

There must be some odd electrical disturbance in the air, I think. Everybody is complaining of being more or less nervously affected. Mr Forster (who has gone, for a change, to Tavistock House) fluctuates like Mrs Brown, and makes slow progress.

Our united regards to her and Mr Brown. I am glad Brighton did him so much good.

154. SEPTEMBER 2, 1852, ADELPHI HOTEL, LIVERPOOL

Your account of Mrs Brown makes me very anxious. Surely it is a singular illness, requiring investigation from a great many points of view. Don't you think it might be well to take Southwood Smith's opinion? Mr Brown knows best, — but Southwood Smith's experience and observation of all the eccentricities of fever, are so great that I should think him extremely likely to have seen cases like it.

My Sanitary Institution has this particular feature that you *can't* subscribe to it. You must be a shareholder. You are only responsible to the extent of your shares. The object in this, is, to assist the poor to help themselves, and not to pauperize them. I will cause the papers descriptive of the Society, to be sent to you. I have no doubt of its being worthy of support.

I sent you a paper from Manchester this afternoon, with a report in it of a dinner to the Guild. With that gallant people at my back — as they always are — I have a more fervent hope than ever, of setting right at last what is very wrong in my calling. I have the object so deeply at heart, and so strongly feel the advantage I have in my present power in such matters (which involves a great duty) that I am in a desperate earnestness that I think must produce something. I am afraid you hardly think with me now — but you will.

I wish you could have seen the opening of the Free Library for the people, at Manchester today. Such a noble effort, so wisely and modestly made; so wonderfully calculated to keep one part of that awful machine, a great working town, in harmony with the other!

We acted — not the dismal comedy, but Used Up and the Farce — ²

---

² These were the concluding performances undertaken for the benefit of the Guild of Literature and Art, at Manchester on September 1 and at Liverpool on

to some 4000 people last night, and finish here tomorrow night. I shall be in town at 12 on Monday — going to Dover — and shall call to ask after Mrs Brown.

ᴄᴬᴼ

155.   SEPTEMBER 14, 1852, 10 CAMDEN CRESCENT, DOVER

I have just heard of what you will have been long prepared for, but what I fear will cause you, notwithstanding, some natural distress. I was walking at Walmer this afternoon, and little thought that the great old man was dying or dead.[3] He had been a steady friend to an uncle of Mrs Dickens who was Colonel of Engineers here; and his son left word a little while ago, while we were at dinner, that the Duke was dead.

I believe that what you write about Westminster [4] is the whole truth and force of that subject, and that there is no better way of doing good, or of preparing the great mass of mankind to think of the great doctrines of our Saviour. If I were to try to tell you what I foresee from your lending your aid to what is so practically and plainly Christian with no fear of mistake, your modest way of looking at what you do would scarcely believe me. But you will live to see what comes of it, and that will be — here — your great reward.

September 3. All told, they cleared more than £ 5000. On the second, Dickens spoke at the opening of the Manchester Free Library, and at a public dinner Lytton spoke brilliantly about the Guild. It will be observed that Dickens's sentiments about the merits of *Not So Bad as We Seem* had notably declined, and that it was dropped from the last Manchester performance in favor of *Used Up* and *Mr. Nightingale's Diary*. The second of these was a screamingly ludicrous farce, a collaboration between Dickens and Mark Lemon, in which Dickens played no fewer than six parts: a lawyer, a Sam Wellerish waiter, a maniacally enthusiastic walker, a hypochondriac, a gabbling Sairey Gamplike old woman, and a deaf sexton.

[3] The Duke of Wellington died at Walmer Castle that day.

[4] The paragraph about Westminster may refer either to Miss Coutts's religious and educational work or to a sanitary project under way there. St. Stephen's Church, which she had built and endowed in memory of her father, Sir Francis Burdett, had been consecrated June 24, 1850, when its altar cloth was presented by the Duke of Wellington, who also gave the church a sixteenth-century silk curtain taken from the tent of Tippoo Sahib at the storming of Seringapatam. Adjoining the church was Miss Coutts's school for boys, girls, and infants, with which were connected Guilds, Working and Friendly Societies, Bible classes, and a soup kitchen that in the course of a few years served over 70,000 dinners to the indigent of this poor district. In addition Miss Coutts was conducting a survey of its tenements that resulted in a plan by which, if the landlords installed sanitary facilities and running water, she agreed to pay them any costs over a given estimated sum.

I felt, when I came back, that I had so much to do with Bleak House that it was not safe for me to contemplate doing nothing next Wednesday. So I proposed to Mr Stone for that day week. As soon as I receive his answer I will write again.

I am glad Southwood Smith will have an opportunity of considering Mrs Brown's case. The results of a great mass of that peculiar experience, *must* be useful in so delicate a matter — if only as confirming your faith in what is being done.

∽

156. SEPTEMBER 20, 1852, 10 CAMDEN CRESCENT, DOVER

When I received your note this afternoon, I intended to write to you tomorrow (after waiting for the morning's post, and getting nothing to the contrary by it) to tell you that although I wrote to Mr Stone as we agreed, I have received no answer from him and suppose he is still out of town.

I will now propose Wednesday week, which will quite suit me. In the Shepherd's Bush matter, a great deal seems to me to depend upon the possibility of getting the two houses under one roof as it were, and managing them with the same staff and at no increased expence for supervision. If that could be done, I should think it might be very desirable to increase the capacity of the Home. But this of necessity so depends upon the nature of the premises that I should like to see them before further considering the subject. If you would like to see them too, perhaps we could go out there on the same Wednesday?

I am quite delighted with your letter, for the double intelligence of your sister and Mrs Brown, makes me feel as if you were throwing down your late troubles altogether, like Christian and his difficult bundle in the Pilgrim's Progress. Heaven grant that it may be so, and that we may soon have Mrs Brown in a good contradictory humour again! I long to have a disagreement with her.

[P.S.] I had a long talk with Charley before he went back, in which he behaved in such a manly manner and shewed himself to be such a fine fellow, that he rather disturbed my judicial equanimity. He told me that he would certainly like the Army. I told him, in return, that he must consider the practical difficulties and drawbacks of the life, as well as the bright side. I set both fairly before him, and he then said he would like time to consider, as he would wish to understand himself and do right. So I settled to go and take a walk with him next month, & decide the question in a perfectly open and unreserved confidence.[5] He is the best of boys now, and I hope will not be among anything but the best of men.

ᴄ⅃ᴐ

157.   SEPTEMBER 23, 1852, 10 CAMDEN CRESCENT, DOVER

The whole Public seems to me to have gone mad about the funeral of the Duke of Wellington.[6] I think it a grievous thing — a relapse into semi-barbarous practices — an almost ludicrous contrast to the calm good sense and example of responsibility set by the Queen Dowager — a pernicious corruption of the popular mind, just beginning to awaken from the long dream of inconsistencies, monstrosities, horrors and ruinous expences, that has beset all classes of society in connexion with Death — and a folly sure to miss its object and to be soon attended by a strong re-action on the memory of the illustrious man so mis-respected.

But to say anything about it now, or to hope to leaven with any grain of sense such a mass of wrong-doing, would be utterly useless. Afterwards, I shall try to present the sense of the case in Household Words. At present, I think I might as well whistle to the sea.

I quite concur with you as to Mr Stone and the Westminster project. The survey is actively going on. Do you think you can let me know, by Tuesday, whether you will go to Shepherd's Bush on Wednesday? If not, a note to the Household Words office on Wednesday forenoon will do as well. I shall be there, at 11.

ᴄ⅃ᴐ

158.   OCTOBER 23, 1852, TAVISTOCK HOUSE

As soon as I came home this week (and consequently, before I received your kind note) I set off to see Mr Austin on the Westminster question. But I found him gone to Wales on a visit of sanitary inspection, though soon expected back. He is not yet returned. When he "turns up" — as my friend Mr Micawber might observe — I will have some talk with him, and should like to see you with him whenever you can appoint a time. I understand the merits of the great encounter

---

[5] Ultimately Charley decided against the Army, in favor of a commercial career.

[6] In an article entitled "Trading in Death" in *Household Words*, November 27, 1852, Dickens denounced the barbarous show and expense of state funerals and quoted a large number of advertisements that had appeared in the *Times* offering for sale seats to view the funeral, autograph letters, and locks of the Duke's hair.

of the Windmills, as Mr Austin stated them to me at Dover. If you were successful in the quixotic attack, you would be saved a very large, and (I am quite convinced) an unnecessary expence. But the scheme must not be paralyzed by the encounter, whether or no.

Your description of the placid Doctor [7] makes me laugh in a most ridiculous manner whenever I think of it. I always feel inclined to take him by the throat and squeeze the words he *won't* say and *won't* be helped to (for if you suggest them he positively refuses to take them but goes floundering on in the profoundest contentment), out of him by force. He is an excellent creature, however, and knows what he is about far better than he seems to — which is not saying much for him, but I mean a great deal more.

We are greatly relieved, and very glad, to hear that Mrs Brown continues to mend. I have effected, and am effecting, several small improvements in the internal arrangements here, which I shall hope to hear both your and her commendation of, by the glow of a winter fire. I bought at Boulogne, a little figure for my study chimney-piece *which was the sign of a tobacconist's shop,* and which, for the most grotesque absurdity, I consider unrivalled.

Tomorrow I am going to Shepherd's Bush. Charley and I hold our council at Eton on Wednesday.

With kindest and truest regards

[P.S.] I am glad you liked the paper on Graves and Epitaphs.[8] Since I came back I have been busily projecting a great variety of subjects for Household Words.

ตัว

159.   OCTOBER 30, 1852, TAVISTOCK HOUSE

On coming home from the Household Words office last night, I found Lord Douro's note,[9] asking me to call there yesterday or today. I was about writing this morning to say I was quite laid up with my cold and would come on Monday, when I received your letter relative to your being there on Monday. I have written Ld Douro to that effect,

---

[7] Unidentified.

[8] "Graves and Epitaphs" was an article in *Household Words,* October 16, 1852.

[9] The Duke of Wellington had been created Baron Douro in 1809 and Marquis of Douro in 1814, and it is probable that his eldest son, Arthur Richard Wellesley (1809–1884) was known by that title during his father's lifetime. Dickens may either have been absent-mindedly calling him by his former name or have been referring to his younger brother Charles (1808–1858). Miss Coutts was a close friend of the family and had been since her childhood a favorite of the great Duke.

and said I will call between 12 and 1 on Monday, while you *are* there.

I went out yesterday to Fulham, and occasioned the most frightful consternation in Auckland Cottage by unexpectedly appearing in the rain. A large young family fled from the back parlor, on a visitor being announced, and took refuge (with their mother) at the top of the stairs — where they stood, as I saw from the passage, like so many Ostriches — with their heads hidden, but their legs plainly visible; and I think I never saw so many legs listening at once, as while I inquired for Mrs Brayne.[1] Being shewn into the vacated back parlor, I was there presently confronted by the wrong Mrs Brayne, a muscular lady with very large bones, to whom I timidly intimated my profound conviction that she was not the ancient artist you had described to me. She replied, "No doubt it was her mother in law I wanted," and, withdrawing, sent in a little bright-eyed old lady in a grey and mulberry-colored knitted polka, whom I perceived to be the right Mrs Brayne. She shewed me the copy. I apprehend there is not much choice of a frame, for it must be fitted in a case to shut up, or it would fade in no time; being a kind of work that will not bear much exposure to the light. I therefore advised her to make the gilt flat frame within the case something wider than usual, and pointed out to her another slight alteration in the usual measurement of such things, which increases the effect. The whole to be fitted in a morocco case. This, I settled she might proceed to do, after Tuesday, if in the meantime she heard nothing to the contrary.

I send you Mr a Beckett's last letter in reference to the girl of whom I spoke to you. There is something in it (that about her telling the children stories) that I connect so strangely with her bruised face when I saw her, that I fancy it will interest you too. She was here with her father (a very decent man indeed, and very sorrowful about her) this morning, and I will give Mrs Morson all needful instructions today.

This brings me to another point about the Home, which I have had in my mind a good deal since I was last there. Talking with Mrs Morson about Susan Matcham's illness, I found (what I have found before) that they are strangely indifferent to one another in sickness, and hardly seem to have the least natural tenderness for the sufferer. Now in their own lives outside, they are so very different in this respect — being generally extremely compassionate — that I take this to be, some-

---

[1] Unidentified.

how or other, our fault in a great measure; and considering the subject further, I am inclined to think that this indifference springs out of our doing too much. What I would propose to try, is, that while Mrs Morson neglects nothing of her kindness and vigilance to a sick young woman, the very circumstance of there being somebody sick in the house, shall be made to change (as it would in any ordinary house) the regular domestic occupations, and that she shall make Nurses of the whole party, one after another, and let them in regular turns sit by the bedside and tend the girl who is ill. I should greatly wish to try this plan, for there is something shocking (and in any other point of view that I can think of, unaccountable) in their being so remiss in one of the most natural feelings of humanity. I shall be going out to the Home on Monday after I see you, and will explain all this to Mrs Morson in its full force, if you approve. It is very desirable to get this right if we by any means can; not only because it is so wrong in itself, but because so many occurrences are constantly taking place among girls, of Anne Johnson's stamp for instance, shewing tenderness in sickness and death which is an uncomfortable thing to set against their being quite hard-hearted to one another in the Home.

I saw the writer of the letters I sent you, yesterday evening — a lady in manners — well educated and sensible, and evidently trying very hard. I found that five and twenty pounds would pay her rent, and enable her to compound for some of her more pressing little debts; but I could not satisfy myself that a smaller sum was likely to be of real service to her. So I gave her £25. We settled how it was to be applied, and she is to write me a letter setting forth in detail what she has done with it, presently.

Lastly, and to conclude this long epistle, I cannot tell you how much I thank you for writing to Charley. It is what I could have most wished, and what I know will be of service and encouragement to him above all things. In sending him the letter, I have consulted his inclinations about the time of leaving Eton, and have told him to write to me on that head.

Mr Trimmer's prospectus I enclose.

With kind regards to Mr and Mrs Brown (and three cheers for Boulogne) ever Dear Miss Coutts

[P.S.] I think of doing something about the Thames Police, and had some of the Toll takers at Waterloo Bridge at the office yesterday to put some questions to them about their experience of Suicide. Their answers were rather curious. Almost all the attempts are by women — a man, quite a rarity.[2]

⁓

160.   NOVEMBER 1, 1852, TAVISTOCK HOUSE

I waited for you at Lord Douro's today, until a quarter before two. I pointed out those peculiarities we spoke of, to Mr Adams,[3] and he made some alterations in that part of the face — *I* think (and I hope you will think) greatly to its improvement. I also found, according to my eye, the mouth much too tight, and a general want there about of a suggestion of flexibility. This the sculptor also worked upon. It seems to me that the best and most hopeful thing that can possibly be done now, is to let the sculptor alone. The bust is far more like than any I have seen, and strikes me as possessing very great merit.

I went to the Home afterwards, and made the enclosed memorandum, on a calculation, about the marks. I told Mrs Morson that we would not announce the value, until after the departure of the next party. I thought it would prevent — or might prevent — any little inconsistencies. There had been some indications of a small assault by Stallion upon the brownish-yellow girl, Youngman. Both had behaved with perfect submission, except in the heat of a moment — both were in fault — and I had both in, and pointed out to them how wrong they were and told them to be friends.

On then coming home to dinner, I found the enclosed from Charley. He hits exactly my apprehension — that retaining him there in that unsettled state, might be a mere loss of time. Shall I write to his "Dame" and Tutor, saying it is *probable* he will leave at Christmas? I shall wait for your answer before doing so.

⁓

MARKS MEMORANDUM

The average earning of Marks is about 170 per week. (rather a high average).

At six and sixpence per thousand, eight thousand marks in a year would be £2..12..0. I have therefore fixed the price at six and six-

---

[2] Dickens does not seem to have written anything on this subject.

[3] I have not identified Mr. Adams, but the remainder of the paragraph makes it seem likely that he was a sculptor, probably working on a bust of the Duke of Wellington.

pence per thousand. I would also propose to allow girls who are ill, to be credited during the time of their illness, *with their usual average gain of marks when well.*

The foregoing calculation proceeds upon the data, twelve months of four weeks each in a year. This leaves a little margin. Calculated at fifty two weeks in a year, the girl would earn some five shillings or so more. But, as I have already noted, 170 good marks a week seems, according to the mass of markpapers, rather a high average.

⟶

161.   NOVEMBER 3, 1852, TAVISTOCK HOUSE
I have writen to Mr Cookesley and Mr Evans, telling them that Charley will leave at Christmas for the purpose of going to Germany.[4]

I shall be very much obliged to you if you will enquire about the German Master. I think the French will be comparatively easy, for his ear was well used to it when he was young, and he could speak quite fluently when we were in Switzerland and in Paris. Mamey and Katey have a french Governess every day, and we could easily make a conversation class of the whole four (Charley being the fourth) in the holiday time.

I am quite vexed about the State Funeral. I think it is altogether wrong as regards the memory of the Duke, and at least equally wrong in the Court estimate it implies of the People. The nonsense of the Heralds' College and Lord Chamberlain absurdities, keep his own soldiers away; the only real links of sympathy the public could have found in it are carefully filed off; and a vulgar holiday, with a good deal of business for the thieves and the public houses, will be the chief result.

You will see an account of an Irish Workhouse [5] in the current No of Household Words, which seems to me rather a good commentary on the rampant Irish nonsense (and worse) about the Saxon.

[P.S.] If you can spare me your box at Drury Lane once or twice during Jullien's [6] concert season, I shall be very glad to use it.

---

[4] It had now been decided that Charley, who was almost sixteen, should not embark upon a military career, but become a businessman. For this purpose he was to acquire a speaking and writing knowledge of German as well as French.

[5] "The Irish Union," *Household Words*, November 6, 1852.

[6] Louis Antoine Jullien (1812–1860), French composer and musical director, who gave a series of popular concerts at the English Opera House 1842–1852. During the following two years he was in the United States.

162.   NOVEMBER 19, 1852, TAVISTOCK HOUSE
First, about the Home.

Shall I write to the woman at Boxley near Maidstone whose letter
you enclosed to me in your last?

It has been necessary to discharge Stallion who turned out to be a
ferocious temper, and probably would have done some serious damage
to somebody if she had remained. Little Willis from the Ragged School
having tried her hand at the Key and Bible business [7] (in bed and in
the dark, knowing it to be wrong) I told Mrs Morson that unless she
behaved very well, she should have no marks for a month. After a
day or two I went out, and she requested to see me, and said — I wish
you could have seen her come in diplomatically to make terms with
the establishment, "O! Without her marks, she found she couldn't
do her work agreeable to herself" — "If you do it agreeable to us," said
I, "that'll do." — "O! But" she said "I could wish not to have my marks
took away." — "Exactly so," said I. "That's quite right; and the only
way to get them back again, is to do as well as you can." — "Ho! But if
she didn't have 'em giv' up at once, she could wish fur to go." — "Very
well," said I. "You shall go tomorrow morning."

Both these dismissals had a very good effect in the house, particularly on the new girl from Mr a Beckett: who was a little dubious, and
to whom I spoke very seriously, telling her that if she once got outside
the gate we knew, better than she might think for now, what she would
give if she could, to come back. Mr Tracey, having sent Stallion, discharged her. She had no clothes of her own, and, it being a very wet
day, they gave her an old but decent bonnet and shawl — which she
immediately threw away in the Lane. To provide for such a case again,
I told Mrs Morson to buy at a slop-seller's, the commonest and ugliest
and coarsest (but still clean and whole) woman's dress that she could
possibly purchase, and invariably to keep such a thing by her. It occurs
to me that they will be very beneficially astonished when we have
occasion to bring it out.

All the rest doing very well, and no complaints.

I cannot by any means find out the truth about Kelly's soup-kitchen,
because it is not in action. But it was certainly found that the Soup
Kitchen and Hospice in Leicester Square had an effect directly the
reverse of that which he predicts, and assembled the sturdy vagrants
from all quarters. His convictions on the subject are so extraordinary,

---

[7] Unexplained.

that I would strongly advise you to do nothing yet, but to let me keep my eye a little while upon the place. With that view, I retain the letter. I can hardly compass the possibility of its having the anticipated result, but we will fairly see.

In the matter of the Household Narrative,[8] I think, on looking back to the previous numbers, that there is nothing to be done, as to the Duke's Memory, beyond a general account of the Funeral Ceremony — unless there be anything that you would *like* to add about his character. If you will send me anything, of course I will take care to append it in the right place. I came home yesterday in time to write an article for the next No of Household *Words* — which I had kept open for the purpose, and which is now at press, of necessity — objecting to the whole State Funeral,[9] and shewing why. I will send you a proof — tomorrow night, I hope — thinking you may like to read it.

The Military part of the show, was very fine. If it had been an ordinary Funeral of a great commander, it might have been impressive. I suppose for forms of ugliness, horrible combinations of color, hideous motion, and general failure, there never was such a work achieved as the Car.

It will be a great satisfaction to us, to know that Mrs Brown keeps well. I have been so busy, leading up to the great turning idea of the Bleak House,[1] that I have lived this last week or ten days in a perpetual scald and boil.

ϛↃↄ

163. DECEMBER 3, 1852, TAVISTOCK HOUSE
I have held a Council today with Mr Austin and our rapid light-

---

[8] *The Household Narrative of Current Events* was a supplement to *Household Words,* presenting without editorial comment a condensation of all important news, under the main headings of Parliament and Politics, Law and Crime, Accident and Disaster, Social, Sanitary, and Municipal Progress, Obituaries, Colonies and Dependencies, Foreign Events, Commercial Record, Stocks and Shares, and Emigration Figures. Although unillustrated, and even more succinct, it was a forerunner of the modern news weekly.

[9] "Trading in Death," *Household Words,* November 27, 1852.

[1] *Bleak House,* No. 9, December (Chapters XXVI–XXIX), in which Mr. Tulkinghorn tries to obtain Captain Hawdon's letters from Trooper George, and Mr. Guppy, interviewing Lady Dedlock about Esther Summerson (the illegitimate daughter of Captain Hawdon and Lady Dedlock), hints that he has discovered the relationship. The discovery and revelation of Lady Dedlock's secret precipitated the catastrophe of the main plot of the story.

comedy friend the Doctor,[2] on the subject of the Westminster Improvements.[3]

The matter is now in this state. The survey and plans are completed, and the detailed estimates made out, for "the block" of houses lying between Willow Street and Cobourg Row, which stand in great need of efficient drainage, connected with good water supply. This district includes rather less than a third (at a rough calculation) of the whole district; and the estimates for the necessary improvements make the total cost (for 150 houses) £420.

These houses belong to about eighteen proprietors, of whom the greater part are reasonably well off; and the largest of these proprietors, one Mr Bennet, appears to be a decent man. Now on going into the question carefully, it appears to us unreasonable that you should pay (if it can possibly be avoided) for the permanent improvement of their property. Our course we therefore propose to take thus: — Mr Austin will see this Mr Bennet, and the next large proprietor or two, and point out to them that for the sake of their poor tenants you have gone to the trouble and expence of having these surveys and estimates made, and of shewing them for how little money they can greatly improve the dwellings. If we find them reasonable, we then propose to put it to them that with such help and encouragement they ought to pay for the alterations on their property, and to use their influence with the smaller proprietors to do the like. (If they seem reasonable, we think it may be well to hold a little private meeting of them all, and talk to them). As it is a regular ingredient in that helpless state of ignorance, to suppose that sanitary improvement is very dear instead of very cheap; and as it is most likely that they will therefore plead a doubt of the estimates; we then propose to say "you may set your minds at rest on that score, for we guarantee to you, on the part of Miss Coutts, that they shall not be exceeded — in other words that if there be any excess, she will pay it." If it should turn out to be absolutely necessary to the good work that you should do more in the first instance, we can consult with you further on that point. But it seems so right that this should be our first attitude, and I feel so confident of your thinking so, that I have set this scheme in motion.

---

[2] Clearly some kind of joke, but "our rapid light-comedy friend the Doctor" cannot be identified.

[3] The project mentioned at the end of Note 1 on Dickens's letter of September 14, 1852.

Our light-comedy friend Young Rapid, and Mr Austin, are now inclined to think that if we could ask the sanction of the Commissioners of Sewers to this portion of the improvements, *with the proprietors'* *consent and co-operation,* they would not throw many obstacles in the way. And we could go to them with this portion of the plans and estimates only, and (their authority obtained) could go to work, while the remainder of the plans and estimates were yet being made out.

No more at present on that point. I now come to the Home.

Everything is quiet and comfortable there. I paid the bills for last month, which (with £5 petty cash to Mrs Morson) amounted to £43..16..0. I wrote to the woman near Maidstone, and she came up here with her daughter — a girl of only 16. She is a very decent woman, whose name is Donovan. Her sister's name is Wallis, and her sister wrote the letter to you, in consequence of Mrs Donovan's "not being a scholar." The girl comes from a bad school (where I dreamed my first dreams of authorship when I was six years old or so), namely Chatham,[4] and I think she may be of rather a shrewish temper; but it is undoubtedly a case to make trial of, and I have given Mrs Morson instructions to fetch the girl.

— No more about that, and now I come to Charley. Doctor Hawtrey has broken up the school a few days before the time, in consequence of the vast quantity of outlying water in the neighbourhood; and the said Charley appeared with his boxes today. The Doctor was very sorry to part with him, and, in proof of his popularity, he brought home nineteen presents of new books from boys. I enclose you his tutor's letter concerning him. The fee to which he refers, is one of three sets of fees amounting to Thirty Pounds which are paid by boys on going away. I quite agree with him on the gross and disagreeable nature of such transactions in such a place, and felt quite uncomfortable in complying with the custom. The companion fee of fifteen pounds to the Tutor, is one of ten pounds to the Doctor. I asked Charley when he gave me notice a week or two ago that these would have to be paid, whether he paid the Doctor's fee himself? He said "Yes. The way it was, was this. The boy called on the Doctor to say Goodbye, and the Doctor went and stirred the fire, and the boy put ten pounds on the table"!

---

[4] A dame school at Chatham that Dickens and his sister Fanny briefly attended; the old woman who conducted it was in part the model for Mrs. Pipchin in *Dombey and Son.*

We hope Mrs Brown continues to do well, and that you get brighter weather where you are (and where I dined yesterday!) [5] than we get here. I look forward to sending you next week, a week or more before its publication, the extra Christmas No of Household Words. It has cost me some pains, and I think is very pretty. [6]

∾

164.   DECEMBER 9, 1852, TAVISTOCK HOUSE
I know a certain Chevalier Bernhard Taüchnitz, [7] at Leipzig, whom I think an extremely likely man to suggest a good place for Charley. He is a publisher by profession (the largest, I believe, in Germany), but is a gentleman of great honor and integrity too, and well acquainted with all the most celebrated men of letters in Europe. I have had many transactions with him, referring to all my books, and am well acquainted with him personally, and with his thoroughly good reputation besides.

I thought of him before, when Mr Engelbach occurred to you. If you approve, I will write to him now. But I shall do nothing until I know that you think well of it.

∾

165.   DECEMBER 16, 1852, TAVISTOCK HOUSE [TO MRS. BROWN FROM CHARLES DICKENS]
You may faintly imagine my astonishment on receiving your packet last night. The enormous number of letters that come here from all parts of the Earth, render general instructions necessary that nothing is to be taken in, on which postage requires to be paid. But of course there are exceptions perpetually, — as in the present inscrutable instance.

---

[5] The Hotel Bedford at Brighton, where Dickens had dined with John Leech the cartoonist after the two had enjoyed a day's walk on the Downs.

[6] The extra Christmas Number of *Household Words* bore the title, "A Round of Stories by the Christmas Fire." In it, "The Poor Relation's Story" and "The Child's Story" were by Dickens.

[7] Christian Bernhard Tauchnitz (1816–1895), the publisher of the well-known Tauchnitz Editions begun in 1841. The first work published in this edition was Bulwer Lytton's *Pelham;* the second, in the same year, was *Pickwick* in two volumes, followed in 1842 by *American Notes*. Although there were no laws of international copyright at this time, in 1843 Tauchnitz visited England and arranged with many leading authors to pay them a fee for authorization to reprint any of their future writings in Germany. Henceforth all of Dickens's books were printed by Tauchnitz from corrected advance proofs that Dickens sent to Leipzig.

A servant whom I have had for twelve years, and who had attained to an almost preternatural sagacity in these things, having left me to be married (and to keep the Household Words office), has been replaced by a pastoral youth under whose administration I feel my brain reeling. Pray tell Miss Coutts of his horrible incapability. What *can* she have thought of my not answering such a letter at once! The idea of having lived for a fortnight with such a cool appearance upon me, makes me almost desperate, and impels me to shake the innocent cause of my degradation in the eyes I most care for.

Between 4 and 5 tomorrow, I will appear in Stratton Street, when I hope I may not be "R E F U S E D" too.

∽

166. JANUARY 7, 1853, 16 WELLINGTON STREET NORTH — STRAND; OFFICE OF *Household Words*

I have been down to this Saint Mark's District today, as a reasonably bad day on which to see it at its worst, and have looked well over it. It is intensely poor in some parts; and chiefly supported by river, wharf, and dock, employment; and by some lead mills. In one corner is a spot called Hickman's Folly (a Folly it is much to be regreted that Hickman ever committed), which looks like the last hopeless climax of everything poor and filthy. There is a public house in it, with the odd sign of the Ship Aground, but it is wonderfully appropriate, for everything seems to have got aground there — never to be got off any more until the whole globe is stopped in its rolling and shivered. No more road than in an American swamp — odious sheds for horses, and donkeys, and vagrants, and rubbish, in front of the parlor windows — wooden houses like horrible old packing cases full of fever for a countless number of years. In a broken down gallery at the back of a row of these, there was a wan child looking over at a starved old white horse who was making a meal of oyster shells. The sun was going down and flaring out like an angry fire at the child — and the child, and I, and the pale horse, stared at one another in silence for some five minutes as if we were so many figures in a dismal allegory. I went round to look at the front of the house, but the windows were all broken and the door was shut up as tight as anything so dismantled could be. Lord knows when anybody will go in to the child, but I suppose it's looking over still — with a little wiry head of hair, as pale as the horse, all sticking up on its head — and an old weazen face — and two bony hands holding on the rail of the gallery, with little fingers like convulsed skewers.

I have no doubt that there would be innumerable claimants upon any little fund sent to the Incumbents, but that may be said with equal truth of twenty places in a breath. There are no better sort of residents whatever — and never have been as I take it; which would account for the smallness of the sum in hand for purposes of charity. I am afraid it is not a promising place in which to try such an experiment as we have so much discussed. There is no lack of little houses to let, but there is no large space of ground; and I think the place to bad to attempt to make an oasis in. It would be of no use to touch a limb of Hickman — his whole body is infected, and would spoil the mended part. An act of parliament would be necessary to clear the place. (There *may* be some such power in existence, for I observed the "Bermondsey Improvement" announced like an official thing on a church wall.) Jacob's Island adjoins Hickman's Folly, and I see that the ditch I described in Oliver Twist has since been filled up. If you would like to see the place, I shall be glad to shew it to you any afternoon. Or I will see the Incumbent if you desire it.

I cannot make out the money account in detail, because you have Charley's bill, and I forget the precise amount. I however enclose the sum in compound addition duly drawn up, and it only wants that item and its results, to be complete.

I would have given anything that you had seen my Birmingham [8]

---

[8] Dickens was given a dinner on January 6 by the Society of Artists at Birmingham, where he was presented with a silver-gilt salver and a diamond ring. He took advantage of the occasion to voice his disbelief in "the coxcombical idea of writing down to the popular intelligence" and his belief in the people. "From the shame of the purchased dedication, from the scurrilous and dirty work of Grub Street, from the dependent seat on sufferance at my Lord Duke's table today, and from the sponging-house or Marshalsea tomorrow . . . the people have set literature free. And my creed in the exercise of that profession is, that literature cannot be too faithful to the people in return — cannot too ardently advocate the cause of their advancement, happiness, and prosperity. I have heard it sometimes said . . . that literature has suffered from this change, that it has degenerated by being made cheaper." But he himself, Dickens asserted, did not believe that to be true. "I believe there are in Birmingham at this moment many working men infinitely better versed in Shakespeare and in Milton than the average of fine gentlemen in the days of bought-and-sold dedications and dear books. I ask any one to consider for himself who, at this time, gives the greatest relative encouragement to the

people yesterday, for I don't think it possible to imagine such a scene quite accurately! I have promised at the end of the year, if all go well, to read the Christmas Carol to the Town Hall full of working people [9] (the salver and diamond ring were not confined to that class); and if there were any hope of your seeing them then, I think I could assure you of one of the most remarkable sights that this country could produce.

I asked the Mayor about the church experiment [1] you mentioned. He said it had failed — had not been required or warranted, as he considered, by the local circumstances — and was being gradually abandoned. I had not the opportunity of asking the same question of Archdeacon Sandford; for he sat at some distance from me at the public dinner there was — and he made such a speech about a certain Writer's books by the bye, that I think you must have heard the cheering at Mivart's [2] — but the mayor was quite confident, and spoke of the thing as a matter of fact.

With best regards to Mrs Brown

ᕗ

167.　　　　　　　　　　　　FEBRUARY 1, 1853, TAVISTOCK HOUSE

I found the foregoing scrap [3] in the Times of today, as I was reading it just now after dinner. Perhaps you may have seen it, but I send it. I had written a most savage and Zoological roaring on the subject for Household Words, this very morning (in pursuance of our parting talk yesterday) — and suppose it must now go among the lost treasures of mankind.

The Board of Health being engaged in some pressing enquiries at

---

dissemination of such useful publications as Macaulay's *History,* Layard's *Researches,* Tennyson's *Poems, The Duke of Wellington's Published Despatches,* or the minutest truths . . . discovered by the genius of a Herschel or a Faraday."

[9] Dickens did give three readings of the *Christmas Carol* the following winter, at the Birmingham Town Hall, December 27–30, in aid of the Literary and Scientific Institute.

[1] The Mayor was the Mayor of Birmingham, but the "church experiment" cannot be identified. Archdeacon Sandford was John Sandford (1801–1873), who was honorary Canon of Worcester 1844, Archdeacon of Coventry 1851, and examining chaplain to the Bishop of Worcester 1853–1860.

[2] A hotel in Brooke Street, London.

[3] At the top of the first page of this letter there is pasted the newspaper clipping referred to, which sets forth the story of a nurse, Mary Ann Oldham, who beat a child at Greenwich Union Workhouse, resulting in its death, and of her arrest and sentence to Newgate to await trial.

Croydon, Mr Austin proposes Thursday instead of Wednesday, for the Bermondsey expedition. As that evening is usually revising evening at Household Words, I will come in at Stratton Street on *Friday evening* if that will suit you. I shall conclude that it does, unless you tell me it does not.

Your note of last night suggests that we might adopt this, as a very good, practical, safe, and sound plan. First build the house. Then, before it is inhabited, make it known through a sensible handbill, plain to the commonest capacity (and well circulated in the neighbourhood) that it will be shewn and explained to all decently behaved people, on certain days. And then, to all who come, and to all the little tradesmen and so forth in the neighbourhood, give another little bill which shall be the history of the objects of the house — which shall state that they are easily attainable, in a considerable degree, by the humblest landlords; to the improvement of their own property, the greater happiness and health of their tenants, and their own peace of mind when they come to think about it — and which shall inform them in conclusion, that on a certain day and hour in every month any small proprietor will find in that Model House two or three gentlemen assembled, for the purpose of shewing him at how small an expence he can improve the houses he now lets — of giving him friendly advice — and even of assisting him to do what is right, if he will only do it. I think this, done from the 'vantage ground of the house itself which they can see and touch like so many Thomases, would be a discreet means of using your generosity to the best account. Perhaps you will think of it too.

[P.S.] I am sorry to say that Susan Matcham is neither at St Thomas's Hospital, nor at Guy's. Mr a Beckett sent this morning, and she had not been received at the one or the other.

∽

168. MARCH 6, 1853, BRIGHTON

I am afraid that "green" is not very verdant, and is near (if I have it in my mind correctly) to a most horrible smell of rotten skins. But I will look at it as soon as I come back, and then report further.

The case you extracted from the paper, is one of the most pitiable class of offences, and one to which the benevolence of the Home would be thoroughly well extended. But the concealment of the birth of a child being a misdemeanour, the poor creature *must* be tried and sentenced. As she will not be committed for trial (so I see by the report you enclosed) until after the lapse of a week, it would be premature to move now. On my return, I will communicate with the Magistrate, and with the chaplain of the prison in which she is, and try — supposing the case to be a good one — if we cannot get her after a short imprisonment. I think we may contrive to do it.

[P.S.] Charley has written from Cologne. He could not go on by the Rhine, as it was full of ice. Was to go to Hanover next day, and to Leipzig *next* day. He was very happy, he said, "except being from home."

∞

169.   APRIL 1, 1853, TAVISTOCK HOUSE

Mr Broderip [4] is the man. He is rather a distinguished Naturalist besides having long been a very good magistrate. I know him intimately. He is getting a little old now, but will do anything and everything in his power. He has often begged me to give you the assurance; but I have not troubled you with it — reserving it for any occasion when you might want his aid.

I concur in all your suggestions as to the Home article,[5] and will devote this evening to it. Everything shall be stated as you wish and I will take care to relieve it of all the little points in doubt. I clearly see the way to smoothing them down. Though it will not be published for a fortnight, it must be got to press now. But it shall not leave my hands until it is perfectly discreet.

Charley certainly seems, I hope and believe, to be admirably placed. I am quite certain they will take as much care of him as could be taken of him here. When he left me I wrote to Professor Müller a description of his character and his little weak points; and I read it to Charley himself, in order that he might know the confidence that was established between them. They seem to have come together in the most natural manner possible.

I am so dreadfully jaded this morning by the supernatural dreariness

---

[4] William John Broderip (1789–1859), lawyer and naturalist, educated at Oriel College, Oxford, called to the bar at Lincoln's Inn 1817, magistrate at the Thames Police Court 1822–1846 and at Westminster 1846–1856, F.L.S. 1824, F.R.S. 1828, founder and fellow of the Zoological Society 1826.

[5] "Home for Homeless Women," an account of the methods and work of Urania Cottage (although its name and location were left deliberately unmentioned) written for *Household Words* and published April 23, 1853.

of Kaye Shuttleworth,[6] that I feel as if I had just come out of the Great Desert of Sahara where my camel died a fortnight ago.

∽

170.   MAY 10, 1853, TAVISTOCK HOUSE

Your account of Anne Johnson has interested me very much indeed. I fancy that her disappointment in respect of that young man, may have more to do with her state of mind than she supposes; but it is a great thing to have that voluntary confession from her, and I shall hear Mrs Morson's account of her interview with her mother, with great curiosity and compassion. — I suppose it will not break the mother's heart to take the younger daughter away from her?

A considerable correspondence about the Home has poured in upon Household Words. I have kept the best part of it for you to read. The object has generally been, either to see the place or to subscribe towards its support. I have invariably answered on the first point that to give any further information would be to interfere with the discipline of the establishment and impose useless trouble on the superintendents. On the second point, I have of course replied that subscriptions are not accepted.

The post that brought me your note this morning, brought me the enclosed. Shall I do anything more?

Mr Lemon [7] the Editor of Punch, came to me privately on Sunday, to say that he had received a bitter letter from some man in Westminster — a lawyer of some sort, as he thought — complaining of the proposed improvements, and of "being put by Miss Coutts under the parsons." Mr Lemon had destroyed the letter as an impertinence, before he thought that I should probably know something about the subject, and might have liked to see it. He could not remember the writer's name, but I think from what he did recollect of the man's statement of his own case, I could pick the gentleman out if he should come to one of the meetings. I mention this, as an additional reason for your giving Mr Tennant a hint (if you think well of it) to be practical and business-

---

[6] Another expression of Dickens's recoil from the utilitarian factuality of Sir James Kay-Shuttleworth's educational philosophy.

[7] Mark Lemon (1809–1870), journalist, dramatist, and novelist, one of the founders of *Punch* and its first editor 1843–1870, one of Dickens's most constant associates in amateur theatricals, and a close friend who had sat up all night with him in 1851 beside the dead body of his infant daughter.

like above all things, *and not on any account to talk to them as if they were children.*

೦೪೨

171.   MAY 19, 1853, TAVISTOCK HOUSE

I think that must be all a mistake about that Suffolk baby your nephew, because (it is a remarkable fact) we have in this house the only baby worth mentioning; [8] and there cannot possibly be another baby anywhere, to come into competition with him. I happen to know this, and would like it to be generally understood.

I return Mrs Morson's letter. It is a very nice child (not being a baby) and will be very pretty and very like the sister. All was quiet on Tuesday. I paid the bills, and administered encouragement to the vicious Cranstone who seems to have been trying to do better. Also to Campbell who has her head shaved (in consequence of her hair falling off) and is low spirited in consequence. As well she may be, looking something between the knob on the top of a pair of tongs — a chinese — and a scraped dutch cheese.

I have Cubitt's plan for the new bedroom, *and* a small sitting room (which Mrs Morson says would be necessary, at cleaning times, with the increased number). It is sensible and practicable, and the estimated expence is £275. The whole could be erected (but of course not dried for occupation) in six weeks. Will you "seriously incline" your mind to the subject, and decide when it shall be done? I am anxious to arrange it all, as I shall be flying to Boulogne, and more peaceable work than London admits of at this time of year even to a paragon of seclusion like myself, early in June. And further, Cubitt's foreman is much distressed that we have no regular supply of water at Shepherd's Bush. He has craved leave to "look into it" and see what it would cost, which I have ventured to give him.

Now, will you read the enclosed from Mrs Matthews [9] (in answer to questions of mine) and tell me what I shall do. Your view of the Scandinavian book is mine, and therefore (?) I thought it very humour-

---

[8] Dickens's youngest child Edward, now only a little more than two, and soon to be known by a variety of fantastic nicknames, "the Plornish Maroon," "the Plornishghenter," "Mr. Plornishmaroontigoonter," usually shortened, however, to "Plorn."

[9] Mrs. Antonina Matthews, a begging-letter writer by whose appeals Dickens and Miss Coutts were for some time favorably impressed, and to whom they gave help, but who ultimately outwearied their patience by her increasingly unreasonable demands.

ous. Why a man who is for ever fainting away, should be making himself limper with Scandinavian poetry, is one of those extraordinary mysteries that the mind cannot fathom.

Being rather limp myself with working since ½ past 5 this morning, I will leave off.

⌒

172.   MAY 21, 1853, TAVISTOCK HOUSE [TO DR. BROWN]

I would not bring forward the proposition of advancing a third of the money,[1] unless on the extremest necessity. For I am inclined to doubt whether the disadvantages of a principle so objectionable, would not counterbalance the advantages of the improvements.

I will call for you in Stratton Street at 3 on Monday, and in the meantime will consider the matter carefully. I think it very important to consider these two points, in reference to Mr Arnold's [2] suggestion.

1. Whether, if we offer a third, the class of persons who would accept it will not immediately get it into their heads that they have only to stand out and get half, or more — in short, to be bribed into consenting? (which I greatly fear.)

2. Whether the better class of opposing persons who are not so base, would be in the least shaken in their objections by such an offer? (which I rather doubt)

⌒

During the previous October, Dickens had passed a week at Boulogne and had liked it so much that he resolved his next summer's vacation should be spent there. One of his Lausanne acquaintances had lived there in the Château des Moulineaux, a villa belonging to a Monsieur Beaucourt, and it was this same dwelling that Dickens now rented from early in June. On a wooded hillside in the midst of a great terraced garden, it was approached by an avenue of hollyhocks and surrounded by thousands of roses and other flowers. In the garden were five summerhouses and fifteen fountains stocked with goldfish; inside the house there were countless little bedrooms and drawing rooms, a billiard room, a dining room looking into a conservatory, and a glitter of mirrors everywhere.

---

[1] Evidently an attempt to move the Westminster landlords to sanitary improvements by offering to pay not just the cost of conversion *above* a given amount, but a flat one third of their costs in any case.

[2] Unidentified.

Dickens had been working at a terrific pace, and despite his steel-coil vitality, felt almost exhausted. He had written more than four fifths of Bleak House's 380,000 words, and dictated over 125,000 of the Child's History of England *to his sister-in-law Georgina. What with these, "and Household Words . . . and Miss Coutts's Home, and the invitations to feasts and festivals, I really feel as if my head would split like a fired shell . . ."* In fact, he fell ill with a severe recurrence of the kidney trouble that had afflicted him at irregular intervals since his childhood, and spent six painful days in bed. As soon as he was able to move, however, he proceeded to Folkestone, and, although he still felt aches and pains when he sat up to write, he crossed the Channel with his family on June 12. In Boulogne he recovered so rapidly that within ten days he was boasting himself *"brown, well, robust, vigorous, open to fight any man in England of my weight, and growing a moustache."*

ౚ

173.　　　　　July 10, 1853, Chateau des Moulineaux, Boulogne

I have not been in London since I left it, ill, or I should have endeavoured to see you there. Nor do I think at present, that I shall journey in that direction until about the twentieth of next month. I am getting my book done in peace, and am (thank God) very vigorous and very brown.

I can't quite make out — *my* fault, no doubt! — the name of the applicant, of Cambridge Terrace, Liverpool Road. If it be Derry, I never heard of her husband. If it be Herry, I never heard of him. If it be Sherry, I *have* heard of him — but only in connexion with the Spanish wine trade. If it be Flerry, I never heard of him. If it be Jerry, I never heard of him. And if it be Henry, Benry, Stenry — Werry or Merry — I never heard of him.

We are all very well indeed, I am happy to say, and hear constantly from Charley who is beginning to make head with his German. The Baby who defies competition, almost disappeared to the naked eye, under the effects of a very bad passage across; but he has since recovered, and is — as he was — unapproachable by any baby whomsoever. The laudable vanity of parents and aunts, in some weak-minded instances induces a belief that there are Babies worthy to hold a candle to him; but this is an innocent delusion and engenders feelings gratifying to the individuals, of which one would be sorry to deprive them.

I am always hoping and expecting to hear of you at the Hotel des Bains — scarcely the less, I think, because you speak of your party as fixed. For there is an occasional eccentricity (I have observed) in some peoples' movements.

We all unite in kindest regards, in which Mr and Mrs Brown (broad faced I hope?) are well remembered. I look forward to shewing you, here, the most ridiculous suite of children's rooms ever imagined — an absurdity of which I am quite proud to be the temporary owner — and a very good one in practice too.

There are rumours here, that the English Hay Market has been surprisingly affected by a sudden glut in the article of New hay. It is thought to have been thrown in from Highgate, and I have no doubt is the Holly Lodge contribution.[3]

They speak of 715,428,673,904000 tons. But I suppose this to be a little exaggerated?

[P.S.] I have seen a very good occasion for giving the poor schoolmistress that Ten Pounds which we agreed to hold in abeyance.

ᕱᕲ

174.   JULY 18, 1853, CHATEAU DES MOULINEAUX, BOULOGNE

I am glad to hear those girls are well away at last.

Susan Matcham is the handsome girl whom it was necessary, under very flagrant circumstances indeed, to discharge; but who, being ill at the time of her discharge, had five shillings given her for coach-hire, together with a letter of recommendation to the House Surgeon — either of St Thomas's or Guy's Hospital: I forget which. She went away with the greatest gratitude, protesting that she would immediately repair to the hospital, and that she was deeply sensible of the kindness with which she was treated. She never went near the place, and has not been heard of, since. My own impression is, that she went to some male acquaintance with whom, by some means unknown to us, she had communicated while in the Home. She came originally from a London hospital — had had a long illness while with us — and had been most tenderly nursed and restored. I believe the acquaintance before-mentioned, to have hung about the house, and to have seen her more than once.

If those other cases referred to, should appear to be of a good kind,

---

[3] The reader will recall that Miss Coutts inherited this property in 1849, when the Duke of St. Albans died.

I think it would be well to take them. But it is desirable to know their circumstances. I have just received an application, apropos of the article in Household Words, respecting two girls — sisters. The circumstances stated, are of a terrible kind; but I doubt the expediency (from what I observe in the letter) of pursuing the matter, at all events until I can see the writer.

It has been blowing great guns here — raining great waterspouts — hailing sugar loaves, and going all up and down the glass in four and twenty hours. We are at present expecting snow.

The baby sends his pity (for the pretended baby), his forgiveness, and respects.

◌

175. AUGUST 7, 1853, CHATEAU DES MOULINEAUX, BOULOGNE [TO MRS. BROWN]

Thinking (as you may suppose) a good deal about that ruffian [4] lately, I had considered your question before I received it from you. I say, without hesitation, that I would *not* prosecute him for the Perjury he has committed in swearing to the Schedule. I would have him before a magistrate on his recommencing any annoyance, but I would not run the hazard of making a Martyr of him (even with the ill-conditioned, addle-headed, or malevolent Idiots who could alone have any consideration for such a scoundrel), coupled with all the annoyance and uncertainty of our monstrous Law.

I am very sorry that I did not see the Daily News, and cannot see it here. But I have written to town for it. I saw, with a thrill of pleasure (in the Times report of the Judgment [5]) that a generous movement of irrepressible indignation pervaded the crowded court when his conduct was — feebly — described.

As to the asinine commissioner's compliments, they are of a piece with so much unreason and sheer rottenness of the same kind, that I feel as if I could strike my head against the wall, in the insupportability of bearing it. That kind of gingerly balancing of black against white, has become one of the Judicial and Parliamentary commonplaces. And we shall perish of common-places at last, if we don't mind what we are about — or if Prince Albert and his relations, interfering in Foreign affairs, leave us any good name or any good thing, long, to perish out of.

---

[4] Richard Dunn, again!
[5] London *Times*, August 4, 1853.

I should very much like (and I have often thought so) to state this Dunn's case, as from a public knowledge of it, in Household Words.[6] I think I could cast a little more reproach and disgrace about the gentleman than the Judges do. I wish you would ask Miss Coutts to think at her leisure whether she sees any objection to it.

And pray tell her that if I were called upon to describe her handwriting I should say — round, full, clear, intelligible, always distinctly made out, very upright, and generally resembling a school-copy in copper plate.

I am confident, and I will die in the confidence, that the Insolvent Commissioners had no right to entertain that man's petition, when they had it in legal evidence before them that it was stated on a false oath.

With kindest regards from all,
    Dear Mrs Brown
    Most Indignantly
    And Ferociously
    Yours
P.S. I hope you will not be shocked when you come here, to see an eminent Englishman of our acquaintance with a Moustache.

∽

176.   August 27, 1853, Chateau des Moulineaux, Boulogne
A thousand thanks for the powders, which I received (to my unbounded amazement) as I was sitting at breakfast in the solitary desert of Tavistock House.[7] I took two, in strict observance of the directions, and came back triumphantly. There was hardly a ripple on the sea, but I have half a mind to believe that the powders had some hand in that.

I found time to get to Shepherd's Bush, where all was going on quietly; one of the delinquents having been just apprehended and being then under remand. The little girl from Petworth is an extraordinary case of restless imposture and seeking after notoriety; but there are chances (not desperate chances, I think) of something better being made of it.

---

[6] He did: "Things That Cannot Be Done," *Household Words*, October 8, 1853.
[7] Dickens had been to London for a brief business trip; the "powders," obviously, were a remedy for seasickness.

Your packet I sent safely to Stratton Street as soon as I arrived in town.

I have just finished my book [8] (very prettily indeed, I hope) and am in the first drowsy lassitude of having done so. I should be lying in the sunshine by the hour together, if there were such a thing. In its absence I prowl about in the wind and rain. Last night was the most tremendous I ever heard for a storm of both; I fear there will be sad shipwrecks in the newspapers a few days hence.

The article in the Daily News [9] was written by my sub editor Mr Wills (who makes those enquiries sometimes, and finds the cupboards of begging letter writers full of provender) in conjunction with the editor of the paper. He has nothing to do with it (I mean the Daily News) himself, but rushed into the subject con amore.

Not having an atom of news to tell, I am troubled with doubts of the justification I have for sending this sheet of paper so far. My publishers [1] have had their festivity here and are gone; I am looking up my Italian again, preparatory to my autumn trip; [2] Christmas numbers of Household Words already importune me to make them all right before I go; and that is all I know — except that I have misty visions of meeting you somewhere by the Alps, and a kind of absolute certainty of dining with you at Townshend's: [3] I hold to my purpose of leaving here on the tenth of October, and going straight to Lausanne by Paris and Geneva.

---

[8] The book now finished was *Bleak House*, of which the last number was published in September.

[9] Unidentified.

[1] Since 1844, when Dickens had severed his connection with Chapman and Hall, his publishers had been Bradbury and Evans, who were also the publishers of *Punch* and who were part proprietors of the *Daily News*, the liberal daily that Dickens had founded in 1846. They came over to Boulogne for a short vacation visit with Dickens.

[2] Dickens was planning to take an eight weeks' vacation trip to Italy that autumn with the painter Augustus Egg and the novelist Wilkie Collins.

[3] The Reverend Chauncy Hare Townshend (1798–1868), whom Dickens had originally met through Dr. John Elliotson, and who, like Elliotson, was interested in mesmerism, on which he had written a book. Although an ordained clergyman, Townshend's religious beliefs were unorthodox, and, being a man of wealth, he spent his time either traveling or living at an estate he had acquired in Lausanne, where Dickens now proposed to visit him on the way to Italy. Later, in 1861, Dickens dedicated *Great Expectations* to him and, when Townshend died in 1868, in accordance with a request in his will, Dickens edited and wrote an introduction for his *Religious Opinions*.

You have seen, I dare say, that disagreeable account of Mr and Mrs Norton [4] at the County Court. It is very odd that they should have become a public topic so soon after our speaking of them as we did. (This reminds me that I send by the same post a letter for Kaye Shuttleworth, on which I place your name conspicuously, for greater certainty's sake.)

I shall look forward to hearing how you like Vichy — how large Mrs Brown's face gets in that air — and how those airy plans of yours seem to be shaping themselves out in the far perspective. Mrs Dickens and her sister, and all the children, send immense packets of messages and loves. — The baby defies competition I need not observe.

The Birmingham people are arranging those readings I promised to give them. They expect to get five hundred pounds for their new Institution (a splendid idea of a Mechanics Athenaeum) therefrom. I am going to read three nights in the Christmas week — to two thousand working people only, on the Friday — the Christmas Carol. You heard the beginning of Bleak House. I wish (and did wish very heartily) you had been here the night before last, to hear the end.

With kind regards to Mr and Mrs Brown

ↄ

177. September 8, 1853, 16 Wellington Street North — Strand; office of *Household Words*

Your account of Vichy gave me a chill from which I have not yet quite recovered. A dim oppressive sense of windy discomfort has been upon me ever since, and I feel inclined to try to warm myself at a bright hard hearted little fireplace which produces nothing but smoke. Concerning Mr and Mrs Hall — S.C. I presume to be the christian initials — I in confidence renounce that amiable couple as the most terrific Humbugs known on earth at any period of its history.[5] And as to their being in my confidence, or knowing my affairs, I can only say that it must be in a magnetic, table moving, or spirit rapping, way — wholly without any participation of mine — and altogether unaccountable and supernatural.

---

[4] The Honorable George Chapple Norton and his wife Caroline, who figured in the notorious Melbourne-Norton trial in 1836.

[5] Samuel Carter Hall (1800–1889), author and editor; edited *The Amulet*, the *New Monthly Magazine*, the *Art Union Journal*, and *Social Notes;* wrote *Baronial Halls of England* and other books, and, in collaboration with his wife, *Ireland, Its Scenery, etc.* He was a pompous man of oleaginous manner, upon whose ways of expressing himself Dickens based those of Mr. Pecksniff, in *Martin Chuzzlewit.*

I have written to Mrs Morson this morning, to say I will come to Shepherds Bush tomorrow. I passed your house yesterday, and it looked tremendously dull — if that is any comfort to you. Painters were at work in Mr Brown's, and a man on a tall thin pair of steps much spotted with whitewash was at work in the middle window of the dining room, according to the usual manner of that class of operative — scraping a little, looking about him a great deal, and singing the dreariest song I ever heard. I suppose that part of London never was so empty. In search of two or three little things I wanted for my trip, I went to one of my tailor's who lives in Piccadilly. He couldn't bear the silence and had gone to Brighton. I went to another of my tailors who lives in Clifford Street Bond Street. He had given up business altogether, for the time, and was playing the piano upstairs, surrounded by his family and mignionette boxes. I then went to my hosier's in New Bond Street, and found the establishment reduced to two of the least illustrious of the "young men", who were playing at draughts in the back counting house. This is really the experience of a solitary traveller in those regions at eleven o'clock yesterday forenoon.[6]

I *didn't* take the powders this last passage, and it was a most forlorn one; the sea washing over us the whole way, the boat rolling violently, and so filled with disappointed sight-seers whom the renown of your Presidential friend[7] had brought over, in a vain hope of seeing the original head-dress that sets the fashion just now and pulls up the feminine eyelid into the temples — that there was no room to be ill in. It was the most disastrous scene of that kind in which I ever acted a prominent part. The after-deck was covered (in several places two or three deep) with wet ladies; and so prodigious was the number of white basins, and so intent were the drooping heads upon them, that

---

[6] Dickens later worked up the observations in this paragraph into part of an article entitled "Arcadian London," one of the series called *The Uncommercial Traveller.* It was first published in his periodical, *All the Year Round,* September 24, 1860.

[7] Louis Napoleon Bonaparte (1808–1873), who had been elected president of the second French Republic in 1848, and proclaimed himself emperor in December 1852. Two months later he married Eugénie de Montijo, whose beauty and style of dress immediately began to set feminine fashions. Miss Coutts knew Louis Napoleon well, and Dickens had met him often both in her house and in Lady Blessington's salon at Gore House in earlier days. Dickens was infuriated by the *coup d'état* that had destroyed the Republic, and loathed Napoleon's autocratic régime.

once when I caught a general view of the scene as the vessel made a dive to the bottom of the channel, it looked like an immense Pic-Nic to which everybody had brought an exclusive pigeon pie. As usual, the moment I set foot upon the pier at Folkestone (where I was received with an encouraging cry of "O, *ain't* he green!") I felt as if I were no relation whatever to the drooping and draggled idiot who had come over in my name.

It is dark now, and raining hard — good suitable circumstances in which to devise a Christmas number, which is my present employment.[8] If you should be in Paris on the 10th of October, I shall hope to know it beforehand, that I may have the happiness of seeing you (and confounding you by naming THE baby) on my way through. With kindest regards to Mr and Mrs Brown

◦↔◦

178.   SEPTEMBER 18, 1853, CHATEAU DES MOULINEAUX, BOULOGNE
Mr Collins [9] will be very sensible, I know, of your kind recollection and invitation. (You remember his father, by the bye? I think I recollect to have seen him at your parties.)

---

[8] The extra Christmas Number of *Household Words* in 1853, called "Another Round of Stories by the Christmas Fire," contained two by Dickens, "The Schoolboy's Story" and "Nobody's Story."

[9] William Wilkie Collins (1824–1889), the well-known novelist, author of *The Dead Secret, The Woman in White, No Name,* and *The Moonstone.* He was a son of William Collins (1788–1847), landscape and figure painter, and a brother of Charles Allston Collins (1828–1873), painter and writer, who in 1860 married Dickens's daughter Katey.

Wilkie Collins came to be a friend of Dickens after he had been induced to take the small part of a valet in *Not So Bad as We Seem.* Their relationship speedily developed into a close-knit and convivial intimacy that in later years rivaled Dickens's friendship with Forster — especially when Dickens was looking for fun and relaxation, for in the course of time Forster had grown steadily more heavy, conventional, and pompous. Collins became a member of the staff of *Household Words,* a number of his stories were published as serials there, and still others, later, in *All the Year Round.* He and Dickens collaborated on several Christmas stories, most significantly on *No Thoroughfare* in 1867, which they did both as a story and as a successful play. Dickens also had a hand in Collins's two melodramas, *The Lighthouse* and *The Frozen Deep,* of which he was both the producer and the leading actor.

The Italian trip upon which they were now to start with Augustus Egg was a milestone in their friendship. Miss Coutts, who was at the moment staying in Paris, through which they would be passing, had invited Dickens to bring Collins to see her there.

But "we are" — not seven, like Wordsworth's children — "three." Mr Egg[1] the painter is the last of the party. Therefore I think the best thing I can do, will be to leave them quietly at our hotel after dinner, and then come round to yours. I do not think we shall remain a day in Paris. Firstly, because I have not the smallest interest in your amiable friend, or in the flowers that grow on the graves of the murdered; and secondly because we have made the staunchest and most inviolable of compacts to dine with Townshend on a certain day. Furthermore I particularly want Mr Egg, who is so fine and picturesque an artist and has never been farther than Holland, to see some good Swiss interiors and backgrounds. And with this view, if the season should be tolerably open, we shall make a push for Chamouni, and try to get the short way through the snow thence to the Simplon. — Not to mention my having vague Swiss notions in my mind myself, and therefore wanting to look about me!

I will bring the box, with the greatest pleasure. It would be best for your housekeeper to send it — *with the key* — to Tavistock House on Wednesday the fifth of October. Will you charge her to send the letters separately, in order that I may put them in my pocket? The book I will not forget. If you should think of anything else you want, pray let me know.

I got out of the Deserted Village (leaving the other man who was there, behind me) as safely as could be expected, and had a really delightful passage back! I had not previously believed in such a thing, but — I — enjoyed — it.

Until the first or second of October any commission will find me here. Between that and the sixth, in town. Do you see Household Words in Paris? If not, I will send you two papers I should like you to read. The first, called *Frauds on the Fairies*,[2] I think would amuse you, and enlist you on my side — which is for a little more fancy among children and a little less fact. The second, called *Things that cannot*

---

[1] Augustus Egg (1816–1863), painter of historical and genre scenes, who had been associated with Dickens in amateur theatricals since the benefits for Leigh Hunt and John Poole in 1847.

[2] "Frauds on the Fairies," an article Dickens wrote for *Household Words,* was published there October 1, 1853. It was a good-natured but effectively satiric attack upon his old friend Cruikshank, who in his mania for total abstinence from alcoholic beverages, had lately taken to re-editing and rewriting fairy tales such as "Hop o' My Thumb" in order to make them propagandist vehicles for these opinions.

be done,[3] relates to the efficiency of the law in the impossible case of a man taking up the trade of deliberately persecuting a lady until she will buy him off with money — shews in short how such a thing could not by any possibility be, in this age and country.

With kindest regards to Mr Brown and our dear obstinacy

[P.S.] This place was decorated, three weeks ago, for the Emperor. All the triumphal arches (made of green boughs) have faded, and look exactly as if they were made of tea leaves.

∽

179.   OCTOBER 8, 1853, CHATEAU DES MOULINEAUX, BOULOGNE

No seeds arrived before I left town. A parcel is coming over to-morrow. They may be in that.

I hope to bring some first rate cider, and some ditto perry.[4] Also some reliable information of the kind you want.

I was at the Home on Tuesday. All was going on quietly.

As you kindly contemplate the invasion of your table by the whole Italian triumvirate, and as I know you will find Mr Egg very modest and agreeable, I think I ought to give "Co" the great pleasure you so considerately offer that part of the Firm, as well as "Self." But as we shall not be presentable by your dinner hour on Monday, and as we shall not go on to Strasburgh until Wednesday morning, I would propose, if you approve, that we dine with you on *Tuesday.*[5]

I expect to be at the Hotel Brighton — if there be any room there — which there never is.

A letter from Charley this morning. He seems to be doing thoroughly well with the German language. In proof of which, he sends me all manner of compositions, translations, journals, and other performances, of which I can't read a word!

I have a game to shew you, which will interest you if you never saw it. We have been playing it here of an evening, with the greatest

---

[3] "Things That Cannot Be Done" was that account of Richard Dunn's persecutions of Miss Coutts that has been previously mentioned as having been published in *Household Words,* October 8, 1853.

[4] Perry: a fermented liquor made from pears.

[5] Miss Coutts had enlarged her invitation to dinner to include all three of the travelers, who accordingly dined with her in Paris on October 11. "Co," of course, means "Company," an expression used by Mark Tapley, in *Martin Chuzzlewit,* after Martin had made him a partner in Chuzzlewit and Company.

success. I think it will put our friend O [6] (if you will say as much to her from me) on the alert.

All unite in kindest regards. You will be sorry to hear that the

Beauty,

Size,

and

Vigor

of the

Baby

are the admiration of the entire population of Boulogne, without any distinction of race or country.

∽

180.   OCTOBER 25, 1853, HOTEL DE LA VILLA, MILAN

When I came to reflect at leisure on what the Prince [7] had said at dinner, I felt convinced that he must labor under some complicated (and I had almost added here, peculiarly Parisian) mistake. Firstly, because travellers crossing the Simplon enter Italy by the Sardinian State, and secondly because Travellers crossing the St Gothard not only come direct from the obnoxious Swiss Canton — which in the other case they do not — but enter Italy at once by an Austrian portal. When I got to Lausanne I made enquiries whether Austria interposed any difficulties in the way of English travellers entering Italy by the Simplon. Nobody knew, or had ever heard, of any such thing. The courier of the mail, who had just come across, utterly rejected the idea; saying that they took passengers, and passed and met travelling carriages, every day. Thus confirmed, I resolved to come by the Simplon — and did. We crossed it on Sunday, when there was not a cloud in the sky, and when the most sublime Sunday service the mind can well imagine pervaded the tremendous silence and grandeur of the whole distance. That night we lay at Domo D'Ossola, and yesterday we came on here. Both at the Austrian frontier and at the gate of Milan we were received with the greatest politeness and consideration. I am bound to say that I never knew the usual Passport and Custom-House regulations more obligingly enforced. So here we are.

We stayed two days with Townshend very pleasantly indeed, and I had the gratification of receiving your note with the Prince's kind en-

---

6 "O": a designation for Mrs. Brown, probably an abbreviation for "Objector."

7 Unidentified.

closure — for which pray thank him in my name — and also of further hearing of you from our host himself, who beamed "like one entire and perfect" soft smile when he produced your hand writing. My old Lausanne friends were all so cordially happy to see me that I felt half ashamed of myself for being liked so much beyond my deserts. Our stay there disposed of, we went on to Geneva and so to Chamounix, which at this time of the year — no visitors, the hotels shutting up, and all the people who can afford it going away — is far more primitive and interesting than as one usually sees it. We went up to the Mer de Glace through pretty deep snow, warmed ourselves at a wood fire on the ice, came down again and stayed a day in the valley, left Mont Blanc at 7 in the morning just reddened on its utmost height by the sun and without a cloud upon it, and crossed to Martigny. These achievements (with a variety of gymnastic exercises with a pole, superadded) I performed on foot, to the infinite satisfaction of the guides, who, pronounced me "a strong Intrepid," and were of the opinion that I ought to ascend Mont Blanc next summer. I told them in return that it had become such a nuisance in my country that there was some idea of authorizing Paxton [8] to take it down and re-erect it at Sydenham.

We go on to Genoa by the Mail tomorrow, where some more of my old friends expect me and are going to hold a small festival on the great occasion. I find my companions so unused to the notion of never going to bed, except in large towns, that Sicily is already erased from the trip, and Naples substituted for its utmost limit. We shall return too, for shortness, by the way of Paris — where I shall probably take up Charley about the 8th or 9th of December. If you should have leisure to write me a few lines within ten days or so — or say a week — after the receipt of this, Poste Restante Rome will find me. After that, Florence. After that, Venice. After that, Genoa again, as we shall return by way of Marseilles.

---

[8] Sir Joseph Paxton (1801–1865), horticulturist, landscape gardener, and architect. Originally gardener to the Duke of Devonshire at Chatsworth, he made a fortune in railway shares, became one of the founding proprietors of the *Daily News* in 1846, and was the architect of the Crystal Palace, erected in Hyde Park for the Great Exhibition of 1851, and subsequently reerected at Sydenham. He was knighted in 1851. He also designed the mansion of Baron Rothschild at Ferrières, France, and organized the army work corps in the Crimea. The joke about taking down Mont Blanc, however, was a reference to Albert Smith's illustrated lecture on his ascent of that mountain, which for six years was a popular entertainment at the Egyptian Hall, in Piccadilly.

It is so strange and like a dream to me, to hear the delicate Italian once again, and to recover the knowledge of it (such as it is) which I almost thought I had lost! So beautiful too to see the delightful sky again, and all the picturesque wonders of the country. And yet I am so restless to be doing — and always shall be, I think, so long as I have any portion in Time — that if I were to stay more than a week in any one city here, I believe I should be half desperate to begin some new story!!!

My two companions have gone out to see the Cathedral and to kill off some other Lions. Mr Egg's face fell prodigiously when we passed the cathedral last night, and he said with a pathetic access of despondency "that he should never be able to do it under a month." I wait for his report on that subject before I close this note. In the meanwhile I can't help saying, for want of more interesting news, that he was very solicitous some year or two ago, to marry Georgina.[9] It would have been a good thing for her, as he is an excellent fellow, and is well off, over and above his professional reputation which stands high. But she said No, though they are very good friends. I took no other part in the matter than urging her to be quite sure that she knew her own mind.

He is very far her inferior intellectually; but five men would be out of six, for she has one of the most remarkable capacities I have ever known. Not to mention her being one of the most amiable and affectionate of girls. Whether it is, or is not a pity that she is all she is to me and mine instead of brightening up a good little man's house where she would still have the artist kind of life she is used to, about her, is a knotty point I never can settle to my satisfaction. And I have been trying to untwist it in my mind on the road here, until it will persist in ravelling itself out on this paper.

They have come back from the Lions, and Mr Egg is very anxious I should explain to you that the cathedral is so "tremendously elabo-

---

[9] Georgina Hogarth (1827–1917), Dickens's sister-in-law, had joined his household on his return from America in 1842, when she was only fifteen, and never left it for the remainder of her life. At first she helped Catherine with the children and taught the little ones to read, but gradually her energy took over from her sister's lethargic hands more and more of the duties of household management until, by the time of this letter, she was practically running the establishment wherever they lived. Her admiration for Dickens was unbounded, and he responded with the warmest gratitude, affection, and regard for both her character and her devotion.

rate" as to render it impossible that he could make any such sketch of it as he would like you to have, in the time available. He hopes you will go to see his pictures on our return, and that he may be able to do something else and something into which he can "throw himself" with greater heartiness of satisfaction, as a reminder of the country we have passed through. They both beg me to send their compliments and acknowledgments of your great kindness.

Dinner time and post time being now at hand together, I break off with my love to O, and friendly regards to Mr Brown. I will write again, probably from Rome.

181.   NOVEMBER 13, 1853, ROME

On sending to the post office here this morning — we arrived last night — I was delighted to find your letter awaiting me. I read it with the greatest pleasure, in spite of the heavy drawback of counsel's advice; and cannot deny myself the further pleasure of writing to thank you for it.

We came from Genoa to Naples — I ought rather to say, went — in the Valetta steamer, an English ship placed upon this route chiefly to convey the Overland India mail from Malta to Marseilles, when it becomes due. Our countrymen and women, and the men and women of all other European regions, are so much attracted by the fame of this ship, that we found it when we went aboard perfectly crammed. There were about forty passengers, without any berths, blankets, seats at dinner, or other accommodation in the way of eating, drinking, or sleeping — the whole having paid heavy first class fares. The first night, we lay on the planks of the deck, with thirty seven unfortunates — of whom thirty two declared all night that they would write to the Times in the morning. You never saw so ridiculous a scene. Insane attempts to make pillows of carpet bags, hat boxes, and life buoys — wild endeavours to screen ladies off with flags, which invariably fell down as soon as they had tied their heads up in extraordinary dimity machines taken out of reticules elaborately worked in worsted — and in the middle of the night a perfectly tropical rain which swept the whole ship clear in a minute and crowded us all together on the cabin stairs, where we remained all night; whenever any desperate creature came below, all tumbling down; and whenever any other desperate creature ascended to the deck, all tumbling up again. As a distinguished Englishman in my way, I became the brother of all the officers in half an hour, and set off with them next day (we being detained at Leghorn four and twenty hours) to see Pisa, which expedition I made with the comfortable assurance that the Valetta could never go without us, while the Captain was in our company. He was so much affected by our sufferings that next night he put Mr Collins and Mr Egg in the store room (opened for the occasion) where they slept on little dressers, with the pickles, spices, tea, fruits, and a very large double Glo'ster cheese in cut — the whole forming a combination of smells of which they were profoundly innocent after they had been there (it was under water too) five minutes, but which, to my senses, had left a general flavor of Chandlery and Grocery about them ever since. I was superbly lodged in the steward's cabin; that potentate sitting in an arm-chair all night, and resigning his bed (four feet and a half by one and a quarter) to me. It was very comfortable though the engine was under the pillow, and the wall extremely nervous, and the whole in a profuse perspiration of warm oil. At Naples, I found Layard [1] — with whom we ascended Vesuvius in the sunlight and came down in the moonlight, very merrily. Talking of Italian, I *must* mention that Emerson Tennent [2] and his family were of the party — they had been in the Valetta — and that he stopped the expedition indignantly, a little way up the cone, to demand "a church" for his daughter. He meant a chair; but he persisted in, and insisted on, having "una chiesa" [3] — to the unspeakable amazement and consternation of the forty screeching vagabonds who formed our escort. My heart misgives me in relating this story even to

---

[1] Sir Austen Henry Layard (1817–1894), archaeologist and diplomat, noted for his discoveries in Asiatic Turkey, the author of *Nineveh and Its Remains, Fresh Discoveries at Nineveh, and Researches at Babylon, Inscriptions in the Cuneiform Character from Assyrian Monuments,* and similar works. Like Dickens, he was a political radical, and as M.P. for Aylesbury violently assailed the corruption and inefficiency of government departments during the Crimean War. He became Under-secretary for Foreign Affairs 1861–1866, Commissioner of Works 1868–1869, Minister to Spain 1869–1877, and Ambassador to Turkey 1877–1880.

[2] Sir James Emerson Tennent (1804–1869), traveler, politician, and author, educated at Trinity College, Dublin, and traveled in Greece, where he met Lord Byron. He married a daughter of William Tennent of Belfast and adopted his wife's last name. As M.P. for Belfast he supported the Reform Bill of 1832. He was Colonial Secretary at Ceylon 1845–1850, and Permanent Secretary of the Board of Trade 1852–1867. Among his writings were *A Picture of Greece, Letters from the Aegean, History of Modern Times, Belgium, Christianity in Ceylon,* and *Natural History of Ceylon.* Dickens dedicated to him *Our Mutual Friend,* his last completed novel.

[3] Instead of saying *sedia* or *seggiola;* Tennent was confusing *una chiesa* with the French *une chaise.*

you, for he wanted to turn his son out of his bed (and stranger still the son wanted to turn out too) when he heard of my lying on the deck. But we laughed about it so ridiculously afterwards, with Layard, that I can't help this little bit of treason.

There has been a wretched business with young Brinsley Norton (the youngest living son of that unhappy marriage) [4] at Naples. He has recently turned Catholic and married a Peasant girl at Capri, who knows nothing about anything — shoes and hairbrushes included — and whom he literally picked up off the beach. They told me about it at the Embassy. He had not been married a fortnight when I was there. One of the attachés had just seen him in his "Island home," translating Longfellow's poems which he is supposed not to understand in the least, into Neapolitan — of which he knows nothing — for the entertainment of his wife — who couldn't possibly comprehend a line under the most favorable circumstances. His brother is supposed to be going to marry a sister of the young lady's, and altogether it seems to be a most deplorable affair.

It was very hot at Naples, and I bear some highly ornamental marks of mosquito bites. The same men, with the same instruments, were singing the same songs, to the same tunes, all along the seashore in the morning, as when I was there nine years ago. Affairs with France looked queer and the French Ambassador left while I was there, in high dudgeon. It made considerable talk. Verdi is still the rage. In a poor enough opera of his — very well done indeed, at San Carlo — there was a Prima Donna who I think will soon make a great success in England. Pompeii has greatly increased in interest of late years; several fine houses having been excavated, and one being left imperfectly dug out, with the ruined and broken roof still upon it — which gives a perfect and admirable idea of the process of destruction. Meanwhile Vesuvius looks on very peaceably — for the present.

I hope to be at Turin on the fifth of December, and to leave it on

---

[4] Caroline Sheridan (1808–1877), one of the three beautiful daughters of Thomas Sheridan. Poet and novelist, she was the author of numerous popular works, including *A Voice from the Factories, The Dream, and Other Poems, The Child of the Islands, Stuart of Dun-Leath,* and *The Lady of La Garaye.* She married the Honorable George Chapple Norton, and was separated from him in the course of a notorious court trial in 1836, in which her husband accused Lord Melbourne, the Prime Minister, of criminal conversation with his wife. Dickens was a reporter at this trial, and heard the verdict go against Mr. Norton. Later Dickens made the acquaintance of the slandered wife, who continued to hold a high place in fashionable society. See also letter of August 27, 1853, note 4.

the sixth, and then to come on very rapidly indeed. I shall hear from Charley there, and learn whether I shall find him waiting at Paris or at Boulogne — or even at Lyons, though I don't think the last place likely. I was amazed by the life and enterprize in Genoa, and the increase in the place since I lived there. If it goes on in the same way, long, its old commercial greatness will be renewed again.

I admit that they do not speak very clearly or sweetly, about Milan and in that country; but they can if they choose, and they do choose when a stranger speaks to them. The language has a pleasant sound in my ears, however spoken almost, which no other has except my own. That preposterous Miss Cunningham [5] was at the hotel at Leghorn when I was there — in attendance on her mother, who seems likely to be the only British martyr of that hollow, ill considered, vain, wrongheaded proceeding. I understand that she always objected to her daughter's taking such propagandism upon herself, and that her alarm and anxiety have made her very seriously ill.

With my kindest regards to O and to Mr Brown, now and ever my Dear Miss Coutts Most Faithfully Yours

∽

182. NOVEMBER 27, 1853, VENICE

I had a letter from Charley yesterday, in which he wisely elected to meet me at Paris.[6] As I think he may be there, one or two days before me — my day will be, as well as I can calculate, either the 9th or the 10th of December — I have told him where you are, and as soon as he has housed himself he will call on you. I have also told him that I will try and write him a letter from Lyons, letting him know by what train I shall come into Paris, in order that he may meet me at the Railroad, if I do not arrive in the night. The said letter I will address to him with your permission — I mean without it — to your care. And if I should by any means miss him at the Railway, I will come to the Hotel Bristol to ask where he is. I suppose we may stay one night in Paris, but that will depend on our not having been previously detained on the road. For they will be anxiously expecting me at home, and I

---

[5] Unidentified.

[6] Returning home from Germany for the Christmas holidays. Meeting Charley in Paris, Dickens found "his arms and legs so grown out of his coat and trousers"— he was now almost seventeen—as to necessitate smuggling him "under cover of night, to a ready-made establishment . . . where they put him into balloon-waisted pantaloons, and increased my confusion."

shall want to get quietly into my own room for a few days, with a view to my Birmingham readings. Seeing that I have, for such a purpose, left the little books some years behind.[7]

We have now had three days rain in two months. It is very cold, but very fine. We posted from Florence to Padua, to take the railroad for this place, and travelled all night, to get an extra day here. It was most severely cold. Our passports had had, each, six brand new Visés at Florence. In the course of that one night they had, each, *Nine More* — written, and stamped, and sanded, and blotted, and blurred, with every conceivable description of utterly illegible formality. Every time, some drawbridge had to be let down, and somebody had to be knocked up. So that I really did at last begin (though the sweetest of travellers) to think it was a little overdone. Again I must say of the Austrian Frontier, and of the arrangements here, that we experienced greater politeness than in any other part of Italy; the duty strictly done, but the doers of it, being treated like gentlemen, invariably responsive, explanatory, and courteous.

For our prodigious sojourn of four days we have established a highly imposing Gondola, rowed by two men in a modestly alarming livery, who are very strict in observing all the old stately forms. Last night we proceeded to the Opera in our gallant bark, with an enormous-Christmas-Pantomimic-lantern in the prow. When we landed, the chief of our two Gondolieri went before, with this terrible machine, and lighted us — not only up to the Theatre door, but up the staircase, through the brilliantly lighted passages (where the lantern became a mere twinkle) and into the box. I don't know that I ever in my life felt more absurd, and I certainly was never so anxious to shave anybody as I was to shave my two companions; whose moustaches, being in their feeble infancy,[8] did not at all accord with the magnificence of this triumphal entry. What I suffered all night, from the fell mis-

---

[7] Scheduled to take place December 27–30. These were really the first public readings from his books, although he had read *The Chimes* to the circle of his friends who assembled to hear it at Lincoln's Inn Fields in 1844. The *Carol* had been published in 1843 and *The Cricket on the Hearth* in 1845, so it might easily have been a number of years since Dickens had last read through them.

[8] In imitation of Dickens's beard and mustache, both Egg and Collins were letting their own grow, achieving results, Dickens said, "more straggling, wandering, wiry, stubbly, formless, more given to wandering into strange places and sprouting up noses and dribbling under chins, than anything . . . since the Flood." Hoping they would follow his example, Dickens seized his razor and shaved off his beard, but they merely observed "with complacency that 'it looks much better.'"

giving that the lantern would reappear, or what temptations were upon me to drop into the pit, I will not wring your heart by describing. But at the end of the ballet, when there was still another act of the opera to come, I opened the box door a very little way, and peeped out — with the intention of sneaking away if the coast were clear. The instant I looked into the passage, the lantern — beaming and radiant — burst out of a corner and blazed into the box again! There was nothing for it but to go back in the same state. I saw nobody laugh; which was my only comfort.

Everything here and elsewhere, of the beautiful kind, looks as I left it nine years ago. Except that I found the old ruins of Rome (the Coliseum excepted) smaller than my imagination had made them in that space of time. I went to see Lockhart [9] at Rome, where, as perhaps you know, he is passing the winter. He is dreadfully changed, even in his changed state, and I should think his recovery very very doubtful. Yet he was cheerful about himself too, after we had walked to and fro in the sunlight a little while, and spoke of himself as "going to be better."

I am sorry to see that there have been some disturbances in Lancashire, arising out of the unhappy strikes. I read in an Italian paper last night, that there had been symptoms of rioting at Blackburn. The account stated that the workers of that place, supposing some of the obnoxious manufacturers of Preston to be secreted "nel palazzo Bull" assembled before that Palazzo and demanded to have them produced; and that thereupon, "La Signora Lawson, padrona del palazzo Bull," appeared at a window and assured the crowd that they were not within. I suppose the Palazzo Bull to be the Bull Hotel, but the paragraph gave no hint of such a thing.

(I wish you would come to Birmingham and see *those* working people on the night when I have so many of them together. I have never seen them collected in any number in that place, without extraordinary pleasure — even when they have been agitated by political events.)

Among the vast multitude of beggars we have seen, there came up one, at nightfall — at a poor little place on the Roman side of Siena — carrying another, a disabled youth — and very heavy — on his back.

---

[9] John Gibson Lockhart (1794–1854), the son-in-law and biographer of Sir Walter Scott. He joined the staff of *Blackwood's Magazine* in 1818, married Sophia Scott 1820, and edited the *Quarterly Review* 1826–1852.

After begging in the usual manner, and with great volubility for some time, and getting nothing (nobody having any small money of the country) he suddenly jerked his burden into a dirty little doorway, and walked off. The burden tumbled down like a sack of flour, and lay there, apparently quite used to it. I suppose he is picked up whenever a carriage is seen coming, and thrown away when there is nothing going on. Another beggar at the same place persisted so long (we were waiting for horses) that I remonstrated, and said "My good man I have told you twenty times that I have no little money. Why do you take so much trouble in vain? Why don't you go home and get to bed?" — "Sir," said he, "I'll give you change" — "Well, but if you can give me change, you can't be very poor." — "O yes I am. I have not eaten for five days" — "And still got change in your pocket?" — "Truly yes, what is a man to do? I must keep change, for English travellers. English travellers are *my only property*, and they never have change."

Although the Grand Canal is undeniably romantic, and the window at which I am writing (close to the Piazza of St Mark) has a noble view of it, my feet are so intensely cold that I must take them to the fire. The unromantic wind is blowing from the East, and, there being a crack in the wooden part of the balcony casement (prodigiously picturesque from the outside) through which I can see the whole of the Trieste Steamboat with a very dirty Turk on board, I am, fortunately for my "gentle reader," prevented from going on into another sheet, which I had had serious intentions of doing.

My kind regards to Mr Brown, and to O. Pray mention to the latter that I am collecting some materials for a pitched battle with her on my return. I expect to be dreadfully puzzled by some of your specimens of the curious game when I am so happy as to see you all again.

ᕲᕛ

183.   DECEMBER 4, 1853, HOTEL DE L'EUROPE, TURIN
I found your kind letter awaiting me at the Post office here, on my arrival yesterday evening. Through the kindness of a Genoese friend, I had beforehand engaged the courier over the Mont Cenis to Lyons, for Tuesday the 6th and I hope this will so bring us to Paris as now to enable me to propose to dine with you *on Saturday next*. My fellow travellers beg me to thank you for your remembrance of them, and to assure you of the gratification with which they respond to it.

I have another favor to ask of you. It is, that you will allow one of your servants to engage an apartment at an hotel, to be ready for us on our arrival. We want an apartment of four bedrooms (Charley's included) and sitting room. As we shall probably leave Paris on Sunday morning, and as I suppose it to be still very full, it will be a great comfort not to have to drive here and there, seeking a shelter. The difficulty is, that, there being no information here concerning the boats up the Saone, or the railway from Chalons to Paris, I do not know whether we shall arrive in Paris on the Friday, or on the Saturday morning; but it would be best, perhaps, to take it for granted that Friday will be the day. I was once at the Hotel Bristol, en garçon, and remember some very good bachelor-apartments looking on the Rue St Honoré. Perhaps one of them might be vacant for our purpose. Anyway, we will drive to the Hotel Bristol, and I will send my servant in, to ask for yours. From whom, we shall know our destiny.

I write in haste, for I understand that the post goes out rather early. My love to O, and kindest regards to Mr Brown. Mr Egg and Mr Collins desire their best compliments.

I find little letters, here from Mamey and Katie, in which they describe *The* Baby as being now — but I, of all people, should not rend your feelings, so I say no more.

P.S. If, in our fast travelling, I have time to anticipate myself by the post, I will still write to Charley, naming the train by which we come; and will address the letter to your care.

I I I
Vast Edges Drear

IN 1838, passing through the Black Country and the industrial Midlands, Dickens had had his first horrified vision of mines like underground dungeons and mills filled with clamor and cruelty. He then swore that some day he would "strike the heaviest blow in my power" for their victims. And in the course of the years he had come to realize that the rapacity of Scrooge, the mercantile power of Mr. Dombey, the landowning power of Sir Leicester Dedlock, were all incorporated into the brutal and ugly world of mechanized industrialism that multiplied their tyranny a thousand times. Defended by laissez-faire economists and approved by the "hard-facts" educators and utilitarians, the philosophy of the industrialists savagely denied that they had any duty to their employees except to pay the wage established by the law of supply and demand, and insisted that the prosperity of the country depended upon high profits and cheap labor. The industrial system established an oppression all the deadlier because it professed to be based upon scientific laws inherent in the very structure of society.

These were the forces that Dickens found himself confronting in this crucial and climactic stage of his career. Hard Times *unmasks the cold-hearted rationalizations of political economy and the greed that used economic "laws" to justify a callous exploitation of the laboring classes.* Little Dorrit *paints this entire system as a vast jail imprisoning every member of society, from the glittering upper-class admirers of Mr. Merdle, the dubious financial wizard, down to the rack-rented slum-dwellers in Bleeding Heart Yard.* Our Mutual Friend, *his last completed novel, depicts society as a vast monetary barbarism in which the wealth that is its goal is symbolized by the dust contractor's heaps of refuse, the supreme goal of the world's greed imaged as filth and ordure.*

Everywhere it was venality and materialism that blocked a decent improvement of the world, that corrupted politics, that imposed the ponderous inertia of countless Circumlocution Offices to wear down the energies of reformers. More and more, Dickens found himself deeply and bitterly skeptical of the whole system of respectable beliefs that cemented society into a monolithic structure stubbornly resistant to significant change. He was contemptuous of the dishonesty and inefficiency of government, indignant over the brutality of a system that condemned the masses to ignorance, suffering, and squalor. But there the monstrous thing lay in the path of progress, in one enormous mass, higher and more invulnerable than any Chinese Wall. Although he was never to cease pouring out criticism, Dickens had almost lost hope.

The House of Commons seemed to him "to be getting worse every day." The dire influence of privilege had so tainted all the potentialities of representative government as to make it "a miserable failure among us." The people were far more honest and efficient than the members of Parliament, but the people had given up in a gloomy disgust. England was in the hands of the Dedlocks and Dombeys, of Boodle and Coodle, of the Tite Barnacles; worse still, of Mr. Gradgrind, Mr. Bounderby, and Mr. Merdle; and, worst of all, England abased itself beneath their feet. The people were "on the down-hill road to being conquered," were "content to bear it," and "WOULD NOT be saved." Though he still fought, it was as on Matthew Arnold's darkling plain, swept with the confused alarms of armies clashing by night, while faith ebbed away:

> I only hear
> Its melancholy, long, withdrawing roar,
> Retreating to the breath
> Of the night-wind down the vast edges drear
> And naked shingles of the world.

Mingling with Dickens's social disillusions were the deepening miseries of his marriage. In David Copperfield his young hero, married to the helplessly inadequate Dora, had forlornly told himself, "There can be no disparity in marriage like unsuitability of mind and purpose," and had explained to himself his misfortune in marrying her as "the first mistaken impulse of an undisciplined heart." "Why is it," Dickens now exclaims to his friend Forster, "that as with poor David, a sense comes always crushing on me now, when I fall into low spirits, as of one happiness I have missed in life, and one friend and companion I have never made?" And, finally, when he and his wife are upon the

*verge of the separation that ultimately parted them forever, "I find
that the skeleton in my domestic closet is becoming a pretty big one."
All these feelings are mirrored in the letters of these later years.
His fierce resentment of the state of England is seen in those letters
to Miss Coutts in which he vehemently supports Austen Layard's
efforts for administrative reform, and belligerently, almost angrily,
lectures her upon the dangers of the situation. His marital bitternesses,
too, after being so long suppressed, here burst out like subterranean
fire. And, finally, the letters written during his feverish and exhausting
tours as a public reader reveal the desperate, suicidal intensity that
hastened him to his grave. But by that time Dickens had ceased to
care what happened to him. Like the weary factory child he had once
been, he was almost impatient, almost glad, to reach his narrow bed.*

184.   JANUARY 2, 1854, TAVISTOCK HOUSE

We have just come home from Birmingham — where I would have
given no small sum if you had been. If you could have seen the two
thousand five hundred workpeople on Friday night, I think you would
have been delighted.[1]

Mrs Morson came here early this morning, to announce the disappearance of one of the girls over the garden wall, immediately after
church yesterday. She had just come home from service, and bodily
vanished in her cloak and bonnet and best gown. This is not the worst
disappearance she came to announce in great trepidation. She is going
to be married!

I will tell you the circumstances under which she is to change her
condition, when I see you. I think them very reasonable and sensible,
and creditable both to herself and her husband that is to be. He proposes the end of February for the event. Of course she has no idea of
leaving until she can be replaced, but of course "she would rather not
put him off, if she can help it."

---

[1] In spite of the enormous size of the Birmingham Town Hall, Dickens made
himself heard perfectly by the audience of two thousand people who listened to the
Christmas Carol for three hours on the evening of December 27 and repeatedly
burst into rapturous applause. On the twenty-ninth he gave an equally successful
reading of *The Cricket on the Hearth*. The twenty-five hundred working people for
whom he read the *Carol*, at reduced prices, on the thirtieth were, he thought, the
best audience of them all. These three readings added between £400 and £500
to the endowment of the Institute; the grateful founders gave Dickens and his wife
a silver flower basket and another piece of plate, and the performance made such a
furore that he was deluged with pleas to read elsewhere.

I have no idea where you are, and am going down to Stratton Street with this, to get enlightenment from Webb. Will you tell Mr Brown with my regards that I have been wondering whether he means to renew his acquaintance with the only Gin-Punch known to mankind, next Friday? I found the children getting up a dull charade for the occasion, and have altered Tom Thumb for them instead.[2] Tom is to be represented by one of our tiniest babies — the smallest size but one — who has a most remarkable ear for music. It will be very droll, and they will all look like little pieces of china. They have derived considerable notions of punctuality and attention from the parental drilling. The undersigned is to enact the Ghost, and Mr Lemon (as great a child as himself) the Queen of the Giants.

I leave it to the last my dear Miss Coutts to wish you many happy years, chiefly because, as I cannot do it heartily and affectionately enough, it seems mere nonsense to try. Will you include O in this abortive demonstration and complete failure?

If you are at Paris, how cold you must be. If you are at Brighton, how cold you must be. If you are anywhere, how cold you must be! I persevered in the cold bath at Birmingham, notwithstanding its being frozen; and not only escaped the least hoarseness or sense of fatigue from three nights of three hours each in that enormous hall (which requires a great effort) but felt as if I could have gone on for three weeks.

ᔔ

185.   JANUARY 4, 1854, TAVISTOCK HOUSE

I was the Committee yesterday, and, it being the close of the year, send you the book.

Rhena Pollard, that girl from Petworth jail, had been (as is sup-

---

[2] Dickens's children had been giving Twelfth Night plays, under his direction, in the schoolroom of Tavistock House, from the first winter after they had moved there. In 1852 the play had been Albert Smith's burletta *Guy Fawkes,* in 1853 Robert Brough's extravaganza *William Tell,* and this year, as Dickens explains, it was to be Fielding's *Tom Thumb.* Dickens, playing the Ghost of Gaffer Thumb, billed himself as "the Modern Garrick," and stout Mark Lemon, playing the Giantess Glumdalca, was listed as "the Infant Phenomenon." Little Betty and Lally Lemon, his daughters, were gravely irresistible as Huncamunca and Dollalolla. A small boy named Alfred Ainger (later Canon Ainger, Master of the Temple and biographer of Charles Lamb) played Lord Grizzle so drolly that Thackeray, who was among the guests, fell off his chair in a helpless fit of laughter. The supreme hit of the evening, however, was the small, helmeted hero, Tom Thumb, acted with solemn conviction by four-year-old Henry Fielding Dickens.

posed) the companion of the girl who ran away last Sunday, and had, in a most inveterately audacious manner, threatened Mrs Morson that she would leave — had pretended indeed, that she waited for the Committee day, as a kind of obliging favor on her part. Accordingly I summoned Mrs Morson when the girl appeared in her turn, and said "Mrs Morson this is the girl who wants to go, I believe" — "Yes." — "Take her at her word. It is getting dark now, but, immediately after breakfast tomorrow morning, shut the gate upon her for ever." I think the girl was more taken by surprise, and more seized with consternation, than anybody I have ever seen in that place. She begged and prayed — was obliged to be taken out of the room — went into the long room, and, *before all the rest,* entreated and besought Mrs Morson to intercede for her — and broke into the most forlorn and dismal lamentations. I told Mrs Morson to give her no hope or relief all night — to have the rough dress down and air it in the long room — and this morning, if the girl again besought her in the same way *before all the others,* to pause and send to me. This she did. I wrote back a letter, which I arranged with her yesterday that she should read them all. I put the case in the strongest and plainest manner possible, and said that you supported that Home, to save young women who desired to be saved and who knew the misery and degradation out of which they were taken — that it was *not* the place for those who audaciously slighted the shelter of the only roof interposed between them and the great black world of Crime and Shame — and that I *would not,* nor would any of the gentlemen who assisted you in its management allow its blessings to be thus grossly trifled with. As it was the great forgiving Christmas time, she was to give this girl one more trial; but only on the condition that if she ever repeated her threat in any way, she was to be instantly discharged. Also that all the rest were to understand that your consent had been obtained to this principle being in all cases severely and firmly carried out. We pitied such deluded creatures, and knew the remorse that always came upon them as soon as they were outside the gate; but the greatest object of our pity was the miserable girl in the streets who really would try hard to do well if she could get into the Home, and whose place was unjustly occupied by such a girl as this.

Both in words yesterday and in the letter today, I was as emphatic as I could possibly be. I think you will approve of the wretched young creature's having one more chance in this bitter weather — but in a just remembrance of what is due to the Home and its Supporter, I could not have given it to her, if she had been other than a stranger in London, and an utterly friendless speck in the world.

Snow two feet deep in the streets today!

༄

186.   JANUARY 14, 1854, TAVISTOCK HOUSE

I have had a long talk with Charley this morning. Before I proceed in that matter, I will first shew you what I have paid for him at Leipzig during the past year, and then I will give you an abstract of the Professor's letter concerning him.

Payments	£	S	D
Three quarter's board etc —	63 . .	15 . .	0
Lessons in German, Music and drawing	11 . .	0 . .	0
Pocket Money, bath and library) subscriptions, Hartz-Mountain-) walk, and general miscellaneous) items)	21 . .	5 . .	0
Total	£96 . .	0 . .	0

The Professor in his letter says that Charley has attained to a good knowledge of German (M. Taüchnitz, in *his* letter, says he speaks "a very good German indeed"), but that if he were to leave Germany now, he thinks he would soon forget what he has acquired. That he and Taüchnitz have both decided that it is not advisable to send him to the commercial school; firstly, because he must be a perfect German before entering it; secondly, because "I do not think that the extraordinarily great and formal severity and very rigorous discipline which is enforced in that establishment would suit the character and individuality of your dear son." That he loves him heartily, and finds him much improved in many little things that displeased him at first; but that he does not find in him a desire to study, and that he (the Professor) is not quite certain "that to be a merchant, is his earnest and fast determination." That he begs me, in sending Charley back, to send with him my opinion on this subject, clearly; as, if that be his real desire, "he must next employ himself in the necessary studies, arithmetic, writing, mercantile knowledge, etc." And that the usual way in which young men attain this aim, is by entering a counting-house, learning business practically, and forming business habits.

I will add next, without the least reservation or embellishment, the result of my own observation of Charley. He is very gentle and affectionate, particularly fond of his sisters, very happy in their society, and very desirous to win the love of those who are dear to him. His inclinations are all good; but I think he has less fixed purpose and energy than I could have supposed possible in my son. He is not aspiring, or imaginative in his own behalf. With all the tenderer and better qualities which he inherits from his mother, he inherits an indescribable lassitude of character [3] — a very serious thing in a man — which seems to me to express the want of a strong, compelling hand always beside him. Nothing but the conviction formed in his infancy that it *must be done*, renders him attentive to the little points of punctuality and order required of him at home. I believe him to have fewer active faults than ninety-nine boys out of a hundred at his age; but his virtues and merits all want activity too. (When I told him this morning that when I was a year older than he, I was in the gallery of the House of Commons; and that when I was his age, I was teaching myself a very difficult art,[4] and walking miles every day to practise it all day long in the

---

[3] Despite Dickens's affection for his eldest son, and his unfaltering belief that the boy was quick and clever, this paragraph and those that follow reveal the first palpable stirrings of those troubled doubts about the capacities and the future welfare of his sons that were to recur and grow stronger with the years.

This passage also represents, in the midst of Dickens's prevailing reticence about his marriage, the first expression in this correspondence of his underlying feeling about his wife. The reader has no doubt observed how little Dickens ever says about Catherine in all these letters. But to a man of his galvanic vitality the quality that he here calls merely "an indescribable lassitude" must have been both incomprehensible and trying. Even so, Dickens was still seeking generously to emphasize her virtues, "all the tenderer and better qualities." Whether Miss Coutts realized how ill-adjusted he and his wife were to each other can only be guessed, but there is testimony from her secretary, C. C. Osborne, that she had never thought Catherine either clever or attractive. She saw nothing unusual in that, however; she thought a large proportion of wives inferior to their husbands and habitually spoke of them with gentle sarcasm. "Poor dear Mrs Dickens" were her epithets for Catherine — words that on her lips, Osborne says, implied an almost infinite, if gentle, disparagement. It should be emphasized, however, that Miss Coutts was always kind to Catherine and apparently even felt a genuine affection for her.

[4] The "difficult art" was shorthand, which Dickens began teaching himself when he was sixteen as the first step toward his cherished ambition of becoming a parliamentary reporter. The system he learned was expounded in Gurney's *Brachygraphy*, then the most celebrated manual of the subject. Dickens's description of his struggles, in *David Copperfield*, is famous:

The changes that were wrung upon dots, which in such a position meant such a thing, and in such another position something else entirely different;

Courts of Law; he seemed to think I must have been one of the most unaccountable of youths.)

We sat down gravely this morning, to discuss the Professor's letter, and the future. Nothing could be more frank, amiable, and expressive of a sincere anxiety to do right, than his manner. But when I pressed him closely as to the Professor's doubt of his "earnest and fast determination," it was perfectly plain that he was doubtful of it himself. Not so much because he inclined to any other, as because he knew that he wanted determination altogether. I put before him the impossibility of his making any way whatever in mercantile pursuits, without the knowledge necessary to the calling; I shewed him that the same truth held good with reference to the bar, or with reference to anything; and that such knowledge was only to be got by a steadfast devotion to its acquisition, and by continuous persevering patience and pains from day to day. I told him (as I told him at Eton when he asked me) that I thought the army a poor pursuit for a young man of no property, and that I doubted if it would bring him to much self respect, contentment, or happiness, in middle life; but I said that for those who were incapable of steady application, it was a better thing by far than failure in any of the many better callings. He still repeated what he had said to me at Eton, and did so in the most modest and affectionate manner; but I deemed it advisable to close our talk thus: — "I don't think Charley that you have really and sincerely made up your mind with the earnestness necessary to a point on which your whole future life de-

the wonderful vagaries that were played by circles; the unaccountable consequences that resulted from marks like flies' legs; the tremendous effect of a curve in the wrong place; not only troubled my waking hours, but reappeared before me in my sleep. When I had groped my way, blindly, through these difficulties, and had mastered the alphabet, there then appeared a procession of new horrors, called arbitrary characters; the most despotic characters I had ever known; who insisted, for instance, that a thing like the beginning of a cobweb meant expectation; and that a pen-and-ink skyrocket stood for disadvantageous. When I had fixed these wretches in my mind, I found that they had driven everything else out of it; then, beginning again, I forgot them; while I was picking them up, I dropped the other fragments of the system; in short, it was almost heart-breaking."

Nevertheless, he persisted. After a year and a half of toil he was sufficiently expert to hold down a post as a court stenographer; within another few years he was the youngest reporter in the galleries of Parliament, and, once there, he rapidly strode to a position of distinction among the eighty or ninety veteran newspapermen, "not merely for accuracy in reporting, but for marvelous quickness in transcript." Said Thomas Beard, a friend and fellow reporter, "There never *was* such a shorthand writer!"

pends; and you had better think of it very seriously, and come to me again on Wednesday morning."

I am afraid my dear Miss Coutts this is a long and tedious story, and I know it is one that I would tell to no one else; but your interest in my dear boy, and my desire that you should know all about him just as I know it, will be — I hope and believe — its sufficient excuse. Ardor in anything that anybody's right hand finds to do, is so important in my sight and includes so much, that I may with some unconscious impatience, exaggerate Charley's one great want. But if I do, your better judgment will restore the balance.

I remember too, that the Eton system is a particularly bad one for such a character, and that a year is not a long time in which to improve upon it. But before you and I speak upon the subject or come to any decision on it, I want you to know the fact as I see it. I should be very undeserving of the friendship which I value as one of my dearest and best possessions, and which I never can reflect upon without a quickened heart, if I could charge myself with the slightest shortcoming on this head.

[P.S.] Walter is 13 next month. I will advise, on the direct appointment question, both with Mr Stone and Mr Trimmer. I hope he will do his duty steadily, anywhere.

187.   JANUARY 18, 1854, TAVISTOCK HOUSE
Your letter is as wise as it is kind, and I am sure it is impossible to say more of it than that. I quite agree with you in every particular. I must be but an unreasonable and insensible creature indeed, if I did not.

Charley re-appeared in my room this morning, and told me that he had thought of it all very much, and that he was quite resolved and determined in his wish to devote himself to mercantile pursuits. We had a little talk together, in which (profiting by your observations) I encouraged him as much as possible, and he left me as if he were far more comfortable in his mind on the subject. He is a very good boy indeed, but I feel sure that I do not mistake his character.

Your speaking to him will have great weight with him, I do not doubt. Don't you think it will be advisable to send him back now, within a fortnight or so? On what terms to send him back — that is, how I am to answer the Professor's queries about finding a counting-house for him — I am anxious to consult with you. But I am disposed to think that it will be best to send him back to the Professor's house, to study German and arithmetic, until midsummer. I am not clear that he is likely to do much good in Germany after that. Whether he might then go into some place of business in France for a little while, to furbish up his French, may be worth considering. I rather think his practical initiation into business had better be in some busy town *here*. The inducement to application on his return to Germany, might be the prospect of his coming home to begin life.

I rather think the Professor is a regular stolid German grub, and that he and Charley have got to the best understanding of which they are capable together. His books, his piano, and his pipe, seem to shut out the prospect of their ever coming any closer.

It has occurred to me that in the short remainder of his holidays, the best thing I can do for Charley will be to send him down to the Household Words office for some three hours every day. There is a great deal of correspondence there, and I will get Mr Wills to dictate some letters to him, and make him abstract some of the innumerable letters and papers that are to be read, and find occupation for him that will require his attention. When you shall have seen Charley, and I shall have seen you, I think it will then be best, for the present, to send him back — always supposing that you are of the same opinion.

I was at Shepherds Bush yesterday, and found everything quiet, and favorable. In Tracey's prison last week, I found Hannah Myers (who is there again) sitting next the last girl who robbed the Home. I send £35 to Mrs Matthews, with an intimation that this closes the correspondence.

I will not attempt to tell you how much I felt your letter and how highly I prize it. It would be hopeless to begin on such a theme after all these years.

With kindest regards to Mr and Mrs Brown

ꙅ

188.   JANUARY 23, 1854, TAVISTOCK HOUSE
Here is the letter of acknowledgement from Mrs Matthews.

I am delighted to hear that you are ascending in the scale of constructed animals! — and I shall expect half a dozen words when you come to town, telling me when I may have the satisfaction of contemplating your re-establishment in the cook and butler, housemaid, kitchen maid, scullery maid etc etc etc forces.

You will be glad I am sure to hear that Mr Wills gives me the best account of Charley at Household Words. He says he is very quick and extremely attentive — "knocks off" writing from dictation, with great vigor — copies with all possible exactness — makes abstracts of manuscripts cleverly — and is as willing and punctual as it is possible to be. He is proud of being so employed, and I think it does him great good. As you leave it to me to proceed, I will prepare him to go back, *next Wednesday week;* and I will tell him that on condition of his working hard at his German and at arithmetic, he is not likely to be at Leipzig more than 6 months. I will also write to the Professor at once — and to Taüchnitz — to the same effect. We shall have time to discuss the next step (by we, I mean you and I) before he leaves Leipzig; but I am strongly of opinion that he will get as much good out of the Professor, with this impulse, in six months as he would otherwise get in twelve. You will be able to see him, I hope, before he goes? Of course he is not tied to a day or two, if it should not suit you to see him within the time I have mentioned.

I have fallen to work again. My purpose is among the mighty secrets of the world at present; but there is such a fixed idea on the part of my printers and co-partners in Household Words, that a story by me, continued from week to week, would make some unheard-of effect with it, that I am going to write one. It will be as long as five Nos of Bleak House, and will be five months in progress. The first written page now stares at me from under this sheet of note paper. The main idea of it, is one on which you and I and Mrs Brown have often spoken; and I know it will interest you as a purpose.[5]

---

[5] The circulation of *Household Words,* after having risen steadily for the first three years of its existence, had slumped badly: the six months' profits on September 30, 1853, had been only around £528, about half what it had been for the corresponding period in the preceding two years. Bradbury and Evans urged that Dickens spring to the rescue by writing a new serial in weekly numbers especially for its pages. It had always been understood that he would occasionally contribute a long story, though at the moment he had intended no effort of the kind for a full year. But the publishers pressed; Forster and Wills concurred; and Dickens agreed.

Hard Times, the resulting novel, more than restored the fortunes of the periodical. Within ten weeks after the story began appearing on April 1, the circulation of *Household Words* had doubled; the final profits make it clear that before the end the increase must have been far more than that. The prosperity of the magazine was never in doubt again. This, although certainly important to Dickens, was not, of course, the "purpose" referred to in his letter. Dickens had long intended "to strike the heaviest blow in my power" against the industrial system and its ex-

Here is your Bleak House too, modestly waiting to be presented. But what would be the use of my sending it to Stratton Street when there was no butler or other male or female administrator in the house! With Kindest regards

○~つ

189.   FEBRUARY 2, 1854, TAVISTOCK HOUSE
You will be disappointed in the appearance of Mrs Marchmont the Shepherd's Bush candidate.[6] She has none of the brightness of Mrs Morson, is common looking, and lumpish. But she is quietly confident herself, and Tracey is so certain of her that he staggers me. His domain is so extremely well kept, and he is such an admirable administrator, that I have no right to think him wrong when he expresses such absolute confidence. But I must add (with the risk of contradiction by experience, before me) that I never should have derived that confidence myself, from any feature in this "good lady's" face.

She could be put under Mrs Morson's direction immediately, and could form herself during the rest of Mrs Morson's stay.

I have received the enclosed letter and accounts as you see them, from Mr Austin.

○~つ

190.   FEBRUARY 6, 1854, TAVISTOCK HOUSE
I have instructed the maker, since the receipt of your letter this morning, to proceed with the warming — I mean drying — apparatus.[7] The mysterious pattern on the back of the drawing has nothing to do with it, I suppose.

If I may advise, I would by no means get Mr Manly to look at the thing until it is completed. I know him very well indeed, and he is an

---

ploitation of the laboring class. *Hard Times* is the accomplishment of that aim, with Mr. Bounderby and Mr. Gradgrind representing the system's two faces of brutal act and harsh theory. And, significantly, Dickens fuses with his indictment of the "hard facts" philosophy of political economy a portrayal of the utilitarian educational practice that went hand-in-glove with it, the fact-cramming emphasis on practicality that frowned upon all imagination, fancy, and emotion and that was only an aggressive formulation of the inhumane spirit animating industrial materialism. In essence *Hard Times* is thus a morality drama, piercing with prophetic denunciation to the very core of the laissez-faire view of human existence.

[6] Mrs. Marchmont succeeded Mrs. Morson upon her retirement from the Home.

[7] A large closet for drying clothes more rapidly. The maker's name is unknown.

ingenious fellow; but the moment this man receives a suggestion, however slight, the responsibility is divided and you give him a something
to escape upon in case anything should go wrong. It being his trade
to make such things, and he having been just now selected for such
work at Tracey's great prison, I would leave him alone — if it were
my case — until he has done his work.

Charley seems to be a more difficult matter than one would suppose. On Sunday I saw Mr Bates,[8] and had a long talk with him, in
which he was extremely sensible and straight-forward. He said, in
confidence, that Barings' House is now full of young men — gentle-
mens' sons — whom he does not even know by name. That it is impossible in such a place to teach them business — that they chiefly
copy letters, and the like — and that they go away as wise as they
come. That nine failures out of ten, among merchants, take place because they don't know their business; and that very few do know it,
and therefore very few thrive. That the only real education would
be to begin at a Broker's in Mincing Lane — know sugars, coffees,
drugs, cottons, all manner of things, by sight and touch — then pass
through a counting house (after perhaps a couple of years) which
would be very easily done, and then be fit for anything. All this and
a good deal more, he wound up by saying that he did not believe he
himself possessed any remarkable qualities, and that he referred his
own success, mainly to his having been one of the few who did all this.

It is remarkable that, as to the Birmingham business, my Birmingham friend Mr Ryland[9] had said so exactly the same, here, that I could
have believed the two people had heard each other, and that the second was copying the first.

Yesterday I received a letter from the managing partner in that
other highly commended house of Huth and Co. in which he says
that it would give him the greatest satisfaction to do anything for a
gentleman etc whose writings etc — but adds that he really believes
their house is "too large" to be really serviceable to my son — again
offering exactly similar advice to Mr Bates's.

In the meantime I am becoming gradually idiotic on the subject.
Pending Mr Bates's speaking to some Broker, I have pointed out to
Charley the kind of drudgery essential to the calling (but without

---

[8] Josiah Bates was managing partner of Baring Brothers.
[9] Arthur Ryland, a Birmingham businessman. Frederick Huth and Company,
mentioned a few lines later, were merchants, located at 10 Moorgate Street, London.

saying that I think it will scarcely call into action the best sort of power he possesses — though I have a misgiving on that head), and have told him to think again and be certain he is still in earnest. Early next week, he is going down to stay with Mr Ryland for a few days, and see the Birmingham Lion's. Such things being quite new to him, we think may be useful in helping him to a decision.

I am going to Paris on Saturday or Sunday, and perhaps on to Bourdeaux — having motes of new stories[1] floating before my eyes in the dirty air, which seem to drive somewhere in that direction. I shall not be above a week or ten days gone. Can I do anything for you with your friend on the ricketty throne,[2] or anywhere else?

The latest joke is, that it is very bad weather for the Ministry to be out in. Considering the thaw, and the knee-deep slush in the streets, it is meritorious enough.

With kindest regards to Mr and Mrs Brown

ᑲᒪ

191.   APRIL 16, 1854, TAVISTOCK HOUSE

I went out to Shepherds Bush yesterday, and found them all in a very unsettled and unsatisfactory state, mainly owing to Frances Cranstone. Louisa Cooper and Ellen Venns complained of her that she was so constantly irritating and mischief-making, that it was impossible for "the quiet ones" to get on at all — that they had been made perfectly miserable (as indeed they looked) — that Cranstone was making a party in the house, against all who were disposed to do well — and that whenever Mrs Marchmont's or Mrs Macartney's back was turned, there was no disguise about it. Louisa Cooper in particular said that the last new-comer already felt this disturbing influence, and that the last but one (Ellen Stanley) seemed to be going in Cranstone's way as a mere matter of necessity. That the house was perfectly changed and made unlike anything it had ever been within her knowledge of it, and that she felt that whoever should have the misfortune to be sent out in the same ship with this girl never could hope for peace and quiet. Upon receiving this complaint from the two best conducted girls in the house, I referred both to Mrs Macartney and

---

[1] Dickens was still writing *Hard Times* and did not finish it until the middle of July; the last installment was published in *Household Words* on August 12, 1854. The opening scene of its successor, *Little Dorrit*, is in a Marseilles criminal jail. He did not, however, actually begin writing this book until May 1855.

[2] Louis Napoleon, the Emperor Napoleon III.

Mrs Marchmont, who said they had no doubt of its truth, but that the girl was so extraordinarily sly in getting others into trouble and keeping herself out of it — just an inch outside — that they could never catch her. I then had Cranstone in, and told her, positively once for all, that such conduct could not be allowed — that it would be monstrous to advise you to send out a girl so suspicious and full of mischief — and that unless she altered altogether in the next ten days my recommendation to the Committee would be to discharge her; which I was perfectly sure they would do; such complaint against her still existing. Thereupon she went back into the long room protesting and lamenting; and that moment (you may see what her influence is) up gets Eliza Wilkin, that girl with the unhappy Father, and boldly says before them all "If you please Mrs Marchmont, if Frances Cranstone is to go *I* wish to go." I immediately had her in, and said "You want to go?" — "Yes Sir." — "Then Mrs Marchmont please to write to her father and tell him she is to be discharged on Monday." And I went into the long room and said before the others "If that unhappy father of yours does not come here by Monday afternoon, you will be discharged alone."

Soon after I left, Cranstone broke out against Louisa Cooper with that violence, that Louisa Cooper (half frightened to death) entreated to be locked up for safety, which was done, Cranstone then demanding to go straightway, and Mrs Marchmont not knowing whether she ought to let her, Cranstone made proclamation to the establishment that she intended in the meanwhile "to be a Devil." Upon which Mrs. Marchmont locked *her* up in another room.

Early this morning comes Mrs Marchmont to me, to know what to do. I told her, immediately to discharge Cranstone, and to do with Wilkin exactly as I had announced before the girls. I think this will crush the bad spirit summarily, for Mrs Marchmont said that Wilkin's being taken at her word, evidently struck the rest with amazement and consternation.

This is a new instance to us, not only of the necessity, but the true kindness of firmness. If we had discharged Cranstone on that old occasion we should have saved Wilkin. Now, that wretched creature says that she and Cranstone have "always kep' together, and that they mean to go together, and that she has been tired of the place this long time." It would have been better to lose a wilderness of Cranstones.

The gates being rotten and falling away, I got an estimate from Border the carpenter for a new pair. They will be within £10, and I told him to get on with them.

Mrs Marchmont is naturally a little disturbed by these proceedings; but her way will be made much easier, she hopes, after this example.

Quite an official report this!

cᴖ

192. MAY 23, 1854, TAVISTOCK HOUSE

I was at Shepherds Bush today (Committee Day), and paid the bills, and transacted all the usual business.

Mr Tennant and I were on the Committee. Mr Tennant had previously spoken to Goldsborough and Campbell, in reference to their refusal of the places proposed by Mrs Boyle.[3] As he wished, however, that we should again go into the subject, we did so. For Goldsborough there appeared not the least justification. In Campbell's case it did appear that the young woman had a real dread that she was not fit for the work which seemed to be required from her. We took pains to get at the truth; and taking into consideration the kind of illness that she sometimes has upon her, coupled with her old mental suffering, the great efforts she has undoubtedly made to controul herself in the Home, and the affliction she was really in, lest she should not be understood to wish to do all she believes she can; we saw great reason for distinguishing between her case and Goldsborough's. We therefore, after consulting both with Mrs Marchmont and Mrs Macartney separately, as to her usual conduct, called her back, and told her that we felt justified in reporting kindly and considerately of *her* refusal, to you. I think well of her, sincerely; but I do not believe her to be equal, either mentally or bodily, to the general run of our girls.

I asked Goldsborough what work she supposed she *was* to do, when she went abroad? To which majestic enquiry she replied with a very limited sense of Committee dignity, "that she didn't suppose, Mr Dickerson, as she were a goin to set with her ands erfore her." Louisa Cooper when her turn came for appearing, expressed herself very properly and discreetly about the Home and the benefits she had received in it (under the impression that she would have sailed before our next meeting), praised Mrs Marchmont's kind conduct

---

[3] Mrs. Boyle had evidently offered the two girls employment of some kind when they should leave the Home and go abroad.

highly, and said that, being new, she had more to bear than she ought to bear, or than Mrs Morson ever would have borne, from "some of 'em." This vague description gradually settling itself down into Goldsborough and Stanley, we enquired into the conduct of the former again, and finding that it was undoubtedly provoking, and that she took advantage of her being first on the list and at the top of the table to incite the rest, I particularly told both ladies to bear no misconduct whatever from her, but on her disregarding their authority in any marked way, immediately to let me know. And upon that I will discharge her.

Stanley, on being remonstrated with for general defiance, told Mrs Marchmont last night that she meant to go and that she (Mrs Marchmont) was to say so, today. Upon that we had them in together; and Stanley beginning a long story about "which blessed will be the day when justice is a-done in this ouse," I said that the only thing we had to do with, was whether she had said she meant to go. To which she rejoined that she had, and that she could turn her hand to anything, she thanked the Heavenly Powers! I remarked that the only thing she had to turn her hand to, at present, was to going; and that she would understand she was to withdraw before tomorrow evening.

The rest were all well and well behaved. Stanley will be an excellent riddance, and I think Goldsborough will earn her discharge. Of course she will not have it otherwise. But she seems to me pretty sure to do us no credit under any circumstances.

"Hall, General Dealer" proposes to take the field.[4] Bagster[5] has insane ideas about the value of the grass that is to grow between this and midsummer. Not to despise his efforts to get something out of that piece of land, we arranged that Hall should have the field from midsummer, at the rent paid (or not paid) by the last tenant.

Rhena Pollard had been troublesome, but was recommended to mercy. General neatness of establishment, greatly improved.

I must make an end of this long story, or you will dread my handwriting. Kind regards to Mr and Mrs Brown, and best remembrances from all here.

Holly Lodge, from the outside, looking beautiful. (I have just been arranging a very small freehold not far from it, where my little child

---

[4] To rent the field for the value of its hay crop and perhaps for pasturage as well.
[5] Unidentified.

Dora, of the ill-omened name, is to lie under the sun instead of re-maining in a vault; and whither my many walks in that neighbourhood will take me, I suppose, at last.)

From "my" lane the other day, your hawthorns were a sight to see. The heath in bloom, delightful too. And the lopped trees — even the lopped trees — really look very little the worse, now the leaves are out.

∽

193. JUNE 18, 1854, PAVILION HOTEL, FOLKESTONE

I called upon you yesterday between 1 and 2, and I should have called on Friday but that I was all day at Shepherd's Bush making up the book.

They were going on very well indeed. The girl from St James's Workhouse — where she had been temporarily sent, until an asylum could be found for her — the daughter of the vestry clerk of St Pancras — I forget whether her name is McMillan or McGahey — spoke to me about her never having been accustomed to hard work, and hoping she might get a nurse's place when she emigrated. I said all that was needful to be said on the subject, as to her requiring to be used to house work, whatever capacity she might hereafter fill; and added that I would mention what she had said, to you. She, did not urge it by way of complaint at all, and was on the housework then. She has been better brought up than the usual run of our inmates.

I sent a man on whom I could depend, to look after Frances Cran-stone. The place is over by Whitechapel. He brought back such an odd account of the house being one of four or five neat little houses, with a man and his wife — apparently — in the parlor whom he "saw doing nothing, through the blinds" — and further of the people having just moved in, and being quite unknown both at the Police Station and the public house, that Mr Wills's curiosity was piqued and he of-fered to go himself on Monday, and pay a visit to Cranstone in the kitchen if it should tend to elicit the truth. I confided the mission to his discretion, and will write you the result. He is sure to know all about it, somehow or other.

Did you mean, in your instructions to Mrs Marchmont respecting the fetching of the Wiltshire girl, Trim, from the Railway Station, that you wished Mrs Macartney to go instead of Mrs Marchmont, and that you wished to substitute an omnibus for the usual Fly? It rather seems to me that, with a view to the discipline of the place, the first impression should be of the principal Superintendent; also, that there are many reasons which render a public conveyance very objectionable. Of course I did not interfere, but I thought Mrs Marchmont scarcely understood what her directions in this respect were.

Mr Trimmer of Putney, after due consideration, has answered the question respecting Walter. Mr Stone fully concurs. The opinion is, that he is decidedly a subject for the direct appointment, and that he would *not* come off with any high distinction at Addiscombe — where, in that case, he would merely go as a form, and escape what are supposed to be great objections and disadvantages in the college to such a boy. They confirm my belief that he is very steady and good, and will always do his duty with great punctuality and a high sense of responsibility, but that he has no uncommon abilities, and least of all in the sciences of mathematics and fortification which would alone enable him to get into the Engineers. Mr Trimmer therefore says he has no doubt whatever on the subject.[6]

I have received a letter, through Mr Lemon, respecting your next presentation to the St Anns Society School at Brixton, and soliciting it for a girl. I suppose it is already bestowed? I only want to answer, according to fact.

The payments I have made, respecting which your mind was so uneasy while you were under the protection of the French Gov't are,

3 months Dr Elliotson's poor ladies — 15	. . 0	. . 0	
Eliza Wilkin's father — 3	. . 0	. . 0	
Shepherd's Bush in May, as pr book — 41	. . 0	. . 0	
£59	. . 0	. . 0	

I think that's all. Whenever you go to the Bank, you can place it to my credit, or I shall be in town, I hope, towards the end of next month, and will write beforehand to notify the important fact of my appearance. It depends on my completion of Hard Times.

Townshend was in a state of great excitement yesterday, at the

---

[6] At the end of his coaching with Mr. Trimmer, Walter therefore entered the school of Messieurs Brackenbury and Wynne, at Wimbledon, instead of going to Addiscombe, and subsequently, in 1857, after passing his examinations, received through Miss Coutts's influence a direct nomination to a cadetship in the East India Company's 26th Native Infantry.

prospect of your dining with him. The Crystal Palace shares, I hear, have been going down fearfully, since the opening. Perhaps your lunching there, yesterday (as I suppose you did) will bring them up again.

— I am a Spanish Merchant,[7] and I deal, I am rejoiced to say, in a sunny morning and a dead calm. For which reason I am going across presently, with Mrs Dickens and Georgina who are with me, and give me all sorts of messages. The children are coming over direct from London Bridge, on Tuesday. My address is, Villa du Camp de droite, Boulogne.

With kindest regards to Mr and Mrs Brown, and a horrible desire to have the sole and entire direction of the furnishing of that wonderful little room, Ever Dear Miss Coutts

ఞ

194.   JUNE 22, 1854, VILLA DU CAMP DE DROITE, BOULOGNE
That is a most infamous proceeding on the part of Mr St George.[8] Those people who are so horribly charitable at other people's expence, and who will commit any duplicity in furtherance of their object — which they call a good one — are among the worst of Imposters. The Bailiff in the Good Natured Man [9] says of his follower "he's a good deal in need of assistance, and as I can't afford to assist him myself I must get you to do it, Master," which seems to me, in comparison, a respectable thing.

Here is the report of my Sub Editor and factotum concerning Cranstone.

"She has been living, since she left the Home, with a single man, to take care of his three children. He is the first floor. There are other lodgers in the House, and I doubt the respectability of the parlor but can't swear against it. She has had the entire management of his little household, to the paying of the weekly bills. She has been honest, but she has not wanted for meat, drink, or lodging — though she has been wretchedly deficient in washing; having been idle and dirty 'to an unbelievable degree.' Her charge left her her liberty to such an

---

[7] A facetious way of saying that he expects an easy Channel crossing. For this summer Dickens had taken another of M. Beaucourt's houses at Boulogne. He left either that afternoon or the following morning.

[8] Mr. St. George and his "infamous proceeding" have passed into oblivion.

[9] Oliver Goldsmith's comedy.

extent that 'she couldn't abear fur to have any one put over her' —
especially my informant, a bright clean good looking woman in mourning, who only came last Friday week, either as the widower's new
wife or sister; I am not sure which, and could not well ask. Consequently, last Sunday, Miss Cranstone "in a artful way' asked leave to
go out for an hour, and up to the date of my visit (4 P.M. Wednesday
June 21st) had forgotten to return."

It seems pretty clear that it will be best not to answer her letter.
I would not send it to the Mendicity,[1] I think, for they might trouble
you.

It is delightful to hear about Watts.[2] She tastes like a sweetmeat
after the St George physic.

We will look after your little friend if he appears. You cannot think
what a delightful cottage we have got. The rooms are larger than
those in the old house, and there are more of them; but the oddities
are almost as great, and the situation — on the top of this hill, instead
of three parts down it — is most beautiful. We have a field behind
the house, with a road of our own to the Column [3] — unbounded air
— capital garden — and all for five guineas a week. I anticipate shewing it to you sometime in the autumn, with great pleasure. And there
are a variety of ingenious devices in the Robinson Crusoe way, effected by the undersigned (who I think has moved every article of
furniture in the house, since Monday afternoon) which must be
studied, to be appreciated.

The camp [4] is not a mile off, and I have been in terror lest I should
hear the drums. I went over, yesterday, to reconnoitre the enemy. It
is a very curious and picturesque scene. The 3 or 4000 soldiers now
here, are building mud huts thatched with straw, for the 50 or 60,000
who are to come. I should think there are about 100,000 trusses of
straw piled up ready for use; and the 3 or 4000 men (lazier than any
men I ever saw) are constantly wheeling little barrows of earth about
— containing twelve tablespoonfulls each, as nearly as I can estimate.

---

[1] The Society for the Discouragement of Mendicity, an organization that investigated the authenticity of appeals for charitable aid.

[2] Unidentified.

[3] The Column of the Grand Army, a marble Doric shaft 176 feet high, capped
by a bronze statue of Napoleon I, and erected to commemorate his intended invasion of England 1804–1805.

[4] The Crimean War had broken out March 28, 1854. This was a French army
camp.

Except that nobody is brisk, it looks like the opening of some capital French play.

Our children arrived on Tuesday by the London boat, in every stage and aspect of seasickness. When I saw them land (Sydney with an immense basket, and a Custom House officer in a cocked hat much bigger than the child, looking into it) Flight seemed the only course open to me. The Nurse was prostrate, and (generally speaking) was carried by the Baby instead of carrying him. That wonderful young creature was the admiration of the sternest mariner aboard — which I never heard of a Suffolk Baby yet — in consequence of the gentleness with which he was perpetually looking out of a white basin and, in the intervals of his paroxysms, pitying his family and attendants. They arrived after dark, with 27 packages, whereof 5 prodigious chests belonged to Mamey and Katey's governess, who is a Frenchwoman, and so small that I should have thought a hatbox might have contained her entire wardrobe. In the dead of the night, when we were all asleep, a vigilant Custom House agent appeared with 22 of those picturesque but screeching women who look after the baggage. The hill being extremely steep, they had harnessed themselves with ropes to the 27 packages. The tremendous uproad is inconceivable.

The Crystal Palace people, I venture to predict, will find the general English sense revolt against those monstrous pretences.[5] I had a very clever paper sent to Household Words, representing, with very good sarcasm, the hard case of Madame Tussaud of the wax work,[6] for whom the Archbishop of Canterbury had never said prayers in Baker Street. I thought it best not to use it, but the point was well put and would have told.

This is my first effort (no, my second) in penmanship of any kind, since I have been here. I suppose I shall get to work tomorrow, but at present I seem never to have done anything in the way of authorship.

With kind regards to O and Mr Brown

---

[5] The Crystal Palace had been re-erected, to house an industrial exhibition, at Sydenham, and, as the preceding letter shows, the shares issued by its speculators were not holding up very well on the stock market. Dickens's letter sounds as if they had persuaded the Archbishop of Canterbury to offer up prayers for the success of the enterprise, a mingling of the celestial and the commercial at which "the general English sense" might well revolt.

[6] Madame Tussaud's famous waxworks show, established in 1802, and located in Baker Street, 1833–1884.

195. AUGUST 6, 1854, VILLA DU CAMP DE DROITE, BOULOGNE [TO MRS. BROWN]

I received your kind note last night (stress of weather in the Channel delayed it), and I think I should certainly have come over, for the pleasure of such an occasion in such company,⁷ if I were not the unfortunate victim of a highly inflamed Ear. It has been very wet here for two days, and I suppose I have taken cold in the course of my long walks in the rain. Whatever the cause, the effect is very painfull; and after feeling disposed to tear my Ear off in the night, I am now going to hide my anything but diminished head (for it is swollen very big) in a cammomile poultice.

Pray give my kindest regards to Miss Coutts and thank her heartily for her remembrance of me. I should have been delighted to come, under more auspicious circumstances. (The obvious practicability of introducing a joke here, about a good Ear for an opera, warns me off the subject).

As to Industrial Exhibitions, big or little, I am disgusted with them and think of turning Misanthrope.

[P.S.] Mrs Dickens and Georgina and all the house send best regards.

196. AUGUST 9, 1854, VILLA DU CAMP DE DROITE, BOULOGNE [TO MRS. BROWN]

I had been saying that I hoped you would write me an account of Grisi's farewell, so when your welcome letter came this morning and I read the description aloud (I trust with becoming emphasis and discretion), I was not only regarded with great favor as having so much that was interesting to tell, but was looked upon as a small Prophet too. It is always a very melancholy thing to take leave of anything or anybody — I have a remarkable weakness and infirmity in the matter of saying Good Bye on any occasion — and upon the whole I begin to be glad now, or I try to persuade myself so, that I was *not* there! It is not a slight thing to let a Genius go, out of any sphere; and out of that bright one where people are never really sick and never really die, but come back tomorrow superior to all the

---

⁷ As the second paragraph of this letter and the first paragraph of the next make clear, the invitation was to hear the farewell performance of Giulia Grisi (1811?–1869) at the opera before her departure for the United States.

hard conditions on which we hold life, it is a sad sensation to see any one depart into real existence.

As the bright side of which, I beg to report my Ear all right again — except being blistered all over, exactly as if it had been burned — and my head no longer tied up in a black silk bundle. I relapsed into my usual beauty, yesterday.

Townshend (from whom I hear today) is more happy I think in his Stratton Street reception and appreciation than he has been in anything for years; and I believe nobody alive has a more exalted admiration of Miss Coutts.[8] I wish I had been with him in one of the smaller rooms in Stratton Street, or in Holly Lodge, at twilight, when there were no strangers among us. He has the finest collection of Ghost stories I ever heard, and his quiet way of telling them gives them a peculiar effect. But he wants, in a Zoological manner, to be poked and aggravated up to the mark.

I have been thinking of the furnishing of that room, and see it all in my mind's eye. If you adhere rigidly to the points adjusted by the Conference, resolutely breaking the Upholsterer's heart and regarding all his tears with a countenance of flint, it will be the perfection of snugness, completeness, and comfort. If you give the Upholsterer his own way in the slightest matter, you are lost.

Many thanks for your letter. With best regards to Miss Coutts, and a heap of kindest loves and remembrances from all here,

[P.S.] You remember Serjeant Bellasis's [9] priestly friend who imitated a donkey in the Pulpit? I find him to be (not a Frenchman or an Italian, as I had supposed) but an Irishman with a terrific brogue. Which explains the story at once.

ᴄⱳ

The name of Louisa Cooper has already occurred more than once as that of a quiet and well-behaved girl at Urania Cottage. In Dickens's letter of May 23, 1854, he speaks of her as soon expecting to sail. On the actual eve of her departure for the Cape of Good Hope she sent

---

[8] Chauncy Hare Townshend, evidently at this time on a visit to England, and received by Miss Coutts in Stratton Street. He had indeed a high admiration for Miss Coutts: when he died in 1868 he left her a large sum of money for the furtherance of elementary education, which was used to found the Chauncy Hare Townshend Schools in Rochester Street, Westminster.

[9] Serjeant Bellasis, his clerical friend, and the joke involving an Irishman imitating a donkey in the pulpit, remain unidentified.

Miss Coutts a note of gratitude and farewell. It is here given exactly as she wrote it.

ↄ

197. OCTOBER 20 [1854], TILLINGTON [TO MISS COUTTS FROM LOUISA COOPER]

As I am about to leave England I am most anxious that one of my last acts should be to thank you my kind Benefactress for all your goodness to me   I cannot find words to express my gratitude but with the help of that kind Providence who will never leave me nor forsake me if I pray to him I will by my future life try to prove it   I often think of your kind and gentle words and the thoughts of them has many times been a comfort to me and will be when I am in a far distant land   we do not sail till the 10th of November   Mrs Boyle[1] goes to Plymouth a week before   may every blessing be yours Dear and Honnored Lady and may all the young people at the Home prove deserving your bounty   it is a comfort to know there is one placed over them who cares so much about them   I can never forget how much I dreaded her coming or how soon I learned to love and respect her   she has been so very kind in writing to me and given me good advice   I often think of Urania Cottage and the many happy hours I have spent there   I have taken the liberty to write to Mr Tennant to thank him for all his kindness to me   with your permission I will take the liberty of writing on my arrival at the Cape   may every blessing be yours' Honnored Madam is the prayer of your Humble Servant

ↄ

198.   OCTOBER 26, 1854, TAVISTOCK HOUSE

But for the sake of our consistency in cross purposes, I should have liked very much to have seen you when you were in town (after all this length of time) if it had been only for a minute.

Cooper's very good letter I return. Poor little thing, I hope she will flourish out there.

I am sorry you are in a Maze about the article to Working Men[2]

---

[1] Probably the same Mrs. Boyle mentioned in Dickens's letter of May 23, 1854, who had offered some of the girls employment abroad when they left Urania Cottage, and who would seem, from this letter, to be sailing with them to the Cape.

[2] "To Working Men," *Household Words*, October 7, 1854, an angry article written by Dickens himself, and provoked by the sickness and suffering in urban

— which was written by a friend of yours. Its meaning is, that they never will save their children from the dreadful and unnatural mortality now prevalent among them (almost too murderous to be thought of), or save themselves from untimely sickness and death, until they have cheap pure water in unlimited quantity, wholesome air, constraint upon little landlords like our Westminster friends [3] to keep their property decent under the heaviest penalties, efficient drainage, and such alterations in building acts as shall preserve open spaces in the closest regions, and make them where they are not now. That a worthless Government which is afraid of every little interest and trembles before the vote of every dust contractor, will never do these things for them or pay the least sincere attention to them, until they are made election questions and the working-people unite to express their determination to have them, or to keep out of Parliament by every means in their power, every man who turns his back upon these first necessities. It is more than ever necessary to keep their need of social Reforms before them at this time, for I clearly see that the War will be made an administration excuse for all sorts of shortcomings, and that nothing will have been done when the cholera comes again. Let it come twice again, severely, — the people advancing all the while in the knowledge that, humanly speaking, it is, like Typhus Fever in the mass, a preventible disease — and you will see such a shake in this country as never was seen on Earth since Sampson pulled the Temple down upon his head.

I wish you would read, in next week's No of Household Words,

slums and the failure of the Government to take any effective steps for their amelioration. He told readers that unless they set about improving these conditions they were guilty of wholesale murder. He warned working people not to be taken in by "high political authorities" and "sharking mountebanks" interested only in "contesting for places, power, and patronage, loaves, and fishes." He charged the workers to make their voices heard, to unite and use the power of their numbers to see to it that men who defied their needs were thrown out of office.

So fiery an appeal had a frightening sound to many readers. Most of the working class had no vote. Was the counsel that they use their numbers to demand their will an invitation to violence? Or, hardly less horrifying, did it mean that Dickens approved of labor unions? (He did; he thought their employers left them no alternative; although, as *Hard Times* made clear, he believed that their leaders were often corrupt demagogues.) The violent tone of the article worried even Miss Coutts.

[3] The Westminster slum landlords who had refused Miss Coutts's appeal to install sanitary facilities even when she promised to meet any costs that exceeded a moderate preliminary estimate — typical, Dickens felt, of the property owners' hardhearted indifference to every consideration except that of extorting a maximum of profit from their holdings.

an article called Our French Watering Place (with a portrait of my Boulogne landlord), and a poem called The Moral of this Year.[4]

If you will let me know when the room is ready, I shall be delighted to convey my critical eye into the midst of it.

The conclusion of your note has greatly agitated my mind. "With all kind regards and —" then a wonderful word, which I at first thought was "Nelsons," but which I now make out to be "Pelows." What is a Pelow? What am I to do with it? To whom am I to give it? Does it require an answer? Is any Pelow supposed to be enclosed, or was it left out by mistake, or can it have dropped out at the Post Office? I never was so disturbed by doubts and difficulties.

With kind regards to Mr and Mrs Brown — and as many Pelows as may be agreeable to them

[P.S.] Our Committee will be Tuesday the 7th of November.

⁀

Shortly before Dickens returned to London on October 17, he had received a remarkable appeal. In the stress of moving, and then of getting settled down in Tavistock House again, he did not answer it immediately, but subsequently wrote a reply making an appointment to see its author. The communication itself, he passed on to Miss Coutts endorsed: "I received the following letter, from a correspondent quite unknown to me, while I was at Boulogne, I think, in the beginning of October."

⁀

199.   OCTOBER 10, 1854, 25 BUTE STREET, OLD BROMPTON [TO CHARLES DICKENS FROM FREDERICK MAYNARD]

I hope you will forgive the strange appeal that I am about to make to you, but, I shall be very grateful if you will read this letter, and,

---

[4] Both in *Household Words*, November 4, 1854. The first, by Dickens, may be found in *Reprinted Pieces*. The poem portrays the epidemics engendered in unsanitary slums as a conqueror sweeping from them through the entire country. (During that summer alone the cholera had slain 20,000 in England and Wales.)

> Not alone in dens of squalor hath this Giant-King his lair,
> With deadly steps he grimly creeps up many a marble stair!
> In such a day small right to pray, when in each street, each lane,
> No drain or sewer with breath impure, but has its list of slain!
> Scant right to call on GOD to move this evil from our door,
> If man cares naught for brother man, and the rich forget the poor!

may I hope, not throw it aside without notice — I will not take up much of your valuable time but come at once to the point —

My elder sister through a series of misfortunes — (the particulars of which, I cannot enter into, in a letter) — became acquainted with a gentleman and lived with him 9 years but I regret to say not as his wife — She was enabled to keep and educate myself and a sister during that time, I being only 10 years of age when first this occurred — I was articled, with a handsome premium to an Architect when 17, but I had not been 2 years so placed before my sister's circumstances changed — Her protector left her and she was plunged in great distress with the chances of a frightful life before her — You can imagine my feelings at this position — My articles were cancelled, which has marred my progress in the profession, and prevented me returning her that kindness which she showered upon me when I was unable to help myself — My difficulty is this — I cannot wholly support her by my earnings; my desire is to obtain for her some employment or situation, from which she could be independent of me, till I had advanced further in the world — The reason of my writing to you is this — I have no friends who would interest themselves in her behalf, neither has she, for hers is a peculiar position — I have heard much of your goodness to unfortunate people — and your writings have emboldened me to pray for your advice — There is not a tale, or article of your writing that has not assured me that your disposition is charitable to the misfortunes, and merciful to the faults of others, and that your mind is above the vulgar prejudices of this world — Upon you I have placed my hopes of receiving counsel that will enable me to place my sister, who has been a Mother to me, in an honest position — If you will take notice of this letter, I will at a future time enter more fully into the particulars that led to this unhappy state of affairs — My dear Sister's anxious wishes are the same as mine — She must not be judged by her unhappy condition, for I affirm in spite of it — a more virtuous minded woman never lived. You I am sure would not judge her harshly did you know all particulars of her past life — I have full confidence in your honour, that if you take no notice of this letter, the contents will not go further, and to prove my confidence, although I have never seen you, I will give you the names of the gentlemen in whose Offices I have been in — I was articled to F. J. Francis, Esqre, Bedford Place, Russell Sq. and I am now in the Office of Henry Clutton Esqre, Charles St. Haymarket — You will therefore have the opportunity, if you please of proving what I have written is true — In conclusion let me pray of you to listen to my appeal — I am young without Father or friend to assist or advise me, and placed in such a serious position with regard to my sister that I tremble to think of it. For placed as she is she can make no personal application to any one — Do not therefore plunge me in despair by refusing me your advice — Hoping for a favourable reply

ᵒᵛᵓ

Dickens received Frederick Maynard by appointment, and had with him the moving interview narrated in the following account, of which the opening is missing. The last three paragraphs are written at the end of the note from the sister immediately following. There is consequently no date, although the circumstances establish that it could not be earlier than November 16. It probably accompanied the note of November 17.

ᵒᵛᵓ

200. [NOVEMBER 16–17? 1854]

. . . On my return to town I wrote to the young man, representing to him that I had scarcely any hope of helping him in so difficult a matter, but that I was unwilling to seem to slight so peculiar a confidence, and that I would speak with him on the subject if he would call on the following Sunday at a certain hour. That was Sunday the 29th of October.

At the appointed time, he came. I found him a very quiet, youthful-looking man of two or three and twenty, with the appearance of being much younger. He was very becomingly and suitably dressed, in black; and his manner and his whole account of himself were in perfect accordance with his letter. He cried, at several parts in our conversation: but he sat in my room with his back to the light, and always made an effort to hide it, and was evidently relieved when I appeared not to notice it.

To make the least of the wretched story, I will only set down here that the person with whom his sister had lived so long, was engaged in commerce, and was ruined. The sister seems to have done a great deal for him, in the management of his house and accounts, and some of his relations declared when he fell into his difficulties, "that she was the only true friend he had." He was quite reduced to poverty when they parted, and he is far away now, and lost sight of, altogether. She has known nothing about him these many years.

She had only one course of life open to her then, and she has pursued it ever since. She has a child; a little girl of two years old, to whom she is devoted. Although she is what she is, in the very house to which the brother goes home every night of his life, he has an un-bounded respect and love for her, which presents one of the strangest and most bewildering spectacles I ever saw within my remembrance.

She educated her younger sister, who is a Nursery-Governess. The mother (with whom they had a miserable home) is living, and has a small situation in Kensington workhouse. The young man said he had no consideration for his mother and no love for her. That this elder sister of his had been such a mother to him always, as he thought few boys had; and that the gratitude and affection with which she had inspired him and his younger sister "couldn't be described." There is no doubt of this being true. I really had a difficulty in col-lecting myself to understand that in the tremendous circumstances of their daily existence, she has not fallen in this brother's *respect*.

He represented her as two or three and thirty; as having acquired no accomplishments, but as having had a good plain education, and being a good housekeeper. He said, she loved her child in the most passionate manner imaginable.

When the break-up took place, it was impossible for the young man to continue under his articles, because he was then unable to support himself without a Salary — which, while articled, he was not to receive. His articles were cancelled, therefore (no part of the pre-mium being returned), and he obtained a situation as architectural Draughtsman — which he holds now — at one pound fifteen per week. This class of people have no rise or advance, he says; but are at the last, what they are at first. If he could make enough to keep his sister and her child he would be heartily thankful, and they would joy-fully maintain a home together, and he would ask no help. He had tried all sorts of things in despair. He had written, only a week or two ago, to Mr Wigan of the Olympic Theatre,[5] applying for a situa-tion to take checks at the door of an evening, to eke out his income. There was nothing that he wouldn't do, to change his sister's life. Not that it had corrupted her — if I would only see her, I should know,

---

[5] Alfred Wigan was the manager of the Olympic Theatre.

before I had spoken to her five minutes, what a nature she had. (And so he began to sob, and said she was the best — the kindest — the least selfish — I don't know what.)

To try how the shock of a separation they had evidently never thought of, would affect him, I asked him if she had ever thought of being sent abroad — to the Cape — to America — to Australia? He was quite stunned by the idea of parting from her, and asked me, Oh Mr Dickens did I consider how the natural ties between them must have been strengthened by this time! I said what I have said so many times to the Home people, and I urged him to consider that if (as he had said) she would do anything for her child's sake, she would do that thing on occasion, hard as I admitted it to be. He didn't know, he answered. He believed she would do almost anything — but she had never thought of this — she was almost as fond of him as he was of her — he couldn't hastily pledge her to such a separation as she had never had in her thoughts. "Ask her," said I. He was going out, and came back, and said, "Mr Dickens, I know it would be utterly in vain to ask her to leave her child behind her — " "No one would propose that," said I. "Let us suppose that she was to take it with her."

This is all I know, as yet. I have not replied, nor have I seen her. I will do both, if you feel interested, and I don't disguise that I hope you do. But I have told the story very coldly, in comparison with the impression it has made upon me. I asked the young man whether there was anyone who could speak of his sister besides himself and herself? He replied "Dr Lavis of Westminster had attended her, was interested in her (he felt sure), and would know the truth of what he had told." This Dr Lavis is the medical attendant at Tracey's prison, and I know him very well.

I cannot be right, without seeing the girl, of course; but I think that if anything could be done for her, or for her brother, it would seem that they had a better chance together than apart.

If you wish to pursue the case, I would first see the Doctor — then her. In any case, I cannot let it rest; for the position of this brother — his perception of his sister's disgrace, and yet his undiminished admiration of her, and the confidence he has grown up in, of her being something good, and never to be mentioned without tenderness and deference — is a romance so astonishing and yet so intelligible as I never had the boldness to think of.

201. NOVEMBER 16, 1854, 23 BUTE STREET, OLD BROMPTON [TO CHARLES DICKENS FROM CAROLINE MAYNARD THOMPSON [6]]

My Brother (Frederic Maynard) has acquainted me with the kind interest you expressed in my unhappy affairs, and of the hopelessness of my securing a situation in England. Altho' as you may imagine I should prefer remaining in this Country, still for my Child's sake I should gratefully accept any honorable opportunity of redeeming my position, even to the breaking of all ties that hold me here — I have no words to thank you for your goodness in listening to my miserable tale, and the hope you have given me of at least one way of escape and which appears to be the only alternative —

Should it lie in your power to aid me in this matter you will confer a lasting obligation on me

☙

On the same day that the sister wrote, the brother also sent a second letter. At the top of the page Dickens annotated it for Miss Coutts: "I made up my mind not to tell you all this, if I had any reason to doubt the strength of their sincerity. On Wednesday [7] — having done nothing but keep quiet in the meanwhile — I received the two following letters." [8]

☙

202. NOVEMBER 16, 1854, 23 BUTE STREET, OLD BROMPTON [TO CHARLES DICKENS FROM FREDERICK MAYNARD]

Not having heard, I fear that I misunderstood you upon leaving your house last Sunday week. [9] You, at first, said that I was to write to inform you, whether my sister was averse to going abroad — Afterwards, I think, you settled that I was *not* to write, until I heard from you —

Fearing I may be labouring under a mistake, and deeply anxious about the unhappy situation of my sister, — I have taken the liberty of again writing, and enclose a letter from my sister, expressing her

---

[6] "Thompson" was the name she used for her illegitimate child.

[7] A mistake in the date: both letters are dated November 16 — which was a Thursday — and could not have reached him before that day, nor was it likely that both letters would be delayed in reaching him until the following Wednesday.

[8] The letter already given, from Caroline Thompson, and the one following, from Frederick Maynard.

[9] Maynard had evidently had a second interview with Dickens on Sunday, November 5.

anxiety to alter her position even by emigrating, if there are no other means left —

I hope that an opportunity will occur of bringing about that which I so anxiously desire, and relieve my mind of the terrible weight that hangs upon it. I thank you much for the kindness and delicacy you displayed towards me, in the interview I had, — I but poorly expressed my gratitude to you upon that occasion, but, believe me, it will ever live in my remembrance.

ᴄ⳾Ꙭ

203. NOVEMBER 17, 1854, TAVISTOCK HOUSE

I send you the astonishing story to which I referred in my note of yesterday.[1] I have regularly paged it, to prevent confusion. You will find it easy to read, I hope, and not half as long as it looks.

ᴄ⳾Ꙭ

204. DECEMBER 11, 1854, TAVISTOCK HOUSE

I have been asked to give you the enclosed letter from Birmingham. I replied that I would do that much, accompanying it with no other remark than that I knew the Institution to be the best in England and of national importance.

I have today seen Mrs Thompson, the sister of the young man whose letters I sent to you, and in reference to whom I received the enclosed report from Dr Lavis. The kind of life she leads, is far from being as bad as you might suppose, and, to prevent its being worse than it is, she has parted with everything in the way of personal ornament. She would willingly go to the Cape and I have the strongest belief that she would do well. I plainly see, and therefore feel bound to mention, that her child is the one great occasion of her desiring to retrieve the past.

She is rather small, and young-looking; but pretty, and gentle, and has a very good head. Her manner was exceedingly natural to the circumstances in which I saw her, and she greatly strengthened my previous disposition to be interested in her. I feel confident that there can never have been much evil in her, apart from the early circumstances that directed her steps the wrong way.

---

[1] The "note of yesterday" is a missing communication, but it evidently referred to the long account of the first meeting with Maynard hypothetically dated November 16–17 (No. 200 in this collection), printed above for the sake of narrative clarity. Probably it and the two letters from the brother and sister were all sent to Miss Coutts with this note of November 17.

She could not be placed on a level with our Shepherd's Bush girls. Her manner, character, and experiences, are altogether different.

It is a very remarkable case. I very much wish you would see her, and judge for yourself of its peculiarity. There is nothing about her from which you could suppose she had come to this. You might see her and her brother a thousand times — you might meet them in the street, every day in the year — and only notice them as brother and sister who were no doubt living together and taking care of one another. I cannot get the picture of her, out of my head. I particularly wish that you could see her and speak to her.

Supposing she were sent abroad, and her child were to die there soon, I am doubtful whether she would not come back — *unless* she had found an opening for her brother and he had gone out to her.

Perhaps you will tell me on Wednesday, when I can speak to you on this case, and also about Charley — in reference to whom I should like to shew you a letter I have from Birmingham.

The Poor Travellers [2] have not yet emerged from the steam engine. As soon as they appear, they shall wait on you. I hope you will like my little story, as the First of them. It has made such an impression on the staff, that I think there must be something in it.

⌘

205.　　　　　　　DECEMBER 26, 1854, TAVISTOCK HOUSE

Many many merry Christmases and Happy New Years to you, and all of you!

I am glad you like the baskets. May they help to make you tidy!

Mrs Dickens is coming to tell you that we hope you and Mr and Mrs Brown will be able, this year, to see the children's Fairy-play. [3]

---

[2] "The Seven Poor Travellers," the extra Christmas Number of *Household Words* for 1854. Of this number, Dickens wrote "The First Poor Traveller" and "The Road."

[3] The Twelfth Night Play for 1855 Dickens adapted from James Robinson Planché's *Fortunio and His Seven Gifted Servants*. The stage was re-erected in the nursery, now billed as "The theatre Royal, Tavistock House," with "Mr. Vincent Crummles" as "sole lessee and Manager." Large-lettered announcements heralded the "Re-engagement of that irresistible comedian, Mr. Ainger," "Reappearance of Mr. H." (Henry Fielding Dickens) "who created so powerful an impression last year!" "Return of Mr. Charles Dickens Junior from his German engagements!" "Engagement of Miss Kate, who declined the munificent offers of the Management last season!" "First appearance on any stage of Mr. Plornishmaroontigoonter (who has been kept out of bed at a vast expense)."

Among the adult actors, a Mr. "Wilkini Collini" played the small part of Gobbler,

As Charley's birthday falls on a Saturday, we mean to keep it on Monday the 8th when will be presented Fortunio and his seven gifted servants, by the entire strength of the company.

As for me, I am away to Bradford, whence I shall get back just in time for the Commercial Travellers on Saturday. The Reading night was a most rapturous affair. I send you a paper containing a little account of it.[4]

[P.S.] I wish you could see the five and twenty children under training — and the gravity and business of the proceedings.

⁂

206. [JANUARY 8, 1855] 23 BUTE STREET, OLD BROMPTON [TO CHARLES DICKENS FROM CAROLINE MAYNARD THOMPSON]

May I hope your kindness will pardon this intrusion, but as you may imagine I am anxious to know if your endeavours for me have been attended with success — [5]

I cannot express the deep gratitude I feel for the kind sympathy and interest you have shewn in my affairs —

Will you tell me if there is a possibility of my being able to leave England soon, as indeed I am very anxious to do so

Yours ever gratefully

---

one of the seven gifted servants, and was "dreadfully greedy" in devouring property loaves. Mark Lemon, under the name of Mr. Mudperiod, made a mountainous Dragon for Fortunio to subdue, and that small hero, the five-year-old Harry, watched with sly relish as the sherry with which he had adulterated the monster's drink demoralized his foe to helpless imbecility. As Mr. Measly Servile, Dickens was "the Expectant Cousin of the Nobility in General," a role which he played with "a fixed and propitiatory smile on his face"; as Mr. Passé he was a testy old Baron, and interpolated a song supposed to be sung by the Russian Czar:

> A despot I am of the regular kind;
> I'm in a fierce mood and I'm out of my mind
> And man was created to swallow the pill
> Of my wrong-headed, Bull-headed absolute will.

[4] On December 19 Dickens had read the *Christmas Carol* at Reading, and on the twenty-eighth he was to read it again in aid of the Bradford Mechanics' Institute in the Town Hall. On the second of these there was "a little fireside party" of 3700 people. The clipping he sent Miss Coutts was presumably from a Reading newspaper.

[5] The deliberation with which Miss Coutts and Dickens were moving makes understandable Caroline Thompson's anxiety. It is probable, however, that Dickens had made some temporary provision for her needs, pending a final settlement of her case, instead of forcing her to continue her old way of life.

207. [JANUARY 11, 1855] 23 BUTE STREET, OLD BROMPTON [TO
CHARLES DICKENS FROM CAROLINE MAYNARD THOMPSON]
I beg to acknowledge the receipt of your letter and to thank you
for your endeavours to interest Miss Coutts in my Story and obtaining me an interview with her
I look forward with hopes that Saturday may be the commencement
of a new and happier life, and trust that my future conduct may prove
to you and that Lady that your goodness has not been shewn to an
unworthy person
You will pardon me I trust for writing my last letter, it was caused
by no thought of your having lost sight of my case, but from a deep
anxiety to know my future fate You will I am sure understand this
feeling and excuse my apparent impatience
I mention this fearing I might have done wrong in writing

ᑲᑎ

208. JANUARY 12, 1855, TAVISTOCK HOUSE
On Wednesday evening, Mr Ryland of Birmingham came here, and
we had a long and careful discussion as to Charley. He had made extensive enquiries in his town, and had no doubt of the feasibility of
placing Charley in Scholefield's house — Scholefield [6] being one of the
present members for Birmingham, and a very agreeable and worthy
man, whom I know. *But* there appeared to be no doubt (and Mr Ryland himself laid stress upon this, as another result of his enquiries),
that the Birmingham business is *not* the business of a general merchant — is exceptional and peculiar — and belongs to that particular
place; the merchants who send Birmingham goods all over the world,
living elsewhere, and trading on a large scale in all manner of
other merchandise too. Now, what Charley most wants to acquire, is,
a knowledge of general business — of home and foreign markets — and
of home and foreign men. Whereas at Birmingham he would only
gain a knowledge of Birmingham business, Birmingham ways, and Birmingham men. Mr Wills, who has a good plain head in all such matters,

---

[6] William Scholefield (1809–1887), banker, merchant, manufacturer, and political radical. He was the first mayor of Birmingham when that city received its
charter of incorporation in 1838, and was elected one of its two M.P.'s in 1847,
1852, and 1857–1867. In Parliament he voted for the people's charter, for repeal-
ing the paper duties and taxes on knowledge, and for preventing the adulteration
of food. He was a consistent encourager of building societies and mechanics'
institutes.

assisted at the council, and we all three came to the conclusion that it would be best to begin with a London house, and then (supposing no opening should present itself in the Turkey direction [7] you spoke of — though I hope for such a thing), to give him a year or so in Liverpool as an active port where a vast deal of business is done. Wills was rather for beginning with Liverpool; but Mr Ryland was strong on two points: first, on the advantage of beginning in London where the tone of commerce is higher and more responsible; secondly, on the great advantage of a youth's being at home, in the outset of his career. Wills has to go to Liverpool on another business next Monday, and I have begged him to see some people we know there, and take their opinion also.

I think I could address myself to no first-rate London merchant's house, at so great an advantage as through some introduction of yours. Will you kindly think of it? I am very anxious not to lose time. I particularly wish to see Charley actually in the path he is to follow — though I will take care that he is not idle in the meantime. Indeed he wishes to be employed and is glad of my making employment for him.

I have appointed Mrs Thompson (as we agreed) to be at Shepherd's Bush at ½ past 11 tomorrow. She wrote a very good letter in reply — very grateful, and, I cannot but think, very honest.[8]

ഹ

209.   JANUARY 21, 1855, TAVISTOCK HOUSE
First, as to the hot closet.[9]
It happens that Mr Tracey's being worn out, a new man is now erecting a new successor to it. This man is ingenious in his trade, and his

---

[7] Miss Coutts had evidently suggested that she might be able to get Charley a position in some mercantile house doing business with Turkey.

[8] Following this letter Miss Coutts asked the Reverend William Tennant, the vicar of St. Stephen's Church, Westminster, to supplement Dickens's investigations by further enquiries. His recommendations will presently appear.

[9] The plan, as the next paragraph makes clear, was to construct a drying apparatus similar to that employed for drying clothes at Urania Cottage, only larger, for use in the military hospitals at Scutari, to which wounded soldiers were brought across the Black Sea from the Crimea. Florence Nightingale had found frightful conditions of inefficiency, dirt, insufficient medical supplies, and suffering when she arrived there on November 4, 1854, ten days after the battle of Balaklava and the day before the battle of Inkerman. The revelations published in the London *Times* of the horrors she uncovered excited widespread indignation.

name and style are William Jeakes, of 51 Great Russell Street Bloomsbury. He *never has* made such a thing to be carried away and put
together, but he is positively sure he can. He thinks it should be 6 feet
square, and 7 high, made of iron with an outside covering of wood.
He would propose to attach a copper to it for the boiling of water
with which to wash *on the spot where the apparatus for drying would
be.* The water in this copper would be always kept hot by what would
otherwise be the *waste heat* of the closet. He would undertake that
twenty five minutes should effectually dry the whole of the closet's
contents, so that it might be filled with wet clothes, bandages etc, every
five and twenty minutes during the day. He would number all the
pieces and component parts, "so that any one who could put a gun-
carriage together, could put this machine together with perfect ease."
(This, in answer to my enquiry whether it would be necessary to send
a man out with it).[1] It would be an expensive thing to make in this
way — he supposes at a round guess it might cost a hundred and fifty
pounds — it could be got ready in three weeks. A drawing, specification,
and contract, would be of course prepared if you were to pursue the
idea. And in that case I would see my very intelligent Turkish friend
immediately — who knows this country, quite as well as he knows that,
and is intimate with our best officers. He also knows Scutari very well.

Secondly, Mr Hardwick wrote to me the other day from Marlborough
Street, about a girl (whom he had committed for seven days as a disorderly, but about whom the police seemed to have been hasty and mistaken, it afterwards appeared), whom he was so anxious to get into
the Home that he was supporting her in the meanwhile at the Jailer's
house, out of the poor box. The Jailer brought her here, by my appointment. I was not so propitiated by her manner as Mr Hardwick
was, and requested that the accounts she gave of herself should be
closely enquired into. It turning out to be true when this was done,
I did not feel justified in objecting to her; and Mrs Marchmont will
fetch her, next Wednesday.

Thirdly, I have made some further enquiries as to Charley, and am
assured that he should decidedly learn what he has to learn, *in London.*

---

[1] In spite of Mr. Jeakes's assurance that his apparatus could be put together by
"any one who could put a gun-carriage together," it was decided to send out a
workman, named George Phillips, to assemble the parts. He wrote Miss Coutts
from Scutari on May 1, 1855, telling her that he would complete setting it up and
return to England by the end of the month.

Barings, I am assured, would be the best house for him; but, to obtain him the full advantages derivable from his being instructed in all its departments, Mr Bates or Mr Russell Sturges (the two principal and most active partners), must be personally interested in him. Do you know either of these gentlemen? If you could introduce me to either of them, I would strike straightway. As a public personage, I should not particularly mind addressing either of them on the strength of their public knowledge of me; but of course I would rather have the advantage of such a presentation to them. I am delighted to tell you that Charley has quite surprised me at the Household Words, where he appears every morning at 10. He writes an excellent business letter, with a system and clearness that are really remarkable, and which, without experience, are quite a gift. Also in this last week, he has abstracted the contents of 600 letters, and made a note of the purport of each on the back — as I am pretty sure that not five boys in a hundred could. And he is naturally so quick that he confounds Mr Wills, by knocking off what he calculates will occupy him a day, in two or three hours.

I have been over to Wimbledon [2] and seen Mr Brackenbury with whom Willy Latouche was. Walter is to go there next Wednesday week for two years; and I have little fear of his passing the examination for the direct appointment as soon as he is old enough — which will be at the expiration of that time. (I don't think I ever saw boys more closely stoned than at that eminent Grinder's by the bye).[3]

I have no idea where you are, but I know you must be warm! The little foundlings had such red noses this morning, that it made one colder to look at them. Your friend the cold shower descended like a storm of frozen hail, previously, but I was certainly the warmest person in church.

We all unite in kind regards to Mr and Mrs Brown if they are with you. I don't know whether you observe that it becomes clearer from day to day, that the Times are distinctly making out their case as to the condition of the army. It is also lamentable to see (from their opponents who would by no means confirm them if they could help it,

---

[2] The location of the school conducted by Messieurs Brackenbury and Wynne, which trained for India and the artillery and engineers. In addition to Walter, two of Dickens's other sons later studied there, Alfred Tennyson Dickens and Henry Fielding Dickens. I have not identified Willy Latouche.

[3] A joking reference to the "Charitable Grinders' School," in Dombey and Son, where Polly Toodle's son Rob was subjected to a savage discipline.

but are now forced to do so) that the winter-clothing sent out with so much blowing of trumpets, is absolutely inefficient.

ༀ

210. JANUARY 25, 1855, TAVISTOCK HOUSE

Your letter having come in while I was reading by my fire, I have shut up my book, to come to my table and answer it at once.

I am told there cannot possibly be a better person for our purpose than Mr Bates. If you will send me a letter to him (with his address upon it), mentioning that I wish to place my son who has been at Eton and in Germany, in their universally respected house, I will lose not a moment in leaving it for him with my card. And, since you so kindly mention the point, I have no doubt that a line (*I* should be inclined to say, *at once*) from yourself to Baring, would be of incalculable service. I have not the least doubt of that.

The drying apparatus, I will immediately proceed with — cautiously. And I will in the first place signify to the artist that a distinct specification and contract are essential to any further consideration of the subject. I am quite of your opinion as to the expediency of sending a workman with it. Let me add that Tracey's opinion on all such points is an undoubtedly good one, and he says "he does not believe it would be possible to send to Scutari, a more thoroughly serviceable thing."

In the main, there is very little difference (if any) between you "politically" on the war subject, and me politically. I think Lord Raglan's [4] position, tongue-tied as he is, a very painful one; but I think the stern necessity of preventing a repetition of these dreadful — and altogether needless — disasters over-rides every other consideration. To be sure that does not justify the Times in being hard on him, but the reverse. Looking to the other newspaper correspondents, and seeing them at last forced upon confirmation of the Times accounts after so long denying them, I have a dreadful belief that the army will be really (virtually) no more in another six weeks.[5] I become particularly un-

---

[4] Lord Raglan, in command in the Crimea, was made the scapegoat for the mismanagement during the winter of 1854–1855. He died on June 28, 1855, only ten days after the failure of the mistimed attack on Malakhov and Redan.

[5] Dickens was not without reason in his fears. Reports were pouring home from the Crimea of the shameful disorganization of supplies, the horrible bungling in the medical arrangements, and the frightful mortality in the military hospital at Scutari. Out of an army of 54,000 men, 40,000 had died in the course of a few months, from wounds, fever, frostbite, dysentery, and cholera. Of the remainder, 9000 were unfit for duty.

easy when I find the Public so apathetic to the inefficiency of the Government. It is a new and unhealthy symptom — the kind of unnatural lull that precedes an earthquake — and I mistrust there being something sullen working among the people, which we don't at all understand. It is manifest that the system of our service anywhere, civil or warlike, is *not* to rally the best men round the national standard, or to know where to find them; and there is no safety for us until we do begin to cruize about in the Victoria and Albert, far out of the official cordons in which we are all in danger of perishing together. I have made up my mind that what one can do in print to wake the sleepers, one is bound to do at such a serious juncture. And I have fired off a small volley of red hot shot, in Household Words next week.[6]

Enclosed, are all the Mrs Thompson papers that I have: including two notes from herself which you have not seen.

As to the good old admiral,[7] what he has got to do, is the most difficult thing he (or any Napier) can be required to do — *keep quiet.* I don't think there is any disposition in the public mind to do him an injustice, but quite the contrary. There has been a slight re-action occasioned by the injudicious friends he had before he went away; but I believe there is a great general fondness for him and trust in him. I should like to see and hear him, very much.

I have been ploughing daily, through deep snow about Highgate, Hampstead, and Hendon — and saw Holly Lodge the day before yesterday with a powdered head, and a great white fur-cloak on. The condition of the streets today, is inconceivable — mud and mire, in many places a foot deep. Mr Stanfield and I were going down Wellington Street North, the other night, in his little carriage, on one of our Theatrical Expeditions to undiscovered theatres, when I took occasion to protest against the infamous paving there, and the jobbing little

---

[6] "That Other Public," *Household Words*, February 3, 1855, which asks with searing irony why it is always some other public, not ourselves, that we blame for not putting an end to the abuses and evils that we perceive quite plainly. "*We* are the sensible, reflecting, prompt Public, always up to the mark — whereas that other Public persists in supinely lagging behind . . ." *Our* Public, the article continues, "have got to the marrow of . . . the condition of the British Army before Sebastopol" and fully understand where the responsibility lies for the "confused heap of mismanagement, imbecility, and disorder, under which the nation's bravery lies crushed and withered. . . . But that other Public. What will *they* do?"

[7] Admiral Sir Charles Napier (1786–1860), who served in the attack on Washington in the War of 1812, and who was in command of the Baltic Fleet in the Crimean War. He had been much censured for refusing to attack Kronstadt.

local boards, and to say that so many horses fell down opposite Household Words that I hardly ever saw the office door without a horse in it.
He laughed at this, and next moment *both our horses* plunged head-
foremost at that establishment, like impatient contributors. The crowd
seemed to think it was our doing, and, when we got out to help, said
"they should have thought we were hearty enough to walk."

We unite in remembrances to Mr and Mrs Brown. I feel a certain
equanimity in your being at my birth place,[8] though I can't say I
usually care much about it. I was taken away from there when I was
two years old and went back when I was thirty; but I had certainly
carried a little picture of it, wonderful, accurate, away with me, and
knew a particular Parade-ground (my nurse must have been fond of
soldiers) minutely. This reminds me to observe that the intelligence
of the Baby [9] is becoming miraculous.

ono

211.   FEBRUARY 9, 1855, TAVISTOCK HOUSE
I enclose a letter I received last night from the drying-apparatus
maker, which seems, in a plain practical way, to anticipate what you
had had in your mind in thinking of Mr Manly. I have written in reply
that I shall be much interested in seeing the machine at work, and that
I dare say you will go too.

Yesterday I was at Shepherd's Bush, where Mr Chesterton also made
his way somehow, through the snow. All was going on well, and Rhena
Pollard was the subject of a specially good report. Mrs Marchmont
called my attention to the state of the carpets in her and Mrs Macartney's rooms, and also of the matting in the long-room. They are all in
rags, and very ill-looking. I told her to get an estimate from the shop
we deal at, of the cost of some strong plain dutch bedroom carpeting,
and also of a new piece of matting of the present tough quality.

The drying-room has been boarded, but Mr Marchant has not yet
sent the stove in. Now, I suggest that he should *not* send it in at all,
as originally designed, but that the drying stove should be such a
one as will heat the water for a common bath to be fixed beside it.
Our round shallow baths are worn out; they are at the best imperfect
substitutes for a good bath; and, now that the place is boarded, a bath

---

[8] Dickens was born at 387 Mile End Terrace, Landport, Portsea, a part of
Portsmouth just north of Portsmouth proper.

[9] The baby — "Plorn" — was now almost three years old.

could be fixed in the corner, beside the stove, without being in anybody's way. With a cistern outside and the water laid on (very easily done), we should have that great aid to health and cleanliness at a small expence.

I enclose the list of bills for the month.

The actual departure of Goldsborough and Fisher has brightened up Campbell with hope, and has evidently had a good effect upon them all.

In the matter of Charley, I am heartily glad that you have heard from Mr Bates, and I hope he will lead us out of the fog. Charley himself says that he is not in the least alarmed by the what-not Bales. He is very anxious to make a beginning. And so, indeed, is his father.

Supposing the snow between Paris and the Interior to be not more than twenty feet deep, I hope to bring you some little souvenir from the place of your old remembrance. My address in Paris will be the Hotel Meurice.[1]

It snowed here, incessantly and heavily, the whole day yesterday. I returned from Shepherd's Bush, like Lot's wife after she became the pillar of salt. On Wednesday (my birthday) I walked from Gravesend to Rochester between walls of snow varying from three to six feet high, through which a road had been hewn out by men. Yesterday evening I went out at 7 o'clock to dine with Cartwright (I always feel a strange satisfaction in doing at least that much to my own teeth in his house),[2] and could hardly get out at my own door, or in at his.

Walter reports joyfully of his new school.

With kindest regards to Mr and Mrs Brown

ᐤ

212.   MARCH 8, 1855, TAVISTOCK HOUSE

The address of Mrs Thompson is, 23 Bute Street Old Brompton.

After I left you yesterday, I went into the City and saw the Secretary of the Protective Institution [3] — in a sort of china-closet at the back

---

[1] Together with Wilkie Collins, Dickens ran over to Paris for a brief vacation February 11–20. I do not know to what "place of . . . old remembrance" for Miss Coutts he was alluding.

[2] Samuel Cartwright (1789–1864), Fellow of the Linnean Society 1833, F.R.S. 1841, was a well-known dentist.

[3] I have been unable to identify either the Protective Institution or its secretary. The "girl," however, is obviously not Caroline Thompson, whose address, which Miss Coutts had mislaid, Dickens supplies in the paragraph above.

of a first floor in the Poultry. They clearly want to use the case as an advertising Puff of their establishment, and don't desire to part with it — evidently looking upon the girl as so much capital. After a short conversation, in which the secretary enunciated a great deal of perilous nonsense (in reference to which I politely suggested to him afar off, that he knew nothing of what he was talking about), I left the matter thus. That if they ever desired to make application for the girl's admission into your Home, it should be considered, but that the case must even then stand upon its own merits and suitability to your Institution. I would not at any time give them money: — I fear a good deal of trading cant prevails in the concern.

The price of the drying machine will be 18 guineas. I have told Mr Jeakes it must be ready to go with the Drying closet, or you won't have it. I am now pressing upon him the necessity of expediting the shipment.

I think I have just got the best ghost story [4] (sent by a lady for Household Words) that ever was written, and with an idea in it remarkably new. My hand is stayed for the moment, however, by an apprehension that the lady cannot have written it. It is so very clever, that I think (though I never saw or heard of it), it must have been written by some wild Frenchman — and I am trying to find out.

~

213.   MARCH 10, 1855, TAVISTOCK HOUSE
I wrote yesterday (necessarily therefore before I received your note), to the brother.[5] I told him all that you had before you in ref-

---

[4] "A Ghost Story," Household Words, March 24, 1855. The story was not by "some wild Frenchman," but by the lady who contributed it.

[5] Frederick Maynard, Caroline Thompson's brother. Mr. Tennant, pompous, ponderous, and slow, had consulted her neighbors and Lieutenant Tracey, the prison official, about her character and her story. Although he accepted from the former bits of twenty-year-old gossip about her father, he had come to the conclusion that she should be helped, as he told Miss Coutts in a letter of February 3, 1855, but he was uncertain how. On February 16 he reported that Mrs. Thompson's mother had died and that both daughters "behaved with great feeling and the best propriety"; he now believed that Mrs. Thompson sincerely desired to be rescued. On Dickens's return from Paris there was a consultation between him and Miss Coutts. It was agreed that Mrs. Thompson could not very well be taken into Urania Cottage: there was the child, and, although he had broached the idea of her going abroad in order to test the devotion of the brother and sister to each other, it seemed cruel to force a separation. He and Miss Coutts were therefore still undecided what should be done.

erence to the sister, and I said "let me now particularly impress upon your sister, through you, that on her thorough earnestness, patience, and perseverance, at this point in her life, her own future and that of her child undoubtedly depend." I added that I would see her, or him, or both, any Sunday at half past one. I will take such opportunity of repeating the caution. I stated the case however, in the plainest and strongest manner that I could possibly employ; and I did so in writing, to the end that it might make a more enduring effect, as being always there upon the paper.

[P.S.] I enclose a note received this morning, from Miss Martineau.[6]

ᵪᵈ

214.   MARCH 17, 1855, TAVISTOCK HOUSE

Mrs Thompson and her brother will no doubt be with me tomorrow morning. What am I to do? I only want to know. I quite agree with you that it is immensely difficult — and yet her position seems plainly to be a perplexed and complicated one.[7]

---

[6] I know nothing of the note here mentioned. Its author was Harriet Martineau (1802–1876), miscellaneous writer. Left penniless in 1829, deaf, and feeble in health, she became a successful writer, the author of *Illustrations of Political Economy* 1832–1834, a series of stories demonstrating the principles of that science, *Poor Laws and Paupers Illustrated* 1833, and *Illustrations of Taxation* 1834. Seriously ill, she tried mesmerism and recovered; came to London as a celebrity, met Wordsworth and other leading writers, and was consulted by cabinet ministers. She visited America 1834–1836, and wrote *Society in America* 1837 and *Retrospect of Western Travel* 1838. Later still she traveled in Egypt and Palestine, and wrote *Eastern Life* 1848. She was strongly antitheological, published Atkinson's *Letters on the Laws of Man's Social Nature and Development* 1851, and a condensed translation of Comte's *Philosophie Positive* 1853. She contributed to the *Edinburgh Review* and the *Daily News*, and until 1855 frequently wrote moralistic fiction for *Household Words*. But toward the close of that year she took furious exception to a series of articles attacking factory accidents which Dickens had been running in the magazine, and wrote a violent and one-sided pamphlet published by the National Association of Manufacturers, based on information supplied by its representatives, in which she accused Dickens of "unscrupulous statements, insolence, arrogance, and cant." *Household Words* replied on January 18, 1856, in an article entitled "Our Wicked Misstatements," impeccably polite in tone, but demolishing her every argument. The interchange ended their association.

[7] The solution finally determined upon for Mrs. Thompson's problem was to rent and furnish for her, in an entirely new neighborhood where she would be unknown, a house in which she could earn her living by taking lodgers. This was accordingly done, but it turned out not to pay very well. Dickens's letter of May 20, 1856, shows that after trying it out for something over a year it was agreed that she should sell the furniture and, using the capital thus obtained, emigrate with her child to Canada.

Charley and I dine with Mr Bates on Sunday, to confer. Mr Bates writes me that he can place him in a broker's house, but would like to talk to him first that he may be sure — or as sure as he can be — that he is not *mis*placing him. You have not seen your Turkish friend?

Perhaps you may like to read the great ghost story before it comes out. I send you my proof therefore. You have only to put it in the fire. All my corrections are made upon a duplicate, and I don't want it again.

Charley is immensely excited by the opening prospect, and is, I really believe, very earnest to begin. I have lately added to my other little occupations, a determined endeavour to reform a misdoing Institution.[8] If you had seen Sir Robert Inglis in the chair (where he was very just and good-natured), beleaguered by your servant for two hours and a half, I know you would have been amused for a week.[9]

O, likewise.

చిం

215. MAY 2, 1855, TAVISTOCK HOUSE

I looked carefully at the Highgate piece of ground the other day, and I think it on the whole very eligible for preservation as an open space.[1]

---

[8] The Royal Literary Fund, which Dickens was indicting for the extravagance and nepotism with which its affairs were administered. Needy applicants, he revealed, were turned down or given doles as insignificant as £5 while the widows of prosperous members received grants as large as £100. Forty per cent of its income was swallowed up in the expenses of management. Its commodious headquarters in Bloomsbury were for the most part empty and unused. In collaboration with Forster and the journalist Charles Wentworth Dilke (1789–1864), who had been one of the later editors of the *Daily News*, Dickens printed a pamphlet entitled "The Case of the Reformers in the Literary Fund." This was answered by the Committee in a pamphlet called "The Royal Literary Fund: A Summary of Facts." Dickens and his associates replied with "The Answer to the Summary." Their onslaught was partly successful; it brought about some reforms in the administration of the Fund, although not as many as Dickens had hoped.

[9] Sir Robert Inglis (1786–1875) presided at the meeting of the Fund at which Dickens brought up his case. It represented an effort of magnanimity for Dickens to praise him, for they were of opposing views on almost every public question: Sir Robert had been against Catholic emancipation, against parliamentary reform, against repeal of the Corn Laws, against Jewish relief — a fixed Tory of the most unyielding cast.

[1] Miss Coutts did not carry out the suggestion Dickens discusses here of presenting a piece of ground in Swain's Lane, Highgate, as an open space; but as an alternative she provided a site for the schools of St. Anne's Church, Highgate.

These are my reasons.

1. It abuts immediately on the lane as you go up to the Cemetery, and consequently never could be diminished or built in upon that margin.

2. If the field opposite to it and below your large summer-house belongs to you, that West side of the ground is wonderfully free.

3. The ground itself is so shaped that it seems scarcely feasible to build anything outside the top wall but one or two villas on the top of the rise, with lawns or gardens sloping downward to the piece of ground. Which would not at all detract from its beauty, and would not too closely hem it in.

4. The plan of building now carrying out on the East or Small Pox Hospital side, suggests that in that direction also, the piece of ground will have gardens turned towards it.

Lastly the ground itself is of a wonderfully appropriate shape for an open space, and is so high in the most ornamental part that the view must always remain. The bottom would make an admirable childrens' playground, and the upper part with a few seats and a few more trees would be a beautiful little Park in itself.

When you happen to be at Highgate and to think of it, will you be so kind as to ask your gardener to go and look at my grave [2] — see where he could plant that tree you proposed to give me (outside the railing, so that it never need be disturbed) — and then explain to the Manager on the ground what he wants to do, and to see how he can get leave to do it? If they want me to pay any more for the spot in which the tree is planted, he can conclude that done. I ask you this favor, because the Manager and I, without the tree or the gardener, might talk about it till Doomsday and get no nearer to a result.

Remind Mr Brown that the beginning of the fulfilment of my prophecy of yesterday, is the Sheffield meeting [3] reported in today's

---

[2] The plot in Highgate Cemetery where his daughter Dora Annie was buried.

[3] A meeting at the Sheffield Town Hall, occasioned by the disasters to the British troops in the Crimea. Resolutions were passed condemning the administration of the army for its neglect of the soldiers' bodily wants and its failure to take proper measures for providing cleanliness, warmth, and health and for tending the sick and wounded. The same resolutions demanded a thorough reform in the constitution of the army, making it possible for men of energy and intelligence to rise from the ranks, encouraging ability and practical experience, and destroying the monopoly exercised over military command by aristocratic incompetence and

Times. I begin to hope the country is waking up. Its doing so, is the only safety for you and me and all well-disposed people.

ᴖ

216. MAY 8, 1855, TAVISTOCK HOUSE

I am delighted to hear of Miss Nightingale's [4] communication to you. Because I regard the thing as done successfully, now. There will be sad use for it, I am afraid, for I hear that there are forewarnings already of pestilence out there. The closet will be, I really believe, invaluable.

I went up to Holly Lodge yesterday, and saw your gardener again about my cemetery piece of ground. His idea is ingenious and pretty, but involves the removal of the stone and railing. I am not quite decided, but I think it will be best to leave it, and to have one or two pretty boxes of flowers (such as one would have outside a window), on the stone.

If you have, either at Holly Lodge or in town, so much coach-room that there is any to spare, will you receive my little Brougham on a visit, when we go to the seaside? My project is, to make Folkestone our summer-place, so that we may go to Paris (to complete the polishing of Mary and Katey) [5] at the end of October, straight. So I shall relinquish stable charges in these Double Income Tax days of mismanagement and waste,[6] when we leave here. Charley's grandfather

---

nepotism. A final volley extended the attack from the military arm to a blast against the incompetence of the entire government, welcomed the news that an association had been formed in London to demand administrative reform in all the departments of state, and called for the formation of a Sheffield Administrative Reform Association to join in striking at the roots of all these evils.

[4] Florence Nightingale (1820–1910), who was still at Scutari, and who was later to found the Nightingale Home for the training of nurses at St. Thomas's Hospital. Author of *Notes on Hospitals* 1859, *Notes on Nursing* 1860, *Observations on the Sanitary State of the Army in India* 1863, and other works. Evidently her communication to Miss Coutts was an appreciation of the drying apparatus at that very time being installed by George Phillips.

[5] Mary and Katey were now respectively seventeen and fifteen years old.

[6] Income Tax had been introduced as a temporary expedient in Peel's budget of 1842, when it amounted to sevenpence in the pound. Successive governments, however, found themselves unable to dispense with it, and, although there were years in which the income tax was reduced, it has never disappeared from the list of British taxes and on the whole has steadily risen. The Crimean War produced the drastic increase of which Dickens here complains — idyllically little as the total tax would seem to the taxpayer today.

and grandmother[7] will keep house for him and be a species of commission in the Regal absence. He seems to be very much interested in his occupation, and we all turn out at 7 every morning with an edifying punctuality.

I am in a state of restlessness impossible to be described — impossible to be imagined — wearing and tearing to be experienced. I sit down of a morning, with all kinds of notes for my new book (for which by the bye, I think I have a capital name)[8] — resolve to begin — get up, and go out, and walk a dozen miles — sit down again next morning — get up and go down a railroad — come back again, and register a vow to go out of town instantly, and begin at the feet of the Pyrenees — sit down again — get up and walk about my room all day — wander about London till midnight — make engagements and am too distraught to keep them — couldn't go to the Academy Dinner — felt it impossible to bear the speeches — pleaded Influenza at the last moment — and am at present going through the whole routine, over and over and over again.[9]

[P.S.] Two old ladies have turned up at Deptford, who are the last descendants (I think Great Grand-daughters) of Samuel Johnson.[1] Mr Carlyle has found them — in great poverty, but undemonstrative and uncomplaining, though very old — with nothing to speak of in the wide world, but the plain fir desk on which Johnson wrote his English Dictionary.

---

[7] Mr. and Mrs. George Hogarth, Catherine Dickens's father and mother.

[8] The new novel was to become *Little Dorrit*, but up almost to the eve of publication Dickens planned to call it *Nobody's Fault* to point up ironically its portrayal of society as a vast impersonal muddle of inefficiency, venality, and wrong, baffling all endeavor to fasten responsibility anywhere.

[9] It is impossible not to feel in the unusual violence of tension here expressed — even though Dickens was always restless when he was turning over a new book in his mind — a reflection of the increasingly feverish state of distraction and unhappiness he felt in his marriage, which had little by little grown into a misery that seldom left him any peace. His personal unrest and his indignation at all the desperate evils he saw around him in the world fused into an almost intolerable agitation of spirit.

[1] The two old ladies at Deptford, one seventy-seven years of age and the other seventy-two, were not descendants of Dr. Johnson, but daughters of Mauritius Lowe, a late eighteenth-century historical and portrait painter. The elder of the two was Johnson's goddaughter, and remembered being made to repeat the Lord's Prayer while seated on his knee as a child. They were given a donation of £100 from the Royal Bounty Fund, and Carlyle, Dickens, and Forster signed a letter that appeared in the *Times* November 1, 1855, appealing to the nation to subscribe £400 to purchase them an annuity.

217.   MAY 11, 1855, TAVISTOCK HOUSE

The £20 safely came to hand. I am truly touched by your note, because I deeply feel at all times your interest and friendship — can scarcely feel anything more. I am impetuous in my affections at any rate.

Layard has made a mistake.[2] The men who would run him to death

─────────────────────────────

[2] In 1851 Austen Layard had given up his archaeological work and embarked upon a stormy political career. Pressing vigorously for administrative reform in all the agencies of Government, he came into violent collision with the Tadpoles and Tapers of the Liberal Party. The scandalous incompetencies revealed by the Crimean War sharpened his attack. He had seen the battle of the Alma from the maintop of the *Agamemnon;* returning to Westminster he launched parliamentary thunderbolts against the disgraceful indifference to human suffering that he denounced as responsible for thousands of evils both at home and on the field. But what else was to be expected, he asked bitterly, of a Government so conscienceless as to "go on vacation for eight weeks without ever summoning a cabinet meeting"? Lord Aberdeen's cabinet was forced to resign, but Layard found no improvement in that of Lord Palmerston. When he asked as M.P. for Aylesbury to have a day assigned on which he could present his proposals to the House, Palmerston said scornfully, "Let the honorable gentleman find a day for himself." When he finally got his motion before the House, it was defeated by a vote of 359 to 46.

Layard's "mistake" was apparently that of involving Lord Hardinge, the commander in chief, directly in his charges of incompetence and irresponsibility. This distinguished soldier, Sir Henry Hardinge (1785–1856), had been with Wellington at Vimeiro and with Moore at Corunna, had had his hand shattered at Vittoria, had been detailed by Wellington to watch Napoleon's movements after the escape from Elba, and had fought beside Blücher at Quatre Bras. He had been a vigorous and able governor-general of India 1844–1847 and been created Viscount Hardinge of Lahore 1846, with a pension of £3000. In 1852 he had taken command at the Horse Guards. He was highly respected, there was no proof that he knew about all the complex details of mismanagement in the organization at whose head he had been placed. The House of Commons did not want to hear Layard anyhow, who had never hesitated to vote and speak against his own party; it did not want to be forced to contemplate the scandal at its door; and therefore with a noble anger it castigated the one possible error in Layard's statements, ignoring everything that was true. He had "made a misstatement about Lord Harding" — a defender ironically echoed the House accusation in a letter to the London *Times* — "Very shocking," and the House, which "plumes itself upon its gentlemanly reputation," "bawls down the traducer."

No doubt Layard was brusque and vehement to the point of recklessness, and his inclusion of Lord Hardinge in his indictment was an error in diplomacy and parliamentary tactics. Subsequent judgments, however, have not exempted Hardinge from a share in the blame. He was loyal to the memory of Wellington and had been unwilling to disturb routine arrangements sanctioned by his great chief. If as commander he did not know, it was his business to know, and to remedy, the manifest want of preparation of the army that suddenly and disastrously revealed itself on every hand under the pressure of war. But at the moment the House of Commons gladly seized on a technical weakness in Layard's attack.

Such an error would not alienate Dickens, who despised the House with im-

have wilfully committed all manner of perversions a thousand times, and have no claim upon my sympathy in their unfair pursuit of him, and every claim upon my suspicion and resentment. Take my knowledge of the state of things in this distracted land, for what it may be worth a dozen years hence. The people will not bear for any length of time what they bear now. I see it clearly written in every truthful indication that I am capable of discerning anywhere. And I want to interpose something between them and their wrath.

For this reason solely, I am a Reformer heart and soul. I have nothing to gain — everything to lose (for public quiet is my bread) — but I am in desperate earnest, because I know it is a desperate case.

You will believe that I have no sympathy with any misstatement of fact, or hesitation in withdrawing it. I wouldn't be unfair, if I knew it, to any human being. I should hate myself if I were.

You think me impetuous, because I sometimes speak of things I have long thought about, with a suddenness that brings me only to the conclusion I have come at, and does not shew the road by which I arrived there. But it is a broad highway notwithstanding, and I have trod it slowly and patiently. Only believe that, and you may think me as impetuous as you like. Think me anything you like, so that you write me letters I am so proud of.

218.   MAY 15, 1855, TAVISTOCK HOUSE
Shortly to resume the Ninevite [3] question:
As I said before, Layard made a mistake — was too much ill treated

---

measurable contempt, and was behind Layard heart and soul. When Layard countered the rejection of his reform demands with a direct appeal to the public, Dickens promised stanch support. He enlisted the aid of *Punch*, and of the *Weekly Chronicle* and the *Illustrated London News* to bring the issues home to their large bodies of readers; he lined up Jerrold and Forster to help; he hammered away himself in the pages of *Household Words*. He wrote an article called "Scarli Tapa and the Forty Thieves," in which the robbers' cave bears "the enchanted letters O.F.F.I.C.E." on the door, and in which Scarli Tapa, instead of slaying the thieves, forms an alliance with their captain. In another article he denounced Lord Palmerston, the Premier, as "the glib Vizier," who never did the work he was hired to do, but instead constantly "danced the dance of Mistapit, and sang the song of Mistafoks, and joked the joke of Jomillah." Parliament, with its "logic-chopping, straw-splitting, tape-tying, tape-untying," and "word-eating," was plainly "the house of Parler and Mentir," the place of wordiness and lies. Any "half dozen shop-keepers taken at random . . . and shot into Downing Street out of sacks," said still another article, could do a better job than these "Red-Tapers" and "Sealing-Wax-Chafers."

[3] Layard, the reader will recall, had made excavations of the ruins of Nineveh, whence Dickens's epithet.

and insulted to be able to repair it then (which would have required a man with great presence of mind and perfectly free from impetuosity — say, for instance, myself [4]) — and so gave his enemies a handle against him, which they use. I differ from you altogether, as to his setting class against class.[5] He finds them already set in opposition. And I think you hardly bear in mind that as there are two great classes looking at each other in this question, so there are two sides to the question itself. You assume that the popular class take the initiative. Now as *I* read the story, the aristocratic class did that, years and years ago, and it is *they* who have put *their* class in opposition to the country — not the country which puts itself in opposition to *them*.

My present position with Layard, is exactly this. I felt (before the mistake — as I remember, a week or ten days before), that he needed support; I was struck, at your house, to see him so changed and anxious; I happened to come into the knowledge of bitter endeavours and private influences that were at work to put him down; and I wrote to him, urging him not to be discouraged, telling him that I thought him, in the circumstances of the time, the most useful man in the house; and that I considered it a positive duty to render him all the help I could, short of going there myself. Such help as I could give him then, I did give him immediately; and he was very sensible of it. He shewed me his resolutions, some days before he made them known in the house, and in the main I approved. Then came the mistake. We dined together on the very next day after it, and I besought him for Heaven's sake to be careful. In another day or two, came the City Administrative Reform Meeting,[6] and proposal for establishing an association. I resolved to become a member of it, and to give (as a kind of example to a large class), Twenty Pounds. I felt that Layard wanted, and I considered in spite of his error that he deserved, some little

---

[4] The last paragraph of the letter preceding this one shows clearly that Miss Coutts considered Dickens himself violently impetuous. Some of the fun, for Dickens, in the present reference, no doubt, was that she would think him to be speaking facetiously, whereas in fact he *did* regard himself as "perfectly free from impetuosity" — with how much cause the reader may decide for himself.

[5] Despite Miss Coutts's humanitarian and liberal tenets, Layard's appeal from Parliament to the people went beyond the point at which she stopped, and aroused in her the fear that he was "setting class against class" — a view that provoked from Dickens this violent rejoinder.

[6] The Administrative Reform Association was founded as a result of this meeting and Dickens did become a member and speak at a Drury Lane meeting on June 27, 1855.

backing, and I wrote him a note saying "Do you tell Mr Lindsay [7] that the association may rely upon me to this extent." Last Saturday, in pursuance of an old engagement made weeks before the mistake, he and I dined at Greenwich, with Paxton and some others. Layard then asked me, Had I heard from Mr Morley,[8] the chairman of that city association, because Mr Morley had asked him whether he thought I could by any means be got to speak at a Meeting in Drury Lane Theatre, if they should decide to hold one there? I considered about it, and said, my impression was that I would speak on such an occasion; but that before I could pledge myself, I must first know everything that was intended to be done, and be sure that I approved of it. I made this a text for again impressing upon him the necessity of being careful under so great a responsibility (putting it as my own feeling about myself), and he earnestly assented; adding "If you go, I will go; but not otherwise, I think." [9]

---

[7] Unidentified.

[8] Samuel Morley (1809–1886), textile manufacturer, and chairman of the Administrative Reform Association.

[9] Layard spoke, however, at a public meeting of the Association at Drury Lane on June 20, when Dickens, although unable to be present, entirely agreed with what he said. The evidence of government bluebooks, Layard charged, revealed "records of inefficiency, records of indifference to suffering, records of ignorance, records of obstinacy," that were a shame to the nation. The Civil Service was grossly overstaffed with men busy making work for each other. Lord Palmerston, personally, Layard denounced for an attitude of levity toward the sufferings of the poor.

Stung by this attack, Palmerston retorted with a sneer about "the private theatricals at Drury Lane." At a second Drury Lane gathering on the twenty-seventh, Dickens as the principal speaker built the first part of his address around Palmerston's contemptuous epithet: "I have some acquaintance with theatricals, private and public, and I will accept that figure of the noble lord. I will not say that if I wanted to form a company of her Majesty's servants, I think I should know where to put my hands on 'the comic old gentleman'; nor, that if I wanted to get up a pantomime, I fancy I should know what establishment to go to for the tricks and changes . . . We have seen the *Comedy of Errors* played so dismally like a tragedy that we really cannot bear it. We are therefore making bold to get up the *School of Reform*, and we hope, before the play is out, to improve that noble lord by our performance very considerably."

England could not "find on the face of the earth," Dickens continued, "an enemy one-twentieth part so potent to effect the misery and ruin of her noble defenders" as she had been herself. In the gloomy silence with which the people stood aloof from the machinery of government and legislation it was "as if they left it to its last remaining function of destroying itself, when it had achieved the destruction of so much that was dear to them." In a state of affairs so menacing, the only wholesome turn things could take was for the people to speak out, to unite, and to achieve a great change in administration.

I am anxious to have a perfect confidence with you on the subject; and now you know all I know. If I can exercise any influence with him, I hope it will be to keep him cooler and steadier. No man can move me on such a matter, beyond what I have made up my mind is right. And as to my ever being tempted into any hot public assertion, I believe if you had ever seen me under speechifying circumstances, you would have a perfect confidence in my composure — in short, in my having left that impetuosity — say in Stratton Street.[1]

I should like to consider your deeply interesting idea,[2] a little longer. I meant this to have been a short note! Enclosed is one from Mr Carlyle[3] you may like to see.

*

219. MAY 24, 1855, TAVISTOCK HOUSE

I have considered your plan[4] from every point of view, and I would *not* try it, until a special occasion shall present itself. God forbid that there should be another great sickness; but there may be, before we grow to be very old, a peace — for example — and I think if some such opportunity were laid hold of, and associated with the design, you would begin at an immense advantage.

I suppose myself writing some little plain appeal to such waterside people, to be circulated among them, explanatory of the project and of its arising plainly out of the teaching of our Saviour — and I feel that the additional and immediate weight to be got from its being ap-

---

[1] He might just as well have left that impetuosity in Stratton Street. Layard was obstructed in Parliament with every procedural dodge, and before the public with every device of misrepresentation. The necessity of prosecuting the war was used as a device for smothering all social legislation at home, and the ponderous inertia of government bureaus interposed an immovable obstacle to all administrative change. Dining at Lord John Russell's, Dickens "gave them a little bit of truth," he said, that "was like bringing a Sebastopol battery among the polite company," and Meyerbeer, the composer, said admiringly, *"Ah, mon illustre ami, que c'est noble de vous entendre parler d'haute voix morale, à la table d'un ministre!"*

[2] The idea here referred to is obviously the "plan" of the following letter, but I am unable to determine what it was. Dickens evidently feared that the "waterside people" and others who were to be its beneficiaries might feel suspicious of it as a social anodyne designed merely "to keep them quiet" rather than to achieve any real good.

[3] Thomas Carlyle (1795–1881). Dickens admired tremendously both Carlyle and his wife Jane Welsh Carlyle (1801–1866), and was to dedicate *A Tale of Two Cities* to Carlyle, whose *French Revolution* he had read again and again. He did not, however, share Carlyle's distrust of the masses or his glorification of a divine-dictator heroic leader. The note from Carlyle has not been found.

[4] See note 2, preceding letter.

posite to something current which everybody knew, would be invaluable. You might or might not ask me to do such a thing; but the principle would be the same, whosoever might do it — and of the additional strength to be got in this way, I have not the least doubt. It would afford that kind of immediate illustration which there can be no doubt, I think, that Christ himself invariably took, even from passing people and adjacent objects.

Whereas at present I doubt very much whether you would attract many people who are now indifferent. Some might come, from interested motives; but there is danger of a prevalent suspicion of the object being to keep them quiet, and put grievances out of their minds. Now, going among them with a reference to something directly concerning and touching them all, would overcome this, more than any amount of reasoning and probability.

Pray be within reach of this house about the middle of next month. We are going to do a *grown-up Play* [5] in the childrens' theatre, with a smaller audience and a larger stage. Mr Collins has written an odd MeloDrama, the whole action of which (of course it is short) takes place in a lighthouse. He shewed it to me for advice, and some suggestions that I made to him involved a description of how such a thing ought to be done in a Theatre — and might be done if there were more sense in such places. So we are going to shew Mr Webster [6] what it means! and Mr Stanfield, full of his nautical and theatrical ardor, has taken possession of the Schoolroom, and will really paint and make out an illusion of a very fine kind, as far as *his* art goes.

So I entreat you to let nothing interfere with your occupation of the place designed for you — urging the same stipulation on Mr and Mrs Brown. I shall be able to let you know the exact day, pretty early next week.

P.S. My condition of restlessness is not improved. All the symptoms are very bad. The only new feature is, that I am actually at work and in the middle of No. One. [7]

---

[5] Wilkie Collins's melodrama, *The Lighthouse.*

[6] Benjamin Webster (1795–1867), the comedian and theatrical manager.

[7] The first number of *Little Dorrit.* Although begun at this time, it did not commence publication until December. The story, with its fundamental metaphor of the world as a vast prison in which jailers and the jailed are equally confined, and with its involved pattern showing all society entangled in a net dominated by the sinister alliance between political leadership and unscrupulous financial interests, bitterly reflects the disillusioned vision Dickens had now achieved.

220.   MAY 29, 1855, TAVISTOCK HOUSE

Mr Stanfield being at present shut up in the Schoolroom with two of the dirtiest artificers I ever saw — who have been dug out of the profoundest depths of some Theatre, appear to have wallowed in gas from their infancy, and are now making chalk lines all over the floor, while the distinguished painter coerces them with an umbrella — I am in a condition to report that the Night is *Saturday the 16th of June.* We shall begin punctually at 8 o'clock and have done soon after 11. I will send you the Bill in the course of the week. It may be advisable to inform O in reference to my being in an extremely low state in the Lighthouse on account of having something on my mind, that it all ends happily. (If you should think of anybody whom you would like to bring — which is just possible — will you let me know *soon,* and I will perform the needful ceremonies.)

I will note a few questions on common useful knowledge, and endeavour to glean one or two from others.[8]

The subscription to that historical table,[9] was a guinea each.

Old Defoe's wife [1] is dead. The old man is going on patiently and quietly, and is immensely comforted by your allowance.

[P.S.] The interlineations in this note, are attributable to my being at work on the new book — which makes me perfectly reckless as to erasures.

৵৶

221.   JUNE 8, 1855, TAVISTOCK HOUSE

I really did think you *were* lost — and have been in a despondent state of mind about it. Having found you again, I am as well as can be expected (please mention to O), with that murder on my mind.[2]

— Which reminds me of Dr Skey. Pray assure him that I will get him in *somehow.* The devices I have been making to get space and

---

[8] Miss Coutts was proposing to offer a series of prizes to the schoolmistresses and pupils of the Whitelands Training Institute and to the pupil-teachers apprenticed in the county of Middlesex, for the best essays on housekeeping, cooking, the repair and making of clothing, the care of sick persons and children, and other such topics. The essays were to be written as replies to specific questions.

[9] "The subscription to that historical table" may have been to a public dinner, perhaps for charitable purposes, but I cannot identify it.

[1] "Old Defoe" and his wife were an indigent couple, possibly brought to Dickens's attention by Charles Knight, to whom, acting for Miss Coutts, Dickens periodically turned over £10 for their use.

[2] Aaron Gurnock, the old lighthouse-keeper whose role Dickens took in the play, is haunted by the belief that he has murdered a man.

ventilation would amuse you, if any amount of paper would be sufficient for their description. We are obliged to do it three nights. With Mr Stanfield's requirements, I can't get in more than 60,[3] and the wildest people hear of it and ask to come — and I am afraid to go out, because I am certain to meet in the next street the person who has never been thought of, and who ought of all others never to have been forgotten.

But I am going (by back ways) to Hackney tomorrow, to see, at the Elizabeth Fry Refuge,[4] two cases for the Home. We have another, as a parting gift, from Mr Tracey — of which he thinks highly. I hope one of the Hackney cases will do, but I am doubtful of the other. I only judge at this present writing, however, from a lady's written description.

I quite agree with you as to preparing beforehand, for your truly christian design. It has frequently been in my mind again, and I am strengthened in my first belief that its being pointed by an occasion would be a great service to it.

I wouldn't be going every day to that enormous wilderness, and making a fishing net of my brain to drag those Courts with, for — well, I would for Mr Dunn's little bill, but for nothing less.[5]

∽

222.   June 19, 1855, Tavistock House

I dispatch a hasty report to you and O. The audience were not so *demonstrative* last night as on Saturday, and the Corps Dramatique were disposed to think them "flat." I observed however that they were crying vigorously, and I think they were quite as much moved and pleased as on Saturday, though they did not cheer the actors on so much — except in the Farce.[6] Everybody played exactly as on the

---

[3] The performances were to take place, like the children's Twelfth Night plays, in the schoolroom, but the stage set that Stanfield had designed for the purpose took up more room than had previously been needed.

[4] Elizabeth Fry (1780–1845), the famous Quaker philanthropist, had done notable work in prison reform, especially in ameliorating the condition of female prisoners in Newgate and other jails, supplying them with clothing and establishing prison schools. She also instituted nightly shelters and soup kitchens for waifs, and founded a district visiting society to relieve the needy.

[5] Richard Dunn's little bill, the reader will recall, had been for £100,000.

[6] *The Lighthouse* had four performances all told at Tavistock House, June 15, 16, 18, and 19, although the first of them may have been for "trades people and the servants' relations," as in the later presentation of *The Frozen Deep.* (Most biographers have followed Forster in saying three, with Saturday, June 16, as the

previous night — including Mr Forster,[7] who buffeted the guests (I am informed) in the same light and airy manner. Mrs Stanfield was mollified, and certainly seemed to have been hustled out of the house on Saturday Night, like a species of pickpocket. Lady Becher [8] was evidently very much impressed and surprised, and Mrs Yates [9] said (with a large red circle round each eye), "O Mr Dickens what a pity it is you can do anything else!" Longman the bookseller was seen to cry dreadfully — and I don't know that anything could be said beyond that! —

I shall send you another report tomorrow. Georgina and I are now going to ticket the seats again.

223.   JUNE 21, 1855, TAVISTOCK HOUSE

I am happy to report the crowning night, a greater success than either of the others! Everything was in complete and thorough train — the audience were brilliant in their recognition — the actors were in great spirits — and some five and twenty of us danced, the maddest Scotch Reels, with all the steps conscientiously executed, until 5 o'clock in the morning.

To sum up all, Charley was off to the city at a quarter before Nine, and the House (that one room excepted), was in its usual condition at Noon. We were not much tired yesterday; but I feel today, for one, like my Invalid-friend in the Farce — with two pains (and nothing

---

first, but *Letters*, II, 672, lists a letter to the police station on June 15 saying that there is to be a performance that evening and asking to have a constable in attendance from 7 until 12 midnight.) There was a subsequent performance for the benefit of the Bournemouth Sanatorium at Campden House on July 10. The farce on all these occasions was *Mr. Nightingale's Diary*.

[7] This and the following sentence are jesting references to John Forster's arbitrary — and sometimes almost incredibly domineering — manner. After a performance of *The Frozen Deep* in 1857 Dickens wrote: "Macready has been here, perfectly raging because Forster bore him away, and positively shouldered him out of the Green Room Supper, on which he had set his heart."

[8] Eliza Lady Becher (1791–1872), actress, the daughter of an actor named O'Neill. She scored her first great success on the stage of Covent Garden as Juliet, in 1814, and was a sensation as Lady Teazle, Belvidera, and Monimia; she was highly praised by Macready and William Hazlitt. In 1829 she married William Wrixon Becher, an Irish M.P. for Mallow, who became a baronet by the death of an aunt. Among other Dickensian roles, she had played Mrs. Nickleby in Stirling's stage version of *Nicholas Nickleby* with Frederick Yates in 1838.

[9] Elizabeth Yates (1799–1860), actress. Her maiden name was Brunton; she had married Frederick Yates in 1823. As an artist she challenged comparison with the best actresses of the period.

else) to represent my arms, two more instead of my legs, and a broad pathway of fatigue – lumbago down my back.

I expect the postmen on this beat, to sink under the fatigue of delivering letters of enthusiasm from the three audiences. They come showering in every hour.

∽

224.   [TO CHARLES DICKENS FROM JOHN SUTHERLAND, M.D.¹]

Some ages ago I received a note from you forwarded to me at Balaklava introducing a drying machine and its bearer for the hospital at Scutari.

I did what I could with people in and out of authority in Scutari to get their aid in putting up the machine, and heard nothing more of it till the day before yesterday. On that day I went over the hospital for the first time these three months and found it in operation. It is well put up, gives great satisfaction and does its work so effectually that the wet clothes, like David Crockett's Coon, *give in*² as soon as they have seen it and dry up forthwith, at least such is the general impression if I can judge from the terms in which it was spoken of.

The Machine does great credit to Miss Coutts' philanthropy and also to your engineering.

∽

From the middle of July, Dickens rented 3 Albion Villas, Folkestone, a pleasant little house overlooking the sea and breezy with the scent of thyme from the downs. Here he worked busily on Little Dorrit *in order to have a comfortable backlog written before it began publication in December. Early in October he read* A Christmas Carol *for the benefit of an educational institution at Folkestone, and a little later presided over a farewell dinner to Thackeray, who was leaving for*

---

¹ John Sutherland, M.D. (1808–1891), promoter of sanitary science and inspector under the first Board of Health, had been sent to the Crimea to investigate the sanitary conditions of the troops. He carried out great sanitary reforms in the Army. This letter was written from Constantinople and dated, according to Osborne, June 27, 1855.

² David Crockett (1786–1836), American frontiersman, hunter, and trapper, who was born in Greene County, Tennessee, and served in the Creek War under Andrew Jackson. The reference is to an anecdote about his being such a dead shot that when he was raccoon hunting one day and leveled his gun at an "old 'coon" concealed in a tree, the 'coon cried out: "Hallo there! Are you Colonel Crockett? For if you air, I'll just come down, or I know I'm a gone 'coon."

*America to give a series of lectures on "The Four Georges." Two days
later Thackeray sailed from Liverpool and Dickens crossed the Channel to Boulogne on his way to Paris, where he planned to spend the
fall and winter. Here he took an entresol and first floor at 49 Avenue
des Champs Elysées, near the Barrière de l'Etoile and the Jardin
d'Hiver. With him were Catherine Dickens and her sister Georgina,
his daughters Mamey and Katey, and Harry and Plorn, the two small
boys, who were not yet old enough to go to school.*

*Dickens had been in Paris less than a fortnight when he learned that
Dr. William Brown, who was at Montpellier with his wife and Miss
Coutts, had died suddenly, after a short illness, on October 23. His
widow was too prostrated to travel. Dickens stepped in and took
charge, brought the body back to London, where Mrs. Brown desired
it to be buried in St. Stephen's Church, and attended to every detail.
From London he wrote Miss Coutts and her companion.*

༄

225.   NOVEMBER 2, 1855, 16 WELLINGTON STREET NORTH — STRAND;
OFFICE OF *Household Words*

I send a duplicate of this letter to the Pavilion at Folkestone [3] — not
that there is any news in it, but because I think it may be a satisfaction to you on your arrival in England to know that your wishes have
been fulfilled.

I have seen Banting [4] and carefully arranged everything with him
for *Wednesday*. The time at the church will be 12 exactly. The mourning carriages three in number, with Lord Harrowby [5] in the place
you wished. The rest of the mourners are invited to the schoolroom
instead of to Stratton Street. Pair-horse, *not* 4 horse carriages. No
difference in the scarves, hatbands etc. supplied, but all the mourners
exactly alike. In this respect as in all others, I hope I have understood
Mrs Brown's feeling and yours. All your instructions I have fully impressed upon Banting and stood over him while he wrote them down.
The two plates on the coffin are now in preparation. After stating that
our poor friend was the beloved husband of Mrs Brown, I have added,

---

[3] Where Miss Coutts and Mrs. Brown would arrive from France as soon as the
latter was able to travel.

[4] Probably the undertaker.

[5] Dudley Ryder (1798–1882), formerly Lord Sandon, now the second Earl of
Harrowby, whose wife Frances was Miss Coutts's first cousin.

after her christian and surname, "formerly Meredith." The vault, by reason of the heating and ventilating apparatus, could not be made exactly in the place you wished; but I am quite sure you will approve of it.

I heard from Banting this morning that on Wednesday night when the workmen were in the church to begin the vault (Mr Alcock [6] and I having charged all parties concerned that there must be no delay) one of your curates objected that the chancel could not be touched without the consent of the Incumbent; and as Mr Tennant is in too delicate a state to have a telegraph message sent to him, they went through the absurd form of waiting to begin work until a special messenger had been sent down to him in the country and had telegraphed back his consent! If this had been made known to me, I should have ventured on your behalf altogether to over-ride the objection as an absurd one. I should have got the consent while the work was going on, but should have represented that to stop it was a piece of folly, amounting almost, though unintentionally, to an impertinence. However, this would merely have been in a natural desire to assert your supremacy in the place and in the case; for everything is ready, and nothing is the worst for it.

At this moment Mr Meyrick [7] has appeared. Banting had appointed the funeral for 12 o'clock exactly at the church, as the most usual, fitting, and convenient time. Mr Meyrick suggested that there was usually a service at that time and that he "supposed Mr Garden [8] would not object" to give notice that such service would not take place. I replied, of course in the most delicate way, that he mustn't object (I did so in effect, not in words), and that the funeral was to take place at that time.

The letters are probably by this time all gone out. My dear Miss Coutts I hope and trust you will find everything in perfect train when you arrive, and that both you and your dear charge will pass through this closing part of the trial, with a tender but not painful grief.

The nature of the service rests with you. That point I have requested to be altogether reserved until you express your wish upon it.

I will come to you at Lady Falmouth's,[9] at 12 on Sunday.

[P.S.] I have received all your three letters, of course.

---

[6] Unidentified.   [7] Unidentified.   [8] Unidentified.
[9] Anne Frances Lady Falmouth (d. 1864), the widow of Edward Boscawen (1787–1841), first Earl of Falmouth.

226. NOVEMBER 3, 1855, 16 WELLINGTON STREET NORTH – STRAND; OFFICE OF *Household Words* [TO MRS. BROWN]

*You will have found (I hope) from a letter I wrote to Miss Coutts at Folkestone that I have anticipated the greater part of your wishes, and that there will only be three carriages from Stratton Street. I am strongly against the proposed innocent fraud respecting the day; firstly, because I do not think it dignified, in the best and right sense of the word; and secondly because it would be fruitless. I am perfectly convinced that whatever lookers-on assemble, would assemble in any case. And Banting (whose opinion I asked as a sensible tradesman when he was here at noon today) had not a doubt of the inefficacy of such an attempt. Now, adding this objection to the first one – which I feel more strongly, both for the sake of the dead and of the living, than I can well express to you – I Earnestly advise you to abandon that idea. I foresee, I am sure, that it would be perverted, moreover, into an attempt to be exclusive; would be twisted into a purpose exactly opposite to your real intention.

As to the clergyman, I think that is a matter of feeling for Miss Coutts. But if I did not have the service performed by the senior Curate, in Mr Tennant's absence, I (speaking as if it were my own case) would have it performed by a personal friend – such as Harness.[1] No reason presents itself to my mind for the calling in of any Westminster or other clergyman in whom you have not an interest. Harness would do it with feeling and emotion. And I cannot but think that this would be comforting to you.

The letters *have all gone out* to the names on Miss Coutts's list. But observe my dear friend how modestly and simply the arrangement stands. Three carriages will follow your beloved husband's remains from Stratton Street – no preposterous show of horses and feathers; but a quiet, unpretending, necessary means of getting to the church – such as I feel sure that his honest pride and manly feeling would have approved. The other followers who come to the Schoolroom are *not*

---

[1] The Reverend William Harness (1790–1869), who went to Harrow with Lord Byron and was an intimate friend of Wordsworth, Southey, and Miss Mitford. In 1825 he published an eight-volume edition of Shakespeare. He was minister at Brompton Chapel 1844–1847, and became Perpetual Curate of Knightsbridge in 1848, supervising the construction of the Church of All Saints, of which he was Perpetual Curate from 1849 until his death. He was for many years a close friend of Miss Coutts's; in 1864, through his advice, she acquired a Shakespeare first folio for £716.

conveyed there in mourning coaches — I perceived the objection to that, and pointed it out to Banting — so that a few gentleman in mourning arrive there, in an ordinary unrecognizable way during half an hour, and merely pass into the church with the rest when the rest come. You know my own strong feeling in the general matter of parade at such a time, and you know (I feel convinced) how delicately and anxiously I consider everything that concerns you now; but I assure you from my heart that I do not see how you could possibly do what is to be done, in a more unaffected manner.

You might, if you thought right, countermand the order for your own carriage and Miss Coutts's chariot, following. That we will speak of, when we meet.

God bless you! Only think what a friend you have beside you, in the noblest spirit we can ever know, and what an inestimable blessing you possess in her. A hundred times, God bless you!

ᕱᕯᕱ

227. NOVEMBER 16, 1855, 49 AVENUE DES CHAMPS ELYSÉES, PARIS
I will not tell you how interested I have been by your letter, or how glad to receive it.

In reference to your enquiry as to a Secretary, however, I am not without hope that I can recommend a very eligible and trustworthy person for your consideration.[2] (I assume for the present that you want done what I cannot do; but I shall ask you when I return home to consider whether a daily messenger with a Dispatch Box could not put me in possession of all such business, and whether I could not, with some small additional remuneration to one of my trustworthy people at the office, do all you want. Of course I should do it in a confidence and with an interest that can hardly be bought to so full an extent, and your friendship will concede to me the right of entreating from

---

[2] Throughout the preceding fifteen years, although Dickens had never formally been Miss Coutts's secretary, he had discharged, as the reader has seen, many of the more important and confidential duties of a private secretary and almoner, investigated the appeals of begging-letter writers, brought to her attention many cases of distress, advised her upon many of her charitable enterprises, laid down the plans for their operation, and even supervised some of them, like Urania Cottage. He was now finding that these many duties made too great demands upon his time — although he still offered to perform all the more confidential parts of them — and Miss Coutts had asked him to recommend a private secretary to take over some of them. As the subsequent letters reveal, he did not cease to take an active part in her work.

my heart to claim a sort of privilege herein. Do not, I beg you, make any such prolonged arrangement for the future as would place it out of your power to discuss this with me. I particularly ask that favor).

I have written to Mr Wills, and told him generally that you will probably write a note to him, asking him to call at a certain time, with a view to helping you to a temporary Secretary. I have mentioned to him two people of different capacities and qualities, of whom he will speak to you. But I have also said to him, as from myself, that I would recommend him also, to suggest *himself*.[3] It is impossible to find a more zealous, honorable, or reliable man. What you would want done would be perfectly compatible with his daily pursuits, and easily discharged along with them. Finally, you need not have (for he is perfectly sensible and manly) the least reluctance to propose it to him as an engagement for a certain remuneration — whatever you may have thought of.

Yes, if you please, and when you please, as to the payment of my account.

I write very hastily to save the post. Affectionate regards to Mrs Brown.

ᴄᴧᴊ

228.   JANUARY 10, 1856, 49 AVENUE DES CHAMPS ELYSÉES, PARIS
    The noble cake arrived in the best condition — was a great surprise — and was received with the loudest acclamations. I think Mrs Dickens will have already thanked you for it, but I cannot omit it from my note in reply to yours received yesterday.

I was very much pleased to receive that note, because I know its effect will be a great pleasure to Wills, and because I am certain of his deserving your confidence, and most zealously, delicately and worthily acquitting himself of any function you entrust him with. My experience of him is close and constant, and I cannot too highly commend him. I feel so much interested in hearing "the arrangements you would prefer to make," that I put a strong constraint upon myself

---

[3] At the same time Dickens wrote Wills, strongly advising that if Miss Coutts offered him the post he should accept it. "The duties," he said, "would not be inconvenient at all — the connexion would be extremely valuable and pleasant to you — the money would not be unacceptable — and the post is fit for any gentleman, in association with such a lady." Miss Coutts, always deliberate, took two months to make up her mind, but then, after consultation with Dickens, offered Wills the position at £ 200 a year. This offer he gladly accepted. He discharged its duties until his retirement in 1868.

in not immediately coming to London. However, I shall try to force
myself to write a No. of Little Dorrit first (I am just sitting down to
one), and that will hold me prisoner, if I submit, until early in next
month. Whenever I come to town, of course I shall come to you within
a few hours.

Next month reminds me of Walter. Being fifteen next month, he will
be able to go up for his examination next month twelvemonth. I found
him so excessively deaf when he came over here, that I felt it necessary
to have him examined by the Chief Surgeon (very famous in that way),
of the Asylum for the Deaf and Dumb. He found him to have an
Ulcerated Tympanum, of a very aggravated and peculiar kind. He
said it was of long standing, must have caused him great pain, and
he should have thought must have forced itself on the attention of the
masters of his school. He has greatly relieved and improved his patient,
but says that his sense of hearing will never be quite delicate. To brush
up the patient's French, I send him to a great school in the Faubourg St Honoré, two hours a day. An omnibus comes round for
the Pupils every morning — a private omnibus belonging to the school
— and the Driver blows a frightful whistle on the box, to announce
himself.

I have made arrangements with a large book-selling-house in Paris
here, for the publication of a French translation of the whole of my
books.[4] A volume will appear about once a month, and it will take a
year and a half or two years to complete. It will be a pleasant thing
to have done in one's lifetime. It is there venture, and they pay me
three or four hundred pounds for it besides. The Portrait for which
I have been sitting to Ary Scheffer, is just done.[5] He is a great painter,

----

[4] The offer came from Hachette et Compagnie; in the agreement finally arrived
at Dickens received £440 in monthly payments of £40 each. In the course of
1857 six of his works appeared in ten volumes: Vie et aventures de Nicolas
Nickleby, Le Magasin d'antiquités, Contes de Noël, Dombey et fils, Bleak House,
and Les Temps difficiles; in 1858 three more in six volumes: Barnabé Rudge, Vie et
aventures de Martin Chuzzlewit, and La petite Dorrit. Others followed in later
years: Les Aventures de M. Pickwick in 1859, Paris et Londres en 1793 1861,
David Copperfield 1862, Oliver Twist and Les Grandes Espérances 1864, L'Ami
commun 1867, and finally Le Mystère d'Edwin Drood 1874. The only omission
was Sketches by Boz, and the edition comprised sixteen works in twenty-eight
volumes.

[5] Ary Scheffer (1795–1858), the well-known French artist. "He is a most noble
fellow," wrote Dickens, "and I have the greatest pleasure in his society." Scheffer
also introduced Dickens to Daniele Manin, the former president of the ill-fated
Venetian Republic, who gave lessons in Italian to Mamey and Katey. The portrait,

and of course it has great merit. I doubt if I should know it, myself —
but it is always possible that I may know other people's faces pretty
well, without knowing my own.

I have omitted to say, in its proper place, that I had *not* communicated to Wills, what passed between you and me. It did not seem
to me quite decided, and I thought there was time enough: knowing
that I could at any time tell him that I had had a reason for reserving
it, and that he would be quite satisfied with that assurance.

There seem to be great misgivings here, that a pecuniary crisis must
come.[6]

My kind love to Mrs Brown, whom I hope to find very much improved when I next see her.

ᏴᎳ

229. FEBRUARY 9, 1856, 16 WELLINGTON STREET NORTH — STRAND
[OFFICE OF *Household Words*]

First, as to Teignmouth,[7] Wills knows it very well. The soil is red
loam, and not naturally damp. But the town itself stands in a rent or
gash made among great hills, by the mouth of the river, and is certainly
moist and low — decidedly *not* advisable for your purpose I should say.
On the other hand, if the house should not be in Teignmouth or in
the valley of the river, but should be on the bold hills which rise about
it, then the objection to it would be removed. The whole question turns

---

however, gave Scheffer considerable difficulty; he said that Dickens looked like
nothing so much as a bluff Dutch sea captain, and, as the sittings prolonged themselves from early November until well into March, the "nightmare portrait," as
Dickens came to call it, made him chafe wildly at a bondage that kept him away
from his desk. When it was finished, Dickens still thought it didn't look like him.

[6] The mania for stock-market gambling in Paris filled Dickens with the foreboding that a crash must be imminent, and incontestably deepened the hues in
which he was later in *Little Dorrit* to paint the widespread ruin following the
Merdle bankruptcy. "If you were to see the steps of the Bourse at about 4 in
the afternoon," he wrote, "and the crowd of blouses and patches among the speculators there assembled, all howling and haggard . . . you would stand aghast at
the consideration of what must be going on. Concierges and people like that perpetually blow out their brains, or fly into the Seine, 'à cause des pertes sur la
Bourse.' On the other hand, thoroughbred horses without end, and red velvet carriages with white kid harness on jet black horses, go by here all day long, and the
pedestrians who turn to look at them, laugh, and say, 'C'est la Bourse!' Such
crashes must be staved off every week as have not been seen since Law's time."
(The eighteenth-century collapse of the notorious Mississippi Bubble speculation.)

[7] Miss Coutts was evidently seeking a winter residence away from London.
In 1860 she took a house at Torquay, south of Teignmouth.

upon the exact position of the house. If it be on the hills, good. If it be in the valley, bad. If it be in neither the one place nor the other, rather dubious.

Secondly, as to Wills himself. I have communicated to him the result of our conversation yesterday, and he is "gratified beyond expression." He says he considers it most generous, and is extremely anxious that I should express his sense of it to you in the most earnest and emphatic words I can employ.[8]

Thirdly, as to Gad's Hill Place [9] — which is the name of my house. If you mean in your kind note, the refusal of it *now*, I am sorry to say that it is not now available. As I told Mrs Brown yesterday, the Rector [1] lives in it, and has lived in it for some years; and the object Wills and I have in view in going down there directly, is to ask him how and when it will suit his convenience to come out — as of course I wish to treat him with all handsome consideration. It is not now a furnished house, but my object is, as soon as I shall have got rid of the tenant, to make it clean and pretty in the papering and painting way, and then to furnish it in the most comfortable and cosey manner, and let it by the month whenever I can. Whenever I cannot, I shall use it for myself and make it a change for Charley from Saturday to Monday. When all this is done, I shall have a delight in taking you down to see it which I shall not try here to express; and if you should like it so well as to think of ever occupying it as a little easy change, I shall be far more attached to the spot than ever. I think you will be very much pleased with it. It is old-fashioned, plain, and comfortable. On the summit of Gad's Hill, with a noble prospect at the side and behind, looking down into the Valley of the Medway. Lord Darnley's Park of Cobham [2] (a beautiful place with a noble walk through a

---

[8] Wills' "letter book" contains a copy of the letter in which he accepted Miss Coutts's offer.

[9] Gad's Hill Place, the rose-brick Georgian dwelling on Gad's Hill, two miles outside of Rochester, which it had been the dream of Dickens's childhood to own. As a rather sickly small boy of eight or nine, when they lived in nearby Chatham, he had admired its bow-windowed façade and the small white bell turret surmounting its gambrel roof. In the summer of 1855 it came on the market, and Dickens immediately entered into negotiations to buy it.

[1] The Rector was the Reverend Joseph Hindle. He remained at Gad's Hill another year, until Lady Day (March 25), 1857. The purchase was concluded on March 16, 1856.

[2] Cobham Wood and Park, directly neighboring upon the Gad's Hill property, were the estate of John Stuart (1827–1896), sixth Earl of Darnley; after Dickens became his neighbor Lord Darnley gave him a key to the gates of the park and

wood) is close by it; and Rochester is within a mile or two. It is only an hour and a quarter from London by the Railway. To crown all, the sign of the Sir John Falstaff is over the way, and I used to look at it as a wonderful Mansion (which God knows it is not), when I was a very odd little child with the first faint shadows of all my books in my head — I suppose.

Mr Austin surveyed it for me, and was greatly struck by it. Large sums of money have been expended on it (for such a small place) at various times, and he found everything about the garden and so forth, in the best order. There is a very pretty garden, and a shrubbery on the other side of the high road, at which the house looks. When I exhibit it to you with all my contrivances accomplished — of course some of them will be wonderfully ingenious — I will tell you what I paid for it.[3]

With love to Mrs Brown, who is looking immensely better.

❧

230. FEBRUARY 12, 1856, 49 AVENUE DES CHAMPS ELYSÉES, PARIS

My Rector, having lived in the house six and twenty years, has an ardent desire to stay there until Lady Day next year. I have of course acceded to his wish. In the meantime he purposes building a house for himself somewhere near, as there are very few indeed in that neighbourhood but Farms, and Farm-laborers' cottages. The only house thereabouts (except mine) that would suit you as a Retreat, is a very good one called the Hermitage. But it is in the occupation of the owner and is not to let.

It has occurred to me that Tunbridge Wells might be a good place for your purpose. It is extremely healthy, very beautiful, very accessible, and has many pleasant houses that are let furnished by the month. Anywhere upon or near the Heath is a very fine situation, on light sand. If you should think well of it, Wills would be delighted to go down and look about for you. Or there is an excellent Hotel — The Calvary — where you might be as private and as comfortable, almost, as in any hired house. If you don't think well of this, anywhere

---

free access to the property for strolling. The walk through the wood was the last Dickens took, on the day before he died.

[3] "After drawing the cheque," Dickens wrote, "I turned round to give it to Wills (£1790), and said: "Now isn't it an extraordinary thing — look at the day — Friday! I have been nearly drawing it half-a-dozen times, when the lawyers have not been ready, and here it comes round upon a Friday, as a matter of course.'"

about Croydon, Dorking, or Guildford, is good, and particularly healthy.

Of course you will let me know where you go. I shall have to be in town about the Tenth of next month.

With my love to Mrs Brown

[P.S.] Mrs Brown will immediately receive from Wills, the result of the London University enquiries.[4] I forgot to speak to you about Mrs Kenney, 192 Faubourg St Honoré. Perhaps it might be painful to her if I were to write to her, as she has not written to me. But the plain truth is, that I have no means of employing translators, and that I never do.

*

231.   FEBRUARY 19, 1856, 49 AVENUE DES CHAMPS ELYSÉES, PARIS

Walter was born on the 8th of February 1841. His name (a mild one) is Walter Landor. Birthday, eighth of February eighteen hundred and forty one. Name, Walter Landor. No vegetable designation, no flower, no beast, no terrors of any description.

I don't know Dr Sandwith.[5]

Your note finds me settling myself to Little Dorrit again, and in the usual wretchedness of such settlement — which is unsettlement. Prowling about the rooms, sitting down, getting up, stirring the fire, looking out of window, tearing my hair, sitting down to write, writing nothing, writing something and tearing it up, going out, coming in, a Monster to my family, a dread Phaenomenon to myself, etc etc etc.

With love to Mrs Brown

*

232.   MAY 13, 1856, TAVISTOCK HOUSE

I have indeed read this letter with great emotion.[6] If you had done nothing else in maintaining the Home — instead of having done so much that we know of, to which is to be added all the chance and by-way good that has sprung out of it in the lives of these women: which I believe to be enormous — what a great reward this case alone would be!

---

[4] I do not know what the London University enquiries were, nor can I identify Mrs. Kenney, in the sentence that follows.

[5] Unidentified.

[6] The letter itself is missing, but clearly it was from one of the women who had been received in Urania Cottage and benefited from its training, like the letter from Louisa Cooper given earlier.

Unfortunately I was out last evening. I went to the Egyptian Hall,[7] and had left home for the Athenaeum before your note arrived. I will come to you on Thursday at half past four. I hope you got well out of the animalculae — your account of which enjoyment in prospect, made me laugh heartily.

I am not without hope that in the winter nights when we are alone here, you and Mrs Brown may be induced to take some interest in what I dare say you never saw — the growth of a play from the beginning.[8] Mr Collins and I have hammered out a curious idea for a new one, which he is to write, and which we purpose, please God, to bring out on Charley's birthday. Mr Stanfield has already been hanging out of the centre back-window of the schoolroom at the risk of his life, inventing wonderful effects and measuring the same. If you and O were to come into the secret from the commencement, and see all the ways and means, and the gradual improvement of it, and the trials of patience to which my young people are submitted, and the general ingenuity and good humour, I think it would pass a few dark evenings pleasantly.

***

233. MAY 20, 1856, TAVISTOCK HOUSE

I have been very much interested in the pamphlet.[9] There is nothing in it that I see, demanding correction, except the paragraph which you pointed out to me and which I marked in Stratton Street.

Mrs Thompson has written me a letter, and I have seen her since its receipt. The lodging-letting does not succeed sufficiently well to be pursued. In June the notice she has given to quit her house, will expire. She will then, by the sale of her furniture and so forth, have from a hundred to a hundred and fifty pounds. With this sum, she

---

[7] The Egyptian Hall, in Piccadilly, was a place of entertainment and exhibition used for many different purposes, from displays of paintings to conjuring performances. In 1846 the artist Benjamin Robert Haydon had shown his pictures there; in 1847 a group of independent artists had held a Free Exhibition. General Tom Thumb had appeared there, and, in 1848, Banvard's Geographical Panorama of the Mississippi and Missouri Rivers. In 1854 Albert Smith used it for his popular illustrated lecture on his ascent of Mont Blanc.

[8] Wilkie Collins's *The Frozen Deep*, a melodrama based on the ill-fated Arctic expedition of Sir John Franklin in 1845–1847, all of whose members died of starvation and exposure. Traces of the expedition confirming its total annihilation were not found until 1859. The performances of Collins's play were not to take place, as this letter implies, until the following winter.

[9] Unidentified.

desires nothing more than to emigrate to Canada along with her child, if she can see any reasonably hopeful prospect of getting employment, as a housekeeper, superintendent attendant on children, companion, manager, any honest thing. She writes very well, is a good plain accountant, and generally neat and handy. Does any means of helping her, occur to you? I am trying among Canada Railway people, but I fear uselessly, as their schemes are in a bad way. I should be very glad to hear from you on this, at your leisure.[1]

You will have fine weather for the new house, I hope, and will enjoy it. With kind regard to Mrs Brown

∾

234. MAY 27, 1856, TAVISTOCK HOUSE

I have made enquiries about the Staff Surgeon who wanted the Fifty Pounds (as we agreed), and there is no doubt of his being a reality, and of his holding a responsible appointment, and of his representation being perfectly true.[2]

I wrote to him to say that I was not rich and had a fearful number of claims upon me, and could not lend him such a sum. But that a friend of mine, generous and able in more cases than I should trust myself to mention, *might* — I by no means said *would* — do so, if satisfied of his merits. That if, on this slight encouragement, he could send me any kind of corroboration, himself, I would shew it to that friend, but could give him no other assurance than that his confidence should be respected.

I enclose his reply, and its accompanying letters. Will you send them back to me with your decision?

Your letter from Oxford I received this morning. A beautiful place indeed! The gowing [rowing?] down from Oxford to Reading, on the Thames, is more charming than one can describe in words. I rowed down last June, through miles upon miles of water lilies, lying on the water close together, like a fairy pavement.

I have held a Committee of One at the Bush, where all was going on thoroughly well. Mr Illingworth's case I will immediately see to. With love to Mrs Brown

---

[1] This is the last mention of Caroline Thompson in the surviving letters of Dickens's correspondence with Miss Coutts. Presumably she did emigrate to Canada.

[2] The name of the staff surgeon is nowhere given, nor is there a more explicit statement of his case.

235. JUNE 1, 1856 ("MID WINTER"),[3] TAVISTOCK HOUSE

I have been so incessantly worked since the receipt of your last note, by Little Dorrit, Household Words, and business, that I have let two posts go by without answering it.

You will see by the enclosed that Mrs Matthews (who assuredly has a deadly perseverance), has written again.

What the Staff Surgeon wants, is a Loan of Fifty Pounds.

The letters of the young La Touches (which have naturally interested me very much), and the letter of Rhena Pollard (ditto) I have returned under cover to you at Stratton Street. The two letters concerning the death of Harriet Tanner, I have retained for Mrs Marchmont. There is a poor mother, who enquired after her at the Home not long ago; and I think that for her satisfaction Mrs Marchmont had best copy the passages that refer to the girl.[4]

The Schools Report, I have also returned to Stratton Street.

You cannot imagine what a wonderful sight Illuminated and Fireworked London was, from the top of St Pauls. I must try my hand at a description of it in Household Words.[5] In the next No. but one, by the bye, I wish you would read an opening paper of mine, with the rather alarming title of "The demeanour of Murderers." It is a quiet protest against the newspaper descriptions of Mr Palmer in court: shewing why they are harmful to the public at large, and why they are, even in themselves, altogether blind and wrong. *I* think it rather a curious and serviceable essay! [6]

I am writing in a great coat and a fur cap.

With my (cold and damp) love to Mrs Brown

---

[3] There was an unseasonable spell of bitter weather.

[4] All these letters have disappeared, but obviously involve cases connected with Urania Cottage. Mrs. Marchmont, it will be remembered, is the matron who replaced Mrs. Morson when she left the Home to remarry.

[5] The fireworks were to celebrate the official termination of the Crimean War on May 29, 1856. Dickens obtained permission from Dean Milman to observe the display from the top of the Cathedral, for the purpose of describing it in *Household Words,* but no such article was published there.

[6] "The Demeanour of Murderers," *Household Words,* June 14, 1856, was a blast against the journalistic tendency to make melodramatic heroes out of such criminals. The murderer was William Palmer, M.R.C.S., who poisoned his wife in 1854 and his friend Thomas Parsons Cook in 1855, and who was tried and convicted at the Old Bailey and hanged on June 14. His "complete self-possession" during the trial, his "constant coldness" in the dock, Dickens saw not as signs of innocence or courage, but of "cruelty" and "insensibility."

236. July 5, 1856, Villa des Moulineaux, Boulogne [to Mrs. Brown]

I owe you many thanks for your kind and interesting letter. I need not tell you that nothing in your account of that occasion surprised me, great and high as the pleasure was, that I derived from it.

I meant to have written to you at once; but I was so busy with Little Dorrit that I could not detach myself from her for any pen and ink purpose. Then I had to go immediately to London, and purposed writing from there; but I found myself continually engaged, and had no peace until I came back here again, yesterday.

Walter and the three smaller boys have all come home with a Prize apiece. In honor of these achievements we have made rejoicings with five franc pieces, running matches, and cricket ditto. Besides the pretty gardens here, I have a field for them, in which they tear themselves to pieces all day long — immensely to their satisfaction and the tailor's. Their bedrooms being in a little cottage in the garden, I have established (by way of a lesson in Common Things)[7] a regular code of laws for the administration of that Institution. The washing arrangements and so forth are conducted on the strict principles of a Man of War. — Nothing is allowed to be out of its place. Each in his turn is appointed Keeper for the week, and I go out in solemn procession (Georgina and the Baby — as we call him — forming the rest of it), three times a day, on a tour of inspection. Meantime Charley seems to get on very well indeed in the city,[8] and is coming here for a fortnight at the end of August.

Poor Mrs Watson [9] went to Southsea a few months ago, to see her second boy through the Naval School before entering the service. There, he fell ill of Scarlet Fever. Having all her children with her, she was obliged to send the rest away into another house, and only to see them, day after day and week after week, from her own sickroom balcony. Nevertheless the little girl took the fever somehow, and then poor Mrs Watson — all alone there, except for a servant — took it herself. The happy conclusion of the story is, that they are all now well again, and that we heard from her this morning. She has

---

[7] An allusion to the prizes for essays on "Common Things" that Miss Coutts had inaugurated at Whitelands Training Institution and other places.

[8] Charley was now employed in Baring Brothers.

[9] The Honorable Mrs. Richard Watson, of Rockingham Castle, whose husband had died in 1852.

gone through a great deal of late years, but has a wonderful force of character.

Mrs Dickens and Georgina and all the children send their loves. How beautiful the country now! We have Millions of roses here, and as I came from town yesterday the luxuriant hay fields were so beautiful that I felt as proud of them as if they were all mine.

ⴰⴰ

237.   JULY 11, 1856, VILLA DES MOULINEAUX, BOULOGNE

First, as to the Common Things. I rather think that if I were you, I would *not* send to any more newspapers just now. The subject has been so well taken up by the best of them, and the Times [1] did it so much service by returning to it the other day in a Leader, that I would not press it. I think by doing so you might bring out some ignorant caviller, and would not be likely to improve on its present position. I would beg Wills to send to the Quarterly and Edinburgh, if I were you; and there, for the present, I would leave it.

I thoroughly agree in that interesting part of your note which refers to the immense uses, direct and indirect, of needlework. Also as to the great difficulty of getting many men to understand them. And I think Shuttleworth and the like, would have gone on to the crack of doom, melting down all the thimbles in Great Britain and Ireland, and making medals of them to be given for a knowledge of Watersheds and Pre Adamite vegetation [2] (both immensely comfortable to a labouring man with a large family and a small income), if it hadn't been for you.

It occurs to me that Punch, which everybody sees, may be useful by just hitting the good nail neatly on the head, and there leaving

---

[1] The London *Times*, July 7, 1856, carried a leading article praising Miss Coutts for the prizes she was awarding for essays on "Common Things." It observed that the contestants wrote far better than "their order" could have done ten or fifteen years ago, but that their information was still scanty, general rather than concrete, and full of moral platitudes. The writers, it went on, did not have the acquaintance with "ordinary things" that was desirable; on household expenses, the cost of clothing and provisions, and the devices of cookery they were "curt, commonplace, and incorrect." If the prizes Miss Coutts had established fostered a knowledge of these things, she would earn the gratitude of the country.

[2] The satire on Mr. Gradgrind's school in *Hard Times*, Book I, Chapter II, is directed against precisely these points. A letter Dickens wrote to W. H. Wills, January 25, 1854, shows that he modeled his description of Mr. M'Choakumchild's pedagogic training and educational methods on the Educational Board's questions for the examination of teachers.

it. I will say so much to Mr Lemon, who may be safely trusted.

I spell Harbor without the letter u, because the modern spelling of such words as "Harbor, arbor, parlor," etc (modern within the last quarter of a century) discards that vowel, as belonging in that connexion to another sound — such as hour and sour. But, if it will be the slightest satisfaction to you, I will take that vowel up again, and fight for it as long as I live. U and I shall be inseparable, and nothing shall ever part us.[3]

Pray give my kind love to Mrs Brown, in which Mrs Dickens and Georgina and all here join. The parcel shall be sent for directly.

I have reserved the subject of Walter to the last, because your kindness touches me so tenderly that I hardly know my dear Miss Coutts how to acknowledge it. I shall have no difficulty, I hope and fully believe, in remitting that sum to India with him; but if, at any time or in any design of my life, I should want such help as your generosity and friendship could give me, I would ask it of no one else in the world and would unfalteringly turn to you.[4]

Having copied all that part of the letter which refers to Walter, I return the original, enclosed.

⌘

238. AUGUST 8, 1856, VILLA DES MOULINEAUX [TO MRS. BROWN]

I have considered your question very carefully, and with that anxious desire to make no mistake, which my interest in the subject naturally awakens.

First, I cannot too strongly agree with you in objecting to leave any discretion to the Committee.[5] Incalculable abuse, perverted intention, and mischief, come of that, nine times out of ten.

Secondly, it would be very objectionable to bind yourself to any division or disposition of the money among the more deserving students. Cases might easily arise in which your help or encouragement

---

[3] Although Dickens has often made playful jokes in the course of this correspondence and has often expressed esteem, gratitude, and affection for Miss Coutts, the reader will observe that this is almost the first example of his writing, even playfully, in a tone of personal intimacy.

[4] Within another year Dickens's son Walter would be taking his examinations and sailing for India. Miss Coutts had evidently offered to give him a letter of credit that would enable him to meet his expenses comfortably. There is no indication of the precise sum she suggested bestowing.

[5] As the letter following this makes clear, Mrs. Brown proposed to endow a prize for medical students in memory of her husband, Dr. William Brown. A committee was to be in charge of making the award.

might be of little value to any of them. On the other hand, cases might arise in which you would most ardently desire, perhaps to give the whole year's money to one of them. Suppose, for instance, a deserving young man just to fall short (in a year when no one was up to the mark) through having fallen ill for a time in the course of his hard and anxious study; or through having had to tend a sick sister; or to having devoted himself to a dying widowed mother. Such an occurrence is not out of the reach of probability — not to stop short at possibility — and might be very affecting and meritorious.

What I recommend you to do, is, to stipulate without any reserve, that in case there should be no candidate possessing the necessary amount of qualifications, the money shall revert to you. Retain, yourself, the power of rewarding any competitor or competitors as you think best, and I am sure you will never repent it.

I conceive this supposititious failure of all the competitors to be very unlikely ever to occur. But it is quite right to provide for it; and, if it should occur, I say let the money come back to you or your representative. In considering the matter before I thought of this, I felt that I was always wandering about among *some* uneasy chances, but, in this direction, the road seems to me to be clear, safe, and light.

This little place looks very beautiful, but the leaves are beginning to be tinged with yellow, and the berries are turning red, and we have already begun to talk sometimes of our return home early in October. They all send best love to you and to Miss Coutts. Mary is acquiring an immense reputation as an arranger of flowers, and we have some new device on the table at dinner every day. The cats at the mill, are still the great topic of the house, and Mr Plornish mentions them after dark, in a low voice.[6] One of the porters at the Pavilion at Folkestone trained and sent him over a little goldfinch who draws all the water he drinks, in a thimble. He hangs in my room all the morning,

---

[6] Two "tigerish and fearful cats" from a neighboring mill were constantly invading the property and stalking Dick, the pet canary. "Keeping the house open at all points," Dickens wrote, "it is impossible to shut them out, and they hide themselves in the most terrific manner; hanging themselves up behind draperies, like bats, and tumbling out in the dead of night with frightful caterwaulings." One of the servants borrowed a gun to shoot them, and tumbled "over with the recoil, exactly like a clown." The children kept watch "on their stomachs" in the garden to give the alarm with "horrible whistles." "I am afraid to go out lest I should be shot." Tradesmen cried out as they came up the avenue, "It's me — baker — don't shoot!" The household was in a state of siege for over a week before the cats were disposed of, and "Mr. Plornish," now four, was solemnly terrified.

that he may be safe from these ravaging cats. I observe that when he draws the thimble up, he has to put a foot upon the tiny cord, to keep it in its place while he drinks — and that he knows that when he takes his foot away, the thimble will tumble down into the glass with a clink that will frighten him. So sometimes he stands thinking about letting it go, without being able to make up his mind to take his foot off the cord — and the moment he at last does so, he flys away to the remotest end of his perch, that he may hear the clink from a respectful distance. He won't drink when I look at him; but I have beaten him by looking in the glass. Then he exults over me (supposing me to have my eye on the cathedral) and drinks bumpers. — which brings me over-leaf to sign myself — which I have no need to do — Ever Faithfully Yours

❦

239.   AUGUST 13, 1856, VILLA DES MOULINEAUX, BOULOGNE

I believe there will always be a qualified competitor, unless the terms of the Exhibition should by an unfortunate mistake, give the qualified competitor [7] a reason for stopping short of full success. By dividing it between two, in the event of no marked superiority on the part of one, you might really (though unintentionally) appeal to a generous mind, to abstain from rising above the level of the next best man, and content himself with half the prize.

Mrs Brown ought certainly to know with distinctness the nature of the examination. That clearly laid down, I should not be afraid of the Committee rewarding an incompetent person. The credit of their School of Medicine would be more impaired by their so doing, than by their admitting "We have no student, this year, qualified for the Exhibition, *who has been a candidate for it.*" They would always have that saving clause.

The deed should by all means be revocable. It is the only efficient protection, I am convinced, against abuse.

Many thanks for the clue to the outfit, which will be of the greatest assistance to me. Charley shall go to the place and make a copy of the whole list.

When I was last at Folkestone, the picture was strongly before me which your note suggests.[8] I have never been there since, without thinking of it, and of you two.

---

[7] For the medical prize mentioned in the preceding letter.
[8] Unexplained.

Pray tell Mrs Brown with my love, that the flowers are beautiful, and that Mary is improving in her powers of floral arrangement every day. In two parts of the garden, we have sweet peas nearly seven feet high, and their blossoms rustle in the sun, like Peacocks' tails. We have a honey-suckle that would be the finest in the world — if that were not at Gad's Hill. The house is invisible at a few yards' distance, hidden in roses and geraniums. The little bird is gradually getting less afraid of his thimble, and draws a world of water this hot weather. He hangs in the drawing room now, with the other two birds; and a tremendous sensation was created yesterday just before dinner by his being found hanging by the leg, upside down, in the cord from which one of their cages depends — twirling round and round as if he were roasting for a course of poultry. It took about half an hour to untwist him. He was prodigiously ruffled, and staggered about as if he had been to the public house; but soon recovered.

I crossed from Folkestone a week ago, and found Townshend [9] on board, fastened up in his carriage, in a feeble wide-awake hat. It was rather windy, and the sea broke pretty heavily over the deck. With sick women lying among his wheels in various attitudes of despair, he looked like an ancient Briton of a weak constitution — say Boadicea's father — in his war-chariot on the field of battle. I could not but mount the Royal Car, and I found it to be perforated in every direction with cupboards, containing every description of physic, old brandy, East India sherry, sandwiches, oranges, cordial waters, newspapers, pocket handkerchiefs, shawls, flannels, telescopes, compasses, repeaters [1] (for ascertaining the hour in the dark), and finger-rings of great value. He was on his way to Lausanne, and he asked me the extraordinary question "how Mrs Williams, the American actress, kept her wig on?" I then perceived that mankind was to be in a conspiracy to believe that he wears his own hair.

Some gravel got into my bath the other morning, and cut my left elbow, deep, in so complicated a manner that I was obliged to send into the town for a surgeon to come and strap it up. This reminds me of the political Surgeons, and of the fearful mess they have made

---

[9] Chauncy Hare Townshend, evidently either painfully susceptible to seasickness or something of a valetudinarian. In the nineteenth century people often traveled *in* their private carriages, both in crossing the Channel and on the railway, having the vehicle hoisted on board ship and lifted onto a flat open truck on the train.

[1] Repeaters were watches with a striking apparatus that sounded the nearest hour when a button was pressed.

of the Peace. But I have never doubted Lord Palmerston to be (considering the age in which he lives) the emptiest impostor and the most dangerous delusion, ever known. Within three months of the peace, here are its main conditions broken and the whole world laughing at us![2] I am as certain that these men will get us conquered at last, as I am that I shall die. We have been feared and hated a long time. To become a jest after that, is a very, very, serious thing. Nobody knows what the English people will be when they wake up at last and find it out. (N.B. This is the gravel that gets into my mind).
    Love from all

                              ∽

240.   SEPTEMBER 8, 1856, TAVISTOCK HOUSE
    We have all come home from Boulogne. A letter of the strongest possible warning, from my friend Dr Olliffe[3] at Paris, induced me to send the children home a fortnight ago. The rest of us have followed by driblets, and I have brought up the rear. You will have seen in the papers, I dare say, that poor Mr a Beckett died there, unconscious that one of his children lay dead in the next room. He was a very conscientious man and an admirable magistrate, and is a real loss.
    I hope to get out to Shepherd's Bush on Wednesday, and forthwith to re-establish the regular meetings. After a plunge of four and twenty hours duration among the wrecks of my dismantled study, I have hap-

---

[2] The main provisions in the peace established by the Congress of Paris (February 25–March 30, 1856) that ended the Crimean War were: the neutralization of the Black Sea, the guaranteeing of Turkey against foreign aggression, the cession by Russia of the mouths of the Danube and a part of Bessarabia to Rumania, and Russia's surrender of her claims to a protectorate over the Christians in Turkey. Within a few months Russia had men-of-war in the Black Sea and was again interfering in Turkish affairs. Dickens called Palmerston "the twirling Weathercock," and, steadfast in the violence of his disgust with the Prime Minister, regarded these violations as only another proof of his incompetence. He was not alone, however, in thinking that the political surgeons who sewed up the peace had made a mess of their operations.

[3] Sir Joseph Francis Olliffe (1808–1869), physician, educated at Paris and took his M.D. there in 1840, practiced medicine in the French capital, became physician to the British Embassy in 1852, and was knighted at Buckingham Palace 1853. In 1841 he married Laura, the daughter and heiress of Sir William Cubitt (1785–1861), a distinguished civil engineer — not to be confused with William Cubitt, the builder previously mentioned, who became Lord Mayor of London. Dickens was on warmly cordial terms with both Olliffe and Lady Olliffe. The physician's warning on the occasion was against the dangers of a cholera epidemic that had broken out in Boulogne.

pily fished up all the fragments of that noble ship and pieced them together. The neat result is afloat again, and looks none the worse. I am sorry to say that Katey has come home the worse for her absence, and is very far from well. She has a bad cough, and lost her usual pretty looks with extraordinary suddenness. I was very anxious for her to be seen by Dr Watson,[4] but we found him out of town and not expected back for a month or six weeks. So I sent her in the meantime to Dr Hastings, who says she will come right. The noble Baby, after having been the admiration of our gallant neighbours, and the most popular person in Boulogne, has returned to defy competition at home.

We all send kindest regard to Mrs Brown and I am ever my Dear Miss Coutts

◦◦

241. SEPTEMBER 26, 1856, TAVISTOCK HOUSE

I grieve to say that I must deny myself a holiday tomorrow. Destiny seems to be against my coming to Prospect Hill. After having been greatly put-out by the unexpected necessity of chopping and changing at Boulogne, I have come home to such an immense arrear of demands on my attention, that I am falling behind-hand with that reserve of Little Dorrit which has kept me easy during its progress, and to lose which would be a serious thing.[5] All the week I have been hard at it with a view to tomorrow; but I have not been in a quick vein (which is not to be commanded), and have made but tardy way. If I stick to it resolutely now, next week will bring me up. If I let a day go now, there is no saying when I may work round again and come right. You will see what a hard necessity it is that makes me decide so much against my wishes.

With kind regard to Mrs Brown

◦◦

242. OCTOBER 3, 1856, TAVISTOCK HOUSE

This is briefly in answer to your kind and considerate note of this morning — briefly, for your sake, not mine.

---

[4] I have not identified either Dr. Watson or Dr. Hastings, mentioned a few lines below. Katey rapidly recovered from her indisposition — which had nothing to do with the cholera — and by mid-October was rehearsing in *The Frozen Deep* with Charley and Mamey, all three of whom, Dickens said, went "through fearful drill under their rugged parent."

[5] *Little Dorrit* still had nine months to run. Throughout most of it Dickens was three installments ahead of publication.

Your remark upon the Deed,[6] I have replied to, for the sake of clearness and having all the case together, in a note to Mrs Brown which accompanies this.

I have no doubt that it will be best for Walter to go out at once. I believe it will be far better for his health, and certainly for his spirits, and no less for his duties. The staying with his brothers and sisters with that unsettled purpose on him and cloud of departure hanging over him, would do him no good and would be (I much suspect from what I see of him), a kind of cruelty. Mr Brackenbury reports that he will be ready for his examination next March, when he will just have turned his Sixteenth year. With a little holiday here, I should like him to be considered ready to go out. His Presidency [7] (if I can choose it?) is of course the Presidency you recommended.

Perhaps you will kindly tell Mr Lock [8] this, as he knows you, and does me the great service for your sake.

Immense excitement was occasioned here last night by the arrival of Mr Collins in a breathless state, with the first two acts of his play in three. Dispatches were sent off to Brighton, to announce the fact. Charley exhibited an insane desire to copy it. There was talk of a Telegraph message to Mr Stanfield in Wales. It is called The Frozen Deep, and is extremely clever and interesting — very serious and very curious.

❧

243.   NOVEMBER 15, 1856, TAVISTOCK HOUSE

I return Derry.[9] I have no doubt it's a capital article, but it's a mortal dull color. Color these people always want, and color (as allied to fancy), I would always give them. In these cast-iron and mechanical days, I think even such a garnish to the dish of their monotonous and hard lives, of unspeakable importance. One color, and that of the earth

---

[6] The deed of gift establishing Mrs. Brown's medical prize in memory of her husband.

[7] British India was divided into the three great presidencies of Madras, Bombay, and Bengal. Walter went to Bengal, which stretches through northern and central India to Calcutta on the eastern coast.

[8] Unidentified.

[9] "Derry" was a cotton material from which Miss Coutts proposed that overalls and other articles of clothing be made for the inhabitants of the Home at Shepherd's Bush. There are several swatches in different dull colors attached to the original letter, and very drab they all are. It is characteristic of Dickens's unceasing emphasis on the importance of color and imagination in peoples' lives that he insists on the desirability of brightness even in these utilitarian garments.

earthy, is too much with them early and late. Derry might just as well break out into a stripe, or put forth a bud, or even burst into a full blown flower. Who is Derry that he is to make quakers of us all, whether we will or no!

You will immediately hear from Mr Wills, with all the information you want, drawn fresh from the fountainhead.[1]

At Shepherd's on Wednesday, all were in excellent order. Mr Dyer[2] and I represented the august Committee. It was very pleasant to see Louisa Cooper, nicely dressed and looking very well to do, sitting with Mrs Macartney in the Long room. She brought me for a present, the most hideous Ostrich's Egg ever laid — wrought all over with frightful devices, the most tasteful of which represents Queen Victoria (with her crown on) standing on the top of a Church receiving professions of affection from a British Seaman.

How long are you going to stay in Devonshire? And don't you mean to come to town at Christmas Time? I always want to know, and you never will tell me.

With kind regard to Mrs Brown
[P.S.] I re-open this to say that I have just received the enclosed from Mr Macready,[3] who is very anxious indeed that you should have it. Would you like Mr Wills to see the boy, and give him a suit of clothes?

ᴐᴖᴑ

244.   DECEMBER 4, 1856, TAVISTOCK HOUSE

I have gone over the additional MS, and hope I have made it quite plain. I enclose my draft. You will observe at the bottom of page 2, that I have used this expression:

— "distinctly shewing how much a workman receiving so much pr week at so many years of age, *could, by properly investing a steady saving from it, accumulate in five years.*" — This I suppose to be the effect of the calculation referred to?

Enclosed, you will also find the Christmas No. I am the Captain of the Golden Mary; Mr Collins is the Mate.[4] We are out very early,

---

[1] Unexplained.

[2] I cannot identify Mr. Dyer beyond the fact that he was a William T. Dyer to whom Dickens wrote on June 3, 1856, telling him that a girl named Mason was to be admitted to the Home from the Elizabeth Fry Refuge.

[3] William Charles Macready, the actor; the enclosure has not been identified.

[4] The extra Christmas number of *Household Words* for 1856 was *The Wreck of the "Golden Mary,"* of which Dickens wrote the first section, "The Wreck,"

as I want it to get all over England Ireland and Scotland, a good fortnight before Christmas Day.

With love to Mrs Brown

[P.S.] It is freezing, thawing, and snivelling. It is also densely foggy. Nobody can stand in the streets, and nobody can quite fall. Mr Stanfield, after undergoing unspeakable perils in the passage from Hampstead, is being held on a board fixed between two tall ladders (on account of Rheumatism, held) by two carpenters.[5] It is exactly like a shabby coat of arms.

⌒

245. DECEMBER 9, 1856, TAVISTOCK HOUSE

I send you the last addition, enclosed. I omitted to say the other day that I thoroughly agree with you on that point of sending girls to school. There is a vast deal of Kayshuttleworthian nonsense written, sung, and said, on that subject; and I turn into a Man-Trap on it very often, and seize unsuspicious holders-forth by the leg, when they supposed themselves to be promenading among flower beds.

Beauty and the Beast[6] are therefore united, amidst the cheers of thousands, as they were in the story.

I should not like to give you an opinion on the arrangement of the little book, without having it complete before me. But when I have the sheets, I hope I shall put it into the most orderly and convenient form it can be made to take.

Charley will be very proud indeed of a letter from you. I shall not tell him you are going to write, in order that he may have the additional pleasure of a surprise.

You delight me by what you say of the Golden Mary. It strikes me as the prettiest Christmas No we have had; and I think the way

---

and the hymn in the second section, and Collins wrote the second and third sections, "The Beguilement in the Boats" and "The Deliverance."

[5] Stanfield was painting the scenery for the second and third acts of *The Frozen Deep*, and William Telbin, a well-known scenic artist who had supplied one of the scenes for *Not So Bad as We Seem* in 1851, was doing the scene for the first act. "Nothing," Dickens wrote Collins on November 1, "could induce Telbin, yesterday, to explain what he was going to do before Stanfield; and nothing would induce Stanfield to explain what *he* was going to do before Telbin." The following month, writing to Macready, Dickens pictures "Stanfield perpetually elevated on planks and splashing himself from head to foot, Telbin requiring impossibilities of swart gasmen, and a legion of prowling nondescripts forever shirking in and out."

[6] Another of those personal touches so rare in Dickens's letters to Miss Coutts.

in which John Steadiman [7] (to whom I shall give your message) has got over the great difficulty of falling into my idea, naturally, is very meritorious indeed. Of course he could not begin until I had finished; and when he read the Wreck he was so desperately afraid of the job, that I began to mistrust him. However, we went down to Gad's Hill and walked through Cobham Woods, to talk it over; and he then went at it cheerfully, and came out as you see. I wish you would read a Petition to the Novel Writers (by him) in last week's Household Words.[8] It strikes me as uncommonly droll, and shrewdly true.

And now I come round to his play — must do it — can't help it. I really cannot bear that it should pass over, without your seeing it. Mr Stanfield's part in the thing will never be seen again, for I am sorry to say he is getting infirm and ill. Nor do I think (if I may say so) that anything like the thing itself will ever be seen again. I have put up a wooden house at the back of the schoolroom (my own architect!) to help the effect, and the stage is 30 feet long. You would be quite charmed, I think, with the girls; and there is a tenderness pervading the whole design which I believe would thoroughly interest and please you. There are no reminders in the place, for it is utterly changed and different. You would have no idea where you were. Finally, I am quite sure (you may suppose I have watched it a little), that its whole influence is softening and good, and that if Mrs Brown could be induced to come, she would afterwards be glad of having done so. Now, I don't suggest her coming when the place would be full of people she knows; but on the night before Twelfth Night, Monday the 5th [9] we do it exactly as it will be done on Twelfth Night, in the minutest respect; and only our tradespeople and the servants' relations come. Couldn't you two sit beside Mrs Dickens that night? Do think of it. It made me quite unhappy last night, looking at Mary, to reflect that you would not see something that seems so fresh and wholesome to me.

---

[7] John Steadiman is the chief mate of the *Golden Mary,* and the narrator of all the later part of the story, most of which was written by Wilkie Collins — hence the name is here used to mean Collins, upon whose handling of the tale Miss Coutts's message had evidently made complimentary remark.

[8] "A Petition to the Novel Writers," *Household Words,* December 6, 1856, a lightly satiric article by Collins, partly deriding those who profess to regard the reading of fiction as a dangerous, time-wasting, and immoral luxury, and partly poking fun at various clichés of characterization in novels.

[9] January 5, 1857.

246.   DECEMBER 13, 1856, TAVISTOCK HOUSE

As we have now both relieved our minds on the subject of the Play, I cheerfully leave the rest to the result that opens out. I could not quite give you up without a struggle; but, having made it, I can be as quiet as a lamb. If you tell me on the morning of the Fifth that you are coming, either alone or with Mrs Brown, I shall have the happiness of expecting you. If you do not, I shall know that you could not see your way to it — and with a perfect faith in your seeing clearly out of kind eyes, shall want no sort of explanation.[1]

Beauty is mistaken in supposing Beast to have retained any scrap of matter, either printed or in manuscript. Beast appeals to habits of order and method as yet unchallenged by Beauty — lays his paw upon his heart — and declares upon his honor, to the best of his knowledge information and belief, "*Not Guilty.*"

B was at S.B.[2] the other day, and held Committee in due form. All most satisfactory. He begs to send his love to Mrs B(rown).

247.   JANUARY 2, 1857, TAVISTOCK HOUSE [TO MRS. BROWN]

Shall we say, one o'clock tomorrow? I will be ready for you at that hour. The preparations, however, are very difficult to understand in the day; because they have been made by the Painters, for their purposes, extraordinarily ingenious, and require the carpenters to handle them and put them together.[3]

---

[1] Miss Coutts's objections, not to the theater, but to Dickens's engaging in amateur theatricals, was deep-rooted and persistent — it was expressed as early as 1851, when he was planning the presentations of *Not So Bad as We Seem* — but nothing in this correspondence reveals her reasons. It is possible though unprovable that she had an uneasy suspicion of what was indeed the fact, that he used the excitements of these dramatic enterprises as an emotional safety valve of distraction from the increasing unhappiness of his relationship with his wife. By the time of *The Lighthouse*, in June 1855, Dickens was no longer even justifying them either by any charitable purpose or by connecting them with the Twelfth Night festivities. Ultimately, on the present occasion, as is shown by his letter to Mrs. Brown on January 2, 1857, Miss Coutts surrendered and agreed to come to the preliminary performance of *The Frozen Deep* on the evening of January 5.

[2] "B" is, of course, Beast, and "S.B." Shepherd's Bush. Playfully realizing that in this context the abbreviation "Mrs. B.," immediately below, is somewhat ambiguous, after writing it Dickens therefore adds in parentheses the remaining letters of the name.

[3] Mrs. Brown had obviously refused to accompany Miss Coutts even to the advance performance, and Dickens was still trying to persuade her to witness the play at this evening's rehearsal, or, failing that, at least to see the stage settings. Possibly Mrs. Brown's refusal was motivated by her still being in mourning for

I should very much like you only to see a Sunset — far better than anything that has ever been done at the Diorama or any such place. There is a Rehearsal tonight (no one here but the company), and this Sunset, which begins the play, will be visible at a quarter before 8; lasting ten minutes. If you came, you need speak to nobody but Georgina and me — and nobody need so much as see you to recognize you. But I don't press you, and don't look for any answer.

Tomorrow at One, if I don't see you in the meanwhile. That's all.

Ever your faithful

[P.S.] Miss Coutts and Lady Falmouth, Catherine will expect on Monday at 1/2 past 7. I am delighted to hear of their coming.

∽

248.   JANUARY 14, 1857, TAVISTOCK HOUSE [TO MRS. BROWN]

The letter printed in the little paragraph[4] I return, is perfectly delightful. The ship is true to her name, and I trust in God will go about the world prosperously, doing good, as long as she floats. It is one of those exquisitely touching and affecting things that make one smile and cry together.

I do not myself doubt the good result of the enquiry at the hospital; nor do I, I must add, doubt the gentlemen engaged in it. If there be a conscientious and humane body of men in existence, I am convinced they are to be found among the honorable and upright medical men who have attained eminence in London. Whatsoever I have seen of them has won my utmost respect; and I am all but sure that those of them who are associated with St George's Hospital can have no desire but to do their duty. Consequently I have a strong trust in their putting this matter right for the future — just as I have in your scholarship helping to raise up worthy successors to them.

I am delighted to hear that Mr Marjoribanks was so much pleased by the Play.[5] Its effect on the three other audiences we have had, has

her husband, which would explain Dickens's assurance in the following paragraph that she need speak to no one and be recognized by nobody. The lighting effects of the opening scene, which Dickens had devised himself, simulated the changing hours of the day, from bright sunlight through crimson sunset to the gray of twilight and the misty blue of night.

[4] On the envelope of this letter there is a note, presumably written by Mrs. Brown, reading: "Mr Dickens Jay 15 1857 returning paragraph concerning the ship Angela Burdett Coutts."

[5] The first night of The Frozen Deep was on January 6, 1857 — Charley's twentieth birthday — and there were three repeat performances on January 8, 12, and

been the same; and I certainly have never seen people so strongly affected by theatrical means. Tonight is our closing night. By an absurd coincidence three fourths of the Judges I know, preferred this night to another. Please to imagine the Lord Chief Justice, the Lord Chief Baron, Mr Baron Bramwell, and Mr Justice Willes, all sitting on the front row tonight, to try the case. Cockburn the new Chief Justice of the Common Pleas,[6] rather spoils the effect of the absurdity in having been here on Monday. He wouldn't go after the Play, but would come and make speeches at the Green Room Supper. I never saw anything better of its kind than the genuine and hearty way in which, without the least affectation, he shewed his pleasure.

ल्ल

249.   FEBRUARY 3, 1857, TAVISTOCK HOUSE

I have no doubt that your excellent interposition will cause the Hospital to manage these sad matters (clearly, I take it, mismanaged before), in a better way.[7] But I am sorry in the letter to you which I now return, to observe, either carelessness or dishonesty. I recollect my written summary distinctly and I do most positively declare — not only

---

14. Close to one hundred people crowded the little schoolroom theater each evening. Dickens's performance as the tragically heroic lover Richard Wardour was so heart-rending that his fellow actors themselves were in tears and members of the audience sobbed audibly. After an intermission the spectators found him as sidesplittingly comic in Buckstone's farce of *Uncle John* as he had been pathetic.

[6] The Lord Chief Justice was John Campbell (1779–1861), first Baron Campbell, who played a leading part in law reform, become Solicitor-General 1832, Attorney-General 1834–1841, Lord Chancellor of Ireland 1841, and succeeded Denman as Lord Chief Justice when he retired in 1850. Campbell published *Nisi Prius Reports* 1809–1816, *Speeches* 1842, *Lives of the Lord Chancellors* 1845–1857, and *Lives of the Chief Justices* 1849, 1857, and his *Lives* of Lyndhurst and Brougham were posthumously published in 1869. The Lord Chief Baron was Sir Jonathan Frederick Pollock (1783–1870), K.C. 1827, who was knighted 1834, became Attorney-General in Peel's first administration 1834–1835 and in his second 1841–1844, and was Chief Baron of the Exchequer 1844–1866. Sir George William Wilshere Bramwell (1808–1892), Q.C. 1851, served on a commission resulting in the Companies Act 1856, became a judge of the Exchequer and was knighted 1856, later Lord Justice 1867–1881, and raised to the peerage 1882. Sir James Shaw Willes (1814–1872) was a member of the commission on common law procedure 1850–1854, was knighted and appointed judge of Common Pleas 1855; later served on commissions on Indian law 1861 and English and Irish law 1862. Sir Alexander James Edmund Cockburn (1802–1880) was knighted and became Solicitor-General 1850 and Attorney-General 1851–1856; he had just successfully concluded the prosecution in the Palmer poisoning case and been made Chief Justice of Common Pleas 1856. He became Lord Chief Justice in 1859.

[7] I have been unable to learn any more about this hospital case of mismanagement than is inferable from the letter itself, and I have not identified Mrs. Bragg.

that it did *not* represent Mrs Bragg to have seen the body in the Hospital — which she plainly stated to me she did not — but, in so many clear words, described it to have been seen by the two men, who, after having dressed it as they best could, *took it to her*. In such a case as this, of all others, there is no defence for carelessness, and it is excessively suspicious. If I were conducting the case, I would most decidedly put them in the wrong on their own Resolution and make them acknowledge it. I don't say you should do so — your position being so different — but I would allow no body of men on Earth to deal so grossly with me as to make their own misrepresentation and then coolly contradict it as mine. I have never seen a worse thing of this kind in my life. The connexion of the word "exaggerated" with the only hint in its support — that is, that Mrs Bragg never saw the body — which you never represented that she did, is Old Bailey from the crown of its head to the sole of its foot — or, untidy and slipshod muddling.

I will go to the Bishop of Exeter [8] on Monday morning; until when, my mornings will be occupied. Publicly, I think he has done about as much harm to real Christian brotherhood and good will by his uniform conduct since he has been a Bishop as any mere mortal man could well do in his lifetime. Privately, I can of course have no other feeling towards him than that you commend him, and that is enough. I will explain everything to him with my utmost pains.

(I find the foregoing two sides and a half, have a savage aspect! I now subside into ethereal mildness.)

The drainage at Shepherd's Bush has got all at once into such a dreadful condition, fraught with so much danger of sickness to the Inmates, that I was obliged on Saturday, after referring the matter to the Builder, to give him directions for going to work to remove the evil, instantly. I was really afraid to wait, to refer the matter to you (the parlor had then become uninhabitable and the whole house was fast becoming so); and I knew besides, that it must unfortunately be

---

[8] Henry Phillpotts (1778–1869), educated at Oxford, chaplain to the Bishop of Durham 1808, Prebendary of Durham 1809, and Bishop of Exeter 1829. He indeed represented in public life everything that Dickens detested. As a writer on public questions from 1819 on, he had defended the existing poor laws and supported the Government's praise of the Peterloo Massacre, opposed Catholic emancipation, come into collision with Earl Grey about the Tithes Bill of 1831, and fought the Reform Bill of 1832. He was a strict disciplinarian and a High-churchman. Almost the only point he and Dickens had in common was that neither had any sympathy with the Oxford Movement.

done. I am going out there today, to see how they are getting on.

I read your letter at breakfast (with great gravity and a general rustic sensation which I associated with the field and a vague idea of a syllabub in the garden), to the effect that "Mr Tennant will probably speak about a C O W." Coming shortly afterwards to an unknown girl in the country (otherwise unintroduced) I found it was CASE.

I don't know who wrote the African articles in the Times [9]; but I will enquire, and tell you. Without at all disparaging Dr Livingstone or in the least doubting his facts, I think however that his deductions must be received with great caution. The history of all African effort, hitherto, is a history of wasted European life, squandered European money, and blighted European hope — in which the generous English have borne a great share. That it would be a great thing to cultivate that cotton and be independent of America, no one can doubt; but I think that happy end, with all its attendant good results, must be sought in India. There are two tremendous obstacles in Africa; one, the climate; the other, the people.

It rejoices me to hear such good news of Nova Scotia.[1]

With kind regard to Mrs Brown, Ever Dear Miss Coutts, Most Faithfully Yours,

P.S. The wildest legends are circulating about town, to the effect that the Queen proposes to ask to have The Frozen Deep at Windsor.[2] I have heard nothing of it otherwise, but slink about holding my breath. Please don't say anything about fine weather when you write. It is too much to bear.

◌◌

250.   FEBRUARY 6, 1857, TAVISTOCK HOUSE

No. I *won't* look upon it [3] in extremis, — but I have an indignant objection to anything like unfair dealing, which puts my blood up to

---

[9] The African articles in the London *Times,* appearing during October, November, and December 1856, excited much attention. Among the questions with which they dealt were the exploration of central Africa, the peculiarities of Africa, Algiers, and the French, and an attack on the Kabyles (the modern Riffs). Dickens's attitude toward the exploitation of Africa is further implied by his satiric portrayal in *Bleak House* of Mrs. Jellyby and her interest in the Borioboola-Gha and by his article "The Niger Expedition" in the *Examiner,* August 19, 1848, criticizing European attempts at the colonization of Africa.

[1] News of progress on the housing project at Nova Scotia Gardens.

[2] As the following letter shows, these rumors were not without foundation, but nothing came of the idea at the moment.

[3] The hospital case discussed in the preceding letter.

boiling point. A blow would not incense me more than a shuffle.

I knew of Mrs Bragg's having offered the money, but wholly separated it from the Hospital treatment of the Dead, because it had nothing to do with it. If *you* had connected the two things, they would instantly have told you that they had no connexion.

The drainage [4] is distinctly our business (I am sorry to say), the main drain being provided. What is being done will cost, according to estimate, from Thirty to Forty Pounds. But I am pretty sure that when you see what it is, you will think the money well spent. We must have had illness without it. It is surprising that some obstinate disorder had not already broken out.

The gas is now at the gate. Would you like it taken into the house? The expense will be the usual fittings and nothing more. If we had it at all, I would recommend a jet in the fanlight, kitchen, wash-house, bathroom, over the chimney piece in each bedroom. Then no light would Ever be carried about the house. Just as we do here.

Between ourselves, I too should feel a little jealous of our own specialty if it should turn out that the Queen resolves to make that request. [5] I *know* now, that she strongly entertains the idea. However, I should of course stipulate for as complete mastery and inaccessibility on the stage, as if we were at home — and should put a cheerful and dutiful face on the matter. Mr Collins would like it very much, thinking it would express to the Theatres that they are not doing their duty, and that their noble Art is sliding away from them. He is of course a great consideration, and, knowing his feeling, I am ready with my reply if I should have occasion to give one.

With love to Mrs Brown

∽

251.   FEBRUARY 14, 1857, TAVISTOCK HOUSE

I have the necessary form of certificates to fill in before Walter goes up for his examination [6]; and it seems to me that you are the proper person to fill up *The First* on the 3rd page of this form. Will you do so, if you see no objection? I was going to fill it up myself, and had almost written on it, when — reading it again — it appeared to me that I ought to ask you. You will see that the first blank in the certificate is for the Presidency.

---

[4] At Urania Cottage.
[5] That a private performance of *The Frozen Deep* be given for her.
[6] Walter took the examination April 7, 1857.

Yesterday at the Zoological Gardens I saw (accidentally, for I had no idea of such a thing until I got into the room), the Serpents being fed with live birds, Guinea Pigs, rabbits, etc. A most horrible spectacle, and I have ever since been turning the legs of all the tables and chairs into serpents and seeing them feed upon all possible and impossible small creatures.

ono

252.   APRIL 9, 1857, WAITE'S HOTEL, GRAVESEND

I am working here for a few days (that I may have an eye on the little repairs at Gad's Hill), and must thank you for your letter. Not that I thought you "queer" for not writing sooner. You must be very much queerer than that, to be queer in my mind!

My uneasiness on the Dress point, arose, first of all, from the nature of the girls' remarks.[7] I do not feel them to be true, and I have a very great misgiving that they were written against nature, under the impression that they would have a moral aspect. I attach no blame to the young women — have not a doubt that they deceived themselves far more than they will ever deceive anybody else — and believe them to have written in a love of commendation; in a rather more disagreeable phase of it than a love of dress would shew.

I have also long felt the question to be an excessively difficult one. Apart from what you so gently and delightfully write in your letter (you must not mind my praising it, because it really does charm me),

---

[7] This is a reference to some of the prize essays on "Dress" among those others on "Common Things," which had been published in a little book. Dickens had disagreed with Miss Coutts by criticizing their tone. "I think them not natural — " he had written her on March 5, 1857, " — overdone — full of a conventional sort of surface morality — disagreeably like one another — and, in short, just as affected as they claim to be unaffected. Catherine Stanley (page 36) who finds out that the reason for not liking a little bit of finery — which almost every young person on earth does, remember — human nature is 'a common thing,' and it is no use to dream of putting it aside — Catherine, I say, who finds out that the reason for not liking it and putting it on, is, that she will be 'more really admired' without it, ought to be her successor — Miss Sly. I should call Catherine the only honest person of those seven.

"With these exceptions — respecting which I nail my flag to the mast with a tenpenny nail at each corner — I have been greatly interested in, and pleased with, the whole book. And I heartily congratulate you upon it."

Although Dickens said that Miss Coutts would probably exclaim to Mrs. Brown, "What a queer man he is! what odd ideas he has sometimes!" his comment in the present letter on her reply makes it clear that he must have convinced her of the justice of his views.

of that little womanly vanity and desire to please, which a wisdom in comparison with which the best of our lights are mere ignorance and folly, has implanted in women, as one of their distinguishing marks, for the happiness of mankind; I have to add an observation which I believe to be a true one. I constantly notice a love of color and brightness, to be a portion of a generous and fine nature. I feel sure that it is often an innocent part of a capacity for enjoyment, and appreciation, and general adornment of everything, which makes a buoyant, hopeful, genial character. I say most gravely that I do *not* know what I may take away from the good influences of a poor man's home, if I strike this natural common thing out of the girl's heart who is going to be his wife.

It is like the use of strong drinks or the use of strong anything. The evil is in the abuse, and not in the use. The distinction between the two, and the perception of the medium in which taste and propriety are to be found, is the result — one of the results — of a generally good, sound, plain Education. The natural tendency of the sex through all its grades, is to a little finery — and I would not run counter to that (I make bold to say), agreeable, wholesome, and useful characteristic. The frivolous women of a better degree who disgust you and all sensible people, have really had no Education whatever that deserves the name.

You will I know be glad to hear that Walter appeared here yesterday, radiant and gleaming. He passed his examination on Tuesday in a most creditable manner, and was one of a small number of boys out of a large number, who emerged from the ordeal triumphant. I have now taken order for his learning to swim, to ride, to fence, to become acquainted with the use of gun and pistol, and to "go in" for a trifle of Hindustanee, in the course of the three months he will probably remain at home.[8] I started him up again last night to his brothers and sisters (Mary, Katey, and Charley are keeping house), laden with his credentials to the different professors of these arts. He was perfectly happy, and they had received him with torrents of applause, and he was very anxious that I should "tell Miss Coutts that he hadn't been spun" — which means, rejected.

Mr Waite, who is one of my particular friends (and whom you liked, I remember) is in great force, and his house is as orderly and

---

[8] Walter was to sail for India on the *Indus* on July 20.

comfortable as ever. If you don't like Gad's Hill, I shall set it on fire —
particularly as it is insured. I have devised an immense number of
small inventions, which it will require a summer's day for you and
Mrs Brown to appreciate. There *is* a little study (I am sorry to say
that the merit of hewing it out of a china closet is Mr Austin's) which —
but you must see it.[9] According to Charley's plans, Walter is to de-
stroy his constitution at cricket in the field, before starting for India;
which will be a great comfort to him. Mrs Dickens and Georgina and
the two little boys are with me, and send best love to you and Mrs
Brown. I add mine, and am ever dear Miss Coutts
P.S. Very much interested in the Geologist.[1]

~

253.   JUNE 3, 1857, GAD'S HILL PLACE
Would Thursday, Friday, or Saturday, *in next week* suit you for a
day here? If neither will do, will you and Mrs Brown appoint your
own day, in the week following. You come from London Bridge Station
(North Kent Railway) to Higham — the station next beyond Graves-
end. A manly figure will of course be awaiting you on the platform.
The train that I think will be most convenient to you, starts at *12*.
Take return tickets, unless you will stay a day or two with us. I have
some faint hopes that you might do even that!
Hans Christian Andersen [2] may perhaps be with us, but you won't

---

[9] The main alteration Dickens made at Gad's Hill was raising the roof on the
garden side to allow the insertion of two third-floor bedrooms facing that way.
The study was on the ground floor, to the right of the small entrance porch. Dickens went on tinkering with the little estate throughout the rest of his life — installing
a schoolroom above the carriage house, enlarging the living room, changing the
breakfast room to a billiard room, building a croquet ground in the old walled
orchard, adding an eight-acre meadow at the rear, constructing a new staircase with
a parquet landing. The last time his daughter Katey saw him, a few days before
he died, he had just completed a conservatory opening from the living room and
dining room, and joked, "Well, Katey, you now see POSITIVELY the last improvement at Gad's Hill!"
[1] Unidentified.
[2] Hans Christian Andersen (1805–1875), the famous Danish writer of fairy
tales. Lady Blessington had introduced him to Dickens at Gore House in 1847, at
which time Dickens had given Andersen a set of his books; a little later Andersen
had dedicated one of his to Dickens. Throughout the intervening years Andersen
had become an adoring admirer. In April 1857, hearing from the Dane that he
was visiting England for a fortnight, Dickens immediately replied inviting him to
stay at Gad's Hill. Arriving in June, Andersen settled down and remained Dickens's guest for five weeks, oscillating happily between Gad's Hill and Tavistock

mind *him* — especially as he speaks no language but his own Danish, and is suspected of not even knowing that.

With love to Mrs Brown and looking for your answer

～

254.   JUNE 20, 1857, GAD'S HILL PLACE
As you and I had a little talk here about the Frozen Deep, in which your kindness and sense were as conspicuous as they always are — and as deeply felt by me as they are always are — I am anxious to let you know what has since passed about it with the Queen.[3]

I had written (at the time we spoke together) to Colonel Phipps[4]

House. His reverence for Dickens was boundless, he thought Catherine charming with her "china blue eyes" and "womanly repose" — he was innocently unaware of the strained feelings between them — and he found all the children delightful to play with in the nearby field of clover. Catherine took him to see Ristori as Lady Macbeth and to hear Handel's *Messiah* sung to an audience of 12,000 in the Crystal Palace, the vast glass-walled fane of which seemed to him like Aladdin's palace; Dickens invited him to the performance of *The Frozen Deep* given before the Queen on July 4, 1857; and Miss Coutts, at her mansion in Stratton Street, saw that he met all the fashionable world.

[3] On June 8, 1857, Dickens's friend Douglas Jerrold died, leaving his family not exactly indigent but in far from prosperous circumstances. Old affection, generous sympathy, and the burning need for distraction that gave Dickens no peace, all made one idea leap impetuously into his mind. They must raise a fund; there must be a series of performances — revivals of Jerrold's *Black-Eyed Susan* and *Rent Day*, a lecture by Thackeray, readings by Dickens, and, of course, a benefit revival of *The Frozen Deep*. A committee was quickly formed, rooms taken for the series in the Gallery of Illustration in Regent Street, and the Queen asked to give her name in support.

[4] Sir Charles Beaumont Phipps (1801–1866), equerry to Queen Victoria, Keeper of the Queen's Purse, and private secretary to the Prince Consort. It was with Colonel Phipps that Dickens had made the arrangements for the Queen's night of *Not So Bad as We Seem* at Devonshire House in 1851. The colonel's elder brother was Constantine Henry Phipps (1797–1863), first Marquis of Normanby, writer and distinguished statesman. Educated at Cambridge, he became M.P. for Scarborough at the age of twenty-one, succeeded his father as Earl of Mulgrave, was made Captain-General and Governor of Jamaica in 1831, became Lord Lieutenant of Ireland 1835, and was created Marquis of Normanby 1838. He was successively Colonial Secretary and Home Secretary in Lord Melbourne's administration, ambassador at Paris 1846–1852, and at Florence 1854–1858.

Dickens knew the entire family well. He became acquainted with Lord Normanby's eldest son, Lord Mulgrave, on the voyage to America in 1842, acted with him in amateur theatricals in Montreal, and formed a warm friendship for him. Lord Normanby presided over a farewell dinner to Dickens just before his departure to Italy in 1844, the two often saw each other during Dickens's stays in Paris in 1846–1847 and 1850, and Dickens dedicated *Dombey and Son* to the Marchioness of Normanby.

in the usual way, stating what I was trying, with others, to do "In remembrance of the late Mr Douglas Jerrold," and adding that I had no poor case to make, or pitiful thing to say — that I had resolved never to travel out of those words. I added that if the Queen would come to see the Frozen Deep, it would be a great honor, etc. To this Phipps replied (as I knew he would), that the Queen could never do anything in that way for the memory of an Individual, as it would involve perpetual engagements or constant grievous offence; but that she very much wanted to see the Play, and could it be done otherwise? Could he and I talk about it? I then went to see him, and he proposed, on the Queen's behalf, its being done at Buckingham Palace. I begged him to represent to the Queen that I felt difficulties on that score — that I should not feel easy as to the social position of my daughters at the Court under such circumstances — and that I would, with all duty and so forth, suggest that the Queen would relieve me of that difficulty by coming, on a private night of her own, to the Gallery of Illustration, and inviting her own guests to see the Play privately. But I added that she had always been most kind and considerate to me on other occasions, and that if she could not act upon my suggestion, we would, however much I might desire to avoid it, go to the Palace. He received it in the best manner, and *she* received it in the best manner; and the result is, that she has a night of her own at the Gallery, a week in advance of the public, on Saturday the 4th of July.[5]

I hope you think this right, as to all parties?

In reference to the point you suggested to me, I spoke confidentially to Collins, who immediately felt with me that your having suggested it or thought of it, at once closed and settled the case. I have turned over in my mind a way of changing the action of that scene; and I think (as you did) that it can be made more affecting and natural, with the change, than without it.

This is all. With kind love to Mrs Brown, Believe me ever

---

[5] Actually the private performance for the Queen preceded the public performances by only four days, the first of these taking place on July 8. Her Majesty's party consisted of some fifty people, among whom was included the King of the Belgians, and Dickens invited some twenty-five guests of his own. The audience "cried and laughed and applauded and made as much demonstration," wrote Georgina Hogarth, as so small a group could. When the curtain fell on the melodrama, though it was past midnight, the Queen forgot her usual preference for early hours in her eagerness to see the farce as well, and gave word that the evening should go on.

255.

I have been obliged to postpone Walter's photograph visit, because, between the outfitter, and the Hindustanee, and the India House, and the Passage preparations, I thought I descried that he was getting dazed, and had best have a few quiet hours with his brothers, just home from Boulogne after a year's absence. I have sent him down to them again today; but tomorrow he will go to King's College. I a little doubt there being time left for him to learn the art to any real purpose — but I have not said this to him; I only say it to you, in order that you may understand that he has not been remiss in his appreciation of your great kindness.[6]

At Shepherd's Bush on Wednesday, all was in excellent order. No complaints or shortcomings of any kind. Alice Matthews however, very poorly again. I went carefully through my proposed alteration, and left instructions with the builder to send me an estimate. When I get it, I will propose an appointment, if you will make one with me, to explain to you exactly what I mean.

I know my plan is a good one — because it is mine! Seriously, I am certain it has the merit of being simple, easy, cheap, rather ingenious, and easily made with the people in the house. It brings in all the existing materials — would make the long room remarkably airy and healthy — would give us a better bedroom (much better) than we now have over it — and a room for a sick girl besides.[7]

At Gad's Hill, we have left off digging for water, and are now boring. I watch the process with the resignation of despair.[8]

---

[6] Apparently the "photograph visit" was connected with an offer from Miss Coutts to have Walter taught the art of photography before his departure for India. The school at Boulogne was conducted by the Reverend James Bewsher and the Reverend M. Gibson. At this time Alfred, Frank, and Sydney were all enrolled there; later Harry also became one of its pupils.

[7] A contemplated remodeling of some of the rooms at Shepherd's Bush, including the "long room" of general assembly.

[8] The well at Gad's Hill ran dry in June 1857 and forced digging for water. In August they were still boring "at the rate of two pounds per day for wages. The men seem to like it very much, and to be perfectly comfortable." When at last, in the middle of the month, they struck water, a pump was needed to get it into the house. "Here are six men perpetually going up and down the well," Dickens lamented, "(I know that somebody will be killed) . . . The process is much more like putting Oxford Street endwise, and laying gas along it, than anything else. By the time it is finished, the cost of this water will be something absolutely frightful." The dug-up garden, the black mud, the drying bath, the delay, and the expense, Dickens exclaimed, were "changing the undersigned honey-pot into a Mad Bull."

We are suffering a good deal from Andersen. The other day we lost him when we came up to the London Bridge Terminus, and he took a cab by himself. The cabman driving him through the new unfinished street at Clerkenwell, he thought he was driving him into remote fastnesses, to rob and murder him. He consequently arrived here with all his money, his watch, his pocketbook and documents, *in his boots* — and it was a tremendous business to unpack him and get them off. I have arrived at the conviction that he cannot speak Danish; and the best of it is, that his Translatress declares he can't — is ready to make oath of it before any magistrate.[9]

With love to Mrs Brown

☙

256. JULY 20, 1857, RADLEY'S HOTEL, SOUTHAMPTON

I hasten to report that I have just now (one o'clock) come back in the Steam Tender, from putting the poor boy on board. He was cut up for a minute or so, when I bade him good bye, and also yesterday morning when he took leave of them in town, and also on Saturday when he left his little brothers [1] at Gad's Hill; but on all three occasions he recovered directly, and conducted himself like a Man. He leaned over the side looking after Charley and me, quite composed and comfortable. He had already found an old schoolfellow on board, and the Captain came away with me to assure me that he should have every possible protection, assistance, and encouragement. He was anxious that I

---

[9] As a guest Andersen gave a good deal of trouble. "His unintelligible vocabulary," Dickens wrote, "was marvellous. In French or Italian, he was Peter the Wild Boy; in English, the Deaf and Dumb Asylum. My eldest boy swears that the ear of man cannot recognize his German; and his translatress declares to Bentley that he can't speak Danish!" Long before he said good-by, Mamey and Katey regarded him as a "bony bore," and when he was gone Dickens stuck a card on his dressing-room mirror, reading "Hans Christian Andersen slept in this room for five weeks which seemed to the family ages." But the household gave his guest no sign of their restiveness, Dickens accompanied him to his train at Maidstone, and the gaunt, angular Dane wept as he "travelled alone in the steam serpent to Folkestone."

[1] The ages of the younger brothers were now: Frank, 13; Alfred, 11; Sydney, 10; Harry, 8; and Edward ("Plorn"), 5. The separation, Dickens felt, was like having "great teeth drawn with a wrench"; it was a mournful thing to realize how Time had "flapped his wings over your head." But Walter was "in good spirits, as little cast down as, at 16, one could reasonably hope to be with the world of India before one." He did gallantly as a soldier, was made a lieutenant before he was eighteen, and was transferred from the 26th Native Infantry to the 42nd Highlanders, but died of hematemesis when he was only twenty-two, on December 31, 1863, just as he was about to return to England on sick leave.

should send his love to you and Mrs Brown, and a thousand thanks to you for your kind letters. I add mine for all your kindness, out of a heart almost full.

I have appointed to meet Mr Bird [2] about my plan, at Shepherd's Bush on Wednesday at 12. As I come back from there, I will take the chance of finding you in Stratton Street.

⌒

257. AUGUST 28, 1857, GAD'S HILL PLACE [TO MRS. BROWN]
The address of that letter to Miss Coutts, which you enclosed me, is about as bad as bad can be. There are not many worse places. However, there may be something in the case for all that; and I have written to Mr Wills upon it (the street is very near the Household Words office), and have told him what I think about it, and have begged him to try to see the writer, straightway.

In Mr Ford's matter,[3] I have caused "A Lady" to be put down for a subscription of Five Pounds.

I have just come back from Manchester, where I have been tearing myself to pieces,[4] to the wonderful satisfaction of thousands of people,

---

[2] I have not identified Mr. Bird. He was probably a carpenter or builder concerned with the alteration of Urania Cottage mentioned in the preceding letter.

[3] Unidentified.

[4] The Manchester performances of *The Frozen Deep* on August 21 and 22 were the last of the Jerrold benefits. The second night there, before a gathering of three thousand, was Dickens's most triumphant appearance in the play. "The trite phrase," wrote Wilkie Collins, "is the true phrase to describe that magnificent piece of acting. He literally electrified the audience."

Although he was "tearing himself to pieces" rendering Richard Wardour's agony and despair, Dickens felt a kind of agitated relief in projecting and symbolizing an emotion not unlike his own. For by now the wretchedness of his married life had become absolutely unbearable. "Low spirits, low pulse, low voice, intense reaction," he lamented. "I want to escape from myself. For when I *do* start up and stare myself seedily in the face . . . my blankness is inconceivable — indescribable — my misery, amazing." To his old friend Forster, who had long known the state of his feelings without speech between them, Dickens at last made desperate confession. "Poor Catherine and I are not made for each other, and there is no help for it. It is not only that she makes me uneasy and unhappy, but that I make her so too — and much more so. . . . God knows she would have been a thousand times happier if she had married another kind of man, and that her avoidance of this destiny would have been at least equally good for both of us. I am often cut to the heart by thinking what a pity it is, for her own sake, that I ever fell in her way . . ."

"What is now befalling me," Dickens wrote in another part of the same letter, "I have seen steadily coming, ever since the days you remember when Mary was born [1838]; and I know too well that you cannot, and no one can, help me.

with Neuralgia — or something like it — in my face half the time. That work is now over, and more than two thousand Guineas are in store for the widow and daughter.

Last Saturday week, the well-workmen here burst at last upon a beautiful spring of bright clear water which is reported to be exhaustless. I am now having a pump made to pump it up. When the first glassful is drunk at the surface, it will have cost £200. But of course there was no going on without it, and I comfort myself (as well as I can) with the reflection that the spring might have lain much deeper, or might not have been at all.

The restlessness which is the penalty of an imaginative life and constitution — we all hold whatever we possess, on the strict tenure that it must and shall be used — so besets me just now, that I feel as if the scaling of all the Mountains in Switzerland, or the doing of any wild thing until I dropped, would be but a slight relief. The vague unhappiness which tracks a life of constant aim and ever impels to some new aim in which it may be lost, is so curious to consider, that I observe it in myself sometimes, with as much curiosity as if I were another man. Wonderful to think how wise the ordering of it is, and how it works to the doing of what is to be done!

Walter has written from Gibralter and Malta. Quite well, and wonderfully settled to his new life. He does not seem, as yet, to have a backward glance or regret. Will you kindly ask Miss Coutts from me whether the Enclosed refers to *that* helmet? [5] I am quite at a loss to understand it, and only get the idea into my head as I write, that it may possibly be so.

All here unite in kind love and regard.

ᙣ

258.   SEPTEMBER 5, 1857, GAD'S HILL PLACE
I think I would head the paper AN INDEPENDENT AND USEFUL CAREER FOR YOUNG WOMEN OF THE MIDDLE CLASSES. — such a heading as that,

---

Why I have even written I hardly know; but it is a miserable sort of comfort that you should be clearly aware how matters stand." Forster responded underlining Dickens's confession that the shortcomings were not all on Catherine's side, reminding him that his own temperament was impatient, overintense. "To the most part of what you say," Dickens answered, " — Amen. . . . I claim no immunity from blame. There is plenty of fault on my side, I daresay, in the way of a thousand uncertainties, caprices, and difficulties of disposition; but only one thing will alter that, and that is, the end which alters everything."

    [5] Unexplained.

something to that effect, arrests the attention directly. So much Boredom and Red Tape, and what I may call Kayshuttleworry, are associated with the word "Education," that I fear it might repel readers.

The paper itself is very good indeed. Very plain, very easily remembered, very direct to the purpose.

Apprehensive, like Mrs Brown, of the moist valleys, I have decided on a foray into the bleak fells of Cumberland. So the idle apprentices [6] go to Carlisle on Monday.

Sometimes of late, when I have been very much excited by the crying of two thousand people over the grave of Richard Wardour, new ideas for a story have come into my head as I lay on the ground, with surprising force and brilliancy. Last night, being quiet here, I noted them down in a little book I keep. When I went into the dining room and mentioned what I had been doing, they all called out *"Friday!"* I was born on a Friday, and it is a most astonishing coincidence that I have never in my life, whatever projects I may have determined on, otherwise — never begun a book, or begun anything of interest to me, or done anything of importance to me, but it was on a Friday. I am certain to be brought round to Friday. It *must* have been on a Friday that I first dined with you at Mr Marjoribanks's!

Mentioning Richard Wardour, — perhaps Mr Wills has not told you how much impressed I was at Manchester by the womanly tenderness of a very gentle and good little girl who acted Mary's part. She came to see the Play beforehand at the Gallery of Illustration, and when we rehearsed it, she said "I am afraid, Mr Dickens, I shall never be able to bear it; it affected me so much when I saw it, that I hope you will excuse my trembling this morning, for I am afraid of myself." At night when she came out of the cave and Wardour recognized her, I never saw anything like the distress and agitation of her face — a very good little pale face, with large black eyes; — it had a natural emotion in it (though it was turned away from the audience) which was quite a study of expression. But when she had to kneel over Wardour dying, and be taken leave of, the tears streamed out of her eyes into his mouth, down his beard, all over his rags — down his arms as he held her by the hair. At the same time she sobbed as if she were breaking her heart, and was quite convulsed with grief. It was of no use for the compas-

---

[6] Dickens and Collins.

sionate Wardour to whisper "My dear child, it will be over in two minutes — there is nothing the matter — don't be so distressed!" She could only sob out "O! It's so sad, O it's so sad!" and set Mr Lemon (the softest hearted of men) crying too. By the time the curtain fell, we were all crying together, and then her mother and sister used to come and put her in a chair and comfort her, before taking her away to be dressed for the Farce. I told her on the last night that I was sure she had one of the most genuine and feeling hearts in the world; and I don't think I ever saw anything more prettily simple and unaffected. Yet I remember her on the stage, a little child, and I dare say she was born in a country theatre.

Very pleasant to know, I submit to you and Mrs Brown? And if you ever see, at Kean's or elsewhere, Miss Maria Ternan,[7] that is the young lady.

---

[7] The Manchester performances were given in the Free Trade Hall, an enormous auditorium in which only an experienced actress could make her action seen and her voice heard, and Dickens was therefore obliged to replace Mamey, Katey, and most of the other feminine members of his cast. On the recommendation of Alfred Wigan, manager of the Olympic Theatre, he offered the roles of Nurse Esther, Wardour's love Clara Burnham, and Lucy Crayford — the last a comparatively minor one — to Mrs. Frances Eleanor Ternan, née Jarman (1803?–1873), and two of her daughters, Maria and Ellen Lawless Ternan. The mother had been praised as superior to both Fanny Kelly and Fanny Kemble, and Dickens had probably seen her as the Countess of Rousillon in *All's Well That Ends Well* at Sadler's Wells in 1852 or as Pauline in *The Winter's Tale* at the Princess Theatre in 1855. Maria had been on the stage since she was a little child; another sister, Frances Eleanor, had acted at least as early as 1855; and Ellen, the youngest, had appeared as Hippomenes in Talfourd's *Atalanta* only the preceding April. Ellen was eighteen, the same age as Dickens's elder daughter Mamey.

During the course of rehearsals and the frenzied last performances in the North, there can be little doubt that he fell desperately in love with Ellen Lawless Ternan, though their relationship, he insisted, was an innocent one: But Catherine Dickens sensed his emotions and her unhappy suspicions deepened the discord between them. Dickens found a despairing relief in describing his feelings to his old friend Mrs. Watson, as if they were merely the familiar restlessness of the artistic temperament: "I am the modern embodiment of the old Enchanters, whose Familiars tore them to pieces. I weary of rest, and have no satisfaction but in fatigue. Realities and idealities are always comparing themselves before me, and I don't like the Realities except when they are unattainable — then, I like them of all things. I wish I had been born in the days of Ogres and Dragon-guarded Castles. I wish an Ogre with seven heads (and no particular evidence of brains in the whole of them) had taken the Princess whom I adore — you have no idea how intensely I love her! — to his stronghold on the top of a high series of mountains, and there tied her by the hair. Nothing would suit me half so well this day, as climbing after her, sword in hand, and either winning her or being killed. — *There's* a frame of mind for you, in 1857."

When the curtain fell for the last time on The Frozen Deep, *Dickens did not know how he was going to bear his existence. In "grim despair and restlessness" he implored Collins to come with him "anywhere — take any tour — see anything," and the two set off together on the trip through the Cumberlands mentioned both in the previous and in the subsequent letter. They went to Carlisle, to Wigton, to Allonby, where Dickens dragged Collins up Carrick Fell in a fog, the two got lost, and Collins sprained an ankle leaping down a watercourse. Dickens feverishly roamed the countryside while Collins was recovering, then hurried him back to Carlisle, on to Lancaster, and from there to Doncaster, where, although Dickens hated horse racing and gambling, they saw "the St Leger and its saturnalia."*

Dickens returned from the trip more desperate than ever. He felt that he could no longer bear sharing the same bedchamber and the same bed with Catherine, as he had done these many years. With a sudden determination he wrote from Gad's Hill to the servant who was in charge at Tavistock House, directing her to transform his dressing room into his bedroom. The washstands were to be taken into the bathroom, and the doorway between the dressing room and his wife's room to be closed by a wooden door, with shelves fitted into the recess.

∾

259.   OCTOBER 4, 1857, GAD'S HILL PLACE

I sent Mrs Matthews £20, on receipt of your letter.

Mr. Collins (who never goes out with me on any expedition, without receiving some damage or other), sprained his leg on our second day out; and I had to carry him, à la Richard Wardour, in and out of all the Inns, Railway Carriages etc, during the rest of the Expedition. You will see our "Lazy Tour" now going on in Household Words.[8] It contains some descriptions (hem!) remarkable for their fanciful fidelity, and two grim stories — the first, of next Wednesday fortnight, that is to say in the Fourth Part, by your present correspondent — a Short Story — a bit of Diablerie.

When I am clear of this Tour, I shall have to go to the Christmas

---

[8] "The Lazy Tour of Two Idle Apprentices" appeared in *Household Words* October 3, 10, 17, 24, and 31, 1857. A joint work by Dickens and Collins, it is mainly a story of their travel adventures, but Chapters II and IV contain two interpolated horror tales.

Number of Household Words [9]; and I fear (as I want to do a great deal to it), that I shall not be in a condition to come, either "here," or there, while you are "here," or "there." But I have put the travelling-scheme in my desk, and shall try.

We have not yet heard from Walter at Calcutta — could not do so, until the next mail — but we have had three letters from him: the last, from Suez. He seems to be perfectly happy, in great enjoyment of the novelties surrounding him, and with no more thoughts of home — as yet, at all events — than if he had never had one.

When you next come to see this place, you won't know it. I have made all manner of changes. *The* glass of water has not been drunk yet, and the process of fitting the Pump (which is proceeding as slowly, and in every respect as *un*satisfactorily as possible) is like putting Oxford Street on end, and laying gas up it.

I observed an extraordinary deterioration in Layard, the last time I saw him. I ventured to hint to him that I thought it came of his not leaving the noble game of Politics to the Knaves and Fools and Pococuranti, until they had ruined us.

When I see people writing letters in the Times day after day, about this class and that class not joining the army and having no interest in arms — and when I think how we all know that we have suffered a system to go on, which has blighted generous ambition, and put reward out of the common man's reach — and how our gentry have disarmed our Peasantry — I become Demoniacal.

And I wish I were Commander in Chief in India.[1] The first thing I would do to strike that Oriental race with amazement (not in the least regarding them as if they lived in the Strand, London, or at Camden Town), should be to proclaim to them, in their language, that I considered my holding that appointment by the leave of God, to mean that I should do my utmost to exterminate the Race upon whom the stain of the late cruelties rested; and that I begged them to do me the favor to observe that I was there for that purpose and no other, and

---

[9] The extra Christmas Number of *Household Words* for 1857 was "The Perils of Certain English Prisoners, and Their Treasure in Women, Children, Silver, and Jewels," a story of a native uprising in one of the Empire's colonial possessions. Its theme was probably suggested by the Indian Mutiny, which had broken out May 10, 1857. Chapters I and III were by Dickens; Chapter II by Collins.

[1] The Indian Mutiny probably also explains the ferocity of Dickens's sentiments in this paragraph. The massacre at Cawnpore had taken place on June 27, 1857, and the siege of Lucknow was still going on.

was now proceeding, with all convenient dispatch and merciful swiftness of execution, to blot it out of mankind and raze it off the face of the Earth.

My love to Mrs Brown, with these sentiments.

∽

By this time Dickens's relations with Catherine were drifting toward shipwreck. "I am incapable of rest," he told Forster. "Much better to die, doing." And to friends in Genoa who had glimpsed their frictions in 1845: "Between ourselves . . . I don't get on better in these later times with a certain poor lady you know of, than I did in the earlier Peschiere days. Much worse. Much worse! Neither do the children, elder or younger. Neither can she get on with herself, or be anything but unhappy. (She has been excruciatingly jealous of, and has obtained positive proof of my being on the most intimate terms with, at least fifteen thousand women of various conditions in life, since we left Genoa. Please to respect me for this vast experience.) What we should do, or what the girls would be, without Georgy, I cannot imagine. She is the active spirit of the house, and the children dote upon her. Enough of this. We put the Skeleton away in the cupboard, and very few people, comparatively, know of its existence."

But as the fall deepened into winter, the misery of both victims grew worse. Although Dickens did not cease to insist that his relations with Ellen Ternan were entirely innocent, Catherine could hardly fail to draw the most significant conclusions from the fact that he now slept in his dressing room with a walled-off door between them. Tavistock House was filled with heartache. There were no children's theatricals on Twelfth Night 1858. Catherine wept in her lonely room, Georgina kept the house going, Dickens debated with himself what he could do. "The domestic unhappiness remains so strong upon me that I can't write, and (waking) can't rest, one minute. I have never known a moment's peace or content, since the last night of The Frozen Deep. I do suppose there never was a man so seized and rended by one Spirit."

Everywhere he went, something brought to his mind the image of that spirit that was rending him. In a play an actor crushed in his hand a letter from the woman he loved, and Dickens protested against the ill-chosen gesture. "Hold it to his heart unconsciously and look about for it the while, he might; or he might do anything with it that ex-

pressed a habit of tenderness and affection in association with the idea of her; but he would never crush it under any circumstances. He would as soon crush her heart."

But no such tenderness animated his feelings for Catherine. In his anguished state, everything she did deepened the gulf between them. When her solicitude for a brother in need of employment prompted her to consult Miss Coutts, although he had himself written in the same brother's behalf, his exasperation was altogether disproportioned to the harmless act, as Catherine's letter to Miss Coutts and his comment on it reveal.

ᴗ

260. [FEBRUARY 1, 1858], TAVISTOCK HOUSE [FROM CATHERINE DICKENS]

In case I am not fortunate enough to find you — and dear Mrs Brown — at home when I call at Stratton Street today, I write to tell you what I would have said to you.

You may remember that Charles wrote to you now some weeks ago about my youngest Brother Edward who owing to one of the great failures in Sheffield lost an excellent position there, and had the world to begin again.

Soon after Charles wrote to you about him, he was offered and accepted a situation in the City as Cashier in a large Wholesale Furniture Silk Warehouse, but for reasons with which I need not trouble you, he finds it impossible to continue in it. I ought however to add that it is from no *fault* of his that he leaves. I venture therefore dear Miss Coutts to ask you if you should hear of any situation likely to suit him, if you would do me the great kindness to bear him in mind, as I need not tell you I am deeply interested in his procuring employment, more particularly as my Father is not able to do much for him, and it is a serious and anxious thing for him, that my Brother should be unemployed.

I know that with your usual friendship and kindness you *will* pardon my thus troubling you on my brother's behalf, and with best love, Believe me always

ᴗ

261. FEBRUARY 2, 1858, TAVISTOCK HOUSE

I am inexpressibly vexed to find that Mrs Dickens, in my absence and without my knowledge, wrote to you yesterday about her brother.

I had not told her of the contents of your last kind note to me, concerning him. That is her only excuse; and I hope you will forgive her more freely and more readily than I do.

❧

Within no more than a few weeks after this, the conflict reached a crisis. Dickens had bought a bracelet to give Ellen Ternan, and the jeweler sent it by mistake to Tavistock House, where it fell into Catherine's hands. Dickens had often before exchanged little gifts and mementos with participants in the theatricals, both men and women; but to Catherine this was different, and she deeply resented it. Jealous of her husband as she had been on past occasions, grieving over their present alienation, already suspicious of Ellen Ternan, she found it impossible to interpret such personal attentions to an eighteen-year-old girl as innocent.

Dickens furiously denied any guilt. He concentrated all his violent will power on battering Catherine into surrender. She could show her confidence in him, he told her, and her belief in Ellen's innocence, by calling on her and her mother. Passing Catherine's door, eighteen-year-old Katey heard sobs from within and found her mother weeping at her dressing table as she was putting on her bonnet. To her questioning, Catherine, with streaming eyes, choked, "Your father has asked me to go and see Ellen Ternan." "You shall not go!" exclaimed Katey, stamping her foot. But Catherine Dickens was not strong enough to defy her husband's will.

Nevertheless, unable to bear her grief, at last she confessed the situation to her father and mother. Mrs. Hogarth insisted that she must leave Dickens at once and demand a separate maintenance. Georgina supported Dickens and infuriated her family by refusing to leave when Catherine took her departure from the house. Dickens tried to bring about some compromise short of a public separation. But his heart was not in it; the Hogarths, furious as they were with him, had unwittingly opened the door on a vista of freedom for which he had not allowed himself to hope. By early May the terms of the separation were worked out. Forster acted for Dickens and Mark Lemon — at her request — for his wife. Catherine was to have a house of her own and £600 a year. Charley would live with her and all the other children with Dickens, but she and they would be free to visit each other at all times.

While the arrangements were still being made, Dickens occupied a bedroom and sitting room at the Household Words *office, as he had frequently done when he had to come into town during the summers, and from there he wrote explaining matters to Miss Coutts.*

∾

262.   MAY 9, 1858

You have been too near and dear a friend to me for many years, and I am bound to you by too many ties of grateful and affectionate regard, to admit of my any longer keeping silence to you on a sad domestic topic. I believe you are not quite unprepared for what I am going to say, and will, in the main, have anticipated it.

I believe my marriage has been for years and years as miserable a one as ever was made. I believe that no two people were ever created, with such an impossibility of interest, sympathy, confidence, sentiment, tender union of any kind between them, as there is between my wife and me. It is an immense misfortune to her — it is an immense misfortune to me — but Nature has put an insurmountable barrier between us, which never in this world can be thrown down.

You know me too well to suppose that I have the faintest thought of influencing you on either side. I merely mention a fact which may induce you to pity us both, when I tell you that she is the only person I have ever known with whom I could not get on somehow or other, and in communicating with whom I could not find some way to come to some kind of interest. You know that I have the many impulsive faults which often belong to my impulsive way of life and exercise of fancy; but I am very patient and considerate at heart, and would have beaten out a path to a better journey's end than we have come to, if I could.

We have been virtually separated for a long time. We must put a wider space between us now, than can be found in one house. If the children loved her, or ever had loved her, this severance would have been a far easier thing than it is. But she has never attached one of them to herself, never played with them in their infancy, never attracted their confidence as they have grown older, never presented herself before them in the aspect of a mother. I have seen them fall off from her in a natural — not *un*natural — progress of estrangement, and at this moment I believe that Mary and Katey (whose dispositions are of the gentlest and most affectionate conceivable) harden into stone figures of girls when they can be got to go near her, and have their hearts shut up in her presence as if they were closed by some horrid spring.

No one can understand this but Georgina, who has seen it grow from year to year, and who is the best, the most unselfish, and most devoted of human Creatures. Her sister Mary,[2] who died suddenly and who lived with us before her, understood it as well in the first months of our marriage. It is her misery to live in some fatal atmosphere which slays every one to whom she should be dearest. It is my misery that no one can ever understand the truth in its full force, or know what a blighted and wasted life my married life has been.

Forster is trying what he can do to arrange matters with her mother. But I know that the mother herself could not live with her. I am perfectly sure that her younger sister and brother could not live with her.[3] An old servant of ours is the only hope I see, as she took care of her, like a poor child, for sixteen years. But she is married now, and I doubt her being afraid that the companionship would wear her to death. Macready used to get on with her better than anyone else, and I sometimes have a fancy that she may think of him or his sister. To suggest them to her would be to inspire her with an insistent determination never to go near them.

In the mean time I have come for a time to the office, to leave her Mother free to do what she can at home, towards the getting of her away to some happier mode of existence if possible. They all know that I will do anything for her Comfort, and spend anything upon her.

It is a relief to me to have written this to you. Don't think the worse of me; don't think the worse of her. I am firmly persuaded that it is not within the Compass of her Character and faculties to be other than she is. If she had married another sort of man she might however have done better. I think she has always felt herself to be at the disadvan-

---

[2] Mary Hogarth (1819–1837), who had lived with Dickens and Catherine, first at Furnival's Inn and then at Doughty Street, from the time of their marriage until her sudden death from a heart attack at the age of seventeen. She and Dickens had been deeply devoted and she died in his arms. A ring that he then drew from her finger he wore himself until the day he died. The sorrow he felt for her loss is re-echoed again and again throughout his novels in his descriptions of the deaths of children or of the innocent and the good dying young; her death inspired and made an almost unbearable anguish to him the death of Little Nell in *The Old Curiosity Shop*.

[3] As a matter of record, after the separation Charley lived with Catherine in the house in Gloucester Crescent that Dickens provided for her until, in 1860, he went to China.

tage of groping blindly about me, and never touching me, and so has
fallen into the most miserable weaknesses and jealousies. Her mind
has, at times, been certainly confused besides.[4]

All this is for Mrs Brown no less than for you. Put a kind construction on it, and hold me in the old place in your regard.

∽

*Suddenly in the middle of May the separation arrangements were
shattered. Dickens learned that Mrs. Hogarth and her youngest daughter, Helen Hogarth, were circulating the story that Ellen Ternan was
his mistress. The news turned him into a maniac of indignant fury.
He had assured Catherine he had not been unfaithful to her. He had
heaped benefits upon the Hogarths. For them to be destroying his good
name, endangering the welfare of his children, was the blackest depth
of falsehood and ingratitude. Stormily he refused to make any agreement, any settlement whatever. Unless they retracted their evil slan-
ders, formally and in writing, in their own names and in Catherine's,
he would do nothing, pay not a penny. His bitterness seethed within
him as if in the crater of a volcano. Meanwhile Miss Coutts tried to see
if she could not mediate between them. But in Dickens's angry state
even Miss Coutts received an answer that was as near being a snub as
he ever wrote her.*

∽

263. MAY 19, 1858, 16 WELLINGTON STREET NORTH — STRAND [OFFICE
OF *Household Words*]

I think I know what you want me for. How far I value your friendship, and how I love and honor you, you know in part, though you can
never fully know. But nothing on earth — no, not even you — no con-

---

[4] A similar statement by Dickens that found its way into print later that summer
has been indignantly denounced as a malignant invention, but there is evidence
that Dickens certainly believed it to be true. As far back as 1851, when there was
no thought of a separation, but when Catherine had been unwell and had been
advised to take the waters at Great Malvern, he had described her case to Dr.
James Wilson, the physician under whose care she was to be. It was, Dickens said,
a nervous one, and he implied that she had been behaving strangely during recent
visits to the homes of friends. (Only a short while before they had been at Knebworth with Sir Edward Bulwer Lytton and at Rockingham Castle with the Watsons,
but there are no known details about Catherine's conduct on these occasions.) Not
only did Dickens have no cause to make up a story of a mental affliction at the
time; he could have had no reasonable expectation that if it were false it could
deceive the doctor who would have Catherine under his constant observation.

sideration, human or Divine, can move me from the resolution I have taken.

And one other thing I must ask you to forgive me. If you have seen Mrs Dickens in company with her wicked mother, I can not enter — no, not even with you — upon any question that was discussed in that woman's presence.

I will come round, almost as soon as your messenger [5]; but I foresee that there is nothing left for us to say.

It may be that Miss Coutts got to Catherine Dickens that same day the news that her attempted intervention had been fruitless. At any rate there is a sad little note to Miss Coutts from Catherine on that date.

264.   MAY 19, 1858, TAVISTOCK HOUSE [FROM CATHERINE DICKENS]
Many many thanks for your true kindness in doing what I asked.

I have now — God help me — only one course to pursue.

One day though not now I may be able to tell you how hardly I have been used.

With sincere love to yourself and dear Mrs Brown

For almost two weeks the Hogarths held out. They thought Dickens would give way. After all these years they still did not know him. As in the days when he had fought to get free of his contracts with his publisher Richard Bentley, he was determined that no court in Christendom could make him yield. They refused to put their names to the document he demanded that they sign and he refused to concede a fraction of an inch. It was not until the end of May that they finally gave way to his ultimatum and retracted their accusations. Even then, it is likely that they still did not credit his denials, but surrendered only for Catherine's sake. Nevertheless, at last Mrs. Hogarth and Helen Hogarth both signed the following statement: "It having been stated to us that in reference to the differences which have resulted in the separation of Mr and Mrs Charles Dickens, certain statements have been circulated that such differences are occasioned by circumstances deeply affecting the moral character of Mr Dickens and compromising

---

[5] The note or letter to which this was a reply had evidently been sent round from Stratton Street by messenger, who waited for Dickens's answer, but Dickens himself was following hard upon his written words.

the reputation and good name of others, we solemnly declare that we now disbelieve such statements. We know that they are not believed by Mrs Dickens, and we pledge ourselves on all occasions to contradict them, as entirely destitute of foundation."

Once separated from Catherine, Dickens flung himself for distraction from his lacerated emotions, into a series of public readings from his books. He had often read for charitable causes before now, but had hesitated to become a professional reader for his own profit. Forster stormed against it as degrading to the dignity of a literary artist. Dickens thought this argument irrational, and when he referred Forster's objections to Miss Coutts, although she was at first surprised, she almost immediately replied that she saw nothing derogatory in the project. "I think upon the whole that most people would be glad you should have the money, rather than other people." Even Mrs. Brown, the General Objector, without knowing what Miss Coutts had said, promptly gave the same opinion.

In the very weeks immediately preceding the separation, therefore, Dickens had embarked upon a series of London readings at St. Martin's Hall, starting in May and extending into June. These were to be followed by an autumn tour of the Eastern counties, the West, Lancashire, Yorkshire, and Scotland, running to some thirty-five or forty all told, and lasting through August, September, and October. The business arrangements were under the management of Arthur W. W. Smith (1825–1861), a brother of Albert Smith, the novelist and showman. In addition to the Christmas Carol and The Chimes, before the middle of June Dickens had devised two more reading programs that included the death of little Paul Dombey and some Sairey Gamp scenes from Martin Chuzzlewit.

His performances were more than reading; they were an extraordinary feat of acting that seized their auditors with mesmeric possession. Without moving from the center of the stage, without a single prop or bit of costume, by changes of voice, by gesture, by vocal and facial expression, Dickens peopled his stage with a throng of characters. His Scrooge was harsh and grating, his Mrs. Gamp snuffy, husky, and unctuous with the oozing corpulence of a fat old woman, his Paul Dombey the weary alto of a tired child, his Bob Cratchit a frightened gasp in the thinnest and meekest of tones. His face could flash from the pinched, avaricious countenance of Cratchit's miserly employer to the beaming looks of the plump sister at the Christmas party crying out

"It's your uncle Scro-o-o-oge!" Simply by drumming on his desk top he suggested all the dash and gaiety of Mr. Fezziwig's ball, and by a licking of the lips and a humbly placatory bob, Trotty Veck's relish for tripe and his respect for Alderman Cute.

His first reading of the Christmas Carol *for charity in 1853 had taken three hours. By more and more drastic cuts he reduced it to two. Descriptions he ruthlessly pruned or left out altogether, conveying the appearance and manner of his characters by sheer histrionic brilliance. He speeded up the narrative, tightened the dialogue, made it more sharply typical of each speaker. In his reading copies, whole areas of text were blocked out in a wash of red ink, and changed wordings were written between the lines or bulged out in encircling balloons. In the margins were stage directions for himself: "Snap your fingers," "Rising action," "Scrooge melted," "Soften very much." He practiced each reading hundreds of times, striving for perfection in every intonation, until he knew every word by heart and could allow himself impromptu variations, "gagging" on sudden inspiration, magnetizing his listeners to his will.*

Everywhere, despite the scandal of the separation, he read to crammed houses and swept people off their feet. Arthur Smith, Dickens wrote, "bathed in checks, took headers into tickets, floated on billows of passes, dived under weirs of shillings, floated home, faint with gold and silver." People roared with laughter so that Dickens could hardly keep his own face straight; they cried unashamedly and undisguisedly. In Ireland, men stopped him on the street, saying, "Do me the honour to shake hands, Misther Dickens, and God bless you, sir; not ounly for the light you've been to me this night, but for the light you've been in mee house, sir (and God love your face!) this many a year." After every performance ladies begged his personal servant, John, for the flower from his coat; one morning, when the petals from his geranium showered on the platform while he was reading "Little Dombey," the women swarmed up on the platform after he had gone, and picked them up *as keepsakes.*

265. August 9, 1858, 16 Wellington Street North — Strand
[office of *Household Words*]

Passing through town to resume my country Readings after two days peace and quiet at Gad's Hill, I write this short note to you. Wills tells me that you want my various addresses, and I am delighted to send them, and have so good an excuse for writing to you.

You will observe that a few of the addresses are at Booksellers' and the like. This is to ensure my getting letters at towns where Mr Arthur Smith does not know — or did not know, when he made out the list — the best Hotels.

Our first week was an immense success. I miss the quiet of my own desk, but I look forward to resuming it — and it is a great sensation to have a large audience in one's hand.

Charley was with us yesterday at Gad's Hill, and talked of passing his fortnight's holiday in Ireland with me. I encouraged him in the idea, as I thought it would do him more good than any other Holiday he is likely to take.

It would be too happy a chance to find you anywhere in the Tour, but I shall hope to hear from you somewhere.

With kindest love and regard to Mrs Brown

∽

266. AUGUST 23, 1858, MORRISON'S HOTEL DUBLIN

I shall address this to Mr Wills, as I am not certain where you may be. I passed through Bangor [6] last Saturday night at midnight, and wondered whether you were there.

My dear friend, I quite understand and appreciate your feeling that there must be no reservation between us, and that we must not have a skeleton in a closet, and make believe it is not there. But I must not enter on the wretched subject under false pretences. I must not do what would make my dear girls out to be a sort of phenomena, and what would make my relations with Mrs Dickens incomprehensible. Since we spoke of her before, she has caused me unspeakable agony of mind [7]; and I must plainly put before you what I know to be true, and what nothing shall induce me to affect to doubt. She does not —

---

[6] The seaport on Menai Strait, nine miles northeast of Carnarvon, in Carnarvonshire, Wales, through which Dickens would naturally pass in going from Liverpool to cross the Irish Sea from Holyhead.

[7] Dickens's distress of mind had indeed been exquisite, although there is nothing to show that Catherine had directly and actively done anything to deepen it. After the separation all literary London seethed with scandalous rumor; going into the Garrick Club, Thackeray was told that the cause was a love affair between Dickens and Georgina. Meaning merely to scotch this more vicious story, "Nothing of the kind," he said with his usual clumsiness, "it's with an actress." The remark came back to Dickens, who was furious. To his seething imagination it seemed that the whole world must be clamoring with the hideous accusation. Feverish with this

and she never did — care for the children; and the children do
not — and they never did — care for her. The little play that is acted in
your Drawing-room [8] is not the truth, and the less the children play it,
the better for themselves, because they know it is not the truth. (If I
stood before you at the moment and told you what difficulty we have
to get Frank, for instance, to go near his mother, or keep near his
mother, you would stand amazed.) As to Mrs Dickens's simplicity in
speaking of me and my doings, O my dear Miss Coutts do I not know
that the weak hand that could never help or serve my name in the least,
has struck at it — in conjunction with the wickedest people whom I
have loaded with benefits.[9] I want to communicate with her no more.
I want to forgive and forget her.

I could not begin a course of references to her, without recording
as between you and me, what I know to be true. It would be monstrous to myself and to the children. From Walter away in India to
little Plornish at Gad's Hill there is a grim knowledge among them as
familiar to them as the knowledge of Day Light, that what I now
write is the plain bare fact. She has always disconcerted them; they

---

delusion, he rushed into action, and against the advice of friends published a personal statement on the front page of *Household Words* on June 12, 1858.

"Some domestic troubles of mine, of long-standing," he told the public, had
"lately been brought to an arrangement" involving "no anger or ill-will," and all
the details of which were known to his children. "By some means, arising out of
wickedness, or out of folly, or out of inconceivable wild chance, or out of all three,
this trouble has been made the occasion of misrepresentations, most grossly false,
most monstrous, and most cruel — involving not only me, but innocent persons dear
to my heart." These rumors, he solemnly declared, were abominably false. He sent
other copies of this statement to the newspapers, where they were published, often
with unfavorable comment. Readers, who knew nothing of the rumors to which the
statement darkly referred, were entirely bewildered, and Dickens writhed in bitterness and anguish.

[8] Demonstrations of affection, clearly, from Catherine toward the children,
meeting at Miss Coutts's, and perhaps from them to Catherine, although Dickens
unequivocally asserts that their part was never more than passive and unwilling.
How far to accept his account of the story the student of Dickens's life must decide
for himself. It may constitute some partial corroboration that when Walter sailed
for India, although Dickens saw him off from Southampton, Catherine did not go
with them. Mary always sided with her father, but Katey, in later years, often
expressed sympathy for her mother.

[9] The Hogarth family, with the exception of Georgina, who remained loyal to
Dickens. His resentment is intelligible enough when one remembers that he had
always been most generous to them and that only a few months before these
troubles he had been trying to aid Mrs. Hogarth's youngest son. Since they had
derived their suspicions about Ellen Ternan originally from Catherine, his feeling
about her is also understandable.

have always disconcerted her; and she is glad to be rid of them, and they are glad to be rid of her. — No more of it here.

The country expedition has been doing extremely well. The expences are large (including Mr Smith's share, about 50 percent), but the returns come out handsomely. At Liverpool last week, I read 4 times. The audiences amounted to about 6,300 people. My clear profit, after all deductions, was £260 . . 9 . . 0. What we are going to do here, I don't know. The Dublin audience are accustomed to do nothing in the way of taking places, until the last moment, or until they actually "take them" by walking in at the Doors. We are therefore quite in the dark. I read the Carol here tonight — the Chimes tomorrow — Little Dombey on Wednesday morning — and the Poor Travellers &c [1] on Thursday evening. We had a 5 hours passage from Holyhead in the night of Saturday, and it was very, very nasty.

I am greatly surprised by this place. It is very much larger than I had supposed, and very much more populous and busy. Upon the whole it is no shabbier than London is, and the people seem to enjoy themselves more than the London people do. The old town of Edinburgh is a thousand times more squalid than the byeplaces I have seen in Dublin, and I have wandered about it for 6 or 8 hours in all directions. It may be presumed that it has greatly improved of late years. There are far fewer spirit shops than I have been used to see in great cities. And even Donnybrook Fair (which is on now, though it ought to be abolished) [2] is less disagreeable than Chalk Farm; and I have seen numbers of common people buying the most innocent and un-lifelike of Dolls there, for their little children.

Among my English audiences, I have had more clergymen than I ever saw in my life before. It is very curious to see how many people in black come to Little Dombey. And when it is over they almost uniformly go away as if the child were really Dead — with a hush upon them. They certainly laugh more at the Boots's story of the Little Elopement,[3] than at anything else; and I notice that they sit with their

---

[1] The "Poor Travellers" was a reading made from the Christmas story of 1854.

[2] Donnybrook Fair, held in August just southeast of Dublin since the time of King John, known for good-humored rioting. Its more obnoxious features had in fact been suppressed in 1855. Chalk Farm, just northeast of Primrose Hill, London, was a place of entertainment devoted to tea-drinking and athletic exhibitions that attracted a sporting audience.

[3] From "The Holly-Tree Inn," the Christmas Number of Household Words for 1855. Dickens had written "The Guest," "The Boots," and "The Bill"; Collins the

heads on one side, and an expression of playful pity on their faces —
as if they saw the tiny boy and girl, which is tender and pleasant, I
think? The Chimes is always a surprise. They fall into it with a start,
and look at me in the strangest way before they begin to applaud. The
Cratchit family in the Carol are always a delight. And they always
visibly lie in wait for Tiny Tim. The little books sell extraordinarily.
Besides being in every bookshop window in every place, my men alone
will sell from 6 to 12 Dozen in a night. I think I have now told you
every bit of egotism I can screw out of myself. But I know that you
and Mrs Brown (to whom I send my love) will be interested in these
scraps.

I shall hope to find another letter from you somewhere, soon, telling
me how you both are, and whether you have found a place to breathe
in. Then I will report further of my proceedings.

∽

267. SEPTEMBER 6, 1858, GAD'S HILL PLACE
I am at home here tonight, after great fatigue (and great success,
thank God!) in Ireland, — for no longer than eight and forty hours.
Charley has come down to see me, and he tells me that he thinks the
present is a time, in which a word of reminder at Baring Brothers,
from a good source, might lead to his removal before long into one of
their business opportunities out of London, no matter where, which
would present a better opening than London does, to a young man of
such capacity, education, and energy, as he possesses.[4]

If you could find an occasion of mentioning this to Mr Bates, would
you object to do so? I know, and I always tell him — I mean Charley —
that his rise must in the main depend upon himself. But I hope and
believe he deserves well, and of course I know that any sign of *your*
interest in him could not fail to serve him.

I would have gone to Mr Bates myself in the course of tomorrow, but
that I have the greatest delicacy in obtruding myself, either on his
kindness, or on that of any other partner in the house. What a private

---

rest. The reading was made from the second story, in which a boy of eight, Master
Harry Walmers, elopes to Gretna Green with his sweetheart Norah, aged seven.
It is supposedly told by the "boots" at the Inn.

[4] Charley had been employed by Baring Brothers since September 1855, been
given a bonus of £ 10 and an increase of £ 10 a year in his salary within four
months, and done steadily better and better there. He was now hoping to be put
in charge of one of the enterprises they controlled.

gentleman need not scruple to do, my consciousness of my own notoriety shrinks from. I have a dread of seeming to force it on attention, when I desire nothing more than to be as quiet and modest under it as possible. Hence it is that I trouble you!

I beg to report myself as strong and well as if I had been doing nothing. With love to Mrs Brown, Believe me ever

∽

268. OCTOBER 27, 1858, HULL

I was very glad indeed to receive your kind note when I went to London for a few hours last Sunday morning. This shall be but a very short reply to it, as this is mainly to say that I hope to be able to call upon you *next Monday,* during another short rest.

My tour is now drawing to a close, and I am heartily glad to think that it is nearly over, and that I shall soon be at home in my own room again. It has been wonderfully successful. My clear profit — my own, after all deductions and expences — has been more than a Thousand Guineas a month.[5] But the manner in which the people have everywhere delighted to express that they have a personal affection for me and the interest of tender friends in me, is (especially at this time) high and far above all other considerations. I consider it a remarkable instance of good fortune that it should have fallen out that I should, in this autumn of all others, have come face to face with so many multitudes.

Mr Arthur Smith is everything I could desire, and has made the way as smooth as possible. His extraordinary practical knowledge, and his great zeal, and his gentle way of dealing with crowds and putting people at their ease, have been of the greatest service and comfort to me.

Many thanks for so kindly writing to Mr Bates about Charley. Charley wrote to me at the time, expressing himself about it, most sensitively and properly.

Mrs Matthews is by far the most perplexing female I have ever encountered in that way. I thought you ought to see the letter, and yet

---

[5] The popularity of the readings had led to the tour being extended far beyond the proportions planned at first. In the course of these three and a half months Dickens had given eighty-seven readings in forty-three different towns and cities in England, Ireland, and Scotland. How astoundingly profitable they had turned out to be is obvious if one realizes that the present purchasing value of the pound would have to be perhaps doubled or tripled to obtain an equivalence.

I feel with you that hers is a most unsatisfactory and difficult case. She has certainly become hardened in begging — gradually and surely, since she first began, as I remember, a dozen years ago, or more — in a very remarkable manner. I suppose her statements are correct. Indeed, I recollect that you once made some enquiries respecting her husband, and yet, granting them all, it seems possible to do her but very little good, and this last remonstrance (for it is quite that), has a dogged perseverance in it that is far from impressing one favorably. When I got the letter, I was so bothered and bewildered by it, that I felt strongly disposed to quarrel with the Postman for not having lost it.

~

269. DECEMBER 13, 1858, TAVISTOCK HOUSE

Wills sent Mrs Brown *her* paper from Manchester, and I sent *you* another paper at the same time.

Mrs Matthews's case is clearly hopeless.[6] I have had another letter from her this morning, which I have put in the fire. Her former letter, and the Bishop's, I enclose.

You will be sorry to hear that Mr Arthur Smith, going over to Paris at the close of our labors, was taken ill there with diphtheria and scarlet fever, and has been in an alarming state. He is now recovering, though very weak and much reduced. The work of our tour was a little too hard for him, I fear. I thank God that I have been, and am, wonderfully well, and that I have never felt the fatigue; though it came upon me under no commonly harassing circumstances, when I would sometimes as soon have laid myself down and given up all, as I would have gone into a bright crowd and read.

It is to be hoped you have brighter weather on the Devonshire coast than we have here. London, I really think, was never so dark for so many days together, as it has been in this present month. It is like living in a large dirty slate. On Saturday I took a foreign friend from Genoa,[7] down to the Crystal Palace. I asked him to try to

---

[6] Mrs. Antonina Matthews's begging-letters, which had long been wearing out Dickens's patience. Which bishop had written in connection with her case this time cannot be determined.

[7] Monsieur De la Rue, a Swiss banker married to an English wife, with whom Dickens had become acquainted during his Palazzo Peschiere days in 1844 and with whom he had corresponded ever since. The De la Rues had been witnesses of Catherine's unhappy and jealous disposition at that earlier time.

imagine the sun shining down through the glass, and making broad lights and shadows. He said he tried very hard, but he couldn't imagine the sun shining within fifty miles of London under any circumstances.

The Coventry people have given me a seventy five Guinea Watch, which is chronometer, Repeater, and every other terrible machine that a watch *can* be. It was very feelingly and pleasantly given, and I prize it highly.[8]

This is all the news I have — except that I send my love to Mrs Brown — which is no news — and that I am ever — which is no news either —

∽

From this point on, Dickens's letters to Miss Coutts — or those that have been preserved, it is impossible to say which — are less numerous and frequent. C. C. Osborne, her secretary in later years, copied a number of which the originals have not survived, and there may have been still others that did not come to his hands. It seems likely, how-ever, that without there being any lessening of friendship the bulk of the correspondence did dwindle. When W. H. Wills had become her secretary on Dickens's recommendation, he assumed a great many of the duties that had formerly obliged Dickens to write weekly and voluminous letters.

Now, as Dickens launched into repeated reading tours involving con-stant, wearing, and onerous travel as well as the most exhausting labor, the demands upon his time and energy were greater than ever. He be-gan publishing his new weekly, All the Year Round, *in 1859, absorbing* Household Words *into it, and built it up to an even more striking suc-cess than its predecessor had ever achieved. With its fifth number it trebled the circulation of* Household Words, *which had never sold more than 40,000 copies; within ten years* All the Year Round *had reached 300,000. The most striking innovation of the new magazine, which helps to explain this success, was that it always carried a serial story by a well-known writer. The opening serial was* A Tale of Two Cities, *starting off with a bang and running for thirty-one numbers. It was followed by Wilkie Collins's* The Woman in White. *Meanwhile Dickens had again begun reading in London, and given twenty-four*

---

[8] This gift was tendered Dickens at a public dinner in his honor on December 4, 1858, as an expression of gratitude for readings he had given in aid of the Coventry Institute.

'more readings between Christmas Eve 1858 and February 8, 1859.
And A Tale of Two Cities had still another month and a half to run
when he began his second provincial reading tour on October 10.

With these furious activities keeping him busier than ever, and with
the increasing proportion of his little leisure that Dickens devoted to
Gad's Hill, many of his old friends saw much less of him than they had
in earlier years. Although during and after his separation from his
wife, Miss Coutts sympathized with Catherine and even attempted
more than once to help end their estrangement, she did not take sides,
and her friendship with Dickens remained unbroken. The tone of his
letters to her, indeed, remained unaltered, and was as warm and affectionate as it had always been.

∽

270.   JANUARY 30, 1860, TAVISTOCK HOUSE

I send you a thousand thanks for your most considerate and kind
letter, and I deeply — deeply — feel it. I trust to God that Charley may
thank you in his life and actions; but he never can do so with a stronger
earnestness than is in his father's heart — many voiced to me — almost
dumb to you.

The difficulty that I feel in reference to Mr Bates, is the careful
delicacy that must be observed in the matter, towards him. He has, no
doubt, felt flattered by your confidence, and would be — naturally —
easily hurt, if he thought it in the least respect withdrawn. I am sure
he would have a respect for Mr Moore,[9] for instance; but I can understand that he might not exactly like the idea of there being another adviser. Do you not think if you wrote to Mr Bates thus, it would be
best? You remind him of the conversation which you have described
to me, and you ask (as Charley's twenty third birthday is just over)
whether he is in the way of yet seeing any opening for him out of
Baring's house? If he replies — No, then, I think that Charley might
himself ask to speak with him, and might take his advice upon Mr
Moore's general suggestion, without saying where it originated.

I have considered the point with great care, and in this kind of
course I seem to descry the safest and gentlest way of dealing with a
man of Mr Bates's position and years. Does it strike you in the same

---

[9] George Moore (1806–1876), a partner in the business firm of Grocock, Cope-
stake and Moore, and a prominent merchant and philanthropist. There is no evidence of what suggestion he had made about Charley's future.

way? I have always impressed upon Charley the same policy (which is indeed, Mr Bates's due and nothing more), and he had always observed that it was suited to his character, and their relative situations. Acting thus, you see, Mr Bates either way is in the position of being consulted; and that is the thing that seems right and necessary and just.

I am very hard-worked just now, for, finding that I could not prevent the dramatizing of my last story,[1] I have devoted myself for a fortnight to the trying to infuse into the conventionalities of the Theatre, something not usual there in the way of Life and Truth. The result will become manifest tonight. I have some hopes that there is a French populace dancing the Carmagnole, which is not like the languid run of unrealities of that kind.

It grieves me to hear that dear Mrs Brown is not yet quite recovered — even under the Torquay sky.[2] Pray give her my love and dear remembrance, and tell her nothing changes me. I have always heard of her, and of you, from Wills, and the old time never grows older or younger with me.

༄

271. MARCH 13, 1860, TAVISTOCK HOUSE

Charley — as you may suppose in his joyful flush and excitement — has been with me often lately, and when he was here last (a week ago) was saying that of course he must appoint a time for coming down to Torquay "to say Good Bye."[3] I said, "of course" too, and I told him to let me know when it would be, as soon as he knew himself, in order that I might come with him, or at least propose myself. — You will have me for a few hours?

You know that I want no bed, but have an adventurous satisfaction in exploring hotels, and am quite as likely as not to leave in the middle of the night for the Coast of Cornwall.

Wills told me about the sick children, or I should have written to

---

[1] *A Tale of Two Cities*, adapted by Tom Taylor and opening at the Lyceum, with the noted dancer and actress Madame Céleste (1814?–1882) in the role of Madame Defarge. Dickens in fact did more even than he claims: he practically directed the entire production.

[2] Where Miss Coutts now had a winter residence near Teignmouth.

[3] With financial backing from Baring Brothers, Charley was sailing to China at the end of April, to buy tea on his own account, before setting up in business for himself.

say this — as indeed I said to Charley I was going to do. But when I heard that you were occupied and anxious, I thought it better to wait.

Charley was waiting at Baring's until his successor should be ready. He thought it likely that Mr Bates would deem it well to send him to Manchester, somewhere about the middle of this month. I suppose he would be free for a flight to Torquay in about a month from this time; but I am at sea about this, until he comes again, because he was out in the wildest Pacific himself.

My Dear friend I cannot trust myself on the ground that lies trembling at the point of my pen. Many reasons, old and new, unnerve me. I think you know how I love you — how I could do anything in your name and honor, but thank you.

My love to Mrs Brown. Tell her that everything stands upon my tables as it used to do, and that Gad's Hill (wonderfully changed now), is the admiration of Rochester. I want to sell this house.

∾

Almost two years after Dickens and his wife had parted, Miss Coutts, on April 4, 1860, seems to have made a further effort to bring about a reconciliation between them. The following fragment and the letter succeeding it, reveal the ineradicable scars both his marriage experience and the struggles of the separation had left upon his spirit.

∾

272.   APRIL 5, 1860, TAVISTOCK HOUSE

. . . I cannot be easy under the chance of *seeming*, through the silence of a week or two, to debate within myself the possibility of what your affectionate kindness suggested yesterday. In the last two years, I have been stabbed too often and too deep, not to have a settled knowledge of the wounded place.

It is simply impossible that such a thing can be. That figure is out of my life for evermore (except to darken it) and my desire is, Never to see it again.[4]

---

[4] In fact, Dickens never did see Catherine again. When his daughter Katey was married to Charles Allston Collins at Gad's Hill on July 17, 1860, Catherine was not among the wedding guests, and when their son Charley married the daughter of Frederick Evans the following year, Catherine was present but Dickens was not. In later years there were a few formal notes between them, and no more.

273.   APRIL 8, 1860, GAD'S HILL PLACE

Don't be afraid of my handwriting, for I hope I can write you a few reassuring words, this blessed morning. — I believe I am exactly what I always have been; quite as hopeful, cheerful, and active, as I ever was. I am not so weak or wicked as to visit any small unhappiness of my own, upon the world in which I live. I know very well, it is just as it was. As to my art, I have as great a delight in it as the most enthusiastic of my readers; and the sense of my trust and responsibility in that wise, is always upon me when I take pen in hand. If *I* were soured, I should still try to sweeten the lives and fancies of others, but I am not — not at all.

Neither do I ever complain, or ever touch that subject. What I have written to you respecting it, I have written merely because I wished you to understand me thoroughly.

Lastly, I do not suppose myself blameless, but in this thing as in all others know, every day more and more, how much I stand in need of the highest of all charity and mercy. All I claim for myself, is, that when I was very young, I made a miserable mistake, and that the wretched consequences which might naturally have been expected from it, have resulted from it. That is all.

Do not think you failed to express yourself to me. You expressed — emphatically — *yourself*, and what more could I have, or what could I more earnestly feel?

Charley is here, and has gained a colour in a dozen hours. I hope you may not have read The Tale of Two Cities, for I have entrusted your copy to his care.

∽

274.   APRIL 8, 1860, GAD'S HILL PLACE [TO MRS. BROWN]

I was so interested and delighted by the receipt of your kind letter, that I must write to thank you for it. — Yes indeed. In seeing Miss Coutts again, I saw you again, and we all understood one another as of old, and knew that we were all doing our best.

Charley told me last night (he came down yesterday) that he was "going" to write you a line today. When last seen, he was lecturing on China, in the garden, to two of his young brothers and a dog. I put the volunteer mettle to the proof, by turning him out at 3 o'clock this morning, on a false alarm of somebody prowling in the garden. We patrolled the place, and he handled the poker with which he was

armed, in a meritorious manner. (I complimented him at breakfast
this morning, on the scrupulous politeness with which he yielded pre-
cedence to his father and made him go first.)

He is full of hope and spirit as well he may be. And you and I know
whom he has to thank for this, and how much hundreds have to thank
her for, that will never be heard of in this world.

God bless her, and you! I never forget you. "Out of sight" is not
"out of mind" with me, my dear friend; nor with you, I very well
know.

ᘓᴥᴥ

275.   August 3, 1860, Gad's Hill Place
Let me send my love — and thanks to you and Mrs Brown. Your
remembrance was the kind remembrance of true friends, in due season. And there is nothing better in the world.

My poor brother's death [5] is a sad calamity, to which there are five
little witnesses. But he had a good, true, striving wife, and I can
trust her with all my heart. This is not the first time I have had occasion to respect her undemonstrative and patiently dutiful character.
It is all that she can call her own, but it is a great deal for me to have
so much to be a friend to.

God bless you, and you, dear Mrs Brown. And both believe me, ever

ᘓᴥᴥ

276.   November 3, 1861, Gad's Hill Place [to Mrs. Brown]
I received your letter at Norwich — I am away, reading,[6] and am
only at home for a day — with many affectionate and cherished re-

---

[5] Alfred Lamert Dickens (1822–1860), who had died on July 27. He had been
a hard-working engineer all his life, but had never managed to do more than earn
a living. Dickens established his widow Helen and her children in a house with
his mother on Haverstock Hill, a little south of Hampstead Heath. John Dickens's
widow was now in a state of senile decay, in which she seldom understood what
was going on around her, but when Dickens visited her in the new home in
November he found her like her old self in one respect. She was "not in bed, but
downstairs. Helen and Letitia were poulticing her poor head, and, the instant she
saw me, she plucked up a spirit, and asked me for 'a pound.' "

[6] *Great Expectations*, which had begun appearing as a weekly serial in *All the
Year Round* on December 1, 1860, had concluded August 3, 1861. At the end of
October, Dickens started out on another tour, this time of forty-seven readings,
beginning at Norwich and ending at Chester on January 30, 1862. They were
followed by a series of ten London readings in St. James's Hall, Piccadilly, between
March 13 and June 27.

membrances, on which I need not dwell to you. When I heard you were at Paris, I often thought of you, you may be sure; but uppermost among all I thought, was a feeling of great gratification and sympathy in your having gone there. It was right and true and wholesome.

In poor Arthur Smith, I have sustained an irreparable loss — not because he was a man who did for me what no one else can ever do, but because I loved him and he deserved it well. But we must all be brave, as good soldiers are, and when the fast-thinning ranks look bare, must close up solidly and march on.[7]

You, and dear Miss Coutts, will be glad, I know, to hear that my readings have begun again most prosperously. Enjoying crowds have been about me, since I recommenced. I have made one reading from Copperfield that I should very much like you both, to hear. It seems to have a strong interest, and an expression of a young spirit in it that addresses people of sensitive perception curiously.

I wish I could hope that Charley's marriage may not be a disastrous one.[8] There is no help for it, and the dear fellow does what is unavoidable — his foolish mother would have effectually committed him if nothing else had; chiefly I suppose because her hatred of the bride and all belonging to her, used to know no bounds, and was quite inappeasable. But I have a strong belief founded on careful observation of him, that he cares nothing for the girl.

I left Colchester yesterday morning, when the town was hoary under a sharp snow storm. Two days before, I had been breakfasting at

---

[7] Arthur Smith, his manager, had died in October. His position was taken by Thomas Headland.

[8] Early in November, Charley Dickens married Elizabeth Evans, daughter of Frederick Evans, the junior partner in the printing and publishing firm of Bradbury and Evans. Dickens had quarreled bitterly with Evans at the time of the separation. He had quarreled with the publishing firm, too, for refusing to print his "personal" statement in Punch, severed his relations with them, and gone back to Chapman and Hall as publishers for his books. Although Dickens was not pleased at his eldest son's choice of a marriage partner, he was reconciled to it, and often had the young couple at Gad's Hill. He refused, however, to be present at the wedding because that would have necessitated his entering the house of the bride's father. These facts may account for some of the oddity of the judgments expressed in this paragraph. There never appeared any later reasons to suggest that Charley did not love his wife, and there is no evidence that the match was made by Catherine. The curious inconsistency of conduct Dickens attributes to her is significant as another revelation of his feelings about the woman with whom he had lived for twenty-two years.

Bury St Edmunds with the window wide open, and bright flowers in all the gardens.

Give my ever affectionate and never changing remembrance to Miss Coutts, and Believe me my dear friend

∽

277. OCTOBER 24, 1862, RUE DU FAUBOURG ST. HONORE, PARIS [TO MRS. BROWN]

On the very day when your letter reached me, I had been walking past the Hotel Bristol, looking up at the windows and thinking of Miss Coutts and you — I found your letter on my table when I came home straight, by the Rue Castiglione and Rue St Honoré.

You know all that I would say — better than that, you know all that I would *do* — in response to your affectionate and tender remembrances. I am so confident in the free masonry between us, that I will write not another word on that almost sacred theme.

It is amazing to behold the changes in this place, and the vast works doing and done. But I notice (having been much in the country parts of France this summer), that as Paris swells, the provincial towns of the second and third degree collapse. "Maison à Vendre" — "Maison à Vendre" — everywhere — Towns falling to pieces — grass growing over the public buildings — population Heaven knows where.

Of the daily lives and exercises of the soldiers, I have seen a great deal, in the out-of-the-way fortified towns where such things are the only business. In all respects of sensible training and an admirable adaptation of the men to the purposes and the purposes to the men, I believe this army, as compared with ours, advances 50 years in every year we live. It is a disquieting consideration, when one remembers that but the other day — when Sydney Herbert went to the War Office — there were two sizes of shoes in the whole line!

Contrariwise, I had a capital french gentleman in the Dover carriage with me, the last time I came across, who summed up his admiration of the order of the London streets (I didn't tell him of people of being knocked down every day and night by ticket of leave men), and of the efficiency of the Police, with the very good remark "Et voyez-vous Monsieur! Tout cela sans un seul chapeau bas!" [9]

For our Christmas No. besides executing the main idea which is a playful kind of joke on our usual scheme of a Christmas No. I have

---

[9] "Without a single hat in hand" — for a tip.

done a little story which I have tried to make a complete Camera Obscura picture of a dull fortified French town.[1] I set myself the task of trying how much I could possibly suggest — of the truth — to the fancy or the recollection, in the compass of five or six pages. Wills will not fail to send the No. to Stratton Street before it is out, and I hope you and Miss Coutts may like the little story. (It was put into my head by seeing a French soldier acting as nurse to his master's — a Captain's — little baby girl, and washing her, and putting her to bed, and getting her up again in the morning, with the greatest gravity and gentleness.)

My daughter and her Aunt were to have met me at Boulogne for the purpose of coming on here.[2] They were out in the great gale — could not get near Boulogne — and were carried, after several ineffectual attempts to make Calais Harbour, into Calais at last: whence Dessin sent me a Telegram to say they were safe. I stood five hours on the end of the pier at Boulogne in the height and fury of the storm, and it was a wonderful sight. To my great consolation I only saw one thing missed in the Copperfield storm. But it was a very picturesque thing. After it became dark, the surf ran out so far (two or three miles perhaps), and so high, that when a greater wave than usual broke, what was seen of its white top was so like light, as to induce the Boatmen over and over again to cry out, "There's the steamer! I saw her fire as she rolled!" This impulse was quite unchecked by repeated failures, and each time it seemed a more dangerous case than before when we were left to the waste of water again.

I find this is getting to be quite a long letter about nothing, so I will wind it up before it gets longer by sending my most affectionate earnest and grateful regard to Miss Coutts, and the assurance to you, my dear Miss Brown, that I continually live over again, the years that lie behind us.

[P.S.] As you date, generally, "Tavistock," I think it perhaps safest to address this to Stratton Street. I remain here until just before Christmas Day.

---

[1] The Christmas Number of *All the Year Round* for 1862 was called "Somebody's Luggage." Dickens wrote the chapters entitled "His Leaving It Till Called For," "His Boots," "His Brown-Paper Parcel," and "His Wonderful End." It was the second of these that described the French provincial town.

[2] Georgina and Mary were with Dickens in Paris from mid-October to the end of December. His daughter Katey had married Wilkie Collins's brother Charles Allston Collins, a well-known painter, on July 17, 1860. All the younger children were still at school.

278. FEBRUARY 12, 1864, 57 GLOUCESTER PLACE, HYDE PARK GARDENS
I have taken this house until June, to be in town when my book is preparing and begins to come out.[3]

I cannot tell you my Dearest Friend — and I know I need not — with what feelings I received your affectionate letter this morning, or how dearly I prize it. Let me give you, briefly, the circumstances of poor Walter's death.

He had always been in debt, poor boy,[4] and I never could make out how, except that I suppose the Regiment to have been ill looked after by the Colonel. When Charley was in India, the two brothers were together for a fortnight, and Charley paid, as he supposed, Everything. Yet before he got back to England, there was more to pay. This led in course of time to Walter's writing to me to say that his difficulties had led to his being placed low on the list for a Company (though he had never failed in exactness in his duty on any occasion), and that he had put his name down for home service. I wrote to him urging the folly of that proceeding and its reduction of his Income, and pointed out to him that although I was very sorry, I was not angry, and that he must now, as a matter of common reason and justice to his other brothers, live upon his own means. Thereupon he wrote to Mary, saying that he had made up his mind to write home no more, "until he was out of debt." So nothing was heard of him for many months. Mary then got — this last Autumn — a short note from him to the effect that he was not well, and would presently write again. Then, about the turn of Christmas, she had another short note from him to say that he had not said how ill he was when he last wrote, for fear of alarming us, but that he had been very ill indeed, and was now packing up to go to Calcutta, to be certified by a medical board there, and sent home on sick leave. He said he was "so weak that he could hardly crawl," but otherwise was much better; and he was in joyful

---

[3] Shortly after Katey's marriage in 1860, Dickens had sold Tavistock House and retired to Gad's Hill when he was not away on his reading tours, only renting a house in London for Mamey's sake during the season. *Our Mutual Friend*, his last completed book, was published in monthly installments from May 1864 to November 1865.

[4] The pattern of John Dickens's extravagance, and that of Dickens's brothers Frederick and Augustus, repeated again; although they were still in the future, there were to be similar troubles with two of Dickens's younger sons. Charley, too, although apparently not extravagant, became a source of financial worry. He was now in business for himself, with a partner, but in 1868 the firm went bankrupt and Charley was personally indebted for a sum of £1000.

expectation of seeing Gad's Hill again. He arrived at Calcutta from the station where his regiment was, on the 27th of December. He was consigned by the Regimental Doctor to the officers' Hospital there, which is a very fine place. On the last day of the old year at a quarter past 5 in the afternoon he was talking to the other patients about his arrangements for coming home, when he became excited, coughed violently, had a great gush of blood from the mouth, and fell dead; — all this, in a few seconds. It was then found that there was extensive and perfectly incurable aneurism of the Aorta, which had burst. I could have wished it had pleased God to let him see his home again; but I think he would have died at the door.

The immediate cause of his death, his sisters and Charley and I, keep to ourselves; both because his Aunt has the same disorder, and because we observe strong traces of it in one of his brothers. Another of his brothers, Frank,[5] I sent out to Calcutta on the 20th of December. He would hear of his brother's death, on touching the shore.

Do not think me unimpressed by certain words in your letter concerning forgiveness and tenderness when I say that I do not claim to have anything to forgive — that if I had, I hope and believe I would forgive freely — but that a page in my life which once had writing on it, has become absolutely blank, and that it is not in my power to pretend that it has a solitary word upon it.[6]

I am beyond measure interested beforehand, by what you are to tell me. Pray write it as soon as you can. Do not suppose that I am

---

[5] Frank was now twenty and, after having shown no particular talent for anything and proved unsatisfactory even on the office staff of *All the Year Round,* had finally expressed a strong desire to enter the Bengal Mounted Police, to which Dickens obtained a nomination for him. Frank proved an excellent officer in India, where he remained for the next seven years. Returning to England after his father's death, he lost a good deal of his share of Dickens's estate in a disastrous speculation in indigo and squandered the rest in extravagant living. When he was penniless his Aunt Georgina and his sisters successfully appealed to Lord Dufferin, the Governor-General of Canada, to grant him an appointment in the Northwest Mounted Police, and advanced the money for his outfit and passage. Subjected to external discipline he again did well, became a subinspector, and rose to the rank of captain. He retired in 1886, dying a little later in the same year.

[6] The wording of this paragraph strongly suggests that Miss Coutts had used the sad occasion of Walter's death to urge upon Dickens once more — almost six years after his separation from Catherine — the possibility of "forgiveness" and reconciliation, and that once again he was here shutting the door on her efforts. This final surviving reference to the subject in their correspondence is as unyielding as Dickens had been from the beginning.

unfit to pursue it. I am at work, though in a rather dull slow way for the moment.

On the last night of the old year I was acting charades with all the children. I had made something to carry, as the Goddess of Discord; and it came into my head as it stood against the wall while I was dressing, that it was like the dismal things that are carried at Funerals. I took a pair of scissors and cut away a quantity of black calico that was upon it, to remove this likeness. But while I was using it, I noticed that its *shadow* on the wall still had that resemblance, though the thing itself had not. And when I went to bed, it was in my bedroom, and still looked so like, that I took it to pieces before I went to sleep. All this would have been exactly the same, if poor Walter had *not* died that night. And examining my own mind closely, since I received the news, I recall that at Thackeray's funeral I had sat looking at that very object of which I was reminded. See how easily a marvellous story may be made.

I enclose a line for Mrs Brown, and am ever My Dear Friend

∽

279. JANUARY 4, 1865, 26 WELLINGTON STREET, STRAND [OFFICE OF *All the Year Round*]

Coming here this morning for the first time since the day before Christmas Eve, I found your dear words of remembrance. I send you out of my innermost heart my wishes for your happiness through many coming years, and my ever grateful and faithful remembrance of many years that are gone.

∽

During these middle years of the 1860s, the industrious pattern of Dickens's life remained the same. He read in London and about the country, he wrote at Gad's Hill and made improvements on his little estate, he went over to Paris for occasional holidays, he took a furnished house in town during the spring season, he worried about his sons. Alfred, after devoting six years to preparing for a cadetship in the artillery or the engineers, either failed to qualify or veered away from the military profession. Hopefully Dickens tried to give him a start in business, obtaining him a post "in a large China House in the City," and looking toward the possibility of his ultimately going out to some firm in Ceylon or China. Alfred was pleased with this idea, but after two years in London decided that he would rather try Australia. This also Dickens aided him to do, and on May 29, 1865, Alfred sailed for Australia.

The fifth son, Sydney, who had always been mad about the sea, had joined the Royal Navy as a midshipman when he was thirteen and was now sailing the seas on the Orlando. But on his first cruise he fell from a porthole and had a concussion of the brain; later on a voyage to Africa he fell ill with African fever, and his subsequent conduct became so wild, extravagant, and irresponsible that Dickens during the last years of his own life was bitterly distressed about him. At the time Dickens died, Sydney had been forbidden to come to Gad's Hill. The youngest child, Plorn, was also worrying his father. Amiable but shy, with no intellectual abilities and small powers of industry, he was displaying even more than Charley had the unambitious lassitude that had so troubled Dickens when his eldest son was growing up. Even Harry, who at sixteen seemed the quickest-minded and most energetic of the boys, disturbed Dickens by announcing that he "did not wish to enter the Indian Civil Service," as his father had planned for him to do — was he going to turn out a waverer like Frank? It was painfully disquieting. Goaded by his sense of parental responsibility, Dickens drove himself still harder to build up a fortune that might keep them all from want when he was gone.

At the end of May, 1865, he went off to Paris for a week's vacation. "Work and worry, without exercise," he wrote his old friend Forster, "would soon make an end of me. If I were not going away now, I should break down. No one knows as I know today how near it I have been." But in Paris he picked up rapidly. June 9, the day of his return, was clear and sunny and the Channel was without a ripple. At Folkestone he boarded the train for London, and was soon spinning along the rails at fifty miles an hour. But a little more than an hour later, going full speed along a straight stretch of track between Headcorn and Staplehurst, the engineer suddenly saw a gap of ripped-up track. A gang of workmen replacing worn timbers had mistaken the hour at which the train was due. When the driver slammed on the brakes it was too late.

The engine leaped a 43-foot gap in the rails, just where there was a marshy dip and a river bed. The guards' van and a coach followed it. The next coach, in which Dickens was seated, jolted partly over the side of the little bridge and remained hung ten feet above the stream.

*The coupling behind broke, and the other coaches ran down the bank,
buckling and turning upside down in the marsh, where four of them
were smashed to matchwood. Seeing that momentarily they were in
no danger, although precariously balanced, Dickens climbed out of the
window of his compartment, found a guard running wildly about, made
him unlock the door, and with the aid of a laborer and a few planks
rescued the other passengers in the carriage.*

*Then he went back for his brandy flask, filled his hat with water,
and began trying to help the injured and dying. The shattered carriages
were projecting wheels upward from the water. The screams of the
sufferers were appalling. There was a staggering, blood-covered man
with a frightful gash in his skull, a lady with blood streaming in a river
over a lead-colored face, a woman crushed to death and laid on the
bank, a mangled corpse. When Dickens had done everything he could,
he remembered that he had left the manuscript of the next number of
Our Mutual Friend in the compartment he had occupied, and coolly
climbed back into the uncertainly balanced carriage to retrieve it. Only
when he was back at Gad's Hill did he begin to feel the shock and
realize how shaken he was.*

*For more than a month he was unable to throw off the effects of
the accident. His pulse was feeble, he felt curiously weak, he often
turned faint and giddy, and even driving from Gad's Hill into Rochester made him very nervous. Railway traveling he could not bear at all.*

*Letters from Miss Coutts and Mrs. Brown were among the first in
the flood of enquiries for his health that poured in upon him and were
among the first that he answered. The following letter is the last but
one that has been found of those he wrote to either of them.*

∾

**280.   JUNE 11, 1865, GAD'S HILL PLACE [TO MISS COUTTS AND MRS.
BROWN]**

My steady heart thanks you better than my unsteady hand for your
kind, kind letters. I was in the carriage that did not go over the bridge
but caught in turning and hung suspended over the ruined brick work.
I worked hard afterwards among the dead and dying, and it is that
shock — not the shock of the stumbling carriage, which was nothing —
that I feel a little. I could not have imagined so appalling a scene.

Your recommendation my dear Miss Coutts to rest a little, shall not
be neglected. I will come to Holly Lodge, to thank you, as soon as I go
to London.

Dickens never fully recovered from the Staplehurst accident. "To this hour," he wrote more than three years later, "I have sudden vague rushes of terror, even when riding in a hansom cab, which are perfectly unreasonable but quite insurmountable. I used to think nothing of driving a pair of horses habitually through the most crowded parts of London. I cannot now drive, with comfort to myself, on the country roads here; and I doubt if I could ride at all in the saddle." When he resumed train travel, as he presently insisted on doing, he would sometimes clutch the arm of his chair when the carriage jolted across switches or over intersections, his face would whiten, and his brow break out in perspiration. Exactly five years after the accident, to a day, he died.

But meanwhile he drove himself as relentlessly as ever. With a new manager, George Dolby, he gave another series of thirty readings in 1866, under the sponsorship of the Messieurs Chappell, of New Bond Street. They were a triumph everywhere, and he got through them in high spirits despite the fact that his pulse was bad and his heart action enfeebled. In addition, he developed severe pains in his left eyeball, pains in the pit of the stomach and in the chest, and recurrent inflammations in the foot that he refused to admit could be gout. Chappells tempted him to begin another series of fifty readings at Christmas. Ultimately he agreed to give forty-two for £2500. They continued into May 1867 and left him almost exhausted.

Even then he would not stop. Despite his friend Forster's disapproval, he determined on crossing the Atlantic for an even more prolonged reading tour in 1867–1868. Everywhere his arrival was a sensation; America had long forgiven or forgotten its fury over Martin Chuzzlewit and American Notes. Lines eight hundred long waited all night to buy tickets. Members of families relieved each other during the vigil; waiters flew across the streets and squares from neighboring restaurants to serve breakfast to people who ate standing in the cold December air; excited men offered five and ten dollars merely to change places with those near the head of the line. But Dickens picked up a hacking cough that he was unable to get rid of throughout the entire tour, and that left him only by some miracle of will power during the two hours that he had to appear on the platform. He journeyed from Boston to New York, to Philadelphia, to Baltimore, to Washington, and then through a series of one- and two-night stands in Buffalo, Syracuse, Rochester, Albany, New Haven, Hartford, Springfield, Worcester,

Providence, New Bedford, on up to Portland, Maine, and then back to Boston and New York again, coming steadily closer and closer to a collapse. During the latter part of his tour, he was hardly able to eat solid food, and subsisted on eggnogs, sherry, cream, brandy, and champagne. Only through an iron determination did he force himself to undergo a great farewell banquet at Delmonico's.

At last he got back to England. He had earned almost £20,000. He rested awhile, and then began another series of readings — one hundred for a guaranteed sum of £8000. He had almost broken down in America giving no more than three quarters of that number. To his repertory he added a new and dreadful piece, Sikes murdering Nancy, which he acted with terrifying and gruesome realism. The need to leave a comfortable fortune to his children had, indeed, long since become only partially a motive for the strain he put upon himself — an excuse for what he had really become an excitement, an indulgence, a distraction. When even Dolby, his manager, pointed out to him that no matter what he read his audiences would still overflow their auditoriums, Dickens became violently angry, and then broke down and wept.

For all his tremendous success, he had never really accepted the world. He felt that the changes that had taken place in his lifetime had merely deepened the dreadful chasm of injustice he had always deplored. At bottom his disquietude was a distress with a world that afflicted him with a dreadful doubt about the way in which it was going. There was the "enormous black cloud of poverty in every town," a "non-working aristocracy," Parliament "the dreariest failure and nuisance." In Our Mutual Friend Boffin's dust heaps are Dickens's symbols for the world's supreme values, the embodiment of wealth and greed: mere piles of dirt, trash, garbage, and the evil-smelling filth of privies.

In his need for distraction, Dickens ignored plain symptoms of paralysis. No one — not his son Charley, nor his friends, nor his physician— could stop him. He was as generous and affectionate with others as always. He was still able to stimulate himself into an effervescence of high spirits that simulated happiness, perhaps even to himself. But underneath, his body was not merely wearing out, he was determined not to relax because he preferred to break down in action. When the readings came to an end, he could hardly bear it. "From these garish lights," he told a deeply moved audience of over two thousand, "I vanish now forevermore, with a heartfelt, grateful, respectful, affectionate farewell." Tears streamed down his cheeks as he limped from the platform.

Down at Gad's Hill he rested awhile, then resumed work on The Mystery of Edwin Drood. But it was destined to remain unfinished; the strain had gone on too long. At dinner on June 8, 1870, his sister-in-law Georgina Hogarth saw that he looked ill. He started to rise, pushed back the crimson damask chair, and almost fell. She tried to get him to a sofa, but he was too heavy, and after a slight struggle he sank heavily on his left side. "On the ground," he murmured. They were his last words. It was a paralytic stroke, an effusion of blood on the brain that left no hope. Stertorous breathing continued all night and all the next day, but there was never a gleam of hope. At ten minutes past six, he gave a deep sigh. His eyes were closed, but a tear welled from under his right eyelid and trickled down his cheek. It was just four months and two days past his fifty-eighth birthday.

The incredulous grief that rolled through the world was more than a testimony to Dickens's fame; it was an earnest of the love in which he was held. "Dickens is dead" sounded a knell in the humblest heart. "Nostro Carlo Dickens è morto," Our Charles Dickens is dead, headlined the Italian newspapers. Overwhelming sentiment demanded his burial in Westminster Abbey. For the two days the grave was kept open, thousands upon thousands of mourners surged past the plain oak coffin in the Poets' Corner. Innumerable visitors paid their tribute of tears and heaped blossoms innumerable, sometimes single flowers deposited by trembling hands. And for months after the grave was closed, no day passed without still other mourners coming and leaving it a mound of fragrant color.

Miss Coutts survived her old friend by another thirty-six years of vigorous continued activity — a period a little over one year more than the entire time they had known each other. Her philanthropies were unceasing. After the retirement of Wills in 1868, she acquired a second secretary, Sir John Hassard, who was followed by a Mr. Clough, who in turn was succeeded by Mr. C. C. Osborne, who remained her secretary until her death. In 1871 she was elevated to the peerage as the Baroness Burdett-Coutts of Highgate and Brookfield, Middlesex. She built further model tenements for the poor, the Peabody dwellings, and founded a garden city on the site of her Holly Lodge estate. She aided the poor of Shoreditch and Bethnal Green. She gave generously to the Society for the Prevention of Cruelty to Animals and founded a small society that led to the Society for the Prevention of Cruelty to Children. In 1877, aided by William Ashmead-Bartlett, a young American living in England, she helped the Bulgarians and the Turkish Compassionate Fund, and in 1878 received from the Sultan the diamond star of the Order of the Medfedie and the grand cross and cordon of the Chafaket (Mercy). In 1881, when she was almost sixty-seven and he was twenty-eight, she married Ashmead-Bartlett. Her interest in the banking house consequently passed to her sister Clara, but by a private agreement she retained two fifths of the income for the remainder of her life. In 1888 she was made a Lady of Grace of the Order of St. John of Jerusalem. On December 30, 1906, well on toward her ninety-first birthday, she died in Stratton Street, where her body lay in state while a stream of thirty thousand mourners filed past. She was buried in the Abbey — the only woman not of royal birth so honored — where Dickens had preceded her on a June day thirty-six years before.

APPENDIX

Publishing History of the Letters

The texts of all letters not otherwise noted are taken from the originals in the Pierpont Morgan Library.

Letter
Number

22 Most of this letter is in Osborne, 50–52, and *Letters,* I, 531–532.

23 Hitherto unpublished.

24 Hitherto unpublished. The original is in the collection of Mr. Roger W. Barrett, of Kenilworth, Illinois, by whose kind permission it is used.

25 Hitherto unpublished.

26 Hitherto unpublished.

27 Hitherto unpublished.

28 All except the first two paragraphs published in Osborne, 53, and *Letters,* I, 546–547.

29 Hitherto unpublished.

30 Hitherto unpublished.

31 Practically complete in Osborne, 56–59, and *Letters,* I, 648–649.

32 Complete in Osborne, 60–67, and *Letters,* I, 663–666.

33 A few sentences from the fourth paragraph are in *Letters,* I, 696, taken from a sales catalogue.

34 Hitherto unpublished.

35 The greater part of this letter is in Osborne, 67–70, and *Letters,* I, 702–703.

36 Hitherto unpublished.

37 The fifth paragraph is in *Letters,* I, 724, taken from a sales catalogue.

38 A single sentence from the first paragraph is in Osborne, 70, and *Letters,* I, 730.

39 Half of the second paragraph is in Osborne, 71, and *Letters,* I, 747.

40 All except the first paragraph is in Osborne, 71–82, and *Letters,* I, 749–754.

41 Only a few sentences from this letter are printed in Osborne, 88, and *Letters,* I, 758–759.

42 All except the first two paragraphs and the last paragraph is in Osborne, 88–91, and *Letters,* I, 772–773.

43 There are a few sentences from two paragraphs near the end of this letter in *Letters,* I, 796, taken from a sales catalogue, but printed in an incorrect order and with omissions and inaccuracies of wording. An even smaller part is in Osborne, 91.

44 Hitherto unpublished.

45 The last paragraph, taken from a sales catalogue, is in *Letters,* II, 4.

46 Hitherto unpublished.

47 Only a few parts of the second paragraph, taken from a sales catalogue, are printed in *Letters,* II, 24.

48 Hitherto unpublished.

49 Hitherto unpublished.

50 Hitherto unpublished.

51 Hitherto unpublished.

52 Less than a third of this letter is printed in Osborne, 92–93, and *Letters,* II, 56–57.

Letter
Number

53 Only about one quarter of the more generalizing part of this letter is in Osborne, 93–99, and *Letters*, II, 57–59. None of the concrete details have been printed before.

54 Hitherto unpublished.

55 Hitherto unpublished.

56 Hitherto unpublished.

57 Hitherto unpublished.

58 Hitherto unpublished.

59 Hitherto unpublished. Although this letter does not bear the name of its addressee, it was found among a considerable group addressed to Dr. William Brown, husband of Miss Coutts's companion, who was undoubtedly its recipient.

60 Hitherto unpublished.

61 Hitherto unpublished.

62 Hitherto unpublished.

63 A few fragments of this letter, taken from a sales catalogue, are in *Letters*, II, 76.

64 Hitherto unpublished. A previous owner of this letter has a note dating it August 1848, but this is unlikely on a number of grounds. Mrs. Fisher's impending departure from her position is mentioned in a letter of December 29, 1847, and Mrs. Graves is referred to in terms that suggest she has already entered upon her duties at the Home in a letter of May 23, 1848. That would place this letter some time between the two. The ending of *Dombey and Son*, mentioned in the postscript, was published April 1, making it likely that the date should be early in April.

65 Hitherto unpublished.

66 Hitherto unpublished.

67 Hitherto unpublished.

68 Only a part of the second paragraph, from a sales catalogue, is in *Letters*, II, 92–93.

69 Hitherto unpublished.

70 The third paragraph is in Osborne, 99–100, and *Letters*, II, 115.

71 Hitherto unpublished.

72 Hitherto unpublished.

73 Hitherto unpublished.

74 This letter and the enclosure are hitherto unpublished.

75 Hitherto unpublished.

76 Hitherto unpublished.

77 Hitherto unpublished.

78 A part of the third from the last paragraph is in Osborne, 176, and *Letters*, II, 122.

79 Hitherto unpublished.

80 Complete in Osborne, 100–101, and *Letters*, II, 126.

81 Hitherto unpublished.

Letter
Number

82   The last paragraph only, taken from a sales catalogue, is in *Letters*, II, 128.

83   The last paragraph only, taken from a sales catalogue, is in *Letters*, II, 128.

84   Hitherto unpublished. A previous owner has a note dating it merely as November 1848.

85   Hitherto unpublished. Though the date has been added in pencil by a previous owner, it is undoubtedly accurate: the letter is headed "Saturday," and the second paragraph identifies the occasion as Twelfth Night, which did not fall on a Saturday again till 1855.

86   Hitherto unpublished.

87   Hitherto unpublished.

88   Hitherto unpublished.

89   Hitherto unpublished.

90   Hitherto unpublished.

91   Hitherto unpublished.

92   All except the last paragraph is in Osborne, 102–103, and *Letters*, II, 148–149.

93   Hitherto unpublished.

94   Hitherto unpublished.

95   Hitherto unpublished.

96   Hitherto unpublished.

97   Hitherto unpublished.

98   Hitherto unpublished.

99   Hitherto unpublished.

100   Hitherto unpublished.

101   Hitherto unpublished.

102   Hitherto unpublished.

103   Hitherto unpublished.

104   Hitherto unpublished.

105   Only two fragments from the first and third paragraphs, taken from a sales catalogue, are in *Letters*, II, 193.

106   Hitherto unpublished.

107   Hitherto unpublished.

108   Hitherto unpublished.

109   Hitherto unpublished. Endorsed in Dickens's hand: "Mrs Gaskell's letter."

110   Hitherto unpublished.

111   Hitherto unpublished.

112   A few parts of the third paragraph and the last paragraph, taken from a sales catalogue, are in *Letters*, II, 203–204.

113   Hitherto unpublished.

114   Hitherto unpublished.

115   Hitherto unpublished.

179   The fourth and seventh paragraphs are in Osborne, 128–129, and *Letters,* II, 494; and the remark about the baby, taken from a sales catalogue and mistakenly dated September 18, is in *Letters,* II, 490.

180   The first four paragraphs are in Osborne, 130–133, and *Letters,* II, 497–499.

181   The greater part of this letter is in Osborne, 134–137, and *Letters,* II, 509–511.

182   Hitherto unpublished. From the collection of Mr. Roger W. Barrett, of Kenilworth, Illinois, by whose kind permission it is printed.

183   Hitherto unpublished.

184   Hitherto unpublished.

185   Hitherto unpublished.

186   Hitherto unpublished.

187   Hitherto unpublished.

188   The second sentence of the fifth paragraph, taken from a sales catalogue, is in *Letters,* II, 537.

189   Hitherto unpublished.

190   Hitherto unpublished. Dickens made a mistake in the date; Tuesday was not the sixth, but the seventh, of February.

191   Hitherto unpublished.

192   The next to the last paragraph, taken from a sales catalogue, is in *Letters,* II, 558.

193   Hitherto unpublished.

194   The first paragraph and the sixth through the eighth paragraphs are in Osborne, 140, and 138–140, and in *Letters,* II, 563–564.

195   Hitherto unpublished.

196   Hitherto unpublished.

197   Hitherto unpublished. The year is established by Dickens's letter, immediately following.

198   The third, fourth, and sixth paragraphs are in Osborne, 142–143 and 177–178, and in *Letters,* II, 599–600.

199   This letter, written on mourning stationery, has been privately printed in *The Charity of Charles Dickens,* by Edward F. Payne and Henry H. Harper, Boston: The Bibliophile Society, 1929. My text, however, is taken from the original letter in the Morgan Library.

200   My text is taken from the original letter in the Henry W. and Albert A. Berg Collection of the New York Public Library, whose authorities have kindly given their permission for its use. This letter is also printed in *The Charity of Charles Dickens.*

201   This text also is taken from the original letter in the Henry W. and Albert A. Berg Collection of the New York Public Library, whose authorities have kindly given their permission for its use, and is also in *The Charity of Charles Dickens.*

202   This letter has also been privately printed in *The Charity of Charles Dickens*.

203   Hitherto unpublished. This note obviously accompanied the two foregoing communications from Frederick Maynard and Caroline Thompson, together with Dickens's annotations on them and the narrative account printed as No. 200.

204   Privately printed in *The Charity of Charles Dickens*.

205   Hitherto unpublished.

206   Privately printed in *The Charity of Charles Dickens*. This letter Dickens endorsed: "Mrs Thompson Received Tuesday 9th January 1855."

207   Privately printed in *The Charity of Charles Dickens*. The date is established by Mrs. Thompson's reference to the Saturday appointment that Dickens mentions in the letter to Miss Coutts that follows.

208   Privately printed in *The Charity of Charles Dickens*.

209   Hitherto unpublished.

210   Parts of three sentences from the seventh paragraph, taken from a sales catalogue, are in *Letters*, II, 618.

211   One sentence from the seventh paragraph, taken from a sales catalogue, is in *Letters*, II, 624.

212   Privately printed in *The Charity of Charles Dickens*. The last paragraph, taken from a sales catalogue, is in *Letters*, II, 639.

213   Privately printed in *The Charity of Charles Dickens*.

214   Privately printed in *The Charity of Charles Dickens*.

215   All except the last paragraph is in Osborne, 143–144, and *Letters*, II, 657.

216   The last paragraph and postscript are in Osborne, 147–148, and *Letters*, II, 659.

217   All except the first paragraph is in Osborne, 149–150, and *Letters*, II, 660.

218   All except the last paragraph is in Osborne, 150–153, and *Letters*, II, 661–662.

219   The next to the last paragraph is in Osborne, 154, and *Letters*, II, 665.

220   The earlier half of the first paragraph and the postscript are in Osborne, 154–155, and *Letters*, II, 666.

221   Hitherto unpublished.

222   All except the first sentence and the last paragraph is in Osborne, 155–156, and *Letters*, II, 672–673.

223   Hitherto unpublished.

224   Previously published in Osborne, 157–158.

225   Hitherto unpublished.

226   Hitherto unpublished.

227   Almost all, except a few sentences at the opening and close, is in Osborne, 31–32, but it was overlooked by the editor of *Letters*.

Letter
Number

228 The fourth paragraph is in Osborne, 160–161, and both this paragraph and an additional sentence from the second paragraph — about writing the next number of *Little Dorrit* — are in *Letters*, II, 726–727.

229 The third and fourth paragraphs are in Osborne, 161–163, and *Letters*, II, 742–743.

230 Hitherto unpublished.

231 Hitherto unpublished. The original letter is in the collection of Mr. Roger W. Barrett, of Kenilworth, Illinois, by whose kind permission it is here printed.

232 The last paragraph is in Osborne, 164–165, and *Letters*, II, 773–774.

233 Privately printed in *The Charity of Charles Dickens*.

234 Hitherto unpublished.

235 The sixth and seventh paragraphs are in Osborne, 165–166, and *Letters*, II, 776.

236 Hitherto unpublished.

237 The second and fourth paragraphs are in Osborne, 166–167, and *Letters*, II, 791.

238 Hitherto unpublished.

239 The third, fourth and fifth paragraphs are in Osborne, 169–172, and *Letters*, II, 795–796, but are printed in both as if they were extracts from two different letters of the same date.

240 Hitherto unpublished.

241 Practically the whole of this letter is in Osborne, 172, and *Letters*, II, 802.

242 The last paragraph is in Osborne, 172–173, and *Letters*, II, 802. The original is in the collection of Mr. Roger W. Barrett, of Kenilworth, Illinois, by whose kind permission it is here printed.

243 The first paragraph is in Osborne, 174, and *Letters*, II, 812.

244 The postscript is in Osborne; the last paragraph and the postscript are in *Letters*, II, 814.

245 Hitherto unpublished.

246 Hitherto unpublished.

247 Hitherto unpublished.

248 Hitherto unpublished.

249 The fifth and sixth paragraphs and the postscript are in Osborne, 178–179, and *Letters*, II, 832.

250 Hitherto unpublished.

251 The second paragraph is in Osborne, 180, and *Letters*, II, 835.

252 The second, third and fourth paragraphs are in Osborne, 181–182; and in *Letters*, II, 842–843, there is in addition the single sentence in the last paragraph mentioning Gad's Hill, probably derived from a sales catalogue, although no source is mentioned.

253 The second paragraph is in Osborne, 184; in *Letters*, II, 852–853, there are in addition, taken from a sales catalogue, the last two sentences of the preceding paragraph.

Letter
Number

254   Hitherto unpublished.

255   The last paragraph of this letter is in Osborne, 184, and *Letters*, II, 860.

256   Hitherto unpublished.

257   Hitherto unpublished.

258   The last three paragraphs are in Osborne, 29–30 and 186–187, and, in addition, although mistakenly placed at the end, the third paragraph is in *Letters*, II, 876–877.

259   The second paragraph and the sixth to ninth paragraphs are in Osborne, 189–190, where they are printed as if they were from two separate letters of the same date. In *Letters*, II, 889–890, they are printed as parts of one letter, but the second paragraph is placed at the end.

260   Hitherto unpublished. This letter can be dated as Monday, February 1, 1858, from Dickens's letter immediately following, which was written Tuesday, February 2.

261   Hitherto unpublished.

262   Taken from a transcript made by Miss Coutts's secretary, C. C. Osborne, and now in the British Museum (Add. MSS. 46402–8); published in "Dickens to Miss Burdett Coutts," by K. J. Fielding, London *Times Literary Supplement*, March 2, 1951. It is printed here by the kind permission of Mr. Fielding.

263   The transcript of this letter is from one sent the editor by the late Comte Alain de Suzannet, of Lausanne, Switzerland, by whose kind permission it is here printed; it has also been printed in "Dickens to Miss Burdett Coutts," by K. J. Fielding, London *Times Literary Supplement*, March 9, 1951.

264   Hitherto unpublished.

265   The first sentence and parts of two sentences from the third paragraph are in *Letters*, III, 37, but with no indication of the source from which they were taken.

266   The text of this letter is taken from the original in the Henry W. and Albert A. Berg Collection of the New York Public Library, by the kind permission of whose authorities it is here printed. Except for the first paragraph, the last paragraph, and the last sentence of the paragraph immediately preceding, it has been published in "Dickens to Miss Burdett Coutts," by K. J. Fielding, London *Times Literary Supplement*, March 9, 1951, from a transcript made by C. C. Osborne and now in the British Museum (Add. MSS. 46402–8).

267   The first sentence, taken from a sales catalogue, is in *Letters*, III, 51.

268   The second and third paragraphs are in Osborne, 192, and *Letters*, III, 65–66.

269   The fifth paragraph is in Osborne, 193, and, in addition, the last sentence from the third paragraph is in *Letters*, III, 79.

270   The fourth paragraph is in Osborne, 193, and *Letters*, III, 148.

Letter
Number

271   Hitherto unpublished.
272   From a transcript made by C. C. Osborne and now in the British Museum (Add. MSS. 46402–8); published in "Dickens to Miss Burdett Coutts," by K. J. Fielding, London *Times Literary Supplement,* March 9, 1951. It is printed here by the kind permission of Mr. Fielding.
273   Hitherto unpublished. The original is in the collection of Mr. Roger W. Barrett, of Kenilworth, Illinois, by whose kindness it is here printed.
274   Hitherto unpublished.
275   Hitherto unpublished.
276   Hitherto unpublished.
277   Hitherto unpublished.
278   The next to last paragraph is in Osborne, 193–194, and *Letters,* III, 379–380, where it is preceded by the very first sentence of the letter without any sign that there is an omission of intervening material.
279   Complete, except for the last clause of the second sentence, in *Letters,* III, 411.
280   The first paragraph, except its opening sentence, is in *Letters,* III, 424.

Index